Ma
Te

- g

2 3

Varieties of Anti-Fascism

Also by Nigel Copsey

ANTI-FASCISM IN BRITAIN

CONTEMPORARY BRITISH FASCISM: The British National Party and the Quest for Legitimacy

BRITISH FASCISM, THE LABOUR MOVEMENT AND THE STATE
(*edited with D. Renton*)

Andrzej Olechnowicz

WORKING-CLASS HOUSING IN ENGLAND BETWEEN THE WARS: The Becontree Estate

THE MONARCHY AND THE BRITISH NATION 1780 TO THE PRESENT (*edited*)

Varieties of Anti-Fascism

Britain in the Inter-War Period

Edited By

Nigel Copsey
Reader in Modern History, Teesside University, UK

Andrzej Olechnowicz
Lecturer in Modern British History, Durham University, UK

Editorial matter and selection © Nigel Copsey and Andrzej Olechnowicz 2010
All remaining chapters © their respective authors 2010

First published 2010 by
PALGRAVE MACMILLAN

Palgrave Macmillan in the UK is an imprint of Macmillan Publishers Limited, registered in England, company number 785998, of Houndmills, Basingstoke, Hampshire RG21 6XS.

Palgrave Macmillan in the US is a division of St Martin's Press LLC, 175 Fifth Avenue, New York, NY 10010.

Palgrave Macmillan is the global academic imprint of the above companies and has companies and representatives throughout the world.

Palgrave® and Macmillan® are registered trademarks in the United States, the United Kingdom, Europe and other countries

ISBN 978-0-230-00648-5   hardback

This book is printed on paper suitable for recycling and made from fully managed and sustained forest sources. Logging, pulping and manufacturing processes are expected to conform to the environmental regulations of the country of origin.

A catalogue record for this book is available from the British Library.

A catalogue record for this book is available from the Library of Congress.

10   9   8   7   6   5   4   3   2   1
19   18   17   16   15   14   13   12   11   10

Printed and bound in Great Britain by
CPI Antony Rowe, Chippenham and Eastbourne

This volume is dedicated to the memory of Paul Tajfel (1955–1985).

Contents

List of Abbreviations

AIA	Artists' International Association
BEU	British Empire Union
BF	British Fascists
BUF	British Union of Fascists
Comintern	Communist International
CP	Communist Party
CPGB	Communist Party of Great Britain
CRA	Constitutional Research Association
ENA	English National Association
BNP	British National Party
GCCS	Government Code and Cypher School
SB	Special Branch
HUMINT	Human Intelligence
IIB	Industrial Intelligence Board
ILP	Independent Labour Party
KPD	Communist Party of Germany
LBC	Left Book Club
MRP	Mouvement Républicain Populaire
NEC	National Executive Committee
NF	National Fascists
IFL	Imperial Fascist League
NJC	National Joint Council
PLP	Parliamentary Labour Party
TUC	Trades Union Congress
ODC	Open Door Council
ODI	Open Door International
RC	Right Club
SPG	Six Point Group
WIL	Women's International League
WEA	Workers' Educational Association
WILPF	Women's International League for Peace and Freedom
YCL	Young Communist League

Acknowledgements

The origins of this volume stretch back to conversations that the editors had following a conference on fascism and the labour movement held at the University of Leeds in November 2003. We both agreed on the overriding need for a new approach to the study of British anti-fascism, one that recognised that not all anti-fascism in inter-war Britain was 'active'. Whilst still retaining an appreciation of the part played by left-wing anti-fascist activists, we felt that other, and potentially equally significant, varieties of anti-fascism had been ignored. For us, a more inclusive definition of our subject (implied but not fully developed in *Anti-Fascism in Britain*) was essential in order to capture anti-fascism's richly variegated form. Supportive of a broader concept of anti-fascism, we then solicited contributions from a range of academics that we thought could extend the scope of study to neglected areas, and offer a far more elaborate and nuanced understanding of anti-fascism in inter-war Britain. Following a lengthy period of project gestation, our contributors finally gathered at a symposium at the University of Durham in March 2008. The papers presented at that symposium form the basis of the wide-ranging chapters in this volume. It is at this point that the editors would like to express their gratitude to the contributors who were most efficient in the delivery of their final chapters. We would also like to thank the History Department at the University of Durham and the History Research Group at Teesside University for their support in both the funding of the symposium and in the preparation of the final manuscript.

Nigel Copsey and Andrzej Olechnowicz,
Teesside and Durham,
May 2009.

List of Contributors

Nigel Copsey is Reader in Modern History at Teesside University. His research interests lie in the study of historic and contemporary fascism and anti-fascism. He is the author of *Anti-Fascism in Britain* (2000); *Contemporary British Fascism: The British National Party and the Quest for Legitimacy* (2004, 2008); and (ed., with D. Renton) *British Fascism, the Labour Movement and the State* (2005). He is currently working on a volume entitled *British National Party: Contemporary Perspectives* as well as a transnational study of anti-fascism.

Janet Dack is a former civil servant who is currently a PhD student at Teesside University. She is writing a thesis exploring areas of similarity and difference in fascist and mainstream views based on a comparison of the British mainstream and fascist inter-war press. Her research interests include democracy, extremism and anti-fascism.

Julie Gottlieb is a lecturer in Modern History at the University of Sheffield. She is the author of *Feminine Fascism: Women in Britain's Fascist Movement, 1923–1945* (2000); co-editor (with Thomas Linehan) of *The Culture of Fascism: Visions of the Far Right in Britain* (2004), and (with Richard Toye) *Making Reputations: Power, Persuasion and the Individual in Modern British Politics* (2005). Her current project – '"Guilty Women": Gender, Foreign Policy and Appeasement in Inter-War Britain' – examines women's resistance to fascism and to war in the 1930s.

Richard Griffiths was formerly Professor of French at King's College London. He has written widely on the British and French extreme Right. His many publications include *Fellow Travellers of the Right: British Enthusiasts for Nazi Germany, 1933–39* (1980); *Patriotism Perverted: Captain Ramsay, the Right Club, and British Anti-Semitism 1939–1940* (1998); and *An Intelligent Person's Guide to Fascism* (2000).

Tom Lawson is a lecturer in History at the University of Winchester. His research interests lie primarily in the field of Holocaust Studies and modern religious history. His recent publications include: *The Church of England and the Holocaust: Christianity, Memory and Nazism* (2006);

and (ed. with James Jordan) *The Memory of the Holocaust in Australia* (2008).

Thomas Linehan is a lecturer in History at Brunel University. He is the author of *Communism in Britain, 1920–39. From the Cradle to the Grave* (2007); *British Fascism, 1918–1939: Parties, Ideology and Culture* (2000); *East London for Mosley: The British Union of Fascists in East London and South-West Essex 1933–1940* (1996); and co-editor (with Julie Gottlieb) of *The Culture of Fascism: Visions of the Far Right in Britain* (2004).

Andrzej Olechnowicz is a lecturer in History at Durham University. He is the author of *Working-Class Housing in England between the Wars: The Becontree Estate* (1997) and editor of *The Monarchy and the British Nation 1780 to the Present* (2007).

Julia Stapleton is Reader in Politics at Durham University. Her research interests lie in British political thought and intellectual history during the first half of the twentieth century. She is the author of *Englishness and the Study of Politics: The Social and Political Thought of Ernest Barker* (1994); *Sir Arthur Bryant and National History in Twentieth-Century Britain* (2005); and *Christianity, Patriotism and Nationhood: The England of G. K. Chesterton* (2008).

Dan Stone is Professor of Modern History at Royal Holloway, University of London. He is a historian of ideas who works on historiographical, literary and philosophical interpretations of the Holocaust, comparative genocide, the cultural politics of the Right and philosophy of history. Among his recent publications are *History, Memory and Mass Atrocity: Essays on the Holocaust and Genocide* (2006) and *The Historiography of Genocide* (2008). He is currently writing a book on Holocaust historiography and editing the *Oxford Handbook of Post-War European History*.

Richard Thurlow is Senior Lecturer in Modern History at the University of Sheffield. His research interests mainly relate to political extremism and the British state in the twentieth-century. His major publications include: *The Secret State: British Internal Security in the Twentieth Century* (1994); *Fascism in Britain: From Oswald Mosley's Blackshirts to the National Front* (1998); and *Fascism in Modern Britain* (2000).

Philip Williamson is Professor of History at the University of Durham. His research interests lie in twentieth-century British politics, especially inter-war Conservatism. He is the author of *Stanley Baldwin: Conservative Leadership and National Values* (1999); *National Crisis and National Government: British Politics, the Economy and Empire 1926–32* (1992); and co-editor (with Ranald Michie) of *The British Government and the City of London in the Twentieth Century* (2004).

Preface: Towards a New Anti-Fascist 'Minimum'?

Nigel Copsey

Our approach to the subject of anti-fascism in inter-war Britain is deliberately pluralistic. Our intention was to transcend exclusive definitions that restrict anti-fascism solely to the politics of hostile activism. We want to represent it in another way. For us anti-fascism is many-sided, a complex phenomenon open to a full spectrum of different understandings and approaches. Whilst no single volume can hope to encompass all its many permutations, the contributions that we present here are genuinely representative of a multifarious and shifting phenomenon. Our pluralistic approach will no doubt have its critics, and there will be those who accuse us of 'conceptual stretching'. In order to pre-empt such criticism, this preface will advance a broader conceptual understanding of anti-fascism. Through reference to each of the contributions in this volume, this more expansive understanding will then find an anchor in an anti-fascist 'minimum'. But let me say that this anti-fascist 'minimum' does not represent a point of consensus between all the contributors to this volume. Rather, in advancing a more elaborate understanding of what opposition to fascism means, and in proposing a new anti-fascist minimum, my intention is only to stimulate further reflection, and give rise to a much-needed conceptual debate.

Of course, on one level, anti-fascism demands very little when it comes to its definition. At its most straightforward anti-fascism may simply be defined as opposition to fascism as an ideology and to the propagators of that ideology (whether a political party, group, movement, individual, or government). However, as soon as we start probing this more closely, we encounter problems. First, should we exclude from our definition all those 'anti-fascisms' where the recipient of opposition was not fascist? As a case in point, was Communist opposition to social-democratic reformism – 'social fascism' – a type of anti-fascism? It seems to me that we cannot delimit 'true' anti-fascism according to academic definitions of who the anti-fascism is directed at. The voice of the historical actors is critical here. The definition of fascism must rest solely with the anti-fascist, regardless of whether or not they assess/define

xiv

fascism correctly. Secondly, opposition refers not only to the *act* of opposing (the hostile action) but also to the *state* of being in opposition (the hostile attitude). As a result, anti-fascism can take both active and passive forms. Yet the division between these forms is not a neat one. With regard to political parties, for example, the term 'passive' anti-fascism is often used to describe the policy of abstaining from militant confrontation. Yet this does not mean to say that a political party's anti-fascism is not 'active' – it just finds expression in less belligerent form. Indoor and outdoor meetings, the distribution of anti-fascist literature, parliamentary debates, petitions, deputations, all spring to mind. This is not 'passive'; hostility to fascism is being acted upon here even if fascism is not being violently resisted. On further reflection such anti-fascism is probably best characterised as 'liberal' anti-fascism since it rejects violence, and respects the legal and constitutional framework of the liberal-parliamentary state.

For sure, the Communist Party's inter-war anti-fascism was the most direct and also the most belligerent. However, as Tom Linehan's first chapter shows in Part I of the book, even this variant of combative anti-fascism could find more indirect and more imaginative cultural expression. As the CP entered the Popular Front era, it embarked on an anti-fascist cultural project that comprised an inventive series of myths, festivals, and rituals. For Linehan, this cultural variant 'gave real impetus to communist efforts to overcome fascism' by binding together a moral community of Communist anti-fascists in a common sacrificial bond. But such cultural variants were less conspicuous elsewhere on the Left, where the Labour Party establishment was clearly more 'passive' in its anti-fascism than both the Communist Party and the many 'dissident' anti-fascists that populated Labour's grassroots. What distinguished the Labour Party's inter-war anti-fascism, as my own chapter emphasises, was the extent to which it failed to find favour with rank-and-file Labourites – the very people who constituted the massed ranks of Britain's popular anti-fascist movement. Nonetheless Labour's 'liberal' anti-fascism was still successful, reinforcing parliamentary government and values, and thus frustrating native fascism. Labour's anti-fascism was also a good deal less 'passive' than Conservative anti-fascism. We need only recall that Baldwin made just one speech attacking the British Union of Fascists (BUF). Yet when viewed from Philip Williamson's angle it is the Conservative Party – the subject of the third chapter – that emerges as Britain's 'leading anti-fascist force'. 'Leading', not in the sense of giving a direct lead to the popular anti-fascist movement but – as Britain's dominant electoral force – in remaining committed to parliamentarianism. For Williamson, the 'fascist moment' (if there was one) occurred during 1929–31. By re-establishing confidence in parliamentary government, it was the Conservative Party's response to this crisis – the formation of the National coalition government – that indirectly destroyed Mosley's (and fascism's) prospects.

What emerges from this study is that the panoply of anti-fascisms is clearly not limited to party-political forms. A further conceptual point to make here is that anti-fascism is not *agency-specific*. On the contrary, its reach can extend beyond political parties far into civil society, the media and the state. Therefore Part II of the book concerns non-party women's organisations, churches, the media, and the 'secret' state, where our contributors locate further sites of inter-war anti-fascism. Julie Gottlieb contends that there was never a 'unified female response to fascism, either to the home-grown or the Continental model'. This is borne out by her comparison of two non-party women's organisations. In mapping how these organisations negotiated domestic but especially Continental fascism, Gottlieb tells of how feminism could lead to the adoption of militant anti-fascism in one case, and how pacifism could transcend anti-fascism in another. Just as there was no single feminist response to fascism, there was no single Christian response to it either, as Tom Lawson's essay reveals. Lawson concludes that whilst both the Church of England and the Roman Catholic Church did express faith-based opposition to fascism, and therefore rightly deserve a place in the historiography of anti-fascism, their anti-communism drastically curtailed the extent to which both churches engaged with anti-fascist activism. The 'shadow cast by Communism', to use Lawson's fine phrase, also stretched much further into the Catholic than the Anglican community. Nowhere was this more apparent than in their respective attitudes to Spain.

The far-reaching survey of mainstream media responses to Mosley and the BUF by Janet Dack also captures the sense in which anti-fascism in inter-war Britain appeared in various guises and gradations. What Dack establishes is that the liberal *News Chronicle* was by far the most anti-fascist of Britain's mainstream newspapers, although by the end of the 1930s all, including the *Daily Mail*, had no truck with home-grown fascism. It would be wrong, Dack concludes, to characterise this as anything approaching a 'united' or 'popular' front. Rather, the mainstream media comprised a '*de facto* front for British democracy that contained distinct strands of anti-fascism within it'. Richard Thurlow then takes us to the secret agencies of the state. Until 1940, British fascism was a second-order concern; the priority was communism (so much so that the state was prepared to collude with British fascism in the 1920s). Nevertheless, the state sought to marginalise and isolate Mosley from mainstream society, even if the primary purpose was to deny the Communist Party a platform (anti-fascism) on which to recruit. For Thurlow, state management of British fascism still constituted a variant of anti-fascism, albeit a 'passive' one based on political surveillance and minor changes to public order legislation. In Thurlow's narrative, the anti-fascism of the state turned 'active' with the 'sledgehammer' of internment and proscription in 1940, only to return to 'passive' anti-fascism with the cessation of hostilities in 1945.

In Part III of the book – intellectual responses – Dan Stone turns the spotlight on anti-fascist émigrés from Continental Europe. Focusing on the contribution of three such exiles, Stone argues that they brought a theoretical seriousness to domestic anti-fascist opinion. For Stone, whilst not necessarily contributing directly to the defeat of Mosleyite fascism, their uncompromising disquisitions on the nature of Nazism helped ready British opinion for the inevitability of war. That is why, for Stone, 'the spreading of an émigré-driven intellectual anti-fascist literature should be seen not merely as a middle-class or academic anti-fascism (that is, one that ultimately *does* nothing), but as a key part of the anti-fascist movement'. Andrzej Olechnowicz then challenges the idea that indigenous anti-fascist intellectuals were less perceptive about fascism than émigrés. While A. D. Lindsay believed re-stating a theory of democracy was the more important scholarly task, Harold Laski developed a theory of fascism by 1943 which combined economic and psychological explanations in a productive fashion. If their scholarship was flawed, this reflected the general state of their academic disciplines. Moreover, both believed that thought and action were complementary, and both participated in not only Labour but also all-party organisations.

Julia Stapleton's chapter on two of Britain's foremost radical Right intellectuals – G. K. Chesterton and Arthur Bryant – compels us to pause momentarily and reflect on the boundaries of both anti-fascism and pro-fascism. Whereas G. K. Chesterton and Arthur Bryant were both Edwardian patriots, Stapleton shows how their patriotism could pull in different directions: Chesterton away from pro-Nazism, Bryant towards it. And yet even Bryant's pro-Nazism had its limits. What held Bryant back, Stapleton reveals, was patriotic faith in the virtues of English local democracy. Similarly, Chesterton sought to expose democracy to fascist critique in order 'to strengthen not weaken it'. Nonetheless, to suggest that both Bryant and Chesterton were 'anti-fascist' would hardly make for a convincing argument given the sympathies that both shared for aspects of Continental fascism – 'non-fascists' perhaps, but not anti-fascists.

This brings us to the final perspectives where Richard Griffiths mulls over Britain's post-war anti-fascist consensus. For Griffiths, whilst this remained strong enough to militate against those domestic right-wing extremists that clung to conspiratorial anti-semitism and biological racism, it did not prove resilient enough to impede Franco's international rehabilitation. From 1950 onwards, pro-Franco sympathisers who inhabited Britain's inter-war establishment re-emerged, Griffiths argues, and openly worked for full diplomatic relations with Franco's Spain. Meanwhile, protest against Franco's international rehabilitation narrowed down to the traditional left-wing constituency that had led Britain's anti-fascist movement in the 1930s. According to Griffiths, it was during this period that one of the lasting myths of fascist studies was created: that Franco was not a fascist but an 'old-fashioned conservative', a distinction that 'would not have been understood either by Franco's contemporaries, or by Franco himself'.

As we shall see, anti-fascism in inter-war Britain was many-hued. The analogy that works best is that of a kaleidoscope through which we encounter different varieties of colour and form. Each variety in this anti-fascist kaleidoscope has a common point of intersection. At the point of intersection we find the anti-fascist 'minimum'. What all anti-fascists shared in inter-war Britain, at a minimum, was political and moral opposition to fascism rooted in the *democratic* values of the Enlightenment tradition. This was true right across the spectrum, including the Communist Party regardless of the totalitarian potential of Leninism-Stalinism. Of course, where one sat on this broad spectrum, whether on the Left or Right, would determine which aspect(s) to the suppression of democratic rights that anti-fascists were most obviously against – be it dictatorship, totalitarianism, ultra-nationalism, the subjugation of the working class, or racial and/or gender chauvinism.

Democracy, it needs hardly saying, is a contested concept. Historically there have been three principal types: liberal democracy, social democracy and people's or workers' democracy. All three have, as their common denominator, the democratic ideal 'of rule by the people'. Moreover, all three are bound up with the fundamental Enlightenment values of humanism, rationalism, progressivism, and universalism. These democratic precepts constitute the wellhead from which the myriad variants of anti-fascism spring. Fascism, needless to say, has its source not in the Enlightenment but in *reaction* to it – a 'counter-Enlightenment' that combined irrationalism, elitism, and national chauvinism in a revolutionary quest for an alternative modernity. As such, fascism represented 'a radical denial, almost the historical antithesis of the principles of the French Revolution that are the essence of all democratic ideologies', as the renowned historian of Italian Fascism, Emilio Gentile, put it.[1]

For the Communist Party, fascism constituted an open dictatorship of capital – a reactionary, frenzied and barbaric attack on the democratic rights of workers. Admittedly, when we speak of democratic rights and values in relation to Communism, we enter controversial and slippery terrain. But we need to speak, initially, not of the values of bourgeois capitalist democracy (liberal democracy) but those of workers' demo-cracy (the abolition of repressive control and its substitution with a radical democracy in which all workers participate). Under the existing regime, and in anticipation of a workers' democracy – the stage at which the workers' dictatorship was *supposed* to disappear – the CP agitated for maximum democratic rights for workers (right to strike, free speech, etc.), for the abolition of the monarchy and aristocracy, and for the right to self-determination in the Empire. Thus Rajani Palme Dutt could declare in 1933 that 'the Communist Party is in the forefront of the fight for democracy, of the fight for freedom, at every stage'.[2]

To begin with, this fight for workers' democracy was understood as a struggle *against* bourgeois capitalist democracy, and in particular reformist social democracy. Then, during the Popular Front era, as the CP looked to broaden the anti-fascist struggle to middle-class liberals and progres-sives, it morphed into a *defence* of bourgeois-democratic rights against fascist attack. As Dimitrov put it, 'All adherents of democracy must bear in mind that the fate of anti-fascist democracy in Europe is indissolubly bound up with the fate of the working class, with the establishment of the People's Front'.[3] At this moment, the democratic motif became more pronounced; democracy became the Popular Front's 'unifying theme'. The consequence, as Geoff Eley points out, was that 'The CPs now claimed the mantle of a nation's best democratic traditions', which meant 'speaking the language of national democracy'.[4] In Britain's case, as Tom Linehan's chapter shows, the CP endeavoured to site Popular Front anti-fascism in an indigenous radical tradition of popular demo-cratic dissent. But as we shall see, and understandably so given the total-itarian and repressive nature of the Soviet system, the claim that the CP stood for democratic values was regarded by many as entirely spe-cious. As evidenced not only in the attitudes of Labour and Conservative parties, but also the media and the secret agencies of state, communism, like fascism, was said to represent not democracy but dictatorship. As a result, in the 'conventional' anti-fascist interpretation of fascism – described by Rajani Palme Dutt as 'the hallmark of the liberal and social demo-cratic schools of thought'[5] – anti-fascism and anti-communism became one and the same.

The anti-fascist minimum that I propose here is only inferred from the British inter-war experience. It is not necessarily diachronically or synchronically generic, that is, not necessarily of universal application *across* history or for any particular period *in* history. Nonetheless, this anti-fascist minimum does counsel us against elevating anti-fascism to the status of an *ideology*. If we understand ideology to be a distinctive configuration of thought and action, then anti-fascism is not an ideo-logy in and of itself. Whilst anti-fascists shared a belief in the need to defeat fascism, they obviously differed when it came to more specific goals about how society should be structured. Moreover, they could also differ when it came to methods. So what then is the relationship between anti-fascism and ideology? 'Central to any analysis of ideologies', if we follow Michael Freeden's lead, 'is the proposition that they are charac-terised by a morphology that displays core, adjacent, and peripheral concepts'.[6] Core and adjacent concepts are essential to the formation of an ideology; peripheral concepts can be reactive, where other ideologies (in this case fascism) drive them on to the ideological agenda. If we put to one side the anomalous example of the former German Democratic Republic, which relocated anti-fascism to the core of state ideology, anti-fascism is probably best understood, in morphological terms, as a peripheral ideological concept that *reacts* to fascism as a phenomenon antithetical to core and adjacent (Enlightenment) conceptions of humanity and society. Whenever the threat of fascism becomes acute, this peripheral ideological component turns increasingly significant to the ideological core, not least because anti-fascism becomes essential to its very survival.

Readers of this volume should leave with an impression of Britain's diverse anti-fascist experience between the wars. But we are acutely aware that much more needs to be said about the historic and contem-porary complexities of anti-fascism, not just in Britain but also else-where. There is, for sure, an urgent need for international comparison. It was in 1985 that Jacques Droz published (in French) a pioneering sur-vey of anti-fascism as a pan-European phenomenon.[7] And yet, little comparative history has appeared since, all the more surprising given that anti-fascism's reach stretches beyond Europe's shores. In his con-tribution to this volume, Dan Stone is right to call on academe to 'inter-nationalise' the study of anti-fascism. Let us finally heed that call and apply ourselves to an international study of comparative anti-fascism with the vigour that has characterised recent studies of generic fascism. Historians 'should look again at the clichéd dualism of "fascism and democracy"', as Tom Buchanan recommends, 'and start treating the democratic side with the complexity and seriousness which quite rightly, they have brought to an understanding of the fascist side'.[8] Further work clearly needs to be done, but in publishing this volume we hope that the subject of anti-fascism in inter-war Britain benefits from the type of serious historical representation that its complexity deserves.

Notes

1 Emilio Gentile, *The Origins of Fascist Ideology, 1918–1925* (New York: Enigma Books, 2005), p. 358.
2 Rajani Palme Dutt, *Democracy and Fascism* (London: Utopia Press, 1933), p. 11.
3 Georgi Dimitrov, *The United Front* (London: Lawrence and Wishart, 1938), p. 205.
4 Geoff Eley, *Forging Democracy: The History of the Left in Europe, 1850–2000* (Oxford: Oxford University Press, 2002), p. 266.
5 Rajani Palme Dutt, *Fascism and Social Revolution* (London: Martin Lawrence, 1934), p. 76.
6 Michael Freeden, *Ideologies and Political Theory: A Conceptual Approach* (Oxford: Clarendon Press, 1996), p. 77.
7 See Jacques Droz, *Histoire de l'antifascisme en Europe, 1923–39* (Paris: La Découverte, 1985).
8 Tom Buchanan, 'Anti-fascism and Democracy in the 1930s', *European History Quarterly* 32, 1 (2002), 54.

Introduction: Historians and the Study of Anti-Fascism in Britain

Andrzej Olechnowicz

The study of anti-fascism requires more care perhaps than many other areas of historical inquiry. For some before 1939 opposition to fascism was already a terrain of moral absolutes (anti-fascism of whatever kind was absolutely good because fascism of all kinds was absolutely evil); but for as many others it was a muddled terrain, a matter of degree, a choice of evils (anti-fascists might appear as totalitarian as the enemy they fought, for instance). After the defeat of Nazism, the evidence of genocide and the fact of collaboration on the mainland of Europe, 'anti-fascism' became almost the only sure and apparently uncompromised basis for post-war 'democratic' legitimacy in many countries. It is important to recognise that this was no less true of Britain. Here, however, rather than 'resistance', the predominant sense of anti-fascism immediately after the war was as anti-appeasement and pro-rearmament: the cardinal sin was not to have challenged Chamberlain's policy of appeasement rather than Mosley's (or Leese's or others') schemes for dictatorship. What seemed most morally reprehensible and practically damaging was the failure to stop Hitler and war by supporting rearmament; by comparison, Mosley's British Union of Fascists had been successfully contained. The BUF had not come close to undermining parliamentary democracy and its potential for collaboration had not been allowed to be tested.

In one sense, therefore, it is not at all surprising that (other than in the form of the many studies of appeasement, one might add) there was still in 1996 'as yet no historical literature of anti-fascism ... written by professional historians, or written with any distance from the events described'; existing studies were limited and local or the recollections of activists.[1] In another sense, however, the absence is striking, not only because of the many studies of the BUF since Colin

1

Cross's *The Fascists in Britain* (1961), but also because anti-fascist campaigns mobilised, not only in the inter-war period, but throughout the twentieth century, many more Britons than fascists were able to.[2] This absence was finally addressed in 2000, when both Nigel Copsey's *Anti-Fascism in Britain* and Dave Renton's *Fascism, Anti-Fascism and Britain in the 1940s* were published.

This overview will therefore first outline the areas of agreement and disagreement in these two ground-breaking volumes. Though Copsey is less exclusive and dogmatic than Renton and acknowledges the contribution of the state in the 1930s, both pay most attention to the contribution of left-wing activists' organisations in fighting domestic fascism. Does this neglect other varieties of anti-fascism? Second, were the internal weaknesses of fascist organisations so severe as to ensure they would remain ineffective? Third, at what moments of economic and political crisis, if any, did fascism have a chance in Britain? Here opinions vary. Martin Pugh's *'Hurrah for the Blackshirts!'* (2005), most notably, identifies several such moments from the mid-1920s onwards. Alternatively, can a stronger case be made for the period 1918–23? Fourth, most historians ultimately agree that the economic situation was the most critical factor: the slump was never sufficiently deep nor prolonged in Britain to cause the mass of the electorate to abandon the established parliamentary parties. Fifth, however, there is less agreement and indeed less clarity about the inoculative power of Britain's 'liberal', 'democratic' political culture. What exactly are the components of this culture? How entrenched were they? What importance should be attached to the fascist sympathisers identified in Richard Griffith's pioneering *Fellow Travellers of the Right* (1980)? Here we would do well to note that although fascists were unmistakably anti-democratic, many progressives also criticised the existing political system in the 1930s but with a view to making it more genuinely democratic while retaining its key features. A further two sections will consider debates surrounding anti-semitism and appeasement. Finally, what is the legacy of the anti-fascism of the 1930s for contemporary society? Does it still (if it ever did) provide the narrative for understanding the modern world as such? Is Britain too in any way part of the 'massive campaign to denigrate the entire anti-fascist tradition' which Enzo Traverso has detected in Italy, Germany and France?[3]

Left-wing anti-fascist activism

Copsey's book was welcomed for correcting 'earlier, simplistic approaches that restricted the study of anti-fascism to anti-fascist *activist militants* and their formal organization'.[4] Instead, Copsey defined anti-fascism as 'a thought, an attitude or feeling of hostility towards fascist ideology and its propagators which may or may not be acted upon. In other words, anti-fascism can be both active and passive. It can take numerous forms, it sources therefore vary and so conceivably encompass responses by both the state and the media'. It made sense to regard a whole political culture as anti-fascist 'even if the vast majority of society refrains from active expressions of hostility towards fascism'. Anti-fascism was, therefore, 'a mosaic, a variegated phenomenon'.[5] It was also, from its origins in 1923 when Communists disrupted the inaugural meeting of the British Fascisti, a reactive phenomenon meaning 'quite simply that the scale of response has been defined by the nature of its stimulus'.[6] As the threat grew, the Communist Party of Great Britain (CPGB), the Labour Party, the Jewish Board of Deputies, the National Council of Civil Liberties, the central state through the Public Order Act of 1936 and usually Labour-controlled local authorities which from the mid-1930s refused to allow the BUF the use of halls for meetings, all responded. There were tensions between and within all these bodies; but Copsey emphasises that, although Labour pursued peaceful protest and education and the Communists direct confrontation, crucially these contrasting policies 'actually worked in tandem'. Labour's 'political moderation and liberalism' helped to marginalise political violence and extremism while the CPGB engaged the BUF in violent confrontations, ensuring that 'Mosley remained outside the political mainstream'.[7] Even so, Copsey argues that the effectiveness of this anti-fascism is 'more difficult to ascertain' for the later than the early 1930s: he accepts, for example, that the 'Battle of Cable Street' stimulated fascist recruitment and that little attention was paid to the middle class attracted by Mosley's turn to an anti-war policy in 1938. He speculates that since fascist and anti-fascist violence was mutually reinforcing, monitoring but ignoring BUF provocations, as the Jewish Board of Deputies' Vigilance Committees did from late 1936, offered, 'one way of breaking the cycle'; and concludes that by the end of the 1930s the local authorities' withholding of meeting halls from the BUF 'probably proved more damaging to the BUF than any remaining physical opposition by anti-fascists'.[8] These are judgements that historians of fascism share;[9] and Skidelsky was, if anything, more positive about the effectiveness of left-wing anti-fascist activity, arguing that it was Mosley's failure to solve 'the tactical problem posed by unrelenting left-wing opposition' which meant that all the big halls were closed to him by the late 1930s (and he was kept off the radio and out of the press).[10]

Copsey had foreseen that his less exclusive and more multi-dimensional view of anti-fascism would prove a 'harder furrow to plough';[11] and so it does compared to Renton's return to that earlier, simplistic conceptual universe (of which Copsey is critical).[12] Nonetheless, Renton's contributions are also meticulously researched and deserve a respectful hearing. The fundamental distinction for Renton is between 'non-fascists' and 'anti-fascists'. The former 'did not act to stop fascism'; the latter did and to that end emphasised the need for activism and organisation: 'if a number of people are going to act against fascism, then it follows that they should work in a collective, organised, efficient and disciplined manner'. A third feature of anti-fascism was the necessity for 'some positive agenda, some alternative values, against which the values of fascism can be counterposed'.[13] Renton emphasises the need for empirical inquiry;[14] but the nature of this definition points inexorably to the conclusion that the history of British anti-fascism in the 1930s is 'a story of the Communist Party'; its organisations such as the Red Shirts, Anti-Fascist League and Jewish People's Council (and Popular Front organisations such as the Unity campaign and Crusade for the Defence of the British People);[15] and its activism, notably the presence of at least 100,000 anti-fascists to block Gardiner's Corner in the Battle of Cable Street, which was straightforwardly a 'fascist defeat'.[16]

What ultimately matters most for Renton (as for some other historians)[17] are the numbers mobilised on the streets;[18] therefore, he is critical of the CPGB's support for the Popular Front in the later 1930s since it 'took the Communists away from their long-held belief in street politics'; nonetheless, the party retained 'some form of radical politics' and still remained the most important organisation 'opposing Mosley on the streets'.[19] By comparison, the Labour Party and the Conservative Party (at least after 1945) were non-fascist, not anti-fascist: in the later 1940s both 'argued against those anti-fascists that aimed to stop Mosley from below'.[20] Yet the unavoidable difficulty with this perspective even for those generally sympathetic to the CPGB is the party's shift to the strategy of a 'People's Peace' pursued between October 1939 and June 1941. For its critics, this was 'revolutionary defeatism', re-defining an anti-fascist war as an 'imperialist war', proposing that 'the defeat of the Churchill government is a more urgent matter for the British workers than the defeat of Hitler and Mussolini' and possibly making peace with the dictators. The shift was undertaken to justify the Nazi-Soviet Non-Aggression Pact of August 1939 but made 'nonsense of everything Communists have said of fascism' and made likely the 'total conquest' of Britain by the Nazis.[21]

There are more fundamental differences still between the two books. Copsey believes that it is possible for a capitalist state to be anti-fascist; Renton does not. He demonstrates that in 1947 the police, for example, were nearly three times as likely to arrest anti-fascists as fascists and colluded with fascists in court, and in the later 1940s acted to keep fascist meetings open. Renton concludes that the police 'acted in collusion with the fascists' and 'favoured the fascists' because the police's function was 'to protect property, and to obstruct anyone that threatened it'.[22] Though Copsey accepts that fascism has ebbed and flowed in Britain since the 1930s (with popular racism providing a platform for the British National Party in the 1990s),[23] Renton is insistent that 'fascism is a recurrent response to the conditions of life under capitalism ... while capitalism survives, fascism will recur'.[24] His engagement as an anti-fascist activist in the Socialist Workers' Party leads him to castigate 'liberal historians' for being pre-occupied with describing a 'fascist minimum' in terms of fascism's ideas, rather than according analytical priority to it as 'a specific form of reactionary mass movement'. His most striking conclusion is that this failure leads liberal historians to 'fail to generate a non-fascist understanding of fascism' and eschew 'the very idea of anti-fascist history'.[25]

Each of these broadsides invites a counterblast; but here it is more useful to note that, in practice, there are marked similarities between Copsey and Renton. Both deal primarily with left-wing and relatively formal organisations; the centre and right of the political spectrum hardly feature; nor do intellectuals. Moreover, anti-fascism for both is about meeting the threat of native fascism; little or no attention is paid to opposition in Britain to European fascism. Recent work has endeavoured to consider other varieties of anti-fascism. Liberal and Conservative anti-fascism has been explored, though as yet the focus has been primarily on individuals rather than institutions.[26] Dan Stone has emphasised the vital political education provided from 1936 by Left Book Club publications and discussion groups, and from 1938 the sixpenny Penguin Specials, which 'often sold in the tens of thousands, occasionally in the hundreds of thousands': 'millions of ordinary Britons' knew what fascism was like, and 'it scared them enough to know that they did not want it'.[27]

The basis (and limitations) of Anglican opposition to Nazism's 'war against Christian theology' have been examined.[28] These anti-fascisms saw little real danger to Britain from the BUF but were appalled by many of the policies of Italian and especially German fascism and feared fascist ideology as a threat to 'Western civilisation'. Other research has tried to go beyond 'the visible and the formal' groups to consider the dynamics of communally-based resistance.[29] Neil Barrett, for example, has examined how community structures 'could transcend political cleavages' in Nelson in the 1930s while among the Jewish population of Cheetham in Manchester opposition to the BUF was weakened by the community elders' anxiety about their own communal authority.[30] Copsey and Renton may have looked at the most obvious anti-fascist forces; but they were by no means the only ones.

The internal weaknesses of the BUF

Copsey and Renton finally share the view that the BUF was a threat (particularly so in 1934 when supported by the Rothermere press); and some contemporary centrist opinion would bear them out. For Lord Meston in 1935, for example, the Blackshirts were 'going to be a factor in our politics which will have, sooner or later, to be reckoned with … here is a fire which will spread'.[31] For many historians of British fascism, however, the various fascist movements including the BUF were subject to the kinds of internal weaknesses which made sustained and purposeful political action unlikely or impossible. The British Fascisti had few supporters (it claimed one million members while Special Branch put the figure at 300–400 activists in 1934), faced a series of damaging splits, and was handicapped by Rotha Lintorn-Orman's poor leadership. Secessionists from the BF formed the more extreme National Fascisti in 1924 (about 100 members at its foundation) and the Imperial Fascist League in 1929 (which was dominated by Arnold Leese's obsessive anti-semitism and had about 150 members in the 1930s). Richard Thurlow writes that these fascists 'were regarded as highly eccentric by the small minority who knew of their activities, and as a nuisance by the police'.[32] Reviewing Cross's book in 1964, Clement Attlee could write, 'I must confess that although an active politician during the whole of the period, I had never heard of Miss Lintorn Orman or Mr. Arnold Leese before reading this book. I knew, of course, that there were obscure groups of Fascists. Every now and again a youth would appear in the police court charged with making a disturbance'.[33] Mosley and the BUF were a different proposition; but in Attlee's recollection still no more than 'a nuisance'.

The BUF's internal weakness can be considered in terms of membership, organisation, finance and ideology. The most widely accepted estimate of BUF membership suggests 17,000 in February 1934, sixteen months after it was formed, a peak of 50,000 in July 1934, a month after the Olympia meeting, 5,000 in October 1935, 10,000 in March and 15,500 in November 1936, with the campaign of anti-semitism and violence in the East End, 16,000 in December 1938 and 22,500 in September 1939.[34] Its bravado aside, this was not a movement which was growing. Nor was it in reality a 'national' movement. Its main areas of support were London, the North West, South Wales, the towns of the south Coast, Bristol, Reading, Birmingham, Leeds, Edinburgh and Aberdeen; the most recent work has also stressed some success in attracting support in rural areas from farmers.[35] Even in these areas active membership could be desperately small: for example, no more than 100 in the North West by 1937. Even in East London, with 2,000 active supporters in 1936, Tom Linehan has demonstrated that a united 'East London movement' in reality did not exist; what did were numbers of shifting groups rooted in local political concerns.[36] The shifting strategies and campaigns of the BUF led to constant changes in its social composition; but, Thurlow argues, its greatest success was among 'retired military gentlemen, some working-class elements, the lower middle classes and "spirited" middle-class women'; and what this disparate band had in common was the sociological fact of possessing initiative but experiencing 'bottlenecks in mobility patterns in society' as a result of economic depression and 'the lingering after-effects of the First World War'. Thurlow draws attention to W. F. Mandle's analysis of the social 'rootlessness' of BUF parliamentary candidates chosen after 1935.[37] C. L. Mowat had also identified black-coated workers and young middle-class men as core groups because the depression denied these two groups 'employment and importance'.[38] If this is the case, then the BUF were fishing for support in a very small pool because, as suggested below, there was little middle-class discontent in Britain in the 1930s. David Baker's biographical study of A. K. Chesterton points in the same direction: Chesterton's career certainly does not support a view of fascism as attractive solely to 'madmen, charlatans, and misfits': he was 'a relatively "normal" individual, of some talent', attracted to fascism because of his 'cultural ideas, social and historical background, and life experiences.'[39] Nevertheless, his experiences were 'far away from [those of] the average veteran or ordinary postwar citizen'.[40]

Hitler was told by a Nazi agent that the BUF had no organisation. This was not quite true; rather the BUF organisation seemed to be in constant flux and change. In Thurlow's opinion, 'those responsible for organization lacked the competence to manage the growth of a political movement'.[41] One cause of this flux was a bitter rivalry between radicals such as William Joyce and John Beckett – who favoured a more demagogic, anti-semitic and confrontational style – and party adminis-trators who wanted the opposite, and the way this rivalry was played out through control of the party machine, resulting in a succession of dismissals and re-organisations. Another cause, however, was the financial precariousness of the movement, since members' subscrip-tions generated relatively little income. By the mid-1930s MI5 was reporting that it was kept going only by secret payments from Musso-lini; when these ended in 1937 the Headquarters staff had to be reduced by over 55 per cent.[42]

Since the publication of Skidelsky's biography of Mosley in 1975, historians have been much fascinated by Mosley's political ideas and the ideological hue of his movement. The broad consensus seems to be that Mosley had a coherent philosophy and programme influenced by Spengler and Shaw, and Keynes and corporatism respectively.[43] The movement's ideas constituted 'to a large degree a cultural revolt' against 'decadent' modern life and democracy which saw in the Shavian 'new fascist man' the 'capacity to overcome the degenerative forces of internal decay that were supposedly debilitating Britain'.[44] Even if these ideas were interesting and impressively articulated (and Spengler-ism and Shavianism were doing the rounds in this period), and even if there had not been a bitter ideological division with the movement resulting in dismissals and resignations,[45] what significance do they have for the political effectiveness of the BUF? As McKibbin has observed, if any aspect of Mosley's thought deserves to be examined in detail, it is the coherence (and, one might add, dissemination and reception) of his economic ideas, since economic distress and decline were mainstream political issues and idioms; moreover, 'Shavian supermen and Faustian angst ... seems a long way from Cable Street and the teddy boys'.[46] The BUF did attempt to project its cultural philosophy;[47] but its identity among the electorate was not defined by it; and even if it had been, it is unlikely there was a wide constituency for these ideas among voters.

Crisis and opportunity?

Was there ever a real opportunity for fascism to gain power in Britain? Pugh clearly thinks so; indeed, that there were several moments of *political* crisis:

> In 1926 a prolonged general strike could well have destroyed Baldwin's government and created the opportunity fascists were looking for. The

crisis of 1931 that led to the creation of the National Government came at a point when no significant fascist alternative existed. When Mosley produced what was by far the most coherent and compelling challenge in the autumn of 1932, he was just too late to catch the parliamentary system at its most vulnerable ... In 1936 the abdication crisis showed just how vulnerable Britain's constitutional arrangements were; but, again, contingency, in the shape of the King's sudden withdrawal, snatched his opportunity away.

In addition, 'Buoyed by the backing of Rothermere's newspapers, sustained by generous funding, and emboldened by the low morale among government supporters, Mosley posed a serious threat to the conventional politicians during the first half of 1934.'[48]

This is nonsense. There were no viable fascist organisations in 1926 and 1931. Moreover, critically in 1931, the party system did not collapse as a result of mounting economic crisis, as Mosley gambled it would with the launch of the New Party in February 1931.[49] Instead, the formation of a National Government addressed the balance of payments crisis and preserved the essentials of the party system and its loyalties: for Skidelsky 'the sheer *political* competence of the English parliamentary system in this period' was remarkable;[50] and an argument could be made that the National Government constituted the main anti-fascist bulwark in preventing a political disintegration which would 'liquefy existing affiliations'.[51] In 1936 constitutionalism was too deeply entrenched within the main political parties and among the public, and Edward VIII too 'unpolitical' and distracted, for the sort of constitutional irregularities proposed by Pugh to be remotely possible (let alone a *coup d'état*). Forty Conservative MPs and peers promising to support the King (out of 429 government members), Lady Houston calling on the King, and a BUF loudspeaker van in Whitehall and the Mall is hardly incontrovertible evidence of a rapidly emerging 'King's Party'. This was not 'constitutional deadlock'; nor December 1936 'the closest fascism came to obtaining a share of power in inter-war Britain'.[52] Pugh argues that in the first half of 1934 the BUF was attracting a 'wide range of support', except from the upper classes even though these had been prominent in the fascist organisations of the 1920s; that Mosley expected to see some BUF MPs in Parliament after the next general election; and that the membership of the January Club, established on 1 January 1934, and in his opinion undoubtedly 'designed as a front organisation for the BUF', 'reflected the fascist sympathies of the right wing of Conservatism'. When a further economic crisis arose, an alliance of BUF MPs and sympathetic right-wing MPs and peers would be well placed to manage a peaceful transition from parliamentary democracy to the corporate state.[53] As it happened, no further economic crisis arose and no BUF candidates stood in the 1935 election. But even if they had, it is most unlikely that any leading and few ordinary Conservatives would have joined in an alliance with the BUF. This was not only because of party loyalty and party discipline; it was because Mosley was seen as an untrustworthy 'renegade' and 'cad'; and because, as Griffiths has argued, in its initial stages the January Club was 'very much a discussion group' and did not mean that 'the majority of members were primarily interested in the BUF'.[54] Indeed, what might have brought them together was a common inheritance from the Edwardian 'radical right'.[55] Moreover, the Conservatives that the January Club attracted – Alan Lennox-Boyd, Hugh Molson, Viscount Lymington, Michael Beaumont and Lord Erskine (Lord William Scott and Duncan Sandys became MPs in 1935) – were almost all back-benchers.[56] In addition, Pugh also identifies Henry Drummond Wolff, Sir Thomas Moore, J. T. C. Moore-Brabazon, Patrick Donner and Earl Winterton as supporting Mosley; but again these were not the Conservatives who mattered.[57] The political system was impregnable to the BUF.

Was discontent with the *social* structure ever so profound in the inter-war period as to destroy existing loyalties and generate support for fascist movements, especially among those social groups identified by Thurlow as their core constituency? The early 1930s are one candidate for such a period of social crisis, as unemployment rose from 10.4 per cent in 1929 to 22.1 per cent in 1932. But virtually all historians agree that a major, even the major, reason for the BUF's failure in the 1930s was the fact that, in Pugh's words, 'Britain's slump was a comparatively modest affair'[58] – and part of the reason for this was the policies of the National Government which was as aware as its own critics that 'the fate of Democracy is linked up with the problem of economic progress'.[59] After 1932 there was a modest recovery, with unemployment falling to 19.9 per cent in 1933, 16.7 per cent in 1934 and 10.8 per cent in 1937. More precisely, the depression hardly affected the middle class: McKibbin points out that 'the *majority* of working men and women in the interwar years were at some moment in their lives genuinely unemployed; the *majority* of the middle classes never faced such unemployment at all'; only actors and musicians among the middle class faced significant unemployment.[60] Moreover, 'almost uniquely among major economies, Britain didn't experience a run on the banks or a threat to people's savings'.[61] Although the predominantly working-class unemployed were not as apathetic and fatalistic as many academic investigators supposed, their politics were circumscribed by the dole; they could not plausibly be presented to, and regarded by, the middle class as a national political threat, rather they were often the objects of middle-class social pity.[62] This quietude of the unemployed (except in 1935) also owed something to the sustained fall in prices in the 1930s, which also, of course, benefited the middle class.[63]

A more plausible period to consider is the early 1920s. Although McKibbin nowhere suggests that the middle class were turning to fascism in 1918 to 1923, his anatomy of what was for some elements of that class a period of 'genuine "crisis"' is reminiscent of at least some of the social conditions which prevailed in Italy and later in Germany. McKibbin proposes that 'it is impossible not to be struck now by the precariousness of life as much of the middle class saw it at the end of the First World War; by the sense of helplessness with which many contemplated their future'. For some elements of the middle class their anxiety about becoming the 'new poor' was misconceived; but the impact of high post-war inflation on other elements was to leave their real earnings 'lower, perhaps significantly lower, than in 1914'. The combination of real and imagined fears produced in this period 'more severe class conflict than at any other time in modern British history':[64] the middle class blamed their plight on the unpatriotic greed of the workers and trade unionists (and 'profiteers', who were shady plutocrats, but also in the pages of *Punch* income-tax paying, suit wearing, work-shy workers).[65] There was a fleeting middle-class anger that the Conservative Party appeared to have abandoned it, which found temporary expression in support for middle-class interest groups, such as the rather transitory People's League of 'Silent Sufferers', and the more established Anti-Waste League and Middle Classes Union, formed 'to protect the great, hitherto unorganized Middle Classes against the insatiable demands of Labour'.[66] Had there been a viable, politically astute fascist movement at this time, it might have made headway as a 'party' of middle-class protest. Even then, the opportunity was not great since, for the middle class, this short period closed with 'a happy ending'. The rapid price deflation from December 1920 and low levels of middle-class (unlike working-class) unemployment rapidly restored most actual losses in middle-class real earnings. Moreover, the Conservative Party – a middle-class party in terms of the social composition of its grass-roots membership *and* the parliamentary party, argues McKibbin

– rapidly re-connected with that class by 1920 through its emphasis on defence of 'the constitution' from left-wing attack, and its adoption of 'deflation', which *clearly* advantaged the middle and *visibly* disadvantaged the working class.[67]

One of the striking absences in Britain in this period (and throughout the inter-war period) compared to, say, Italy in '*il Biennio Rosso*' was a strong Communist Party and a credible 'red scare'. This is not to deny that there were alarming episodes (such as 'Bloody Friday' in Glasgow on 31 January 1919) or that the middle-class fantasy of a 'red scare' could be stronger than the reality; but these did not require forces other than the 'normal' forces of law and order (some British equivalent of the Italian fascist paramilitary *squadristi*) to deal with them. Critically, by 1920, when the CPGB was founded, the post-war 'crisis' had already been decisively resolved in favour of the middle class. The Communists had only around 4,000 members. Had they managed to win over the Independent Labour Party (ILP), with its 45,000 members, they would have represented an altogether more formidable force; but, according to David Marquand, their willingness to take directions from the Comintern, which had little understanding of British labour, meant that that real possibility was squandered.[68] For Eric Hobsbawm the 'insurmountable handicap' of British communism was the impossibility of creating in British conditions 'strong local communities politically identified with a class party' as in the Paris 'red belt'.[69] Whatever the causes of its weakness, the CPGB was weak; and British fascism's claim to be defending the nation from 'Bolshevism' correspondingly weak as well.

Indeed, looked at from the perspective of comparative historians of fascism, fascist lack of success in Britain (and northern Europe generally) is 'in no way surprising, since nearly all the conditions listed by most analysts as likely prerequisites for the emergence of fascism were lacking', namely problems of nationalism, ethnicity or international status;[70] or, in another formulation, a weak Conservative Party, a powerful extreme Left, an unstable rural population, conflict between traditionalist Christians and a secular state and 'undemocratic' attitudes among employers.[71] This has taken us a long way from Copsey and Renton; but it has important implications for their approach: fascism would have had no chance in Britain, even if no anti-fascist organisations had ever existed. It was not as if Mosley had not been warned: 'Oswald Mosley had a terrific dressing down from him [Mussolini] when he had bn to see him in Rome & announced his intention of founding British Fascism. Musso: told him it was quite unsuitable for England.'[72]

Political culture

For many British historians the main reason fascism stood no chance of success in Britain, even without the existence of the anti-fascist organisations studied by Copsey and Renton, is Britain's 'liberal', democratic political culture; or rather the main form of Britain's anti-fascism was the nature of its political culture.[73] As Attlee later opined, the British people were 'too democratic and too experienced to fall for a rabble-rouser like Mosley'.[74] The elements of this culture included a deep belief in parliamentary democracy and constitutionalism across all three main parliamentary parties, with the monarchy as 'the even-handed guarantor of the class-neutrality of Parliament' (meaning that, as we have seen, the number of Conservative MPs sympathetic to fascism – and, we should add, Labour MPs sympathetic to communism – was very small);[75] a commitment to liberal freedoms of free speech and assembly; and an antipathy to political violence in a nation celebrated as a 'peaceable kingdom'.[76]

There is undoubtedly much truth in this;[77] but three qualifications are worth entering. Firstly, the concept of 'political culture' lacks overall coherence and is too vague: as one reviewer of Robert Benewick's book in this vein complained, 'one's understanding is not substantially advanced by such broad generalizations'.[78] Above all, is a political culture a fixed 'inheritance' shaping a society?; or a set of tendencies which need constantly to be reproduced by identifiable agencies? Secondly, there continues to be speculation that the 'establishment', including King Edward VIII, was 'pro-Nazi';[79] but this appears to be on the basis of unwarranted inferences. Griffiths has shown, for instance, that the January Club 'certainly attracted the Establishment', including members of the then Prince of Wales's circle;[80] but this was not, as we have already seen, reliable evidence of support for the BUF. Edward VIII appears to have been more motivated by anti-communism and a desire for peace in his dealings with the Nazis;[81] but, crucially, in any case, the court did not represent the centre of executive decision-making in Britain. Thirdly, many supporters of this culture in the inter-war period feared that it was being undermined from within by the extension of police powers: in 1937 G. D. H. Cole saw in this extension the foundations 'being laid for a gentlemanly semi-Fascism'.[82] Thurlow has made a powerful case that the Home Office was generally concerned to protect public order *and* civil liberty; that the security services were pragmatic and unbiased; and that while the Public Order Act was obviously intended to limit free speech, its impact in practice was inconsistent. Moreover, contrary to left-wing claims, the police (at least at the highest levels) were not pro-fascist, indeed the Metropolitan Police Commissioner Sir Philip Game strongly argued for the banning fascists and outlawing anti-semitism.[83] The evidence of Ewing and Gearty for the view that it was 'a case of freedom for all except those who dissent' is, however, also striking;[84] the 'discrepancy' might be explained, but at best only in part, by the additional focus of this latter work on 'the politics of the judiciary'. Fourthly, Griffiths detected a widespread 'weariness of democracy' in the first half of the thirties, certainly among admirers of the fascist dictators, but also among some of their detractors, such as the socialist Harold Laski or the Liberal Ramsay Muir, who published *Democracy in Crisis* (1933) and *Is Democracy a Failure?* (1934) respectively.[85]

'Democracy' was manifestly under attack between the wars; but, again, this requires qualification. First, the total number and influence of its outright detractors in Britain was not great. Second, many supporters believed that the most fundamental threat to democracy came from the way modern technology, bureaucracy and the mass media was creating a 'mass society'; fascism was but one possible symptom of this momentous shift from the liberal, bourgeois society created in the nineteenth century.[86] Third, as Tom Buchanan has reminded us, there was a 'multiplicity of conceptions of democracy' in the thirties;[87] some were obviously incompatible with British parliamentary democracy but others were not or not much (Laski might be a case in point; or Attlee, at least in *The Labour Party in Perspective*).[88] Thus, a few attacked Britain's democracy in order to destroy it, but more to preserve it. Fourth, and most importantly, there was a massive ideological campaign by politicians of all parliamentary parties, academics and writers to defend Britain's extant parliamentary democracy in speeches, newspaper and journal articles and books, and through organisations such as the Liberal E. D. Simon's cross-party Association for Education in Citizenship formed in 1934. Philip Williamson has demonstrated Baldwin's significance to this defence, as he developed from the winter of 1933–34 an anti-totalitarianism which 'went deeper than ordinary party and government concerns'.[89] This co-existed with (and partly shaped no doubt) a broader conservative temperament in the 1930s extending beyond simply the party which valued 'moderation, neutrality, impartiality' and 'the liberties of the known and the familiar' as 'part of that retreat within the middle classes from the more gung-ho expressions of national confidence'.[90] The missing link in this emphasis on the Conservative strengthening of the extant political culture, however, is the absence of a definitive study of Neville Chamberlain along these lines. The existing impression is that these anti-fascist themes were not very prominent in his rhetoric.

Two other aspects of the broader public culture that historians have recently suggested were significant in inhibiting fascism are the ubiquitous ideology of 'national character' and the prominence of voluntary associations in Britain. Matthew Grimley notes that although in origin a Liberal discourse, 'national character was appropriated by writers of all parties in the interwar period' and celebrated the 'gentle' virtues of 'tolerance, modesty, eccentricity, and individualism' and the importance of cultural factors, notably religion. This was an 'inward' rather than public religion, and one that 'did not erase denominational distinctions but, rather, was superimposed upon them' through the common Puritan inheritance of Anglicanism and Nonconformity, which denoted 'independence, adherence to conscience, tolerance, high seriousness and hard work'. Moreover, this was allied to the 'survival of a low-key providentialism in national character writing and in political rhetoric'.[91] What is most striking in Grimley's account is his insistence that this ideology had a wide audience 'in the sitting rooms of suburbia through popular histories, radio talks, and the middlebrow press' *and* that it was employed to meet a number of political challenges, including that of Nazi Germany.[92] Vagueness envelopes the notion of 'national character' and its use by historians. Is the further and far-reaching claim being made that this is how the British people truly were?[93] Were there not a plurality of sometimes contradictory notions of 'national character'? Where, for example does 'humour' fit in?; for Attlee 'Cockney humour' was important in 'debunking Mosley's theatrical displays'.[94]

A key feature of Grimley's 'religion of Englishness' was the part Nonconformist voluntarism played in it.[95] Helen McCarthy's research on inter-war voluntary associations such as the National Federation of Women's Institutes, Rotary International, British Legion and League of Nations Union leads her to conclude that the extension of the franchise in 1918 led to 'the establishment of new kinds of civic association, often secular in character, strongly invested in a discourse of active citizenship, and committed to creating and defending a space within associational life which was free of partisan or sectarian conflict'. Their 'pluralist values and political centrism' provided 'important insulation against the currents of political extremism which convulsed other European societies in this period'; and they were 'routinely invoked by politicians on both the left and right as living proof of

Britain's special genius for democracy' (thereby entrenching the fact that British democracy worked).[96] However, it is cautionary to remember that historians of the collapse of Weimar demonstrate that 'participation in organizations of civil society did link individuals together and help mobilize them ... but in the German case this served not to strengthen democracy but to weaken it'.[97] This suggests that voluntary associations (which were, of course, not, as some inter-war writers would have it, uniquely prominent in Britain – rather 'their multiplication is one of the features of a modern civilized community' throughout the world)[98] reflected, not constituted, the political cultures of their societies. It follows that McCarthy is perhaps too ready on too little evidence to reject McKibbin's argument that the latent function of many of these associations was to reinforce the 'informal Conservative hold on bourgeois associational life'.[99] It further suggests the need to pay very close attention to their publications and activities; and to distinguish between an explicitly anti-fascist *role* (in the same way as the Left Book Club) and anti-fascist *effects*.

Finally, historians' laudatory accounts of the inter-war political culture are usually silent on issues of racism and anti-semitism; and, as a general proposition, the near-silence of European anti-fascists in the face of 1930s anti-semitism and ultimately Auschwitz has seemed 'difficult to fathom'.[100] Although historians of fascism differ as to the precise character of Mosley's and the BUF's anti-semitism, that it is right to describe the movement as 'anti-semitic' is agreed, even if Mosley's biographer 'attempts to show that Mosley's anti-semitism was half-hearted and imitative'.[101] The question which requires an answer here, though, is how far anti-semitism was mainstream in British politics and society. Holmes concludes that a 'non-theoretical form of anti-semitic social discrimination in Britain was apparent and abundant evidence of attitudinal hostility towards Jews which assumed different forms' at times of social pressure; but there was no 'official government anti-semitism'.[102] Tony Kushner suggests a fundamental ambiguity in liberal democracies towards Jews, for 'to attack Jews *as Jews* was anathema, yet many western cultures held deeply ingrained views of the "Jew"'.[103] The ideology of 'national character' was important here, because nearly all writers in that mode emphasised the notion that the English were 'racially mixed and could not be distinguished from other European peoples'; hence the prominence of cultural factors that has already been noted.[104] Nonetheless, many 'anti-fascist' intellectuals and bodies did not make anti-semitism a prominent feature (or at all) of its analysis of fascism. Many left-wing intellectuals saw anti-semitism as an epiphenomenal propaganda tool of fascist regimes, which were reactionary forms of monopoly capitalism intent on first and foremost destroying workers' movements. Considered in a broader liberal context, the puzzle presented by Nazi anti-semitism was 'explaining the *ferocity* of Nazi antisemitism within a liberal framework' of rationality. Since it was manifestly irrational, it could not possibly be central to Nazism; and since it was not central, reports of its ferocity must have been exaggerated.[105] Lawson has demonstrated that Anglicanism's understanding of Nazism as a form of anti-Christian totalitarianism 'discouraged specific engagement with the nature of Nazi anti-Semitism', with clearly anti-semitic outrages such as *Kristallnacht* being redefined as new forms of 'disguise for the anti-Christ'.[106] Even so, between November 1938 and September 1939 the British government accepted 40 per cent of the Jews fleeing Nazi-controlled Europe, though Kushner points out that this was not as 'generous' as it initially appears; that it did not necessarily increase popular understanding of anti-semitism, with the belief that it 'could be rationalized by blaming Jewish behaviour' proving remarkably durable; and that British trade unions continued to see refugees as a threat to jobs.[107] Overall, Britain's political culture was 'liberal' enough not to prove fertile ground for the BUF's brand of anti-semitism, but not 'liberal' enough to condemn Nazi anti-semitism incessantly and unequivocally, nor to act accordingly to the very limits of the possible.[108]

The legacy of anti-fascism

Britain was spared much of the bitterness and confusion experienced by the Continent at the end of the Second World War,[109] because it won without being occupied, had dealt with potential 'collaborators' in 1940, and dealt quickly with those few generally believed to be clearly guilty of high treason.[110] In Britain no less than on the Continent 'anti-fascism' became a core component of the legitimacy of the post-war political order. But unlike the Continent, where 'resistance' was the proof of anti-fascism,[111] in Britain it was support for rearmament and opposition to anti-appeasement. This is not the place to consider the constraints on British foreign policy in the 1930s.[112] What is important here is that although sympathy for fascism at home or abroad and anti-appeasement were not mutually exclusive,[113] 'the vital badge of respectability in post-war politics' became solely the ability plausibly 'to imply retrospective membership of what became a surprisingly large band of pre-war fellow-travellers with Churchill'.[114] This was due partly to the impact of *Guilty Men* in July 1940 which presented 'MacDonald-Baldwin' as leading the British Empire to 'the edge of national annihilation' by their policy of 'ostrichism' while the 'fearful menace of the new Nazi Imperialism had been appreciated and forcefully exposed for five years past by a few clear-eyed and courageous figures in British public life, chief of all Mr. Winston Churchill';[115] and partly to the extraordinary dominance that Churchill's own account of the later 1930s and 'the Unnecessary War' achieved following the publication of *The Gathering Storm* in Britain in October 1948.[116] For Churchill, resisting an aggressive Continental power (and only from 1938 opposing Nazism) meant fighting appeasement; as David Reynolds points out, there is little in *The Gathering Storm* about domestic politics since that might have required Churchill to acknowledge his repeated seeking of office from the 'culpable figures' Baldwin and Chamberlain. Since the claims of many *on all sides* to this retrospective membership of the 'anti-appeasers' were tenuous, mutual forbearance emerged. As Williamson writes, 'Labour and liberals had potentially still greater embarrassment as opponents even of the National Government's rearmament, let alone Churchill's calls for accelerated rearmament'.[117] Moreover, mutual tolerance had been practised by ministers since the formation of Churchill's coalition government in May 1940: 'until 1945 one prop of the wartime electoral truce was the formula that all parties shared the blame for any earlier shortcomings in defence and foreign policies'.[118] Even in the 1945 (and 1950) general election 'foreign policy never generated much interest: the identity of the "guilty men" was never much of an issue' compared to housing.[119]

Copsey has written that 'after 1945, the incorporation of anti-fascism into British national identity proved the most decisive factor in fascism's continued marginalisation'.[120] But this raises the complex question of which of various 'anti-fascisms' was incorporated. Certainly the Churchillian brand;[121] but there was a post-war equivocation from the political centre ground about left-wing, anti-fascist organisations such as, eventually, the Anti-Nazi League. Already, in 1945, Orwell was asking, 'how much of the present slide towards Fascist ways of thought is traceable to the "anti-Fascism" of the past ten years and the unscrupulousness it has entailed?'[122] This was, however, an equivocation, not a denigration; and the British state and people do not, I think, seem intent on renouncing or re-imagining Britain's anti-fascism in the 1930s in order to 'normalise' or 'historicise' fascism, as some historians believe is happening on the Continent. In one sense, no great upheaval is required in the British national narrative to 'normalise' the BUF, that is to say, study it empathetically: it failed and therefore objectively, in reality, performed no *great* evil which empathetic understanding might excuse. The BUF (like the CPGB) can be accommodated into a 'liberal' narrative emphasising tolerance of (limited) difference. But the last word should be from Tim Mason's brilliant, difficult meditation occasioned by 'The Italian Economy between the Wars 1919–1939' exhibition in Rome in 1984: in a different context empathetic understanding has to do with the 'emptying of the political culture of its moral and historical reference points'; leaving fascism 'as some sort of an evolutionary stage in a *natural* history of the present-day society and state' and anti-fascism as 'synonymous with prejudice, lack of historical curiosity, fighting yesterday's battles, finger-wagging moralism and being gratuitously divisive today'.[123] To guard against this is a fundamental obligation of those who study anti-fascism.

Notes

1 Dave Renton, 'A Provisional History of Anti-Fascism in Britain in the Forties', www.dkrenton.co.uk/old/old2.html; Nigel Copsey, *Anti-Fascism in Britain* (Basingstoke: Macmillan, 2000), p. 189.
2 Mike Cronin, 'Review', *American Historical Review* 106 (2001), 1459.
3 Enzo Traverso, 'Intellectuals and Anti-Fascism: For a Critical Historization', *New Politics* 9 (2004) at www.wpunj.edu/newpol/issue36/Traverso36.htm.
4 Tom Linehan, 'Review', *English Historical Review* 116 (2001), 1007.
5 Copsey, *Anti-Fascism*, p. 4.
6 *Ibid.*, pp. 5, 189.
7 *Ibid.*, pp. 41, 79.
8 *Ibid.*, pp. 40, 74, 79–80. See also Robert Benewick, *Political Violence and Public Order: A Study of British Fascism* (London: Allen Lane, 1969), p. 266.
9 On the Battle of Cable Street, see e.g. Richard Thurlow, *Fascism in Britain* (London: I. B. Tauris, 2006), p. 81; Martin Pugh, '*Hurrah for the Blackshirts!*' (London: Jonathan Cape, 2005), p. 227.
10 Robert Skidelsky, 'Great Britain', Stuart Woolf (ed.), *Fascism in Europe* (London: Methuen, 1981), p. 275.
11 Copsey, *Anti-Fascism*, p. 4.
12 *Ibid.*, p. 4.
13 Renton, 'Provisional History'.
14 Dave Renton, *Fascism: Theory and Practice* (London: Pluto Press, 1999), Conclusion.
15 Renton, 'Provisional History'.
16 Dave Renton, *This Rough Game: Fascism and Anti-Fascism* (Stroud: Sutton, 2001), pp. 140–7.
17 See e.g. Nigel Todd, *In Excited Times: The People Against the Blackshirts* (Whitley Bay: Bewick, 1995), pp. 39–45, 54–8, ch. 5.
18 There is a similar emphasis in his account of the Anti-Nazi League in the 1970s: Dave Renton, *When We Touched the Sky* (Cheltenham: New Clarion Press, 2006), p. 175.

19   James Eaden and Dave Renton, *The Communist Party of Great Britain since 1920* (Basingstoke: Macmillan, 2002), pp. 49–50. For more positive evaluations of the Popular Front, see Jim Fryth, 'Introduction: In the Thirties', in Jim Fryth (ed.), *Britain, Fascism and the Popular Front* (London: Lawrence and Wishart, 1985), pp. 11, 19, 22, 24; Eric Hobsbawm, 'Fifty Years of Peoples' Fronts', in *Politics for a Rational Left* (London: Verso, 1989), pp. 103–16. As a Trotskyite, Renton looks rather to the tactic of the United Front and Trotsky's view that its immediate task of united self-defence should turn into a process of anti-fascist offence; in general, the adoption of the Popular Front means 'conciliating to the mass support of the fascist party': Renton, *Fascism*, pp. 73, 110; David Beetham (ed.), *Marxists in Face of Fascism* (Manchester: MUP, 1983), p. 37.

20   Renton, 'Provisional History'.

21   Victor Gollancz (ed.), *The Betrayal of the Left* (London: Gollancz, 1941), pp. xviii, 167.

22   Dave Renton, 'An Unbiased Watch? The Police and Fascist/Anti-Fascist Street Conflict in Britain, 1945–1951', www.dkrenton.co.uk/old/old1.html.

23   Copsey, *Anti-Fascism*, p. 192.

24   Renton, *Fascism*, pp. 115–16. See also Alex Callinicos, 'Could fascism take power today?', *Socialist Worker*, 21 June 2008, www.socialistworker.co.uk/art.php?id=15231.

25   Renton, *Fascism*, pp. 23–9, 101–9; Renton, *Rough Game*, pp. x–xiv. This theoretical framework leads Renton to unfairly accuse innovative historians of getting too close to the fascists: see e.g. Dave Renton, 'Review', *American Historical Review* 106 (2001), 1881.

26   See e.g. Julia Stapleton, *Englishness and the Study of Politics: The Social and Political Thought of Ernest Barker* (Cambridge: CUP, 1994), chs 6 & 7; Andrzej Olechnowicz, 'Liberal Anti-Fascism in the 1930s: the Case of Sir Ernest Barker', *Albion* 36 (2004), 636–60; Philip Williamson, *Stanley Baldwin: Conservative Leadership and National Values* (Cambridge: CUP, 1999), ch. 10.

27   Dan Stone, *Responses to Nazism in Britain, 1933–1939: Before War and Holocaust* (Basingstoke: Palgrave Macmillan, 2003), pp. 5–6. See also Stuart Samuels, 'The Left Book Club', *Journal of Contemporary History* 1 (1966), 65–86. There was also traffic in the opposite direction: see Dan Stone, 'The "*Mein Kampf* Ramp"': Emily Overend Lorimer and Hitler Translations in Britain', *German History* 26 (2008), 504–19.

28   Tom Lawson, 'The Anglican Understanding of Nazism, 1933–1945: Placing the Church of England's Response to the Holocaust in Context', *Twentieth Century British History* 14 (2003), 112–37 at 122.

29   Tim Kirk and Anthony McElligott, 'Introduction: Community, authority and resistance to fascism', in Tim Kirk and Anthony McElligott (eds), *Opposing Fascism: Community, Authority and Resistance in Europe* (Cambridge: CUP, 1999), p. 11.

30   Neil Barrett, 'The anti-fascist movement in south-east Lancashire, 1933–1940: the divergent experiences of Manchester and Nelson', in Kirk and McElligott, *Opposing Fascism*, pp. 48–62.

31   Meston, 'Review: *B.U.F.: Oswald Mosley and British Fascism* by James Drennan [William Allen]', *International Affairs* 14 (1935), 575. Meston was president

of the Liberal Party from 1936 and a leading light of the Institute of International Affairs.

32 Thurlow, *Fascism*, p. 30, ch. 2; Julie Gottlieb, 'Orman, Rotha Beryl Lintorn Lintorn-', *ODNB Online;* Richard Maguire, '"The Fascists ... are ... to be depended on."' The British Government, Fascists and Strike-breaking during 1925 and 1926', in Nigel Copsey and Dave Renton (eds), *British Fascism, the Labour Movement and the State* (Basingstoke: Palgrave Macmillan, 2005), pp. 6–26. There were, of course, other, still smaller 'proto-fascist' organisations. One which has received close attention from Stone is the English Mistery, out of which emerged the English Array following a split in 1936: see Dan Stone, 'The English Mistery, the BUF and the dilemma of British fascism', *Journal of Modern History* 75 (2003), 336–58; Dan Stone, 'The Far Right and the Back-to-the-Land Movement', in Julie Gottlieb and Tom Linehan (eds), *The Culture of Fascism: Visions of the Far Right in Britain* (London: I. B. Tauris, 2004); Dan Stone, 'Ludovici, Anthony Mario', *ODNB Online;* D. Stone, 'The extremes of Englishness: The "exceptional" ideology of Anthony Mario Ludovici', *Journal of Political Ideologies* 4 (1999), 191–218. Their exotic and eccentric ideological brew is obviously of interest to historians of ideas, and they do demonstrate the existence of 'indigenous strains of fascism, however weak, within British thought'. However, they represented no political danger in the 1930s. Even Stone's guarded view that this indigenous fascism 'in very different circumstances might have been nourished into more vigorous growth' seems questionable: it is difficult to conceive of *any* circumstances in which their esoteric concerns could have commanded wide support.

33 Earl Attlee, 'Review', *Political Science Quarterly* 79 (1964), 109.

34 Gerry Webber, 'Patterns of Membership and Support for the British Union of Fascists', *Journal of Contemporary History* 19 (1984), 575–606.

35 Pugh, *Hurrah*, pp. 140–1.

36 Tom Linehan, *East London for Mosley: The British Union of Fascists in East London and South-West Essex, 1933–40* (London: Cass, 1996).

37 Thurlow, *Fascism*, pp. 99–101. See also Tom Linehan, *British Fascism 1918–39: Parties, Ideology and Culture* (Manchester: MUP, 2000), pp. 6–7.

38 Charles Mowat, *Britain between the Wars 1918–1940* (London: Methuen, 1955), p. 473.

39 David Baker, *Ideology of Obsession: A. K. Chesterton and British Fascism* (London: I. B. Tauris, 1996), pp. 4, 211.

40 Kathleen Paul, 'Review', *American Historical Review* 103 (1998), 519.

41 Thurlow, Fascism, p. 102.

42 Skidelsky, 'Great Britain', pp. 268–75; Alan Sykes, *The Radical Right in Britain: Social Imperialism to the BNP* (Basingstoke: Palgrave Macmillan, 2005), pp. 68–71; Thurlow, *Fascism*, p. 107; Garry Love, '"What's the Big Idea?": Oswald Mosley, the British Union of Fascists and Generic Fascism', *Journal of Contemporary History* 42 (2007), 453–7.

43 Robert Skidelsky, *Oswald Mosley* (London: Macmillan, 1975), chs 7 and 15; Sykes, *Radical Right*, pp. 55–64.

44 Tom Linehan, 'Comment on Roger Griffin', *Journal of Contemporary History* 37 (2002), 273–4. See also Thurlow, *Fascism*, ch. 5; Julie Gottlieb and Tom Linehan, 'Introduction: Culture and the British Far Right', in Gottlieb and

Linehan, *Culture of Fascism*; Michael Spurr, '"Living the Blackshirt Life": Culture, Community and the British Union of Fascists, 1932–1940', *Contemporary European History* 12 (2003), 305–22.

45   Philip Coupland, 'The Blackshirted Utopians', *Journal of Contemporary History* 33 (1998), 255–72 and '"Left-Wing Fascism" in Theory and Practice: The Case of the British Union of Fascists', *Twentieth Century British History* 13 (2002), 38–61.

46   Ross McKibbin, 'Review', *English Historical Review* 91 (1976), 166–7.

47   Julie Gottlieb, 'The Marketing of Megalomania: Celebrity, Consumption and the Development of Political Technology in the British Union of Fascists', *Journal of Contemporary History* 41 (2006), 35–55.

48   Pugh *Hurrah*, pp. 153, 215.

49   See Philip Williamson, *National Crisis and National Government: British Politics, the Economy and Empire, 1926–1932* (Cambridge: CUP, 1992), pp. 146–8, 230–1, 468–9.

50   Skidelsky, 'Great Britain', p. 277.

51   This striking phrase is Williamson's: Williamson, *National Crisis*, p. 148.

52   Pugh, *Hurrah*, pp. 248–51. On the political and ideological context of the abdication 'crisis', see Philip Williamson, 'The monarchy and public values 1900–1953', in A. Olechnowicz (ed.), *The Monarchy and the British Nation 1780 to the Present* (Cambridge: CUP, 2007), 223–57.

53   Pugh, *Hurrah*, pp. 147–53.

54   Richard Griffiths, *Fellow Travellers of the Right: British Enthusiasts for Nazi Germany 1933–9* (London: Constable, 1980), pp. 50–3.

55   Sykes, *Radical Right*, pp. 1–8.

56   Erskine became an assistant whip in 1932 but then moved to Madras as its governor in 1934. Lennox-Boyd only entered government in 1938 as parliamentary secretary at the Ministry of Labour.

57   Moore-Brabazon had been parliamentary secretary to the Ministry of Transport from 1923 to 1924 and 1924 to 1927.

58   Pugh, *Hurrah*, p. 196; Benewick, *Political Violence*, p. 19; Dan Stone, 'Review: "Democracy versus Dictatorship": Die Herausforderung des Faschismus und Kommunismus in Grossbritannien, 1932–1937 by Christina Bussfeld', *English Historical Review* 119 (Apr. 2004), 467, 468; Thurlow, *Fascism*, p. 279.

59   Harold Macmillan, *The Middle Way* (London: Macmillan, 1938), p. 375; Skidelsky, 'Great Britain', pp. 280–1.

60   Ross McKibbin, *Classes and Cultures: England 1918–1951* (Oxford: OUP, 1998), p. 60. Nonetheless, left-wing opinion in the thirties imagined that the 'new' middle class of managers, technicians and clerical workers in the thirties was 'not satisfied with the existing order', making it 'capable of being either on the side of Fascism or of Socialism' in an economic crisis: see e.g. 'The Revolutionary Middle Class', *New Statesman and Nation*, 5 May 1934, 664–5.

61   Ross McKibbin, 'What can Cameron do', *London Review of Books*, 28 Oct. 2008.

62   Ross McKibbin, 'The "Social Psychology" of Unemployment in Inter-war Britain', in *The Ideologies of Class: Social Relations in Britain 1880–1960* (Oxford: Clarendon Press, 1990), pp. 252–8.

63   G. D. H. and Margaret Cole, *The Condition of Britain* (London: Gollancz, 1937), p. 422 on the significance of the 'dramatic collapse of world prices during the economic crisis of the past few years' (which the Coles regarded as nonetheless 'temporary and evanescent').

64   McKibbin, *Classes*, pp. 50, 52–8.

65   See e.g. the *Punch* cartoons of 20 Feb. 1918, 16 Oct. 1918, 12 Feb. 1919, 9 Apr. 1919.

66   Quoted in Garry Runciman, *Relative Deprivation and Social Justice: A Study of Attitudes to Social Inequality in Twentieth-Century England* (London: Routledge & Kegan Paul, 1966), p. 130.

67   Ross McKibbin, 'Class and Conventional Wisdom: the Conservative Party and the "Public" in Inter-war Britain', in *Ideologies of Class*, pp. 259–71. Even so, H. G. Wells saw in the 'rentier type of mind' exemplified by Dean Inge the basis for a fascism 'of a more indoor and defensive type' in the thirties: H. G. Wells, *The Common Sense of War and Peace* (Harmondsworth: Penguin Books, 1940), p. 39.

68   David Marquand, *The Progressive Dilemma* (London: Heinemann, 1991), pp. 44–5. See also Jim Callaghan, *The Far Left in British Politics* (Oxford: Blackwell, 1987), pp. 27–8.

69   Eric Hobsbawm, 'Cadres', *London Review of Books*, 26 Apr. 2007, 23. Hobsbawm also notes that Lenin and the Comintern did not have high expectations of Britain; Comintern's main interest in Britain, he argues, was as a channel to colonial Communists.

70   Stanley Payne, *A History of Fascism, 1914–1945* (Madison, Wisconsin: University of Wisconsin Press, 1995), p. 303.

71   Carl Levy, 'Fascism, National Socialism and Conservatives in Europe, 1914–1945: Issues for Comparativists', *Contemporary European History* 8 (1999), 116. See also Roger Griffin, 'Pre-conditions for fascism's success', in Aristotle Kallis (ed.), *The Fascism Reader* (London: Routledge, 2003).

72   *The Times and Appeasement: The Journal of A. L. Kennedy, 1932–1939*, ed. by Gordon Martel (Camden Fifth Series 16) (London: RHS/CUP, 2000), p. 64 (14 Oct. 1932).

73   For instance, Benewick writes that 'the introduction of Fascism was inappropriate and irrelevant in terms of British political development and that its chances of success were therefore remote': Benewick, *Political Violence*, p. 12.

74   Attlee, 'Review', 111.

75   Ross McKibbin, 'Why was there no Marxism in Britain?', in *Ideologies of Class*, p. 18; and pp. 20–3 on 'the place of parliament in the public mind'.

76   Jon Lawrence, 'Forging a peaceable kingdom: war, violence and fear of brutalisation in post-First World War Britain, *Journal of Modern History* 75 (2003), 557–89 and 'Fascist violence and the politics of public order in inter-war Britain: the Olympia debate revisited', *Historical Research* 76 (2003), 238–67; and the debate between Pugh and Lawrence: Martin Pugh, 'The British Union of Fascists and the Olympia debate', *Historical Journal* 41 (1998), 529–42; Martin Pugh, 'The National Government, the British Union of Fascists and the Olympia debate', *Historical Research* 78 (2005), 253–62; Jon Lawrence, 'Why Olympia mattered', *Historical Research* 78 (2005), 263–72. Pugh maintains that not all politicians were

shocked by the violence at the Olympia meeting since they had grown up in a period when violence had been a normal part of local political life.

77   Pugh would not agree, writing that the explanation for the failure of fascism in Britain 'does not lie primarily in British political culture'; but this has to follow from his insistence on there being a number of moments when fascist movements could have succeeded – but did not for purely contingent reasons: Pugh, *Hurrah*, p. 215.

78   Henry Steck, 'Review', *American Political Science Review* 67 (1973), 646. For a critique of the concept, see Dennis Kavanagh, *Political Culture* (London: Macmillan, 1972).

79   For a compendium of the main charges relating to the King, Lynn Picknett, Clive Prince, Stephen Prior and Robert Brydon, *War of the Windsors: A Century of Unconstitutional Monarchy* (Edinburgh, 2002); also Martin Allen, *Hidden Agenda: How the Duke of Windsor Betrayed the Allies* (New York, 2002).

80   Griffiths, *Fellow Travellers*, p. 52.

81   Philip Ziegler, *King Edward VIII: The Official Biography* (London, 1990), pp. 266–72. Strobl argues that the Nazis did not see Edward VIII as a traitor; but 'there is something one comes across only very rarely in Nazi utterances: genuine respect; the respect felt for an equal' because of his modernity, vigour, determination and his *Volksnahe* – 'proximity to the people': see Gerwin Strobl, *The Germanic Isle: Nazi Perceptions of Britain* (Cambridge, 2000), pp. 108–10.

82   Cole, *Condition*, p. 436; also Kinglsey Martin, *Fascism, Democracy and the Press* (London: New Statesman Pamphlet, 1938). The National Council of Civil Liberties had its origins in concern about the abuse and extension of police powers, initially against the hunger marchers: Mark Lilly, *The National Council for Civil Liberties: The First Fifty Years* (London: Macmillan, 1984), ch. 1.

83   Thurlow, *Fascism*, pp. 82–5; Richard Thurlow, 'The Security Service, the Communist Party of Great Britain and British Fascism, 1932–51', in Copsey and Renton, *British Fascism*, pp. 27–45; Gerald Anderson, *Fascists, Communists, and the National Government: Civil Liberties in Great Britain, 1931–1937* (Columbia: University of Missouri Press, 1983). Anderson does, however, find that in Cabinet discussions communism rather than fascism was usually regarded as the greater threat.

84   Keith Ewing and Conor Gearty, *The Struggle for Civil Liberties: Political Freedom and the Rule of Law in Britain 1914–1945* (Oxford: OUP, 2000), p. 35, chs 5, 6, 8.

85   Griffiths, *Fellow Travellers*, pp. 26–31.

86   Olechnowicz, 'Liberal Anti-Fascism', 650–1; Williamson, *Stanley Baldwin*, p. 316. The influence of José Ortega y Gasset's *The Revolt of the Masses* is often evident: see David Callahan, 'The Early Reception of Ortega y Gasset in England, 1920–1939', *Forum for Modern Language Studies* 26 (1990), 75–88.

87   Tom Buchanan, 'Anti-Fascism and Democracy in the 1930s', *European History Quarterly* 32 (2002), 39–57 at 54.

88   Clement Attlee, *The Labour Party in Perspective* (London: Victor Gollancz, 1937), ch. 7.

89   Williamson, *Stanley Baldwin*, p. 317, ch. 10. For examples, see Stanley Baldwin, 'The Authentic Note of Democracy' (1930), 'Our Freedom Is Our Own' (1934) and 'This Torch of Freedom' (1935), in *This Torch of Freedom* (London: Hodder and Stoughton, 1937).

90   Alison Light, *Forever England: Femininity, Literature and Conservatism between the Wars* (London: Routledge, 1991), pp. 85, 144.

91   Matthew Grimley, 'The Religion of Englishness: Puritanism, Providentialism and "National Character", 1918–1945', *Journal of British Studies* 46 (2007), 889–96, 902–3.

92   *Ibid.*, 889, 897–901; Matthew Grimley, *Citizenship, Community, and the Church of England: Liberal Anglican Theories of the State between the Wars* (Oxford: Clarendon Press, 2004), p. 183–201; Philip Williamson, 'Christian Conservatives and the Totalitarian Challenge, 1933–40', *English Historical Review* 115 (2000), 619–28.

93   Stone notes that Bussfeld writes of a 'specifically English mentality' which he believes is 'hard to prove historically' but 'should not be underestimated': Stone 'Review', 468.

94   Attlee, 'Review', 110. Attlee recalled a meeting at which Mosley came onto the stage with his arm lifted, at which point a voice said, 'Yes, Oswald dear, you may go to the lavatory.'

95   Grimley, 'Religion of Englishness', 891, 898, 903.

96   Helen McCarthy, 'Parties, Voluntary Associations, and Democratic Politics in Interwar Britain', *Historical Journal* 50 (2007), 891, 893, 909.

97   Sheri Berman, 'Civil Society and the Collapse of the Weimar Republic', *World Politics* 49 (1997), 408; Bernd Weisbrod, 'The crisis of bourgeois society in interwar Germany', in Richard Bessel (ed.), *Fascist Italy and Nazi Germany: Comparisons and Contrasts* (Cambridge: CUP, 1996), pp. 23–39.

98   Alexander Carr-Saunders and David Caradog Jones, *A Survey of the Social Structure of England and Wales as Illustrated by Statistics* (Oxford: Clarendon Press, second edition, 1937), p. 77.

99   McCarthy, 'Parties', 893, 901; McKibbin, *Classes*, pp. 96–8.

100   Traverso, 'Intellectuals'.

101   McKibbin, 'Review', 166; for Sykes too Mosley's 'cultural, derivative anti-semitism allowed him, in contrast to biological racists like Leese, to discriminate between "good" and "bad" Jews': Sykes, *Radical Right*, p. 66. Pugh sees Mosley buffeted by anti-semitic recruits who were beyond his control but it is not true that the BUF was wholly dominated by anti-semitism by the later 1930s: Pugh, *Hurrah*, pp. 219–21. For Thurlow the use of political anti-semitism by the BUF represented a 'genuine belief', but Mosley's anti-semitic attacks were 'not highly conceptualized nor did anti-semitism ever represent a total ideological explanation': Thurlow, *Fascism*, 126–7. Holmes argues that Mosley's hostility revealed a hostility towards Jews which was expressed within an ethnocentric and conspiratorial framework ... [and] in relatively restrained and sophisticated terms' whereas Joyce and Chesterton emphasised racial hostility towards Jews: Colin Holmes, *Anti-Semitism in British Society 1876–1939* (London: Edward Arnold, 1979), pp. 180–2.

102   Holmes, *Anti-Semitism*, pp. 227–31, ch. 13. McKibbin detects 'a comparatively discreet but almost universal anti-semitism within the English

middle class': McKibbin, *Classes*, p. 55. For Skidelsky what was critical about Britain was that there was 'no anti-semitic ideology of any importance': Skidelsky, 'Great Britain', p. 276. There is comparatively less on inter-war racism (and its limits); it is likely politicians and the people were endemically racist: McKibbin observes that Mosley was 'a "racist" in the conventional sense of the term: long before he had discovered the Jews he flung about "nigger" and "hottentot" with all the insouciance of Lord Salisbury': McKibbin, 'Review', 166.

103 Tony Kushner, *The Holocaust and the Liberal Imagination: A Social and Cultural History* (Oxford: Blackwell, 1994), p. 36.

104 Grimley, 'Religion of Englishness', 890.

105 Kushner, *Holocaust*, pp. 36–40; Griffiths, *Fellow*, pp. 186–7.

106 Lawson, 'Anglican Understanding', 112–37; Tom Lawson, *The Church of England and the Holocaust: Christianity, Memory and Nazism* (Woodbridge: Boydell, 2006), p. 66.

107 Kushner, *Holocaust*, pp. 42–81, 277.

108 The (non-) response to the Holocaust during and after the Second World War is the heart of this controversy: see David Cesarani, 'Review: *The Myth of Rescue: Why the Democracies Could Not Have Saved More Jews from the Nazis* by W. Rubinstein', *English Historical Review* 113 (1998), 1258–60 and *Justice Delayed: How Britain Became a Refuge for Nazi War Criminals* (London: Mandarin, 1992), pp. 1–8, ch. 8.

109 Tony Judt, *Postwar: A History of Europe since 1945* (London: Heinemann, 2005), chs 2 and 3; Istvan Deák, Jan Gross, and Tony Judt (eds), *The Politics of Retribution in Europe: World War II and its Aftermath* (Princeton: Princeton University Press, 2000); Pieter Lagrou, *The Legacy of Nazi Occupation: Patriotic Memory and National Recovery in Western Europe, 1945–1965* (Cambridge: CUP, 2000).

110 Peter Martland, *Lord Haw-Haw: The English Voice of Nazi Germany* (Kew: National Archives, 2003), pp. 78–84; Adrian Weale, *Renegades: Hitler's Englishmen* (London: Pimlico, 2002), pp. 178–82. John Amery was executed on 19 December 1945 and William Joyce on 3 January 1946. Mosley, of course, was quickly rehabilitated in 'high society': see, for instance, *The Letters of Nancy Mitford and Evelyn Waugh*, ed. by Charlotte Mosley (London: Hodder and Stoughton, 1996), p. 147.

111 Therefore, 'resistance' became an essentially contestable term, nowhere more than in Germany: Ulrich von Hassell, *The Von Hassell Diaries 1938–1944: The Story of the Forces Against Hitler Inside Germany* (London: Hamish Hamilton, 1948); Konrad Jarausch, 'The Failure of East German Antifascism: Some Ironies of History as Politics', *German Studies Review* 14 (1991), 85–102; *Questions on German History: Ideas, Forces, Decision from 1800 to the Present* [Historical Exhibition in the Berlin Reichstag Catalogue] (Bonn: German Bundestag Publications' Section, 1992), pp. 348, 364, 413; Marjorie Lamberti, 'German Antifascist Refugees in America and the Public Debate on "What Should be Done with Germany after Hitler", 1941–1945', *Central European History* 40 (2007), 279–305; and especially Bill Niven, *Facing the Nazi Past: United Germany and the Legacy of the Third Reich* (London: Routledge, 2002).

112 See, however, David Dutton, 'Proponents and critics of appeasement', *ODNB Online* and *Neville Chamberlain* (London: Arnold, 2000); Andrew Crozier,

'Chamberlain, (Arthur) Neville', *ODNB Online*; Maurice Cowling, *The Impact of Hitler: British Politics and British Policy 1933–1940* (Cambridge, 1975) and 'The Case Against Going to War', *Sunday Telegraph*, 20 Aug. 1989; R. A. C. Parker, 'British Rearmament, 1936–39: Treasury, Trade Unions and Skilled Labour', *English Historical Review* 96 (1981), 306–43 and *Chamberlain and Appeasement: British Policy and the Coming of the Second World War* (Basingstoke: Macmillan, 1993); McKibbin, 'Class and Conventional Wisdom', pp. 285–91; Nicholas Crowson, *Facing Fascism: The Conservative Party and the European Dictators, 1935–1940* (London: Routledge, 1997).

113   John Ramsden, *The Age of Balfour and Baldwin 1902–1940* (London: Longman, 1978), p. 348.

114   Philip Williamson, 'Baldwin's Reputation: Politics and History, 1937–1967', *Historical Journal* 47 (2004), 138.

115   'Cato' [Michael Foot, Frank Owen, Peter Howard], *Guilty Men* (London: Gollancz, 1940), pp. 19–20; David Dutton, 'Guilty men', *ODNB Online*.

116   David Reynolds, 'Churchill's Writing of History: Appeasement, Autobiography and *The Gathering Storm*', *Transactions of the Royal Historical Society* 11 (2001), 221–47. *Guilty Men* sold 200,000 copies in six months, Churchill in two weeks. Between 1948 and 1954 Churchill's six-volume history of the Second World War was serialised in 80 magazines and newspapers worldwide and was published in hardback in 50 countries and 18 languages.

117   Williamson, 'Baldwin's Reputation', 138. On varying assessments of Labour foreign policy in the 1930s, see G. D. H. Cole, *A History of the Labour Party from 1914* (London: Routledge & Kegan Paul, 1948), pp. 284–91, 354–8; Ben Pimlott, *Labour and the Left in the 1930s* (Cambridge: CUP, 1977), chs 9 and 10, esp. pp. 90, 106; David Blaazer, *The Popular Front and the Progressive Tradition: Socialists, Liberals, and the Quest for Unity, 1884–1939* (Cambridge: CUP, 1992), chs 6 and 7, p. 195; Martin Pugh, 'The Liberal Party and the Popular Front', *English Historical Review* 121 (2006), 1327–50.

118   Williamson, 'Baldwin's Reputation', 138.

119   Steven Fielding, 'What Did "The People" Want?: The Meaning of the 1945 General Election', *Historical Journal* 35 (1992), 635; Ronald McCallum and Alison Readman, *The British General Election of 1945* (London: OUP, 1947), p. 30; Herbert Nicholas, *The British General Election of 1950* (London: Macmillan, 1951), pp. 50–1.

120   Copsey, *Anti-Fascism*, p. 192.

121   Richard Weight, *Patriots: National Identity in Britain, 1940–2000* (London: Pan, 2003), pp. 15, 338–45, 458–64; for its reassertion by Labour and Conservatives during the Falklands War in 1982, see Anthony Barnett, *Iron Britannia: Why Parliament waged its Falklands War* (London: Allison & Busby, 1982), pp. 47–62, 94.

122   George Orwell, 'Appendix I Orwell's Proposed Preface to *Animal Farm*', in *Animal Farm* (London: Penguin Books, 2000), p. 105. Orwell had in mind the demand by anti-fascists that Mosley should remain interned without trial: 'Make a habit of imprisoning Fascists without trial, and perhaps the process won't stop at Fascists.'

123   Tim Mason, 'The Great Economic History Show', *History Workshop Journal* 21 (1986), 28, 31.

Part I
Political Parties

1
Communist Culture and Anti-Fascism in Inter-War Britain

Thomas Linehan

Introduction

As the chapters in this volume will demonstrate, anti-fascism came in a variety of different forms in inter-war Britain. Even within a particular form of anti-fascism, one can find diversity and a range of responses. This was the case with British communist anti-fascism between the wars. On the one hand, it displayed a quite distinct profile and one could speak of it as a quite specific form of anti-fascism. In this sense, it was a particularly aggressive form of anti-fascism. The Communist Party of Great Britain's (CP or CPGB) anti-fascism was belligerent, had a tendency towards direct confrontation with fascism and seemed to have a clear focus on the nature of the fascist threat. Here communist anti-fascism was informed by carefully considered theory, which lent Party judgments on fascism an aura of 'pontifical infallibility' and told Party activists that the fascist threat was violently reactionary, had an international reach and imperiled social progress and culture. Certainly, the historiography and popular memory abound with positive images of resolute communist opposition to fascism between the Wars, not least the spectacular mass anti-fascist mobilisations featuring communists, as at 'Cable Street' in October 1936, and of idealistic young communists embarking for Spain to defend the Republic against the incursions of 'international fascism'. This is the positive history but there is a less impressive history to set against this. At other 'moments', particularly during the 1920s and early 1930s, the prevailing characteristics of British communist anti-fascism were confusion, misunderstanding, tactical ineptitude and a lack of focus. That said, however, to this less positive picture should be added a further variant of inter-war communist anti-fascism. This was the 'cultural anti-fascism' that appeared during the Popular Front years, a form of anti-fascism which displayed a high degree of inventiveness and imagination and which gave real impetus to communist efforts to overcome fascism. The bulk of this chapter will deal with important aspects of this cultural anti-fascism, but before this the communist anti-fascism of the preceding period will need to be considered.

Communist anti-fascism, 1919–34

Confusion, misunderstanding and a lack of focus were evident in CPGB commentary on fascism from an early date. In 1925 the CPGB's leading intellectual Rajani Palme Dutt claimed that fascism arises when a powerful working-class movement in an advanced capitalist country reaches a stage of development which inevitably puts revolution on the agenda, but then that revolution fails to materialise. In Russia, 'where the issue of the revolution was faced', Dutt continued, there was no regression into fascism.[1] This idea, that fascism was the product of the failure or 'delay' of the proletarian revolution outside Russia, would form part of the staple diet of Dutt's and the CPGB's thinking on fascism through the remainder of the 1920s. It would still feature in communist thinking into the 1930s, as in Dutt's *Fascism and Social Revolution* which appeared in early 1934. Fascism, he wrote, using even more vivid language, represented the 'punishment of history', a punishment that history had inflicted on the proletariat for failing to carry out its 'world historic task' of completing the revolution begun in Russia in 1917.[2] It is likely that Dutt derived this view from Communist International (Comintern) sources. The 'punishment of history' version of fascism first appeared in official communist thinking in June 1923 in a speech to the Comintern given by the veteran German communist Klara Zetkin. The genesis of such thinking precedes the Comintern, however, and can be traced back to the understanding within classical Marxism that capitalism was always pregnant with crisis. Prior to fascism's arrival, the Marxist attitude to capitalist crisis was one of some optimism in that the moment of crisis seemed to herald the imminent arrival of a better future. In this dialectical process, there was always the promise of proletarian insurrection which heralded the advance to a liberating proletarian future. Objectively, this perfected future was to arrive courtesy of a providential history moving the historical process and the social order through the evolutionary stages to a brighter era beyond capitalism, in a manner similar to the eschatological stages of the Christian cycle. This sense of optimism, the equating of capitalist time 'running out' with proletarian revolution and a better future, heightened after the October Revolution in Russia and the founding of the Comintern in March 1919. The capitalist order was about to embark on the so-called 'First Period', a passage of time supposedly characterised by capitalist weakness and genuine revolutionary opportunity which would eventually comprise the years 1919–23. Prophecies of 'the end' of capitalism would permeate the Comintern's earliest declarations. The platform drafted by Bukharin for the Comintern's First Congress in March 1919 contained the ringing declaration that: 'A new epoch is born! The epoch of the dissolution of capitalism, of its inner disintegration. The epoch of the communist revolution of the proletariat'.[3]

Three years later, however, and even before the First Period had expired, the communist attitude to capitalism in crisis had registered a marked change. By the time of the Fourth Comintern Congress in 1922, there was no longer an unbounded confidence that capitalist crisis was the precursor to a brighter proletarian future. Instead, with the arrival of the first significant fascist 'reaction' in Italy, the Comintern believed that a new and particularly nasty symptom of capitalism in crisis had appeared which contained the potential to check the proletarian revolution. As the Theses on Tactics adopted by the Fourth Congress proclaimed, fascism was the counter-revolutionary instrument of the industrial and commercial 'bourgeoisie'. Henceforth fascism was cast not just as a derivative of capitalism but as a particularly 'terroristic' form of capitalist reaction to crisis. As the Comintern's May Day Manifesto for May 1923 explained it, 'fascism is capitalism preparing for its final passage of arms with the proletariat'.[4] More specifically though, and a line of argument which found its way into Rajani Palme Dutt's thinking, fascism would be linked the failure of the working-class movement in Western and Central Europe to fulfil its historic obligation to exploit capitalism's serious post-war crisis and carrying on the revolution which had begun in Russia.

This thinking, that fascism was not just an ugly symptom of capitalism at the point of crisis but that it emerged as a consequence of the failure or 'delay' of the proletarian revolution would invariably impact on the character of communist anti-fascism. The stark message for the working-class movement was that it should seek to complete the task that history had set for it or face the terrible punishment of fascism. Thus the surest safeguard against regression into fascism was to press home the proletarian revolution outside Russia, particularly at moments of capitalist weakness as had materialised during the First Period. With anti-fascism construed, at least in this regard, in terms of completing the proletarian revolution, the next step in the analysis was to understand and explain the causes of the revolution's delay. This led to even further misrepresentations and errors of judgment which surfaced at the Comintern's Fifth World Congress in 1924. The Fifth Congress convened at a point when the First Period had apparently concluded and given way to a new passage of capitalist development. This new time-frame, or 'Second Period', was meant to correspond to the condition or health of international capitalism at this particular stage of its evolution. This was deemed to be a period of capitalist consolidation and more restricted revolutionary opportunity which eventually, for the Comintern, ran to 1928. Statements on fascism emerging from the Fifth World Congress not only consolidated the ever-hardening Comintern orthodoxy which defined fascism as a particularly violent anti-proletarian capitalist offensive but reinforced the linkage first established by Klara Zetkin between fascism and abortive proletarian revolution. It is the Congress's explanation for this frustrated revolution that particularly interests us here, for it was partly blamed on 'the absence of a leading revolutionary class party' at the point when the workers had taken up the struggle for power.[5] This judgment, with its implicit attack on 'reformism', the assumption that reformism would always conspire to check the aspiration to revolution, was to be most telling in regard to the development of communist anti-fascism for the Fifth Congress became the stage for the first official appearance of the notorious Comintern line that social democracy differed little from 'classical fascism' in that both were complementary instruments used by large capital at its point of crisis for securing capitalist domination over the proletariat. As the 'Resolution on Fascism' adopted by the Congress explained it: 'as bourgeois society continues to decay, all bourgeois parties, particularly social democracy, take on a more or less fascist character. ... Fascism and social democracy are the two sides of the same instrument of capitalist dictatorship'.[6] This allegation would feature in the thinking of the CPGB's leading strata from an early date. As Rajani Palme Dutt stated in July 1925, 'fascism arises where a powerful working class movement reaches a stage of growth which inevitably raises revolutionary issues, but is held in from decisive action by a reformist leadership. ... Fascism is the child of Reformism'.[7]

Dutt never wavered from this sectarian position throughout the remainder of the 1920s and into the 1930s. In early 1934, in *Fascism and Social Revolution*, he repeated the accusation that social democracy was fascism's 'twin' before proclaiming that both were 'instruments of the rule of monopoly capital. Both fight the working class revolution. Both weaken and disrupt the class organization of the workers'.[8] No doubt, Dutt's thinking again registered the influence of the Comintern, namely the line of the Comintern's Sixth World Congress in 1928 which linked social democracy even more unambiguously to fascism. This 'new' hard line was announced to coincide with the perceived ending of the recent phase of capitalist stabilisation and the arrival of a new international conjuncture thought to herald the onset of a major, systemic capitalist crisis. In this 'Third Period', it was now assumed that capitalism was tending remorselessly in fascism's direction, with the latter again being viewed as the last desperate fling of a dying system. Within this analytical framework, the 1924 Comintern identification of fascism with social democracy was reaffirmed but in more strident terms leading, by July 1929, to the notorious label of 'social fascism' being attached to social democratic parties.

Little wonder then, given that social democracy, particularly its upper strata, was held responsible for delaying the proletarian revolution and thereby colluding in the birth of doomed capitalism's 'misshapen progeny of fascism', that British communists poured much of their anti-fascist invective during the 1920s and particularly the Third Period on 'reformist' institutions and representatives. These striking errors of judgment and crass misrepresentations of the nature of 'reformist' social democracy were not restricted to Rajani Palme Dutt's comments. In contending that 'the whole dominant tendency of British capitalism is now in the direction of fascism', the CPGB's Central Committee in May 1931 concluded that 'the Labour Party and the Trade Unions in adapting themselves to capitalism must also adapt themselves to fascism; in this lies their character as social-fascist organs. They play an important role in the transformation giving rise to the new Fascist state'.[9] Clearly, the message for the workers was to eschew reformism, develop revolutionary awareness under the CPGB's tutelage and continue the revolution begun in Russia as the best means of averting fascism.

Communist anti-fascism could also assume more aggressive and direct forms. As mentioned in the Introduction, CPGB anti-fascism could be belligerent, confrontational and have a clear focus on 'open fascism'. Although these traits were much more apparent from c.1934 they did appear in the earlier years, particularly the mid-1920s. The CPGB was faced with a number of home-grown manifestations of 'open fascism' during these years. The most significant were the British Fascisti (BF; formed May 1923), the National Fascisti (NF; formed late 1924) and the Imperial Fascist League (IFL; formed November 1928). An assortment of smaller formations, some of which had splintered from the more prominent fascist organisations, also made an appearance though the majority did not remain long.[10] Some of these organisations clearly displayed characteristics which, for the CPGB, seemed to confirm the Comintern's assessment of fascism as a 'terroristic' form of capitalist reaction. Fascists attached to such groups adorned themselves in paramilitary paraphernalia and emulated the *squadristi* tactics of the Italian Fascists. NF activists, for example, wore the Black Shirt, a black peakless cap, a badge displaying the lictor's axe and fasces and set about disrupting communist, socialist, trade union and other left-wing activities, often violently as when revolver-wielding NF activists commandeered a *Daily Herald* delivery van in October 1925.[11] The BF espoused a more 'moderate', constitutional version of fascism than the NF but even here we find outbursts of abusive, reactionary anti-Leftist rhetoric. In an official policy statement in July 1926 the BF pledged 'efficacious hostility towards all Bolshevist, communist, socialist and other subversive and anti-Christian movements to be continued until such time as the Empire is purged of all seditionists, disloyalists (sic) and degenerates'.[12] The mid-1920s also saw periodic fascist attacks on CPGB premises and personnel, the latter even extending to the 'kidnapping' of leading CPGB official Harry Pollitt in 1925.[13]

Home-grown fascist aggression towards the Left did not go unchallenged by the CPGB. If the rather melodramatic accounts of the BF's founder, Rotha Lintorn-Orman, are to be believed, when the BF sought to bring the 'patriotic' fascist message to the 'Red' districts of east London during the 1920s they were met by opponents wielding a variety of weaponry that included drawn razors, life preservers and 'stockings full of broken glass'.[14] Beyond the more sporadic episodes of confrontation, there were also efforts to militarise this resistance, as when the CPGB sought to build anti-fascist 'Workers' Defence Corps' an initiative which led to the formation of a Defence Corps during the General Strike. The Defence Corps would eventually mutate into the Labour League of Ex-Servicemen.[15] Clearly, the CPGB leadership was alive to the potential dangers posed by home-grown fascism during the 1920s, particularly at junctures when it seemed as if there was a heightened fascist threat, as during the 1926 General Strike.[16]

That said, we should not exaggerate the extent or significance of direct communist opposition to 'open fascism' in this period. As Nigel Copsey tells us, it was sporadic, involved small numbers of committed activists, was mostly geographically confined to London and rose and fell in proportion to the political fortunes of domestic fascism.[17] The same held true for the early 1930s, when the sectarian 'social fascist' policy of the Third Period led to a disastrous slump in membership and encouraged the CPGB to expend even more of its ever-waning energies attacking social democracy rather than open fascism. As yet, there was no mass-based communist opposition to open fascism, nor even a clear understanding of fascism or the strategies needed to oppose it. Just as importantly, from the point of view of this chapter, there was no discernible anti-fascist 'culture' within the communist movement, which could give impetus and imagination to communist efforts to defeat fascism. These novel elements would not appear until the CPGB managed to free itself from the constraints of sectarianism.

About turn: From sectarian anti-fascism to the Popular Front

The new approach to fascism of the Popular Front was formally announced at the Comintern's Seventh World Congress which ran from 25 July to 21 August 1935. There had been no sudden conversion to the new approach, however. Shortly after the launch of a dangerous 'new fascist offensive' in Germany signalled by Adolf Hitler's advent to the Chancellorship in January 1933, the Comintern called on individual communist parties to make efforts to establish anti-fascist united fronts with social democratic organisations. The Comintern statement of 5 March 1933 also instructed communist parties to refrain from attacks on social-democratic bodies.[18] Although the 5 March initiative signalled a move away from the Third Period's overtly sectarian approach towards social democracy, political hesitancy, Stalinist bureaucratic inertia and lingering sectarian attitudes meant that there was to be no immediate drive towards a more expansive anti-fascist policy. It required a number of developments in early 1934 to precipitate a further lurch towards the Popular Front. The violent suppression of 'Red Vienna' by 'Dollfuss fascism' in mid-February warned of an ever-widening fascist offensive, while the Paris General Strike of 12 February demonstrated the depth of local 'grass roots' feeling for a more unified and expansive policy towards fascism. April then saw the appointment of George Dimitrov to the position of Comintern General Secretary, signalling Stalin's support for those pressing for a more decisive 'about turn' in policy. The following months saw Dimitrov undertake a thorough revision of policy. Stalin approved the new Popular Front line in December 1934, while the Comintern's Political Secretariat ratified it the following month.[19] The ingredients of the new policy were then outlined by Dimitrov and Palmiro Togliatti in two detailed reports to the Seventh World Congress.

If anything, the failings that continued to afflict Comintern anti-fascist policy even after Hitler became Chancellor were even more marked amongst some strands of the CPGB leadership. As we have seen above, Rajani Palme Dutt continued to pour invective on social democracy and link it to fascism as late as May 1934. By the summer of 1934 he seemed to be moving towards a less sectarian stance when he, along with Harry Pollitt, called for a broad anti-fascist coalition to include even 'bourgeois liberal elements'.[20] No doubt Dutt and Pollitt were becoming alarmed by the rapid advance of Oswald Mosley's British Union of Fascists (BUF) which, having just been formed in October 1932, had by the early summer of 1934 built a membership of 40,000. Nevertheless, in May 1935 Dutt could still be found applying the term 'social-fascism' to social democracy.[21] Additionally, Dutt seemed to have regarded Hitlerism as a temporary phenomenon. In *Fascism and Social Revolution* he wrote that 'the German working class revolution is not defeated, despite the temporary retreat of 1933. ... On the contrary, Germany is nearer to the final victory of the proletarian revolution than any country in the capitalist world'.[22]

In passing into the Popular Front era, the CPGB entered a new temporal sphere. This new temporal sphere was liminal in that communist politics and communist anti-fascism were in transition to a new state of being. What was being created through the efforts of the Popular Front was a new dispensation, a new departure or era, to replace the previous discredited Third Period of communist sectarianism and isolation which was passing away. As we shall see below, it was hoped that this new phase of communist politics would bring heightened awareness of fascism based on feelings of communal self-discovery. As a result, in its profile, outlook and orientation, Popular Front anti-fascism would look very different to the anti-fascism of the 'First', 'Second' and 'Third' periods. Eric Hobsbawm has described the Popular Front as a 'set of concentric circles of unity', with the united front of the working-class movement at its centre. The united front was to then serve as the basis for a much broader anti-fascist people's front embracing progressive elements of the middle strata, an alliance which in turn formed the basis for an anti-Axis front at the national level. It was envisaged that an international front of all peoples and governments against fascism and war would then form the outer circle of unity.[23] Thus, whereas CPGB anti-fascism during the 1920s and early 1930s, on the occasions it did confront 'open fascism', was a small-scale mostly London-based affair, the Popular Front sought to become a mass movement with a broad political and social-class base.

Popular Front anti-fascism as a cultural project

Popular Front anti-fascism was also a cultural project, in that it aimed at a common universe of values and outlook within this mass movement. This was to be a new moral community of anti-fascists bound together by a sense of a shared mission to defend liberty, social gains, the Jewish minority, and culture against the threat of fascism. It is generally recognised that the Popular Front sought to build this new moral community through encouraging engagement in mass action against fascism, whether through direct confrontation with Mosleyite fascism as at Hyde Park in September 1934 and Cable Street in October 1936, or through more 'voluntary' means as with the 'Aid Spain' movement. Building anti-fascist awareness was not restricted to mass action of this type, however. At times it worked very indirectly, requiring great patience and a high degree of imagination. Here the Popular Front's cultural project operated differently, as Popular Front anti-fascism expressed itself aesthetically through a particular political style and through myths, festivals and rituals either appropriated from or reflecting past traditions or created specifically for the purpose of socialising members of this new moral community towards faith in the eventual defeat of fascism. In different ways to the forms of mass action just mentioned, these Popular Front myths, festivals and rituals aimed to not only appeal to the moral conscience and heighten communal awareness of the fascist threat but also worked to build sacred enthusiasm for anti-fascist goals even to the point of encouraging activists' willingness to shed sacrificial blood to achieve this end. The following sections will focus primarily on this dimension to the Popular Front cultural project.

Artists and writers

Artists and writers would play an important role in this aspect of the Popular Front cultural project. It was Dimitrov's definition of fascism given to the Seventh Congress that paved the way for the invitation to artists and writers, as progressive elements of the middle strata, to join the anti-fascist people's front. When he described fascism as the 'open terrorist dictatorship of the most reactionary, most chauvinistic and the most imperialist elements of finance capital' Dimitrov seemed to simply restate the reductionist 'agent theory' of fascism that had dominated 1920s and early 1930s Comintern thinking, namely that fascism was but a violent symptom of capitalism in crisis. Nevertheless, in confining fascism to the narrow upper reaches of 'monopoly capital' he opened the way for an appeal to other elements of the 'bourgeoisie', those of a liberal and democratic persuasion, to fight fascism. Once recruited, artists and artists' groups would bring much needed colour and inventiveness to Popular Front festivals and other occasions, clothing these moments of communal defence and celebration in dramatic and emotional expression. The Artists' International Association (AIA) was the principal forum for communist and other anti-fascist artists during the Popular Front period. Originally founded as the Artists' International in 1933, the AIA had recruited over 600 members by mid-1936. The AIA staged a number of well-attended anti-fascist events, such as the 'Artists against War and Fascism' exhibition in late 1935 in Soho Square. The exhibition was attended by 6,000 people and *Left Review* described it as 'something between a demonstration and a national gallery'.[24]

Similarly, imaginative writers were recruited to help stir the emotions, rouse the moral conscience and build anti-fascist awareness. Following the lead of the AIA, the British Section of the Writers' International was founded in February 1934. Its journal, *Left Review* (1934–38), became the main outlet for the many communist and non-communist anti-fascist writers, novelists and poets who featured in Popular Front politics. John Lehmann's *New Writing* (1935–40) performed a similar role, as did the Left Book Club (launched May 1936) which had recruited an estimated 50,000 members by 1937. Participation in the International Congress of Writers for the Defence of Culture which first met in Paris in June 1935, then London in 1936 and Madrid in 1937 enabled British anti-fascist writers to forge international links and experience international solidarity.[25] CPGB cultural writers spared nothing in their efforts to highlight the anti-cultural tendency within Nazism in particular and said that bourgeois artists and writers had a moral obligation to join communist artists in the 'people's front' to defend the 'cultural heritage' from fascist barbarism and debasement. This invoking of the cultural heritage would become one of the foremost mobilising myths of communist Popular Front anti-fascism. By engaging with fascism and defending this heritage, artists and writers were assured that vitality would return to their art. As Ralph Fox, one of the Party's foremost cultural writers explained it: 'It is our fortune to have been born at one of those moments in history which demand from each one of us as an individual that he make his private decision. ... We are a part of that spiritual community with the dead of which Wordsworth spoke, we cannot stand aside, and by our actions we shall extend our imagination, because we shall have been true to the passions in us'.[26] Fox was calling for an engaged art that had a relation to contemporary political struggles, one which drew its themes and inspiration from life and expressed the feelings of the times. This engagement would not only help foster a more creative, imaginative art but would bring the artist into closer communion with 'the good, the brave, and the wise, of all ages', that spiritual community of the dead of which Wordsworth had written. Shortly after he penned these words, Fox entered this spiritual community of the dead when he was killed trying to halt the Axis offensive in Spain. Other 'bourgeois' intellectuals did not stand aside either. John Cornford, Christopher Caudwell, Charles Donnelly and G. C. MacLaurin also died defending the Spanish Republic. Another was the artist Felicia Browne whom we shall meet below. Their participation in the anti-fascist fight in Spain and subsequent deaths in battle represented the pinnacle of engaged art, its most sublime and noble expression.

The Popular Front: Walking with the dead

Popular Front anti-fascism sought to connect with the 'spiritual community of the dead' in another sense. As stated, the Popular Front comprised a series of concentric circles of unity with the united front of the working-class movement at its inner core. In keeping with the Popular Front's non-sectarian approach, the broad British labour movement was to be addressed without prejudice to any of its institutions or personnel and on the basis of new narrative strategies, one of the most important of which had its foundation in an emotive appeal to labour's radical past. In this celebratory narrative the workers' centuries-long tradition of heroic struggle to fight tyranny and defend and extend hard-won democratic liberties was invoked, imaginatively suggesting continuity between past and present historical time in the way it claimed affinity between this 'radical tradition' of popular struggle and the Popular Front effort to quell fascism. 'If England is to be saved from becoming one great graveyard, one great fascist prison, or one great battlefield', the *Daily Worker* stated in September 1936, 'then we, the people of England, must take our mighty past in our hands and use it as a giant sword.'[27] As with the emotive myth of the 'cultural heritage', this invoking of the past and the dead would help to establish the CPGB's radical interpretation of history as one of the principal mobilising myths of Popular Front anti-fascism. It was also a strategy consistent with Comintern Popular Front policy. In his report on fascism to the Seventh Comintern Congress, Dimitrov had urged member communist parties to enlighten the masses on their past traditions of struggle and to link this past with the present struggle to defeat fascism.

According to Richard Fenn, when a community fears its very survival is at stake in the face of an imminent and deadly external power, when it feels that time is pressing in, it calls on the spiritual resources of the past to help subdue this threat.[28] This summoning of the past and the dead into the present restore to a community the potency of ancestral virtues and strengths, helping it to both control the temporal anxiety and regenerate itself in preparation for the struggle to combat the external threat. Temporal anxiety, the fear that time was running out, certainly gripped the Popular Front community, particularly when a new fascist offensive opened in Spain in mid-1936. Writing in November 1936, the communist intellectual Cecil Day Lewis felt that 'every day the formation of a People's Front becomes more imperative'.[29] For Day Lewis, as with the CPGB more generally, the hope of the 'People's Front' lay in the 'regeneration of the Labour Movement' but before this could come about its fighting spirit, 'almost quenched by the General Strike', needed 'to be kindled into flame again'. The past and the dead were to figure in this effort at collective reawakening, for the working class movement would be regenerated if it was reminded 'of the greatness of its past history'. Art should again feature here according to Day Lewis. Art, particularly imaginative writing, could play a great part in reminding the rank-and-file of the labour movement of their ancestral heritage because of its unique power to stir the imagination and appeal to the emotions and 'idealism latent in man'.[30] A variety of modes of Popular Front written narrative would seek to bring about labour's collective epiphany. The drama of particular historical incidents of heroic struggle would be recalled in movement publications, such as the anthology of writings and poetry from twelve centuries of the English radical past collected by Jack Lindsay and Edgell Rickword which Lawrence & Wishart published in 1939 under the title *A Handbook of Freedom.* Another was Jack Lindsay's poem 'Who are the English?' which was published as a *Left Review* pamphlet. Through such written forms of celebration was the British labour movement's past ennobled. Just as importantly, from the point of view of this chapter, this ongoing celebratory narrative helped ensure that the spirit of the workers righteous past was inserted into the Popular Front's evolving communal identity as part of its broader goal to build anti-fascist awareness.

Theatre and festival

Theatre and festival were still more potent cultural forms utilised by the Popular Front to celebrate labour's righteous past as a means of regenerating its vigour in the present. Dramatised versions, both single recitations and 'mass declamations', of Jack Lindsay's celebratory poem 'Who are the English?', for example, were performed by Unity Theatre groups.[31] The constraints of space do not allow for a lengthy appraisal of the use of agitprop theatre as a weapon to combat fascism during the Popular Front era. This topic, in any case, has already received extensive treatment.[32] Communist or Popular Front festival, on the other hand, has received much less attention. Of all the CPGB's efforts to build anti-fascist awareness during the Popular Front period, the use of festival was arguably the most imaginative. The festival performance, even more than agitprop theatre, if staged effectively, had a strong creative potential and public focus, was genuinely participatory and collective, drew on a variety of media, and achieved an emotional reach far beyond that of other forms of communist persuasion, including the written narrative. The Popular Front festivals that sought to tell of labour's radical past were the CPGB-inspired pageants of history which were staged with some frequency in areas of communist and Popular Front strength from late 1936. In terms of the historical pageant's basic generic structure and narrative format, it usually involved costumed re-enactments of specific historical episodes in a manner not dissimilar to the Elizabethan chronicle-play, or long parades featuring scenes or visual images, the latter emblazoned on banners in the case of the communist pageants, of selective historical events deemed to be of significance to the narrative story being told. One of the pageant's key functions was to offer a preferred, usually heroic and unashamedly congratulatory, version of the communal, national or political past and suggest continuity and affinity between present and past historical time. Most importantly, though, in terms of this chapter, the historical pageant was a dramatic public ritual with a rite-of-passage format. In other words, the intention of the pageant ritual was to effect a transformation in outlook of the pageant participants and spectators with a view to bringing forth a new communal orientation based on a heightened awareness of the best of the communal past.

Rituals provide an important means by which communities cope with crises and stress. When communities feel under particularly acute threat, they are inclined to engage in emotive rituals of ancestral restoration which call on the dead to participate with the living in the process of communal regeneration and survival.[33] The Popular Front historical pageants can be read as rituals of ancestral restoration. Here the intention was to effect a transformation in outlook of the pageant participants and spectators with a view to bringing forth a heightened anti-fascist consciousness. At one level, the ritual of ancestral restoration underpinning these pageant processions worked to bring about this heightened communal and anti-fascist awareness by honouring labour's past struggles. The pageant ritual, however, operated at a more opaque, even primordial, level as we shall see below.

Celebrating the blood sacrifice

For Mike Wallis the function of the Popular Front historical pageant was to show the Communist Party 'as a site of celebration, tradition and community' and provide it with an opportunity 'to popularise the Party's claim "that communism is English", the natural heartbeat of the common people, the proper outcome of their long struggle'.[34] It cannot be denied that the Popular Front pageants performed the celebratory role that Wallis describes. Indeed, the historical pageant operated on a number of levels, one of which was to celebrate labour's radical tradition of struggle against injustice, as mentioned above. Another of its celebratory roles was, as Wallis claims, to suggest continuity between the CPGB and the 'English radical tradition' of popular struggle and to bring the pageant participants and spectators to an awareness of this supposed line of continuity. That said, there is a need to re-conceptualise these Popular Front pageants, particularly their celebratory visual narratives. According to this chapter's reading, one of their primary modes of celebration was to celebrate the blood sacrifice tradition in British radical history, to suggest continuity between those radicals of the past who had spilled blood 'for liberty's sake' and the anti-fascist dead of the Spanish Civil War, and to make the pageant participants and spectators conscious of this ongoing tradition. According to this interpretation of the Popular Front pageants then, they were public rituals which celebrated the blood sacrifice, while the commemorative march of history which formed the core of the performance was a sacrificial procession.

In September 1936 the *Daily Worker* reported that the 'ghosts of England's fighters for freedom, ghosts of stalwarts, dead and gone, must have marched yesterday through London streets'.[35] The occasion on which 'they must have marched, those old defenders of liberty', was the first of the major CPGB-inspired historical pageants which was staged on 20 September 1936. This was an extraordinary mass Popular Front spectacle involving 20,000 marchers, a long procession and carnival of flags, banners and colour which wound its way from the Embankment via Hyde Park to its eventual termination point in Shoreditch in London's East End. The literally hundreds of banners on display, many of which had been prepared by AIA artists, depicted heroic episodes and characters from Britain's radical past, all of which were arranged and appeared to the pageant spectators in chronological sequence to evoke a sense of an unfolding radical tradition to which the Popular Front struggle against fascism was an heir. There were banners dedicated to Lilburn's Levellers, the Tolpuddle Martyrs, Robert Owen, the Chartists, Keir Hardie and William Morris amongst others. But what is most interesting from this chapter's reading of the event, were the prominent banners dedicated to Wat Tyler, John Ball, the Peterloo victims, James Connolly and even individuals that one would not normally associate with radical labour history, namely Simon de Montford and Thomas More. The final visual image presented to the spectators, which marked the end-point of the procession and narrative story being conveyed, was a 'great portrait' of Felicia Browne. Browne's portrait was flanked by a Red Flag and the Spanish Flag, alongside the caption: 'A communist dies fighting for liberty in Spain – so is her story told'. Browne, a then thirty-two year old CPGB activist and sculptress who had studied at the Slade Art School, was killed on the Aragon Front on 25 August 1936. She was the first Briton to die in battle in the Spanish conflict. What united Tyler, Ball, de Montford, More, Connolly and the Peterloo victims was that they were not solely stalwart fighters for liberty as the *Daily Worker's* report on the pageant explained it, but that they had endured what subsequent martyrisers would call a sacrificial death 'for Truth's sake'. In other words, they had all met a premature and bloody end 'for liberty's sake' at the hands of a violent or retributive ruling power. Thus, the tradition and community represented in the 20 September London pageant, conjured up by the presence of these banners to the martyred dead of past struggles was one that came into being, to a large degree, through the blood sacrifice. This sense was further reinforced by the literally hundreds of Red Flags in evidence in the London procession, the Red Flag being, of course, the ultimate symbol of the communist and British labour movement dead, the Left's sacred totem which represents the sacrificial blood of its martyred dead.[36]

As mentioned, one of the key devices of the historical pageant ritual was to collapse linear time and suggest continuity and affinity between present and past time. The presence and prominence of Felicia Browne's portrait in the pageant's gallery of the martyred dead, therefore, situated her death in a powerfully emotive tradition of blood and sacrifice. The presence of Browne's portrait in the pageant's gallery also endowed her blood sacrifice with eschatological purpose, whereby her sacrifice was presented as an important, even necessary, element in that long historical struggle towards arriving at the final liberating goal of freedom from tyranny, whether feudal, Victorian capitalist or fascist. It was the hope of the Party elite that a stronger collective identity, that is the strident anti-fascist identity of the Popular Front, would emerge out of awareness and appreciation, arrived at through participation in the pageant ritual, that a member of the community had shed sacrificial blood for its benefit. This association between sacrificial blood and communal benefit, the idea that blood offered willingly brings advantage to the community, has a long ancestry and resonated in the collective memory of many cultures, including communist culture. There is a traditional belief in the power of blood in another sense. If sacrificial blood was thought to be efficacious, it was also thought to spawn new life. In other words, it was seen as the ground of rebirth and regeneration, the seed of renewal. This powerful association is evident in the Christian martyrological tradition, as in the well-known assertion by the late second century theologian Tertullian that the blood of the early Christian martyrs was the seed of the Church. This association is also evident in communist martyrology. Thus when the writer Ralph Fox followed Felicia Browne to the grave, Rajani Palme Dutt was moved to write in *The Labour Monthly* that: 'through the blood and travail of the present time a new and deeper revolutionary movement is growing up in Britain on the foundation of the old, a revolutionary movement whose character and whose sacrifices constitute the guarantee of future victory. In the building of this revolutionary movement in Britain, Ralph Fox, and those who have fallen with him in Spain, will hold an honoured place'.[37] Sacrificial blood, it seems, impresses the imagination and arouses the emotions. It also ensured firmer communal bonds, inspired commitment and was thus the seed of anti-fascist resistance.

The Popular Front historical pageant as a funeral rite

In situating Felicia Browne's death in the emotive blood sacrifice tradition, the Popular Front historical pageant also fulfilled the function of a ceremonial ritual in a manner similar to the funeral rite by helping to ensure her passage into the realm of the sacred, that exclusive place reserved for those who had shed blood for liberty's sake. Indeed, what is striking about the anti-fascist dead in Spain is that they were usually buried where they fell in battle, in the hard earth of Spain. We are thus talking about deaths without a body. These are deaths where the grieving political community of which the deceased was a part was unable to effect that incorporation into the world of the sacred dead through the staging of the crucial funeral rite *and* generate sacred enthusiasm for the Cause for which the deceased had lived and died. In previous eras of popular struggle, when radical movements were hit by the death of one of their activists they proceeded to stage elaborate funeral ceremonies to help heal the wound to the community caused by the passing and to help ensure that the dead person received due recognition by being reconstituted on to a higher plane than was the case with ordinary deaths. This higher plane was perceived to be a sacred realm, an exclusive place usually reserved for movement martyrs, the 'Lords of the dead' of the movement. One just has to think of the funeral staged for the Chartist Samuel Holberry in Sheffield on 27 June 1842. An extraordinary spectacle and statement of Chartist efforts to confer martyr status on the dead 'patriot', it was estimated that c. 50,000 people participated in this ritual event.[38] The highly choreographed ceremony and theatre of the radical funeral then, would announce the passage of the revered 'patriot' or comrade into the world of the martyred dead and would constitute the first and most important stage in the memorialising process. Just as crucially, the highly choreographed and elaborate ritual ceremonies just described also served the purpose of building sacred enthusiasm within the political movement for the Cause for which the deceased had lived and died.

With the British anti-fascist deaths in Spain, there could be no solemn processional cortege bearing witness to the passing of a revered comrade, no emblems and symbolism on display during a 'red funeral' ceremony announcing the passage into the realm of the sacred, no burial service dignified by the mass recitation of a hymn especially composed for the deceased, and no eloquent graveside oration ringing with exhortations to the assembled multitude of mourners to honour the dead comrade by continuing the 'good fight'. How, then, to ensure the deceased's passage into the realm of the sacred and build sacred enthusiasm for the martyr's ideals? In one sense, this function was carried out by the CPGB's memorialising written narratives. A written narrative though, while important for finding an audience and conveying a message was not, unlike the funeral rite, a form of public ritual which could generate sacred enthusiasm. Rather, as this chapter claims, it was the popular cultural form of the historical pageant procession which fulfilled some of the key functions that were normally carried out through the performance of the passage rite at radical funerals. This was not only because reverence for the blood sacrifice informed its underlying ritual pattern, but that in its dramatic, participatory, visual, emotional and rite-of-passage format it resembled some of the features of the radical funeral's elaborate ceremony and theatre. Both forms had a capacity to elevate the dead to the realm of the sacred, heal the political community, build communal awareness and generate sacred enthusiasm for the struggles that lay ahead. Apart from the rite-of-passage format underlying the event, there were other funeral motifs in evidence at the Popular Front historical pageants. For example, when Felicia Browne's huge portrait was carried into Hyde Park on the occasion of the 20 September London pageant, the huge throng of some 20,000 spectators uncovered their heads and stood in respectful silence as it passed by, a scene resembling those displays of collective mourning at the radical funerals of the past.[39] It was through such acts of collective sharing in the appreciation of the blood sacrifice that the anti-fascist community of the Popular Front came together.

To the artist Felicia Browne goes the honour of not just being the first Briton to die fighting fascism in Spain, but the honour of being the first to be incorporated into the Popular Front movement's sacred realm of the sacrificial dead. Moreover, the memorialising frame which enabled the CPGB to sacralise Browne's death, extract meaning from it and represent it to the wider Popular Front community, the idea that this was a sacrificial death in the best radical martyrological tradition and the seed of new political life, would also serve as a template for the Party's memorialising of subsequent anti-fascist deaths in Spain. In this memorialising process, the historical pageant ritual would continue to play an important part not least because, as this chapter has sought to demonstrate, in its format it resembled some of the features of the radical funeral's elaborate ceremony and theatre. Take the example of another historical pageant which the CPGB's Lancashire District Committee staged in Manchester in July 1937. As with the September 1936 London pageant, the martyred radicals of the English past again featured prominently in the performance, including Wat Tyler, Simon de Montfort and the Peterloo dead. Again, as with the London pageant, a comrade recently killed in Spain, the Manchester communist George Brown, was memorialised at the pageant thereby situating his death in the powerfully emotive martyrological tradition of the blood sacrifice.

Yet again, as with the London pageant and Felicia Browne, apart from the rite-of-passage format, funeral motifs were in evidence, as when the pageant opened with a tribute to George Brown and the 'great crowd' present responded by standing and baring their heads in respectful silence while a band played the Funeral March.[40]

Jewish communist resistance to fascism

It needs hardly saying that one cannot discuss inter-war communist anti-fascism without reference to Jewish involvement in CPGB-led anti-fascism. Because the CPGB did not classify its members according to ethnic background, there are no reliable figures as to the numbers of Jews who actually joined the CPGB. Even so, it is clear that during the 1930s the escalating Nazi persecution of Jews in Germany, the BUF's turn towards anti-semitism in September 1934, and the passive response of the official Anglo-Jewish and Labour Party leadership pushed many working-class Jews towards support for the CPGB's more aggressively confrontational form of anti-fascism. The important Jewish contribution to the 1930s anti-fascist struggle is usually measured in terms of the occasions of direct confrontation between Jewish communists and home-grown representatives of 'open fascism'. Indeed, communist Jews could be found confronting Mosley's BUF in small-scale street-level clashes and through participation in mass CPGB-led counter-demonstrations. Although there were street-level clashes between BUF activists and Jews in London during spring 1933, this opposition began in real earnest in 1934. A significant Jewish communist presence was noted at all the major anti-Mosley mobilisations in London from 1934, most notably at Olympia on 7 June 1934, Hyde Park on 9 September 1934 and even Bermondsey on 3 October 1937. Jewish anti-fascists from the CPGB's militant Stepney Branch which boasted 230 members by 1936 were in regular attendance at these gatherings.[41] The impressive Jewish contribution to the mass 'oceanic' anti-BUF gathering at Cable Street on 4 October 1936 is well known. At Cable Street, and during the wider effort to counter the BUF's often violent anti-semitic campaign in East London, mention should also be made of the collaborative work that Jewish communists engaged in with contemporary radical Jewish anti-fascist organisations, particularly the Jewish Peoples' Council Against Fascism and Anti-Semitism (formed July 1936) and the Ex-Servicemen's Movement Against Fascism (formed July 1936). Less well known is the belligerent Jewish communist opposition to the BUF beyond London, particularly in Manchester and Leeds, the latter as displayed in opposing the Mosleyite open-air rally at Holbeck Moor in September 1936.[42]

Finally, there was another dimension to Jewish communist resistance to fascism that should be acknowledged and which speaks to one of this chapter's main themes. This was the willingness to shed sacrificial blood to defeat fascism, which relates to the remarkable and heroic role played by Jewish anti-fascists in the International Brigades during the Spanish Civil War. Some 35,000 to 40,000 volunteers from fifty different countries fought in Spain and, in spite of many Jews using aliases, it is estimated that as many as 25 per cent of this number were Jews.[43] There were approximately 2,000 British anti-fascists in Spain and it is estimated that the Jewish presence may have been as high as 22 per cent and certainly no lower than 11 per cent, that is between 440 and 220 volunteers. These percentages should be seen in the context of a then Jewish population in Britain of 0.5 per cent. The exact number of Jewish communists within these estimates is difficult to assess though one can assume that their presence was substantial. As many as one-quarter of the 2,000 British volunteers died in the Spanish conflict. At an extremely conservative estimate, 10 per cent of those killed were Jews, certainly more given the issue of non-Jewish aliases. It was this willingness to shed sacrificial blood to defeat fascism, demonstrated by both Jewish and Gentile anti-fascists in Spain, many of whom were communists, that stands as the most impressive and enduring feature of that direct, combative and belligerent form of anti-fascism favoured by the CPGB at important intervals during the inter-war period.

Notes

1 *Labor Monthly*, July 1925.
2 Rajani Palme Dutt, *Fascism and Social Revolution* (London: Martin Lawrence, 1934), p. 289.
3 See Jane Degras (ed.), *The Communist International, 1919–1943. Documents, Vol. 1, 1919–1922* (London: Frank Cass, 1971), p. 18.
4 Jane Degras (ed.), *The Communist International, 1919–1943 Documents, Vol. 2, 1923–28* (London: Frank Cass, 1971), p. 22.
5 'Extracts from the Resolution on Fascism Adopted by the Fifth Comintern Congress. July 1924', in *Ibid.*, pp. 137–40.
6 *Ibid.*, p. 139.
7 *Labour Monthly*, July 1925.
8 Dutt, *Fascism*, pp. 150 & 155.
9 CPGB, *To Fascism or Communism. A Resolution of the Central Committee of the CPGB* (London: CPGB, 1931), p. 23.
10 All these groups are discussed in Thomas Linehan, *British Fascism, 1918–1939: Parties, Ideology and Culture* (Manchester: Manchester University Press, 2000).

11 *Ibid.*, p. 126.
12 *British Fascists. Policy and Practice* (1 July 1926).
13 See *Labour Monthly*, July 1925.
14 *The Patriot*, 12 September 1929.
15 Nigel Copsey, *Anti-Fascism in Britain* (Basingstoke: Macmillan, 2000), pp. 9–10.
16 *Ibid.*, p. 12.
17 *Ibid.*
18 Jane Degras (ed.), *The Communist International, 1919–1943 Documents, Vol. 3, 1929–1943* (London: Frank Cass, 1971), pp. 253–4.
19 These developments are discussed in Kevin McDermott and Jeremy Agnew, *The Comintern. A History of International Communism from Lenin to Stalin* (London: Macmillan, 1996).
20 Jim Fyrth, 'In the Thirties', in Jim Fyrth (ed.), *Britain, Fascism and the Popular Front* (London: Lawrence & Wishart, 1985), pp. 13–14.
21 Mentioned in Degras (ed.), *The Communist International, Vol. 3*, p. 357.
22 Dutt, *Fascism*, p. 286.
23 Eric Hobsbawm, 'Fifty Years of People's Fronts', in Fyrth (ed.), *Britain*, p. 240.
24 *Left Review*, 2, 4 (January 1936).
25 See *Daily Worker*, 25 June 1936.
26 Ralph Fox, *The Novel and the People* (London: Lawrence & Wishart, 1937), pp. 154–5.
27 *Daily Worker*, 14 September 1936.
28 Richard Fenn, *The End of Time. Religion, Ritual, and the Forging of the Soul* (London: SPCK, 1997).
29 *Left Review*, 2, 4 (November 1936).
30 *Ibid.*
31 See *Left Review*, 3, 1 (February 1937).
32 For example, see Jim McCarthy, *Political theatre during the Spanish Civil War* (Cardiff: University of Wales Press, 1999).
33 Fenn, *The End*, pp. 57–60. Fenn cites the Ghost Dance of the Sioux as an example.
34 Mike Wallis, 'Heirs to the Pageant: Mass Spectacle and the Popular Front', in Andy Croft (ed.), *A Weapon in the Struggle* (London: Pluto, 1998), p. 50.
35 *Daily Worker*, 21 September 1936.
36 One just has to think of the opening lines of Jim Connell's *The Red Flag* (1889): '*The people's flag is deepest red, It shrouded oft our martyred dead, And ere their limbs grew stiff and cold, Their hearts blood dyed its every fold*'.
37 *Labour Monthly*, February 1937.
38 See *The Northern Star and Leeds General Advertiser*, 2 July 1842.
39 *Daily Worker*, 21 September 1936.
40 *Daily Worker*, 12 July 1936.
41 Copsey, *Anti-Fascism*, pp. 26, 34, 56 & 71.
42 *Ibid.*, p. 46.
43 For these and the following estimates, see Martin Sugarman, *Jews in the International Brigade* (London: AJEX Museum, 1990), and David Diamint, *Combattants Juifs dans l'Armee Republicaine Espagnole* (Paris: Renouveau, 1979).

2
'Every time they made a Communist, they made a Fascist'[1]: The Labour Party and Popular Anti-Fascism in the 1930s

Nigel Copsey

Introduction

For far-Left critics, the Labour Party contributed little if anything to the 1930s struggle against fascism. Repeatedly, the Labour establishment spurned invitations by the Communist Party (CP or CPGB) and Independent Labour Party (ILP) to form either a united anti-fascist proletarian front or an anti-fascist People's (or Popular) Front. Following events at Olympia on 7 June 1934, the National Joint Council (NJC), representing the Labour Party, the Parliamentary Labour Party (PLP) and the Trades Union Congress (TUC), 'repudiated entirely every form of organised interruption at fascist meetings'.[2] At regular intervals, the Labour Party's rank-and-file were told to refrain from agitating against Mosley's British Union of Fascists (BUF), whether in Hyde Park in September 1934, in the East End in October 1936 or at Bermondsey one year later. The Labour establishment – Morrison and Dalton on the National Executive Committee (NEC); Bevin and Citrine on the TUC General Council – insisted that confrontational anti-fascism would advertise the BUF and that 'the silence of the absent', to borrow the words of one contemporary journalist, was a 'strong refrigerator'.[3] When BUF activity and support subsided towards the end of the 1930s, it was 'no thanks to the Labour Party and trade union leaderships', one Marxist historian felt compelled to write.[4]

Yet it should not be forgotten that even if led by the CP and ILP, the mass opposition to Mosley came from ordinary members and supporters of the Labour Party. Writing in 1946, Frederic Mullally spoke about the 'fierce flame of hatred against Mosley [that] consumed all sectarian differences among the rank and file of the working classes and, time after time ... they assembled in their tens of thousands to demonstrate the strength of their anti-fascist conviction'.[5] As Communist Party historian, Mike Power also appreciates, 'Some of the biggest demonstrations in British Labour history were mounted against organised fascism'.[6] Furthermore, since anti-fascist crowds all too often outnumbered fascist gatherings, historians have concluded that popular antifascism dispirited the BUF and halted it in its tracks.[7]

Regardless of whether or not such displays of mass opposition were responsible for delivering the crushing blow to Mosley's ambitions, that thousands of workers brushed aside the Labour establishment and confronted the BUF is clear. To all intents and purposes, these were the people that constituted Britain's popular anti-fascist movement. 'We are talking of an opposition to Mosley which runs into millions', Joe Kahn, a former CP member put it, and 'about a Communist Party which had effectively very few thousand over the entire country... One has to put this whole thing in perspective'.[8] Whilst impossible to be exact, one historian suggests that the greater part of perhaps half a million political and trade union activists, 'were involved in one or another of the anti-fascist and working-class campaigns' of the 1930s.[9] How, then, are we to account for the popular resonance of this active (rather than passive) anti-fascism? What was it about Labour's antifascism that gave rise to dissent, and how should this dissent be understood? With regard to its own working-class constituency, was the Labour Party's anti-fascism a 'failure'? Yet, in absenting itself from confrontational anti-fascism, did the Labour establishment not shore up democratic institutions and thereby frustrate the aspirations of native fascism?

Fascism, communism and democracy

In answering these questions, our central focus falls on the period after the formation of the BUF in October 1932. Of course the history of British fascism precedes the BUF and so too does the history of antifascism. Yet the Labour Party scarcely features in this narrative. Since no fascist organisation that antedated the BUF could lay claim to any real significance, the Labour Party attached little to no importance to the domestic forerunners of Mosley's Blackshirts. In fact, it was in 1924, under a Labour government that the British Fascists were granted their articles of association as the British Fascisti Ltd, and legal recognition for the first time. Whilst the CP critiqued Labour in 1925 for paying insufficient regard to the dangers of domestic fascism, there was little reason for the Labour establishment to take the threat of home-grown fascism seriously. Across the Labour press, Britain's fascist movement attracted seldom more than light-hearted derision. In any case, for the most part it was the CP and not the Labour Party that had been on the receiving end of (minor) fascist provocations.[10] One ironic exception to this rule was none other than Labour MP Oswald Mosley. In December 1926, after his meetings were disrupted by fascists, Mosley ironically mocked those 'black-shirted buffoons' who made 'a cheap imitation of ice-cream sellers'.[11] Less than five years later, when Mosley was expelled from the Labour Party, he would incite a further round of antipathy – this time from the ranks of the labour movement. But there was little incipient anti-fascism in Labour Party opposition to the New Party. This was driven more by anger at Mosley's upper-class treachery than by anger at Mosley's 'embryonic fascism'.[12]

It follows that we must look to 1933 as our starting point. 'Before 1933', as Michael Newman recognised, 'the Labour leadership had not devoted that much attention to the problem of fascism: Hitler's triumph in Germany ended this complacency'.[13] Developments in Germany – the destruction of Europe's strongest labour movement – brought the potential threat of fascism much closer. On 5 March 1933, as Germany went to the polls, the Communist International (Comintern) called for a united front against the 'Fascist offensive of the bourgeoisie'. The idea behind the 'United Front' was for Communist and Social Democratic Parties to participate both nationally and internationally in a joint programme of working-class action against fascism, during which time Communists promised to desist from attacking Social Democratic organisations. Joint action by Communists and Social Democrats, in the Comintern's disquisitions, would then inspire all other strata of working people, be it the urban lower middle class, intelligentsia or peasantry to form a far broader anti-fascist 'People's' or 'Popular Front'. The ultimate objective, as Georgi Dimitrov, the Comintern's general secretary explained, was to find a 'common language' that would 'draw increasingly wide masses into the revolutionary class struggle and lead them to proletarian revolution'.[14] In other words, the 'United Front' was *both* a defence against fascism *and* a tactic to push communism.

The month before, the Labour and Socialist International – the body to which the Labour Party was affiliated – had already issued a call for unity. The Labour and Socialist International advised those parties affiliated to it to refrain from separate negotiations until contact between the two Internationals had produced definite results. But before any agreement had been reached, the CP had contacted the Labour Party and the ILP with proposals for a united front. Although uneasy about collaborating with the CP, the ILP agreed to a series of joint meetings that would call public attention to the fascist danger. The Labour Party was far less receptive. It point-blank refused a deputation from the CP and ILP and then published its reasons in a short manifesto, *Democracy versus Dictatorship.*[15]

This manifesto, issued by the NJC on 24 March 1933, conveyed both Labour's steadfast commitment to parliamentary democracy, and its loathing of dictatorship, whether fascist or communist. If the manifesto reassured Labour moderates, it also gave short shrift to those on the Party's radical wing, in particular the Socialist League, declaring that collaboration with Communists was out of the question. Communism and fascism, it said, led directly to dictatorship, and Labour was opposed to individual or group dictatorship whether of the Right or of the Left. If truth be told, Labour's main attack was not directed against fascism but against Communism. As the CP's Rajani Palme Dutt noted, the manifesto directly attacked Communism or Bolshevism by name seven times but only referred to fascism four times.[16] The British Union of Fascists was not mentioned at all. Although it was clear that Labour understood fascism to be right-wing and reactionary, no definition of fascism was forthcoming either. Labour's manifesto also offered little practical guidance as to how workers should fight fascism other than calling on workers to re-affirm their faith in the fundamental principles of democratic government, and in democratic socialism. The point that Labour made, and this would determine its anti-fascist policy throughout the 1930s, was that fascism grew concurrently with communism; communists were to blame for dividing the German working class, for undermining Weimar democracy and for radicalising the German middle class. The logic that followed: 'To defeat Fascism, root out Communism'.[17]

Naturally, the CP decried Labour's manifesto. By way of reply, Dutt inveighed against Labour's record on democracy, claiming that when Labour was in power, its governance of 420 million colonial peoples had been through armed dictatorship. Meanwhile, Labour's administration of the Tory Trade Union Act, Dutt argued, had turned Labour into an agent for the capitalist class. Moreover, the CP retorted that although a workers' dictatorship existed in the Soviet Union, this was a transient dictatorship of the majority over the minority and would be replaced by free forms of social administration. It was therefore disingenuous for Labour to equate a workers' dictatorship with a fascist dictatorship. The refusal of the Labour Party to unite against fascism meant that Labour had joined a united front of capitalists (and fascists) against Communism, Dutt argued.[18]

Yet Labour's position, even if dismissed by the CP as 'pathologically' anti-Communist, was still anti-fascist. Behind Labour's permutation of anti-fascism was democratic and moral opposition to dictatorship of any kind. And since Labour also held that it was fear of communism that had invited fascism in the first place – 'The fear of the Dictatorship of the Working-class in turn has evoked the iron Dictatorship of Capitalism and Nationalism'[19] – its immediate priority was to repudiate all co-operation with the Communist Party.

A principal author of *Democracy versus Dictatorship* was moderate TUC general secretary, Walter Citrine. For several years Citrine had been speaking out against 'the cancer of communist influence' in the trade union movement. President of the International Federation of Trade Unions from 1928, he had frequently travelled to Berlin, observing the rise of National Socialism at first hand. He was also the NJC's chief spokesperson on foreign affairs.[20] Citrine was anxious to make sense of the rise of Hitlerism and to work through its implications for the British labour movement. In *Dictatorships and the Trade Union Movement* (1933), Citrine identified the factors behind the Hitler dictatorship, and then asked whether there was any similarity between Germany and conditions obtaining in Britain. His conclusion was that economic depression and unemployment was the only common factor.

For Citrine, there were obvious variances between the socio-political cultures of Britain and Germany: the absence of a strong democratic tradition in Germany; the role of the German Communist Party which had prepared ground for National Socialism by dividing the labour movement and 'sapping' the strength of the Social Democratic Party; feelings of resentment and injured national pride for which the peace settlement was to blame; 'vertical divisions' throughout German society whereby political parties had their own trade unions, sports and youth organisations. These divisions were further carried through into the militarisation of political life, whereupon paramilitary organisations such as the Red Front and Brownshirts charged the political atmosphere 'with all the potentialities of disorder and civil war'.[21] For fascism to have any chance of success in Britain, Citrine concluded, the economic situation would have to deteriorate further, at which point a loss of faith in democratic government might ensue. It was therefore incumbent on trade unionists to re-affirm their democratic principles and reject demands for a united front with the CP – a party that stood for dictatorship not democracy.

Although it recoiled from co-operating with Communists, the NJC, taking its cue from a meeting of the International Federation of Trade Unions at Zurich in April 1933, did issue an appeal to raise funds for German workers and recommended that trade unionists boycott German goods.[22] The NJC also organised protests against Hitlerism, first at the Albert Hall in April and then at its London May Day demonstration. That same month the NJC published *Down with Fascism*, a pamphlet written by Joseph Compton, then Chairman of the NEC with a forward penned by Citrine. However, much like *Democracy versus Dictatorship*, it made no mention of Mosley or the BUF. It is probably no exaggeration to conclude that the NJC, even if shaken out of its complacency by the Nazi seizure of power, did next to nothing to counter domestic fascism during 1933. Then again, there was no need. Indeed, Citrine had warned against precipitate overreaction. 'Against what Fascism? Against the 6,000 stalwarts of Sir Oswald Mosley?', he had remarked to the Trades Union Congress in September 1933.[23]

How, then, was the NJC position received by Labour's rank-and-file? What is clear is that support for it was not unequivocal, and this despite the fact that Mosley's Blackshirts had yet to benefit from Rothermere's largesse. When Labour gathered for its annual conference in October 1933, although the leadership won the conference vote, Labour left-wingers dissented. Ellen Wilkinson, representing the Jarrow constituency, and having also witnessed the rise of Nazism at first hand, voiced her disapproval. 'If you just sit there and say we will not have anything to do with the Communists or with the I.L.P', she declared, 'I say the rank and file, whom we represent, will not listen'.[24] Alex Gossip, representing the National Amalgamated Furnishing Trades, recorded 'with pleasure that many affiliated labour parties and Co-operative Guilds' had ignored official Labour Party policy, and 'had taken their place alongside those determined to struggle against War and Fascism'.[25]

Much local-level research is still needed before Gossip's claim can be corroborated. However, there is certainly evidence of grassroots involvement in the loose patchwork of local anti-fascist committees that was already beginning to emerge across Britain in 1933. To take one example, future leader of the Labour Party, Hugh Gaitskell, supported an anti-fascist committee in Chatham and shared a platform with local Communists.[26] Often the Young Communist League (YCL) would court Labour League of Youth branches, especially those eager to assert a more radical identity.[27] As early as June 1933 the North London branches of the Labour League of Youth had dispatched a memorandum to the NEC objecting to official policy on the united front.[28] Moreover, as Dylan Murphy has shown in his work on Leeds, at least three League of Youth branches from the city came out in support of the united front during 1933.[29]

Following the violent suppression of Social Democrats in Austria by the 'fascist' dictatorship of Dolfuss, the possibility that Labour might warm to a renewed call for a united front was raised in early 1934. While Labour Party secretary Arthur Henderson met privately with the ILP's Fenner Brockway and James Maxton, the sticking point had been the inclusion of the Communist Party, and Henderson stood his ground. Since Communists did not believe in parliamentary democracy and were hostile to the Labour Party, wanting to destroy its influence and disrupt its membership, there was no prospect of a united front with the CP, Henderson insisted.[30] The only unity that Labour supported was unity of democratic working-class movements, that is to say, unity between the Labour Party, the TUC and the Co-operative Movement. 'We are united front', Herbert Morrison had maintained, 'and I ask you to stand by the Executive in maintaining the united front we have got'.[31]

All the same, and much to the irritation of the Labour Party's Executive, rank-and-file members continued to co-operate with Communists in local united front committees[32] – and in the case of Tyneside some even donned the grey shirts of the militant Anti-Fascist League.[33] Whether a local left-wing tradition was inclusive or exclusive would often determine whether joint action took place.[34] The existence of a moderate Catholic bloc on Liverpool's Labour Party, as Neil Barrett points out, inhibited joint activity on Merseyside, but in Manchester co-operation was easier to sustain.[35] It certainly did not help Labour's leaders when prominent members of the party, such as Ellen Wilkinson and Labour's chief whip in the House of Lords, Lord Marley, openly associated with organisations deemed ancillary to the Communist Party. Raising the hackles of the Labour establishment in particular was the involvement of both in the Relief Committee for the Victims of German Fascism – an organisation sponsored by the Comintern's Willi Muenzenberg.[36]

Opposing fascism in theory; stifling opposition in fact?

While claiming to have been alert to the BUF from the very beginning, it was January 1934 before Labour's leaders decided to act against domestic fascism. The reason why was the lauding of Mosley's BUF by the Rothermere press which, at an instant, handed British fascism mass circulation publicity. Labour Party investigations revealed a rapid influx of Fascist recruits. At the beginning of February 1934, an official Fascist source revealed that membership of the BUF had jumped to 17,707.[37] What's more, Mosley was trying to reach into the workplace. The BUF had established its own trade union subsidiary – the Fascist Union of British Workers,[38] the *Fascist Week* (2–8 February 1934) had carried a front-page appeal to trade unionists, and Blackshirts had appeared at several industrial disputes, notably the Firestone strike in Brentford the previous year.

In responding to the BUF, Colin Cross has written that 'On the left there was quick, decisive action'.[39] In reality, Labour took its time. Its first step was to ascertain more about the activities of the BUF across the country. The intention was to identify those constituencies where a national educative campaign could be targeted, involving meetings, demonstrations, and the distribution of anti-fascist literature. However, it was 8 June 1934 before the Labour Party's 'Notes for Speakers' was devoted to the subject of 'Fascism in Great Britain', and 12 June 1934 before the Labour Party's questionnaire[40] on fascist activity had been sent out to its divisional parties. Even if in preparation, as of late June 1934 the Labour Party had still not published its statement on fascism at home and abroad. On 28 June Citrine had reported to a joint meeting of the TUC, NEC and PLP that no draft document on the subject of fascism was presently available for submission to either the Congress or the party conference.[41] Moreover, there had been no general circulation of anti-BUF literature.[42] It was also as late as 27 June 1934, and only when prompted to do so by the National Union of Railwaymen, that the NEC contacted the press declaring that members of the BUF were ineligible as individual members of the Labour Party, as delegates to the Labour Party locally or nationally, or as candidates for the Labour Party in parliamentary or local government elections.[43]

In truth, whilst drafting its response to the BUF, Labour was overtaken by events. Towards the end of May, the London District Committee of the CP had written to the London Labour Party, London Trades Council and the ILP calling for a display of working-class opposition to Mosley's proposed rally at Olympia on 7 June 1934. The Labour Party made no response but the Harrow, North Tottenham, East Islington, Stoke Newington and West Ham branches of the Labour League of Youth all joined the counter-demonstration. Perhaps sensitive to League of Youth participation, but clearly anxious to dissociate itself from the activities of the counter-demonstrators, the brutal scenes witnessed at Olympia led Labour Party HQ to emphatically repudiate any suggestion that it condoned organised interruptions at public meetings.[44] Labour expressed its concern that the Metropolitan Police, by failing to prevent Blackshirt stewards forcibly ejecting hecklers, had not used powers available to it under the Public Meetings Act (1908). Prior to Olympia, the Home Secretary, Sir John Gilmour, had hinted that the government was considering a ban on political uniforms, and a Labour Party deputation[45] further impressed on Gilmour that the Government was allowing the militarisation of politics 'to become accomplished fact'.[46] Taking heed of lessons from Germany, Labour insisted that this militarisation had to stop. 'Mosley is recruiting an army', Labour leader George Lansbury warned, 'His drilling and preparing for emergencies ought to be stopped – and stopped now'.[47]

If the disturbances at Olympia had helped turn the popular mood against Mosley's fascists, more than anything else, it was the Night of Long Knives on 30 June 1934 that had 'caused a profound revulsion of feeling against the whole spirit and practice of Fascism', the Labour Party leadership believed.[48] To quote one historian of the BUF, 'When Hitler shot Roehm [sic] in Munich the bullet ricocheted and perhaps shot Mosley's hopes to ribbons'.[49] Rothermere's break with Mosley was communicated to readers of the *Daily Mail* in July. Meanwhile, the government also seemed ready to act. The Air Ministry refused members of the BUF permission to fly in air clubs subsidised by public monies, and in a number of areas Special Constables were requested to either resign or give up membership of the BUF. For the moment at least, the National Council of Labour[50] believed that little further action was necessary.

That the wind had already turned against Mosley partly accounts for why Labour was so impervious to the Co-ordinating Committee for Anti-Fascist Activities.[51] This committee, established on 25 July 1934 and led by former Mosley acolyte John Strachey, had called for a massive counter-demonstration of London's workers against a BUF rally in Hyde Park on 9 September 1934. Strachey believed that a show of force by the BUF would impress the middle classes; the Labour establishment thought that a show of force by anti-fascists would frighten them. As Alfred Wall (Secretary of London Trades Council) and Herbert Morrison (Secretary of London Labour Party) said, 'One of the greatest lessons of Germany is the importance of Socialist education among the salaried workers – usually known as the middle classes. ... The "middle classes" must not be neglected by Labour if they are to be saved from the clutches of reaction'.[52] Strachey further claimed that large numbers of workers would spontaneously demonstrate in Hyde Park and without effective co-ordination, they would run the risk of being attacked by Fascists with all the 'calculated brutality' that had characterised Olympia.[53] But the Labour Party leadership countered that the threat from Mosley's fascists had now receded, and an anti-fascist demonstration would only lead to widespread disorder, which as the *Daily Herald* put it, 'would advertise far and wide the claims of Fascism'. If Labour were to win power, that is to say, by reaching out to those who do not ordinarily support it, 'we must have our hands clean of violence', the *Herald* explained, and so it pleaded with its readers not to go to Hyde Park.[54] Labour's response was also determined by the belief that, as an official circular sent to all Labour-affiliated organisations in the Greater London area made clear, 'Most of the signatories of the Co-ordinating Committee are either known as active Communists, or are associated in one form of another with Communist activities'.[55]

As it turned out, such was the depth of popular antipathy towards fascism, both in the wake of Olympia and events in Germany, that Labour's pleas went unheeded. The *Manchester Guardian* (10 September 1934) estimated that the Blackshirt contingent was outnumbered by around twenty to one with Home Office reports putting the total number of persons present in Hyde Park at 60,000.[56] The *Daily Worker* claimed 150,000; one platform speaker inflated to over 200,000.[57] Many working-class Londoners had acted on their own initiative, and whilst no local Labour parties were represented, possibly as many as 30 branches of the Labour Party League of Youth, 34 trade union branches, two trade union executives and two trade union district committees had supported the anti-fascist demonstration. To those Labourites in attendance, who refused to be 'stifled' by tactics of the Labour Party and TUC, Strachey offered special praise:

> You know what those tactics were – stay away from the Fascist demonstration; ignore Fascism; it will blow over. I believe it is true to say that the Labour Party have not yet issued a single leaflet or pamphlet on the subject, and definitely tried to prevent all members of the Labour Party from taking part in a demonstration of this sort ... I especially thank every labour man and every trade unionist who has come here tonight to help make this demonstration the mighty success which it has been made.[58]

The *Herald* claimed that one reason why Mosley's rally had ended in a 'fiasco' was due to the 'good sense of London workers ... who took no part in the counter-demonstration'.[59] Incensed by this, local

Communists publicly burnt a copy of the *Herald* in Brighton – the ashes returned to the *Herald* offices in a large envelope.[60]

An exultant CP declared that 9 September 'will live for ever in the story of the working-class movement'.[61] Yet it was soon brought down to earth. Even if this anti-fascist gathering had been huge – possibly the largest crowd in Hyde Park in memory – it did not presage the collapse of Labour's ban on the united front. The CP wanted to build on Hyde Park by securing the election of militant delegates to an all-London conference on fascism to be held later that month. Strachey's intention was to use this conference, which had been called by the London Labour Party and London Trades Council, as the platform to launch a nationwide anti-fascist movement.[62] But Communists were deemed ineligible to attend and the all-London conference merely rehearsed the Labour establishment line. Likewise, Pollitt's hopes that a 'monster demonstration' would impact on the Labour Party's conference at Southport the following month were also frustrated.[63] So perhaps unsurprisingly, when the BUF opened its winter campaign with a rally at the Albert Hall in October 1934, divisions were already emerging within the London CP. Springhall, the London CP organiser, wanted a show of force. Some were in favour of a peaceful demonstration; others considered the threat from the BUF had diminished.[64] Branches of the Labour League of Youth (e.g. North Kensington and Balham and Tooting) once again offered their support but with little to no publicity in the communist press, opposition was muted. And without the force of organised Labour behind it, it was not long before Strachey's Co-ordinating Committee lost impetus. Nonetheless, popular anti-fascist opposition soon revived, occasioned first by Mosley's militant anti-semitism, which saw the BUF concentrate its attack on London's East End (and to a lesser extent Manchester); and second, by the outbreak of the Spanish Civil War in July 1936.

Barring the road to fascism: Labour and anti-fascist unity 'from below'

The BUF set in motion a militant anti-semitic campaign in the East End from late 1935 onwards. How, then, did Labour respond? At Westminster, the group of East End Labour MPs, including South Hackney MP Herbert Morrison and Poplar MP and former Party leader, George Lansbury, raised the issue of Jew-baiting with the Home Secretary, Sir John Simon. Yet others, such as Dan Frankel, Jewish Labour MP for Mile End absented himself from parliamentary debates on fascist/

anti-fascist disturbances in the East End.[65] The response from local Labour-controlled councils was also mixed. Whilst Bethnal Green council deployed the machinery of local government in a bid to thwart fascist activity, due to its more moderate Irish-Catholic composition, the opposition of Stepney Council was less resolute.[66] Not only was Irish Catholic dominance over Stepney Labour Party a likely factor in Frankel's reticence, it almost certainly discouraged others (such as Morris Davis, Jewish leader of the Labour group on Stepney council) from more meaningful engagement with anti-fascism. Joe Jacobs, secretary of Stepney CP, approached local Labour branches and Stepney's three Labour MPs (Attlee, Frankel and Hall) with an open letter calling for a united front with the CP in June 1936. Despite being reported in the *East London Advertiser*, it was ignored by the local Labour establishment.[67] Nonetheless, Stepney's anti-fascist coalition did contain grassroots Labour members, as Jacobs's autobiography reveals.[68] The same was true for Manchester. Admittedly, Jews from the Young Communist League undertook the majority of anti-fascist activity. However, it was a branch of the city's Labour Party that had established the North Manchester Co-ordinating Committee Against Fascism in May 1936, and this committee counted the Cheetham and Crumpsall branches of the YCL as affiliated bodies.[69] There is thus some truth in the remark by a South Wales Communist that 'unity' was 'not a formal question to be decided at a Labour Party Conference. It was something "real and alive" which existed in the communities from which they came'.[70]

If fascist-related anti-semitism encouraged anti-fascist unity 'from below' in the areas directly affected by it, the issue of Spain resonated much further. Spain was far more significant in terms of 'uniting' the Left than any street battles against the BUF, James Jupp believes.[71] Labour Party leader Clement Attlee shared platforms with Communists on the issue of Spain, and across a number of areas rank-and-file Labour Party members worked side by side with Communists raising funds, collecting food and clothing, and providing medical aid in support of the Republic. With over 1,000 local committees and millions of people involved in one capacity or another, the Aid Spain campaign was 'the biggest movement of international solidarity in British history'.[72] Neither should it be forgotten that, as far as existing records reveal, 110 Labour Party, 5 Labour Party League of Youth and 6 Socialist League members also joined the International Brigade.[73] However, many of the Aid Spain campaigns were de-politicised and turned into a humanitarian issue.[74] Meanwhile, the Labour establishment, supported by the trade union block vote, remained wedded to anti-Communism. In

January 1936 the NEC had rejected the CP's application for affiliation, maintaining that 'the victories of the Fascist dictatorships were in part facilitated by the campaigns for Communist dictatorship that preceded them'.[75] It then dissociated itself from the CP-organised Brigade, and up until October 1937 – in the belief that it would contain the conflict – supported a policy of non-intervention in the Spanish Civil War.

It need hardly be added that the battle cry of anti-fascists in Spain – 'They shall not Pass!' – was adopted by those who mobilised against Mosley's proposed march through the East End in October 1936. Despite pleas to stay away from both leaders of the Labour Party and Anglo-Jewry, this mass anti-fascist protest – the 'Battle of Cable Street' – saw between 100,000 to 300,000 people take to the streets. Phil Piratin recalled that 'Communists were condemned as "trouble-makers", but in spite of all this slanderous misrepresentation the appeal of the Communist Party was responded to by thousands of Labour Party members and supporters. On that occasion the leadership of the Communist Party was undisputed.'[76] 'All along the route people were preparing in their thousands to swell the ranks of the counter demonstration', as the ILP told it. 'Here is just one indication of this feeling: a Labour Party collector in Poplar who usually collected late on Sunday mornings was out very early in order to get to the "other end" (Aldgate) and asked others to follow suit, against the declared policy of the Labour Party'.[77] Local branches of the Labour Party League of Youth were certainly involved;[78] the Socialist League, which campaigned against East End fascism during October 1936, also supported the mobilisation.[79] Morrison privately admitted that whilst he could instruct Labour people to stay away from fascist meetings in the East End, he felt such pleas would be useless unless the Communists agreed to refrain from attending such meetings also.[80]

Cable Street had coincided with Labour's annual conference, and in his speech to delegates in Edinburgh, Morrison, representing the NEC, declared no sympathy for those on both sides that incited disorder. He distanced Labour from the CP-ILP organised counter-demonstration, and called on the Home Secretary to pass legislation banning political uniforms.[81] Whilst concerns were raised in due course about possible restrictions that the Public Order Act might place on labour movement activities, the Labour establishment held fast to the principle that the democratic state should legislate against fascism. In the East End, the London Labour Party Executive responded to Cable Street by establishing an advisory committee. Its membership was comprised of local Labour Party mayors, councillors, officers and agents. Six demonstrations for 'Socialism, Peace and Democracy against Fascism' were organised, to be addressed by Morrison and Dalton, amongst others.[82] Meanwhile, in order to keep the rank-and-file committed to democratic socialism the NEC disaffiliated the Socialist League, which had launched a unity campaign with the ILP and CP in the aftermath of the 1936 party conference. It also tried to silence the League of Youth, first by disbanding its National Advisory Committee, before disbanding its national leadership in the summer of 1939.

For Morrison, it was the Public Order Act that finally 'did the trick', smashing Mosley's private army and finishing it off. But although it was used to good effect – banning political processions in the East End – the spirit of it still allowed the BUF to march through the capital. In July 1937 local Labour Party officials organised a petition against a proposed BUF march through St. Pancras but decided against any counter-demonstration.[83] Then, in October 1937 the BUF was directed through the solidly working-class district of Bermondsey in South-East London. Once again Labour called for the proposed march to be banned. This time, however, supported by both the CP and ILP, the local Labour Party defied official policy and declared its intention to demonstrate. A call by the London Labour Party to boycott the march, and 'thus reveal the small numbers and limited importance of Fascism in South London' fell on deaf ears,[84] as did the statement issued by Bermondsey West Labour MP, Dr. Alfred Salter, who declared that any breach of the peace will be caused by 'Communists and Socialists, who are adopting Fascist methods to crush their political enemies'.[85] In the event around 50,000 anti-fascist demonstrators gathered to oppose some 3,400 fascists. Fireworks, missiles and stones were thrown into the fascist procession, and in some of the worst street fighting London had seen, scores were injured. Over 100 anti-fascists were arrested.[86] Yet again, domestic fascism had provoked such popular indignation that Labour Party calls for self-restraint were simply ignored by the rank-and-file, and in the case of Bermondsey, even by the Borough Labour Party.[87]

Conclusion: Success or failure?

> Fascism cannot be conquered by standing at a safe distance and blowing loudly upon a trumpet – tactics which have not succeeded since the capture of Jericho (*New Statesman and Nation*, 8 September 1934).

As told here, the 'passive' side to Labour's anti-fascism did not resonate with many in its working-class constituency. The call to stay away from direct agitation failed to prevent large numbers of Labour Party people from taking part in demonstrations against Mosley. The reasons why are clear enough: first, the strength of anti-fascist feeling arising from events abroad, the most significant of which were the persecution of the labour movement and Jews in Germany, the repression of Viennese workers in Austria, and the Spanish Civil War. These and other events too, such as Mussolini's 'rape' of Abyssinia, all found an echo in Mosley's Blackshirts. The second factor was the willingness of the CP and the ILP to take the lead and promote active opposition from across the labour movement. Significantly, this was achieved less through class-based appeals to communism than appeals to the moral revulsion felt by thousands towards fascist barbarism, first on the continent and later elsewhere; the picture of a Chinese baby 'deliberately murdered, with thousands of kiddies and mothers, by the Japanese Fascists' being reproduced on one CP leaflet at Bermondsey. Not surprisingly, within such an emotionally charged atmosphere, arguments about not helping supporters of one dictatorship defeat another carried little weight. In any case, the Soviet dictatorship hardly attracted the same degree of popular antipathy.

For Labour, three conditions had given rise to fascism on the continent: economic dislocation, depression or decay; weak parliamentary government; and the existence of a strong Communist Party.[88] In the first place, encouraged by economic recovery, by Rothermere's apparent break with Mosley and by the tide of public opinion, Labour never became hysterical about the threat of fascist dictatorship in Britain. Secondly, Labour reinforced parliamentary government by placing its faith in the capacity of democratic institutions to take decisive and effective action when needed. Thirdly, the Labour establishment refused to ally itself with the Communist Party, further reducing the possibility that the middle class (or indeed, the Conservative Party) would radicalise towards fascism. Electoral strategy also guided Labour's anti-fascist position, which after the 1931 election defeat underscored moderation rather than radicalisation. The dividends had been reaped at the 1935 general election, and the issue it faced thereafter was how to win over the remaining two million or so voters that stood in the way of an election victory. What would be the point of a united front with the CP, Morrison asked, 'Will it weaken Toryism? I do not think so'.[89]

So was Labour's anti-fascist policy a success? For Power, if 'the advice of some of the principal trade unions and Labour Party leaders, to ignore demonstrations by the fascists in the hope that they will go away, had been heeded then undoubtedly the (fascist) movement would have grown even stronger'.[90] But the fascist movement in Britain was never *that* strong, and in rejecting left-wing extremism and in remaining committed to parliamentary government and moderation, Labour's variety of anti-fascism contributed to a socio-political order that denied domestic fascism political space. So even if large-scale anti-fascist demonstrations diminished BUF confidence, or negatively associated the BUF with violence, it was surely this wider context of *both* working-class and middle-class moderation that sealed the fate of inter-war British fascism. In this sense, Labour's anti-fascism was undoubtedly successful. Yet we also have to acknowledge the sense in which Labour's anti-fascism *failed*. Thousands of grassroots members and supporters went against the Labour establishment. For sure, we might ordinarily expect some manifestation of dissent given that inter-war Britain was, after all, a democracy. Moreover, the only real authority that the Labour Party and the TUC had over its grassroots members was 'moral authority' – 'all that we can do is to persuade them that the course we believe ought to be followed', as one of the NJC deputation had confessed to the Home Secretary in June 1934.[91]

'What Communist parties all over the world, including that in Britain, had begun to understand', according to Noreen Branson, 'was that if you can lead people into action on some issue on which they feel strongly, the very experience itself can bring about a change in their ideas ... you seldom convert anyone to socialism by preaching from the sidelines'.[92] This is almost certainly true but in the majority of cases co-operation in anti-fascist activity did not translate into wider militancy, not least because the working class in the 1930s remained integrated into capitalist society.[93] This is not to say that anti-fascist unity 'from below' did not result in, to use Branson's phrase, 'more and more' Labour Party members joining the CP.[94] There is no doubt that the CP was 'greatly aided by its ability to present itself as the party that truly fought fascism' as Tom Buchanan has observed.[95] CP membership grew from 7,700 in 1935 to 17,756 by 1939, and circulation of the *Daily Worker* also increased from 30,000 to 80,000.[96] Yet for all this, the CP remained tiny (especially when compared to the KPD) – not that many Communists were made, and so few fascists were made also. Clearly, Labour's attempts to curtail anti-fascist political expression did not occasion mass radicalisation or mass alienation from the Labour Party itself. Individual membership of the Labour Party increased from 366,013 in 1933 to 430,694 by 1936, daily circulation of the *Daily Herald* ran to over two million copies, and two-thirds of constituency parties still voted against the 'United Front' at Labour's 1937 party conference.[97] In relation to the International Brigade, Sarah Jackson has characterised Labour Party volunteers as 'dissidents of Labour Party policy, rather than deviants of the Party *per se'*.[98] My closing thought is that this characterisation might equally apply to most grassroots Labourites who actively confronted home-grown fascism – 'dissident anti-fascists' who captured the real depth of popular anti-fascism in 1930s Britain.

Notes

1 Walter M. Citrine, General Secretary of the TUC, Speech to 65th Annual Trades Union Congress, September 1933.
2 See L(abour) H(istory) A(rchive) and S(tudy) C(entre): National Joint Council circular regarding projected meeting of the British Union of Fascists on 9 September 1934 (dated 22 August 1934).
3 *Manchester Guardian*, 5 November 1936.
4 See Chanie Rosenberg, 'The Labour Party and the Fight against Fascism', *International Socialism* 2, 39 (1988), 55–93 at p. 66.
5 Frederic Mullally, *Fascism Inside England* (London: Claud Morris, 1946), p. 68.
6 Mike Power, *The Struggle Against Fascism and War in Britain 1931–39* (History Group of the Communist Party: Our History Pamphlet No. 70), p. 15.
7 Martin Pugh, for example, see Martin Pugh, 'The British Union of Fascists and the Olympia Debate', *Historical Journal* 41, 2 (1998), 529–42 at p. 542.
8 Quoted in Daniel Weinbren, *Generating Socialism: Recollections of Life in the Labour Party* (Stroud: Sutton Publishing, 1997), p. 114.
9 Jim Fyrth, 'Introduction: In the Thirties', in Jim Fyrth (ed.), *Britain, Fascism and the Popular Front* (London: Lawrence & Wishart, 1985), p. 23.
10 See Rajani Palme Dutt, 'Notes of the Month', *Labour Monthly* 7, 7 (July 1925), 385–98. It should be noted, however, that the National Council of the ILP did organise a series of protest meetings against the Director of Public Prosecutions for withdrawing the charge of larceny against four members of the National Fascisti who hijacked a *Daily Herald* delivery van in October 1925.
11 See *Daily Herald*, 22 December 1926.
12 On labour movement opposition to Mosley's New Party, see Nigel Copsey, 'Opposition to the New Party: An Incipient Anti-Fascism or a Defence against "Mosleyitis"'?, *Contemporary British History* 23, 4 (2009), 46–75.
13 Michael Newman, 'Democracy versus Dictatorship: Labour's Role in the Struggle against British Fascism, 1933–1936', *History Workshop* 5 (1978), 67–88, at p. 68.
14 Georgi Dimitrov, *The United Front* (London: Lawrence & Wishart, 1938), p. 92.
15 This manifesto appears as the appendix to John Strachey, *The Menace of Fascism* (New York: Covici Friede Publishers, 1933), pp. 268–72.

16 See Rajani Palme Dutt, *Democracy and Fascism: A Reply to the Labour Mani-festo on "Dictatorship and Democracy"* (London: Communist Party of Great Britain, 1933), pp. 6–7.

17 Rajani Palme Dutt, *Fascism and Social Revolution* (London: Martin Lawrence, 1934), p. 277.

18 See Dutt, *Democracy and Fascism*, esp. pp. 5–11.

19 Strachey, *Menace of Fascism*, p. 269: *Democracy versus Dictatorship*, paragraph 7.

20 See Neil Riddell, 'Walter Citrine and the British Labour Movement, 1925–1935', *History* 85, 278 (2000), 285–306.

21 *Trades Union Congress Report* (1933), p. 321.

22 The following year, various organisations that supported a boycott met in London and the World Non-Sectarian Anti-Nazi Council to Champion Human Rights was established, with Citrine elected Committee Chair.

23 *Trades Union Congress Report* (1933), p. 336.

24 *Labour Party Annual Conference Report* (1933), p. 222.

25 *Ibid.*, p. 220.

26 David Turner, *Fascism and anti-Fascism in the Medway Towns, 1927–1940* (Kent: Kent Anti-Fascist Action Committee, 1993), p. 18.

27 For more on League of Youth opposition to the BUF, see *New Nation*, September 1933–March 1934. On the relationship between the League of Youth and the YCL, see Joel A. Lewis, *Youth Against Fascism: Young Communists in Britain and the United States, 1919–1939* (Saarbrücken: VDM Verlag Dr. Müller, 2007).

28 LHASC: Minutes of the NEC Finance and General Purposes Sub-Committee, 26 June 1933.

29 See Dylan Murphy, 'The West Yorkshire Communist Party and the struggle for the United Front against Fascism during 1933', *North West Labour History* 23 (1988/90), 29–39.

30 See LHASC: Labour Party National Executive Minutes, 27 February–1 March 1934.

31 *Labour Party Annual Conference Report* (1933), p. 222.

32 LHASC: Labour Party National Executive Minutes, 16 May 1934.

33 See Nigel Todd, *In Excited Times: The People Against the Blackshirts* (Whitley Bay: Bewick Press, 1995).

34 Neil Barrett, 'The anti-fascist movement in south-east Lancashire, 1933–1940: the divergent experiences of Manchester and Nelson', Tim Kirk and Anthony McElligot (eds), *Opposing Fascism: Community, Authority and Resistance in Europe* (Cambridge: Cambridge University Press, 1999), pp. 48–62.

35 See Neil Barrett, *Organised Responses to British Union of Fascist Mobilisation in South Lancashire 1932–1940* (University of Manchester PhD thesis, 1998), p. 151.

36 Muenzenberg founded a series of Comintern-front organisations, including International Labour Defence and the International Workers' Relief Fund.

37 According to the *News Chronicle*, 6 February 1934.

38 On the Fascist Union of British Workers, see Philip M. Coupland, '"Left-Wing Fascism" in Theory and Practice', in Nigel Copsey and David Renton (eds), *British Fascism, the Labour Movement and the State* (Basingstoke: Palgrave-Macmillan, 2005), pp. 95–117.

39   Colin Cross, *The Fascists in Britain* (London: Barrie and Rockcliff, 1961), p. 118.

40   See LHASC: LP/FAS/34.

41   See LHASC: Minutes of the Joint Meeting of the General Council of the TUC, NEC and Executive Committee of the PLP, 28 June 1934.

42   Huddersfield Labour Party League of Youth had taken the opportunity to distribute its own anti-BUF leaflet – *The True Meaning of Fascism* – on 15 June outside Temperance Hall where the BUF's John Beckett spoke.

43   See LHASC: Labour Party National Executive Minutes, 27 June 1934 and Minutes of the Joint Meeting of the General Council of the TUC, NEC and Executive Committee of the PLP, 28 June 1934, Press Statement 'For Morning papers Only', dated 27 June 1934.

44   *Daily Herald*, 11 June 1934.

45   The deputation was comprised of Citrine, Attlee, Conley, Smith and Toole.

46   LHASC: National Joint Council Statement on Fascism at Home and Abroad, 28 July 1934.

47   *Daily Herald*, 11 June 1934.

48   *Ibid.*

49   John Brewer, *Mosley's Men: The British Union of Fascists in the West Midlands* (Aldershot: Gower, 1984), p. 82.

50   In 1934, the National Joint Council was renamed the National Council of Labour.

51   On the formation of this Committee, see [T]he [N]ational [A]rchives HO 45/25388/400–4.

52   LHASC: Joint Consultative Committee of the London Trades Council and the London Labour Party: 'The Labour Movement and Fascism: A Special Memorandum', August 1934.

53   See Co-ordinating Committee for Anti-fascist Activities Circular: 'To Secretaries of Working Class Organisations and All Opposed to Fascism', TNA MEPO 2/3074/308–9.

54   *Daily Herald*, 8 September 1934.

55   LHASC: National Joint Council circular, dated 22 August 1934. See *Daily Telegraph*, 23 August 1934. Pollitt was on the Committee but so too was Marley, and former Labour MP and former NEC member, Leah Manning.

56   TNA: HO 45/25383/602–7: Special Branch Report on BUF meeting in Hyde Park, dated 9 September 1934.

57   TNA: MEPO 2/3074/62.

58   TNA: MEPO 2/3074/74.

59   *Daily Herald*, 10 September 1934.

60   Ernie Trory, *Between the Wars: Recollections of a Communist Organiser* (Brighton: Crabtree Press, 1974), p. 46.

61   CPGB: *Drowned in a Sea of Working-Class Activity – September 9th* (1934), p. 13.

62   See TNA: MEPO 2/3077/121: Committee for Co-ordinating Anti-Fascist Activity, 'September 9th and After'.

63   See TNA: MEPO 2/3078/318.

64   TNA: MEPO 2/3077/29.

65   See Elaine R. Smith, 'Jewish Responses to Political Anti-Semitism and Fascism in the East End of London, 1920–1939', in Tony Kushner and Kenneth Lunn (eds), *Traditions of Intolerance: Historical Perspectives on Fascism and Race*

Discourse in Britain (Manchester: Manchester University Press, 1989), esp. pp. 57–61.

66 See Thomas Linehan, *East London for Mosley* (London: Frank Cass, 1996).

67 Henry F. Srebrnik, *London Jews and British Communism 1935–1945* (Ilford: Vallentine Mitchell, 1995), pp. 53–4.

68 See Joe Jacobs, *Out of the Ghetto: My Youth in the East End Communism and Fascism 1913–1939* (London: Janet Simon, 1978).

69 Barrett, 'The Anti-Fascist Movement in South-East Lancashire, 1933–1940: The Divergent Experiences of Manchester and Nelson', p. 57.

70 Hywel Francis, *Miners Against Fascism* (London: Lawrence & Wishart, 1984), p. 113.

71 Jupp, *The Radical Left in Britain, 1931–1941*, p. 123.

72 Fyrth, 'Introduction: In the Thirties', p. 19.

73 See Richard Baxell, *British Volunteers in the Spanish Civil* War (Pontypool: Warren & Pell Publishing, 2007), p. 22.

74 See Lewis Mates, *The Spanish Civil War and the British Left: Political Activism and the Popular Front* (London: I. B. Tauris, 2007).

75 Letter from J. S. Middleton, Secretary of the NEC to Harry Pollitt, dated 27 January 1936, in *Labour Party Annual Conference Report* (1936), p. 51.

76 Phil Piratin, *Our Flag Stays Red* (London: Lawrence & Wishart, 1978), p. 20. Piratin was former CP MP for Mile End (1945–50).

77 *THEY DID NOT PASS. 300,000 Workers Say NO to Mosley* (London: Independent Labour Party, 1936), p. 7.

78 See Aubrey Morris, *Unfinished Journey* (London: Polemicist, 2006), pp. 51–5.

79 Paul Corthorn, *In the Shadow of Dictators: The British Left in the 1930s* (London: I. B. Tauris, 2006), p. 110.

80 See Colin Holmes, 'East End Anti-Semitism, 1936', *Bulletin of the Society for the Study of Labour History* 32 (Spring 1976), 26–33 at p. 26.

81 See *Labour Party Annual Conference Report* (1936), pp. 164–5.

82 *Jewish Chronicle*, 11 December 1936.

83 See TNA: HO 144/21086/141–7: Special Branch Report, 3 July 1937.

84 See LHASC: London Labour Party circular re: Bermondsey, dated 20 September 1937.

85 *Daily Worker*, 22 September 1937.

86 See *Daily Herald*, 4 October 1937.

87 See Bermondsey Trades Council: *Bermondsey says 'No' to Fascism* (1937).

88 See 'The Labour Movement and Fascism: A Special Memorandum', August 1934.

89 *Labour Party Annual Conference Report* (1937), p. 161.

90 Power, *The Struggle Against Fascism and War in Britain 1931–39*, p. 15.

91 See TNA: HO 144/20141/52–7.

92 Noreen Branson, 'Myths from Right and Left', in Fyrth (ed.), *Britain, Fascism and the Popular Front*, p. 127.

93 See Andrew Thorpe, '"The Only Effective Bulwark Against Reaction and Revolution": Labour and the Frustration of the Extreme Left', in Andrew Thorpe (ed.), *The Failure of Political Extremism in Inter-War Britain* (Exeter: University of Exeter, 1989), pp. 11–27.

94 Noreen Branson, *History of the Communist Party of Great Britain 1927–1941* (London: Lawrence & Wishart, 1985), p. 157.

95   Tom Buchanan, *The Spanish Civil War and the British Labour Movement* (Cambridge: Cambridge University Press, 1991), p. 33.
96   See Fyrth, 'Introduction: In the Thirties', p. 16.
97   *The Times*, 7 October 1937.
98   See Sarah Jackson, 'The British International Brigades as Labour Party dissidents', *International Journal of Iberian Studies* 18, 1 (2005), 3–21.

3
The Conservative Party, Fascism and Anti-Fascism 1918–1939

Philip Williamson

The inter-war Conservative Party provides a challenge for recent historical definitions of British anti-fascism. Distinctions between 'non-fascism' and 'anti-fascism' and between 'passive anti-fascism' and 'active anti-fascism' have been valuable in stimulating debate about the character of resistance to fascism, but as Andrzej Olechnowicz has demonstrated these categories have been used to give priority to the political Left – the Communist Party in some accounts, the Labour Party in others – while overlooking the substantial range of 'liberal' anti-fascism that included numerous Liberals and Conservatives as well as Labour figures.[1] His focus is on cross-party or non-party organisations, and as Helen McCarthy has also shown such associations which promoted citizenship and other democratic causes are certainly a notable and under-studied feature of inter-war British political culture.[2] The Conservative Party, however, raises a different range of definitional issues, and not only because it formed the main element in the most important cross-party body, the National Government formed with the main Liberal groups and a few Labour leaders in 1931. Notoriously, a number of Conservatives admired fascism in one or more of its British or foreign forms, and some historians have taken this as indicative of wider Conservative sympathies. Yet the party as a whole was, at the very least, the largest 'non-fascist' political organisation. There are several reasons to go further. The Conservative Party's dominance of not just most of the political Right but also large expanses of the political centre constituted a more decisive barrier to the growth of British fascism than the explicitly anti-fascist bodies of the political Left.[3] As many of its actions and statements had anti-fascist effects, the party might well be categorised as 'passive anti-fascist'.[4] Further, from 1933 leading Conservatives mounted an ideological and moral resistance towards dictatorship and totalitarianism, which should certainly be classified as 'active anti-fascism'.

In considering the inter-war Conservative Party's attitudes towards fascism and more especially British fascists, the 'party' is taken here to mean its leaders, its ministers in Conservative and coalition governments, the strategists and publicists in its national organisation, Conservative MPs, those Conservative peers significant in national politics,[5] and regional and local officials – rather than the penumbra of journalists and other publicists who expressed various Conservative opinions, but very few of whom were important for Conservative politicians. As a necessary preliminary, the first section of this essay will comment on suggestions that the Conservative Party contained a significant pro-fascist element, and that decisions by the party's leaders in the mid-1930s were affected by fears of losing support to the British fascist groups. It will then be argued that the Conservative Party provided a considerable indirect resistance to fascism. While pursuing its main political concerns, the party had the largest role in preserving stable government, maintaining confidence in existing institutions, and containing challenges from the Far Left which might have provoked greater interest in fascism. At the same time it accommodated or emasculated various radical 'right' groups which might conceivably have defected to fascism. The third section will consider Conservative anti-fascism in the direct sense, the expression of arguments and values in opposition to British and international fascism.

Conservatives and fascists

It is now well established that British fascism was not simply a foreign import but had substantial native sources, chiefly the imperial-protectionist, radical Right and diehard movements within or associated with the Edwardian Unionist alliance, as re-energised by certain effects of the Great War and early post-war political, economic and imperial dislocations. In some significant respects inter-war British fascist groups and elements of the Conservative 'Right' shared a common ancestry.[6] Wider points of apparent similarity are obvious: anti-communism, anti-socialism, and opposition to direct-action trade unionism were shared by all Conservatives. Many Conservatives were concerned about the effects of the extended parliamentary franchise created in 1918 and 1928. Some wanted institutional reform of Parliament, and some were interested in 'corporate' economic ideas. Some had anti-semitic prejudices. In the 1930s many wished to prevent another European war and were prepared to be conciliatory toward the Italian fascist and German Nazi governments, and some wanted support for Franco's Nationalists. But such views are not adequately understood if the Conservative Party is conceived of as a 'party of the Right', with its members located in neat ranks on a political spectrum which blended into fascism – and so liable to tumble into wholesale adoption of fascist ideas and methods.

The Conservative Party was a 'liberal' party. It was integral to a parliamentary and electoral party system, sharing substantial ideological ground with the Liberal and Labour parties, and was neither a unitary body nor a simple span along a spectrum but a cluster of groups gathered together for largely contingent reasons. Each group expressed a mixture of interests and opinions drawn from various sources and which commonly pointed in different directions; the groups themselves shifted in composition and concern according to circumstances.[7] Just as Mosley's fascism derived some ideas from Conservatives and some from socialists, so the varieties of Conservatism did not form coherent ideological packages: it was perfectly possible to be interested in or to admire some fascist notions yet be indifferent or hostile towards some or most of the other fascist ideas and methods. This was not just true among Conservative diehards or imperial protectionists, but also some progressive Conservative 'modernisers'. For example, during the furore after the fascist rally at Olympia in June 1934, the Conservative junior minister R. A. Butler privately expressed interest in the 'Corporative State' and a hope that the presence of the British Union of Fascists (BUF) would stimulate Parliament to give greater attention to 'the conception of modern organisation'. He nevertheless 'sought to preserve our liberties and to avoid copying foreign models and regimenting our nation'. Such qualifications were characteristic of Conservative observations on fascism. Butler added that all he and other modernisers such as Walter Elliot, the Minister of Agriculture, wanted was 'to organise our industry within a framework of ordered liberty', and that it was wrong to assume that 'those of us who talk about reorganisation and planning or the corporative state necessarily believe in Fascism'.[8]

It is not surprising that similarities existed between some fascist ideas and the opinions of some Conservatives. It is certainly also the case that various Conservative or Conservative-minded publicists, 'society' figures and local activists embraced 'hard right' views or were culpably naïve about fascist movements and governments. Some publications (those of the Britons, *The English Review, The Saturday Review*) and some writers (Jerrold, Petrie, Webster, Yeats-Brown, Ludovici, Bryant) have attracted particular attention.[9] But while these groups assist understanding of

British fascism, they establish little about Conservative politics: they were far from representative of the party as a whole, and the writers had no influence with Conservative politicians.[10]

Rather, it is notable how *few* Conservative politicians and organisers were attracted by fascism as such and were associated with fascist or pro-fascist groups; and how very *rarely* references to British fascist groups or to bodies favourable towards foreign fascist movements appear in Conservative Party records and in the letters, diaries and speeches of Conservative politicians.

Martin Pugh has argued that 'so far from fascism being repudiated and marginalised by the conventional politicians, there was a flourishing traffic in ideas and in personnel between fascism and the Conservative Right throughout the inter-war period'.[11] Accordingly, in the mid-1920s 'a number of mainstream politicians took the British Fascists very seriously and sympathetically'. However, by his account just four backbench MPs had some association with British Fascist (BF) meetings. Several more found BF members useful as stewards for their own meetings, including those for an unofficial 1926 campaign 'to protest against Soviet interference in British affairs'.[12] Apparently more impressive was the earlier willingness of Joynson-Hicks, the Home Secretary, to include them with members of other 'patriotic' volunteer organisations as recruits for emergency arrangements during a national strike; as Richard Maguire also comments, this indicates some level of political acceptability.[13] Yet as Richard Thurlow, Thomas Linehan and others have shown, until the late 1920s the British Fascists were fascists in name only, and not a distinct party but an anti-communist and anti-direct-action organisation committed by their leaders to uphold the established constitution and to vote Conservative. Their distinctive feature was precisely preparation for supporting the *existing* state in a civil emergency – for which purpose they even offered their services to the 1924 Labour government.[14] Even so Joynson-Hicks, often considered a right-wing 'diehard', insisted that they could participate in the emergency strike organisation only as individuals, refusing to recognise the BF as a corporate body so long as they maintained a 'semi-military organisation' and claimed to act 'in any sense in contradistinction to the work of the Executive Government'.[15]

None of this amounted to 'ideological' approval for fascism; nor do such attitudes towards nominal 'fascists' in the 1920s necessarily indicate sympathy for genuine fascists in the 1930s. On Pugh's evidence, perhaps a handful of Conservative MPs had meaningful associations with both the BF and BUF. But if John Gilmour as Scottish Secretary in 1924 regarded the BF as potentially helpful in maintaining law and order in the event of an emergency, as Home Secretary in 1934 he pressed for legislation to curb the BUF's para-military organisation as 'in principle inconsistent with our free institutions', as well as 'in practice ... the source of repeated and serious outbreaks of disorder'.[16] Of over 450 Conservative MPs in 1934 and over 380 after the 1935 election, Lymington and two others were members of the fascist English Mistery, and according to Thurlow's review of evidence from security service and police surveillance three other MPs showed interest in the BUF.[17] Pugh's more expansive interpretation – including membership of the January Club, a discussion network established by Mosley to draw non-fascists into a presentation of fascism in a 'respectable' conservative form[18] – produces around twenty MPs in some sense favourable towards the BUF. Much of his argument turns on the House of Commons debate in June 1934 on the BUF's Olympia meeting, from which he classifies eight mostly Conservative MPs as defending the methods of fascist stewards in silencing protestors. This number is contested – Jon Lawrence proposes four – but what is more doubtful is Pugh's description of these eight as 'pro-fascists', who 'defended or justified the movement' and showed 'genuine appreciation of Mosley and his organisation'. In reality just two suggested such views: the rest explicitly denied support or sympathy for the BUF's politics, or regretted that it was winning support.[19] Those MPs and peers who did sympathise with the BUF – or like Thomas Moore declared that there was no 'fundamental difference of outlook between the Blackshirts and ... Conservatives' – mostly misunderstood the character of fascism, and retreated after Olympia and the publicity given to Hitler's murderous political purges in late June.[20] They were a minority even among the Conservative Right; in contrast the great diehard cause of the mid-1930s and the dominant issue for Conservatives during the month of Olympia – resistance to Indian constitutional reform – had support from about 80 MPs.[21] No prominent diehard politicians were associated with the BUF or the January Club, not even Page Croft, the leader of a purported precursor of British fascism, the National Party of 1917–21.

Those Conservative politicians who drew attention to the BUF's growing membership during early 1934 did so not from any desire for closer relations with the movement nor from anxiety about defections to fascism, but as ammunition in an argument within the Conservative Party – for changes in party policy and for removal of non-Conservative leaders of the National Government.[22] Use of the BUF as an instrument within Conservative politics was also the purpose of its chief newspaper supporter, Rothermere, who for this reason instructed his journalists to use the term 'blackshirt' instead of 'fascist'.[23] The BUF certainly did not provide, as Pugh asserts, 'the most compelling and coherent alternative' to the National Government: for its Conservative critics, the 'obvious alternative' was an independent Conservative government. Nor did the BUF constitute a 'dire electoral challenge' to Conservatives, or cause the Cabinet to postpone public-order legislation from 1934 until after the 1935 general election.[24] The substantial increase in BUF membership from January 1934 before its collapse from July belongs less to the history of fascism than to the history of newspapers. It was an ephemeral 'bubble' generated by short-lived support from Rothermere's newspapers, comparable with Rothermere's Anti-Waste League in 1921–22 and United Empire Party of 1930–31, and Beaverbrook's Empire Crusade of 1929–31. Indeed, the BUF secured fewer members than the Empire Crusade (some 200,000 members; the BUF 50,000) and had much less impact than any of these earlier newspaper movements on Conservative politics.[25] In contrast to the anxieties those movements caused for party managers, the BUF barely registers at all in Conservative organisational records. The Primrose League noted 'a certain amount of interest' in the Fascists.[26] In Lancashire, where the BUF supposedly posed a particular electoral threat, the Conservative Party's provincial council made no reference to it. The northern provincial area wanted 'immediate steps to combat' the 'menaces' of both Fascist and Communist doctrines.[27] As for Conservative constituency associations, Stuart Ball's comprehensive study of their surviving records has found hardly any mention at all of the BUF, and no evidence of significant concern.[28] Insofar as some Conservative politicians did not rule out fascism entirely in the mid-1930s, the concern was not with the current or any seriously expected political situation. Rather, during a period when Cripps's Socialist League advocated the seizure of 'emergency powers', it arose from speculation about an alternative, conceivable, but very undesired future: what might be preferred if parliamentary government were to collapse after a period of calamitous 'socialist' government. For Conservatives, in some ultimate choice between communist dictatorship and fascist dictatorship, fascism could be the lesser evil – but nonetheless still an evil.[29] Such remarks were not 'pro-fascist'.

Rather more Conservative politicians expressed admiration or support for foreign fascist regimes or movements. Richard Griffiths and others have identified at most fifty MPs who in some degree or at some time were 'enthusiasts' for Fascist Italy, Nazi Germany or Franco's Nationalists. Not all of these MPs admired all of these governments or movements, some actively disliked one or the other, and very few also supported any British fascist group.[30] As is well established, what most of these Conservatives admired was precisely *foreign* fascism – as appropriate for other countries, a barrier to Soviet Communism, or (supposed) pre-server of European peace – not as a model or import for Britain itself. So for instance Churchill, while in Rome speaking as Romans expected, declared in 1927 that if he had been Italian he would have been 'whole-heartedly with you ... in your triumphant struggle against the bestial appetites and passions of Leninism', but that 'in England we have our own way of doing things'.[31] Ten years later Lennox-Boyd, apparently a strong case of a Conservative 'pro-fascist', stated that 'he viewed with horror the establishing in England of any system remotely resembling the dictatorships of the continent'.[32] Lennox-Boyd was one of twenty MPs belonging to bodies which supported Nationalist Spain, while around twenty-five Conservative MPs and a similar number of Conservative peers (most prominently Lords Mount Temple and London-derry) were members of the Anglo-German Fellowship.[33] Again these were just a small proportion of parliamentary Conservatives; taking another measure, 'there were more Jewish Members of Parliament on the Conservative benches than members of the Anglo-German Fellowship'.[34] Nor did such admiration for foreign fascism influence the policy-makers. Government ministers and their large numbers of Conservative sup-porters had their own policy reasons (international, strategic, economic and financial) to avoid war with Italy or in Spain, and to be conciliatory towards Germany. 'Appeasement' was certainly not identical with 'pro-fascism' or 'pro-Nazism'.[35] Conservative membership of the Anglo-German Fellowship fell as the nature of Nazi government became evident with the Austrian and Czechoslovakian crises and then *Kristallnacht*. Mosley's 'British Union' peace campaign was entirely irrelevant for gov-ernment policy-makers and Conservative politics.[36] In mid-1939 perhaps just a dozen MPs were involved for various reasons with the anti-semitic and 'patriotic' Right Club.[37]

Historians of British fascists and pro-fascists tend to slide into stating that 'many' Conservatives were interested in fascist groups or fascism, where 'some' would be a more accurate term, and for Conservative politicians 'a few' and usually 'very few'. This was plain to the party's Liberal and Labour opponents. Lloyd George occasionally accused the Conservative Party of fascist leanings during his anti-Conservative phases following the overthrow of his Coalition government and into the later 1920s;[38] so too did Stafford Cripps during his anti-capitalist Socialist League phase in 1934–35.[39] A few further cases might be found, but such language was the obvious 'negative stereotyping' of party-political rhetoric. Rather more interesting were suggestions by some Labour leaders during the height of appeasement in 1938 that Neville Chamberlain was sympathetic towards the fascist dictatorships.[40] What is again striking is the rarity of such statements: most Liberal and Labour politicians did not mistake the views of a few on the Conservative Right for those of Conservatives in general, and even when arguing party-political points hardly any considered, and none found, that the charge of pro-fascism could be made to stick on the Conservative Party or the National Government.

Conservative government and the National Government

The two most general explanations offered for the marginalisation of British fascism are 'political culture' and 'economic conditions'. For historians who regard Conservative 'pro-fascism' as politically sub-stantial, the first seems just something received, amorphous and frail. This makes the second – the relative mildness of the international depression in Britain, and economic revival from 1933 – the decisive element, but also something independent, almost a force of nature.[41] Yet 'political culture' is constantly renewed as circumstances change. The transformation in political conditions and in the conventional party system from 1914 into the 1930s, particularly with the Liberal Party's disintegration and the Labour Party's arrival as a major force, brought new vigour to political argument, values and assumptions. It also brought changes in economic and social policies. 'Politics' and the 'economy' were not separate spheres, and in inter-war Britain 'political culture' contributed to policies and arguments which affected the character and the public perception of 'economic conditions'.

The Conservative Party had always been fundamentally a constitu-tional party. British politics had for centuries turned upon constitutional issues: not only the parliamentary parties but even most extra-parliamentary radicals admired the established constitution and espoused a version of British history in which the rule of law and representative institutions had secured and safeguarded popular liberties, religious toler-ation, social cohesion, political stability, national prosperity, and superi-ority over other nations. This so-called 'Whig' interpretation of history was at the core of 'national identity' and patriotic loyalties, shaped and re-shaped over generations of contrast to Roman Catholic, Spanish, Bourbon, Napoleonic, Tsarist and Prussian 'despotisms'. Constitutional ideology united the main political parties more than any issue divided them, with

the effect that disagreements were tolerated and in time accommodated, while extra-parliamentary radicals sought less to destroy existing
institutions and procedures than to modify and gain access into them.
The primary distinction between the two main parties was that Whigs
and then Liberals were the party of constitutional reform while Tories,
Conservatives and Unionists were successively the party of constitutional
defence. Even the Labour Party, while seeking priority for social and economic issues, accepted the existing institutional structure and procedures:
it assumed parliamentary democracy as the foundation for democratic
socialism.[42] Such deep ideological roots carried greater influence from
being integral to the hard realities of historical experience, political self-
interest and practical success. Parliamentary methods were the means to
power, and provided party leaders with claims to authority over followers
and to support from voters; for radicals and socialists they supplied the
means for reform, for Conservatives and Unionists the means to preserve
the social and economic structure, and for all the means to avoid a breakdown in political order in which no cause would escape damage.[43]

When in November 1917 Bonar Law as Unionist leader reviewed the
prospects of a new post-war political world with an extended parliamentary electorate and a powerful, socialist Labour movement, he
declared that 'our Party on the old lines will have no future in the life
of this Country'.[44] He did not conclude that the party should turn to
the radical Right and resist democracy and reform; rather, the Unionist
leadership allied with the pre-war progressive radical Lloyd George,
expanded their party's electoral organisation and accepted policies of
social reconstruction. Similarly when post-war inflation, industrial militancy and imperial pressures generated support for 'middle-class',
Rothermere-led and diehard 'revolts',[45] the party leaders did not acqui-
esce in any protests against 'democracy' but treated these revolts as a
disagreement about the Lloyd George Coalition government's ability to
appeal to 'central' opinion. The influence of the radical Right dissolved
with the replacement of the Coalition by a Conservative government
in October 1922, and was not revived even when this government lost
a general election in circumstances which allowed socialists to form a
government in January 1924.

Conservative leaders had two main assumptions about how best to
defend the established order. One was to seek a 'political' balance in
economic and social policies. From 1920 Conservative leaders helped
establish a 'deflationary' budgetary and monetary regime which stabilised
the financial system and reassured property owners and the *rentier* and
salaried 'middle classes'.[46] But they also maintained the unemployment

insurance system and made only limited attempts to restrain its rising cost. In 1923 Baldwin proposed protection as a solution to unemployment and as an electoral appeal to the working population, and when that failed the Conservative leaders replaced it with a social reform programme on a broadly 'new liberal' basis. In 1925 Baldwin resisted proposals to reduce direct taxes by means of social-service cuts as 'a most one-sided policy' which would seem 'an attack upon the working man' and undermine the aim of 'combating Socialism'.[47] That early post-war economic conditions did not produce large-scale alienation from the established party and parliamentary system owed much to Conservative policy decisions.

The other means of defence was to win elections. At some level most Conservatives, including most of their leaders, feared the effects of democracy, but the party's reaction was to make intensive efforts to ensure that parliamentary democracy worked to its own advantage. This involved not just acceptance of the implications of a mass electorate from 1918, but taking the initiative in extending the franchise further in 1928. It included continued adherence to the conventions, restraints, frustrations and occasional defeats of the party-political struggle, even though this meant acceptance of the Labour Party as the main, and legitimate, opponent. Labour was treated largely and usually – though not wholly and always – as an ordinary electoral and parliamentary rival. No extraordinary measures were taken in 1924 and 1929 to obstruct the formation of minority Labour governments, with the purpose of encouraging its leaders' acceptance of existing institutions and political conventions, and their ability to restrain or defeat more extreme types of socialists. But this strategy had further implications. In order to defeat Labour at elections or prevent it forming a majority government, the party had to be spread as widely as possible, across a very broad range of opinions, seeking 'to tie together the moral, industrial, agrarian, libertarian, Anglican and nonconformist bodies of resistance' to socialism.[48] This also meant a determination to ignore or resist disaffected Conservative diehards, whose aims would be self-defeating because fatally narrowing the party's appeal. From 1924 the strategy involved taking every opportunity to win over Liberal voters, to divide the Liberal Party and to capture Liberal politicians. In 1931 it involved a repeat of 1918, agreeing to serve in another coalition under the leading progressive politician, even though MacDonald had been the Labour prime minister. The creation and perpetuation of this National Government is crucial for understanding the weakness of the British Union of Fascists.

It is often observed that British fascism's great opportunity came during the first half of 1934, with the high point of the BUF's membership and national prominence. But if there was any 'fascist moment' in Britain this came earlier, before the BUF's creation, indeed in the circumstances which explain Mosley's decision to form the BUF. From late 1929 to autumn 1931 there was a general and deepening sense of national crisis, with no obvious solution – just that combination of severe economic, financial and political difficulties, and disillusionment with established politics that Mosley later expected would provide the BUF with its opportunity for power. With considerable political intelligence, during those two years he anticipated much of what would happen in national politics from August 1931. With the onset of the world depression, there was much discussion of radical changes in economic policy: hence Mosley's successive economic programmes while a Labour minister and MP from February to December 1930. With all the main parties divided, there was speculation about reconstruction of the party system: hence Mosley's departure from the Labour Party in March 1931, to form the New Party. With a weak government without a parliamentary majority, there was concern that the restoration of strong government might require major institutional changes: hence Mosley's proposals for a small cabinet, armed with special 'general powers' to legislate without Parliament and involving 'a certain surrender of political liberty'. In these years Mosley commanded serious and impressive political attention, listened to with interest and respect not just by Rothermere but by Beaverbrook, the Liberals Lloyd George, Sinclair and Keynes, and the Conservatives Churchill, Lloyd and a younger generation of Elliot, Oliver Stanley, Boothby, Macmillan, Moore-Brabazon, O'Connor and Mond. One example of a widespread sense of crisis is that in early 1930 some of these younger Conservatives indulged in speculative conversation with Mosley (then still a Labour minister) on 'the decay of democracy and parliamentarianism' and (with pre-Hitler innocence) 'whether it would be well to have a fascist coup'.[49] As Mosley intended, his New Party gave him weight during mid-1931 in some proposals for a coalition or cross-party opposition. But much of what he wanted in terms of party re-alignment was pre-empted in August with the formation by the Conservative, Liberal and some Labour leaders of an emergency National Government. Even then Mosley retained some chance of power: at a difficult moment when the new government might have disintegrated and left the Conservative Party to fight an election alone in risky circumstances, Neville Chamberlain very briefly entertained a Mosley overture for an electoral alliance.[50]

What destroyed Mosley's prospects and electorally obliterated the New party was the Conservative leadership's readiness to remain within the coalition government and turn it into a great anti-socialist alliance for a general election in October 1931, at which the Labour Party was crushed. With the coalition winning a parliamentary majority of 500, there was now a strong government which for the foreseeable future was unassailable by the socialist Left and created an assurance of political stability and civil order. Although the emergency National Government had failed to prevent devaluation of sterling, it took measures to restore 'sound finance' and financial confidence and so ensure the security of the banks, rents, investments, and savings. Despite controversial reductions in government spending including unemployment payments which provoked protest demonstrations in the early 1930s, it was even more conscious than governments after 1920 of a need to minimise social and political alienation: by raising direct taxes it had taken care to create and publicise some degree of 'equal sacrifices' and to maintain the unemployment insurance system close to pre-depression levels, in terms of real prices. The elected National Government introduced long-desired Conservative policies, above all protection and imperial preference, yet also what had earlier been regarded as radical monetary measures to boost recovery: a managed currency, managed exchange rates and 'cheap money'. These policies further enabled opportunities to promote 'corporative' industrial and agricultural re-organisation.[51] The National Government thus had a substantial effect in easing 'economic conditions', mitigating the worst effects of the international depression and the worst anxieties about the domestic depression. From 1932 it could claim credit for economic recovery and, for a substantial part of the population, a 'dawn of affluence'.[52]

Consequently the establishment of the National Government was not just a disaster for the New Party; it also destroyed any prospects of fascism becoming a force in national politics. It removed its political justifications; it introduced economic policies similar to those which Mosley and his economist and Conservative friends had wanted in 1930–31; and it cost him potential Conservative allies, with Elliot and Stanley becoming ministers in the National Government while the rest understood that it provided the best means of achieving their aims. If, as is often stated, Mosley was unfortunate in his timing, this was not because the BUF's creation in October 1932 occurred as the economy began to revive, but because he had taken the plunge in the winter of 1930–31 and so was left out of the party re-alignments during autumn 1931.

For Mosley, formation of the BUF was an act of desperation: a response to political exclusion, a bid to regain public prominence and a gamble on a political crash. What he needed was a more severe version of the 1930–31 crisis, forcing not just another re-alignment of parties and policies but a breakdown in the parliamentary regime. This was never likely under the National Government. Certainly the government experienced difficulties and by-election setbacks in 1933–5; certainly there were Conservative critics, a few of whom expressed doubts not just about the government but about parliamentary democracy. But a sense of historical proportion is needed. These problems and complaints were less serious than those of 1920–2 and 1929–31, and were well within the capabilities of experienced government and party management. Of the various critics of the National Government in 1934, the BUF was 'the least significant'.[53] Most Conservative diehards, when not preoccupied with the India issue, were exercised by German rearmament and pressure on the government to undertake British rearmament, as it began to do in July 1934. Their criticisms and those of other Conservatives were more easily contained because one alternative to the National Government was a Labour Party which from autumn 1931 had moved to the Left, become committed to socialist planning and pacifism, and had members flirting with the Communist Party. If the largest political change the sternest Conservative critics wanted was reversion to a purely Conservative government, in contrast the best-supported Conservative statement during 1934 (in the week after Olympia) was from over 100 backbench MPs calling for continuation of the National Government.[54] Government and Conservative Party concerns with 'public opinion' and electoral prospects centred not just on the Labour Party but even more on the possible loss of support from 'liberal opinion'. This, and not anxiety about Conservative 'pro-fascist' opinion, was the party context for the postponement of public-order legislation during 1934. The political and official 'establishment' was hostile towards the BUF's politics and methods, but Gilmour's efforts to restrict its activities faced two obstacles. The first was his officials' difficulties over legal definitions and their 'liberal' concern to preserve civil liberties. The second, related to this delicate civil liberties aspect, was a Cabinet desire for all-party agreement, which ministers could not obtain; in other words, the political obstruction came not from concern about Conservative opinion but from Labour and opposition Liberal leaders.[55] Nevertheless the extent of Conservative as well as Labour and Liberal criticism after Olympia forced a shift in BUF methods;[56] and this, together with the bursting of its membership bubble, made legislation seem unnecessary. The BUF now almost entirely disappeared as a political concern. The strategy, issues and date for the November 1935 election were related to calculations about the Labour Party and liberal opinion and to issues in foreign and defence policies – not at all to concerns about the BUF. The introduction and passage of the Public Order Act some twelve months later arose from renewed Cabinet determination to deal with BUF incitement of disorder after riots in the East End of London, and from the belated agreement of Labour and opposition Liberal leaders to co-operate. Mosley's hope that the BUF would gain new impetus from the issue of Edward VIII's proposed marriage was another instance of desperation, not least because the opposition parties firmly supported the government on a primary element of constitutional principle, that the monarch must accept ministerial advice.[57]

The character of the National Government is central to understanding British anti-fascism. It re-stabilised government, party politics, the financial system and economic policies; it also upheld the British parliamentary system's inherent resistance to non-parliamentary movements. Although Conservative-dominated, and often unthinkingly presented by historians as a 'Conservative' government, it was certainly not reactionary or 'right-wing'. Indeed, an attraction for Conservative leaders was that by diluting the influence of the 'diehards', it increased their range of policy options, most clearly in enabling them to pursue the tri-partisan reform process for Indian government. The government's Conservative leaders carefully preserved its claims to retain wide 'national' and 'liberal' support, and regarded its Liberal National and National Labour members as important. Because its leaders upheld liberal values and so tolerated the expression of illiberal opinions (fascist, communist and others), this did not mean that they approved of these opinions. Because prevention of another terrible war seemed to require conciliation of foreign fascist regimes, this did not mean an absence of ideological resistance to fascism as well as communism.

The Conservative Party and anti-fascism

Conservative Party attitudes towards fascism cannot be understood in relation to fascist parties and governments alone; nor were they just integral to its character as a liberal parliamentary party. They were also affected by the dynamics of the party system – by the stances it adopted towards its main opponents, the independent Liberals and more particularly the Labour Party.

While the main Conservative strategy for restraining the political Left was to encourage the Labour Party's development as an ordinary parliamentary party, Conservative leaders still wanted not just to defeat the Labour movement but to discredit and disarm its challenges to the established order. In some senses and at most times it was presented as acceptable and even admirable; in other senses and for some periods as doctrinaire and disruptive – as a danger to democracy. From the early 1920s this became a central feature of Conservative Party strategy and identity. Its official publicists and its leaders, especially Baldwin, revived and extended their party's role as defender of the constitution. They presented it as the upholder not just of established institutions but of the whole cross-party 'Whig' constitutionalist ideology, and therefore with defence of democracy and as the guarantee equally of stability, freedom and progress, of 'ordered liberty'. By merging the historical functions of the Conservative and Liberal parties, the aim was to act as the ostensibly non-partisan champion of the 'constitutional classes', rallying both Conservative and liberal opinion against the various challenges from the Labour movement.[58] In one voice, parliamentary democracy was celebrated as robust and supplying all reasonable resources for a responsible Labour Party; in another voice it was described as fragile and vulnerable to the dangerous purposes of irresponsible socialists. The new democracy was 'immature', an 'experiment' balanced between anarchy on one side and tyranny on the other: to maintain it would require restraint, exertion, vigilance, dedicated service, good citizenship and political education – and, explicitly, resistance to the undemocratic tendencies and elements inherent in the Labour Party. This was a powerful political and discursive strategy. In the mid-1920s the heckling or 'rowdyism' of Labour supporters at Conservative election meetings was presented as a Labour Party threat to free speech and constitutional government.[59] At the 1924 election the Labour government was attacked with considerable effect as soft towards Soviet 'bolshevism'. During the trade union troubles of 1925–6, the Conservative government changed the argument into a constitutional issue: the General Strike was 'a challenge to Parliament, and ... the road to anarchy and ruin'. At the 1931 election the National Government was said to be preserving 'democracy' and 'parliamentary government'. From 1933 to 1935 the Socialist League's calls for special emergency powers were used remorselessly to assert that the whole Labour Party aimed to establish a 'Socialist Dictatorship'.[60]

This strategy towards the Labour movement reinforced the Conservative Party's opposition to fascism: taking the constitutional and democratic high ground against the first required that this should also be sustained against the second. This explains Joynson-Hicks's very strict line in 1926 against British Fascists who were not actually fascist. It also contributed to Conservative 'active anti-fascism' in the 1930s. This is not to say that Conservative leaders and producers of party literature made extended criticisms of the BUF. In part this was deliberate strategy: denying attention and significance to Mosley's party, which ministers and party officials also recommended to newspapers and the BBC,[61] was politically crippling. Mosley certainly regarded poor media publicity as a considerable handicap. In part it arose from an accurate assessment of its prospects: as Baldwin stated after Olympia, 'Mosley won't come to any good, and we need not bother about him'.[62] Nevertheless Baldwin did make a lengthy public comment on the BUF a few days later, giving a once-and-only admonition to prospective Conservative defectors. Pugh has remarked that this contained an 'inept' concession that fascism and Conservatism were on the same spectrum: 'the policy of Fascism is what you may call an Ultramontane Conservatism. It takes many of the tenets of our own party and pushes them to a conclusion which, if given effect to, would ... be disastrous to our country'. Yet the meaning is clear – 'ultramontane' in the sense of an unacceptable and disastrous absolutism – and the decisive drawing of the line came in Baldwin's following sentence: British fascism had 'taken from the Continent one thing which is completely alien to the Englishman, and that is a desire ultimately, common to the Communists, to suppress opposition and to be able to proceed by dictatorial methods'.[63] Such statements recur in Conservative Party literature and guidance for speakers: in the BUF's meaning the corporate state was 'Dictatorship, pure and simple', and this meant an end to justice, the rule of law and the freedoms of speech, the press, public association, collective bargaining and democratic government.[64]

The main reason why the BUF received limited specific criticism was that Conservative leaders and party publicists subsumed it within a more fundamental defence of democracy against all forms of dictatorship, authoritarianism or totalitarianism. Most evidently, this became Baldwin's characteristic rhetorical strategy, merging rejection of fascism and Nazism with attacks on communism and socialism, and treating them all as the common enemy.[65] The approach had particular purposes in domestic party politics. From 1933 to 1935 it supplied a new justification for continuation of the National Government, both against a possible Conservative diehard rebellion over the India bill and against a Labour Party revival: 'if you have a weak or feeble Government ... you may see a slide here ... to some form of Bolshevism or Fascism'. From 1934 it assisted the delicate task of justifying rearmament in the face of the Labour and Liberal oppositions and considerable popular attachment to peace. When Baldwin was urged to impress on the electorate the possibility of another European war, he re-defined the issue in ideological terms: 'he would not put it that way. I would say that we are the only defenders left of liberty in a world of Fascists'.[66] When concern about Hitler's and Mussolini's ambitions increased during 1935 and made still greater rearmament desirable, he modified the strategy in order to seek still wider national co-operation. He now switched to embracing the Labour movement within the constitutional order: it was a 'great stabilizing influence' and a 'bulwark of popular liberty' against communism and fascism. But if party and ministerial purposes played a substantial part, these were based upon genuine ideological opposition to fascism as well as communism, expressed in many of Baldwin's speeches and broadcasts and in much party literature. Fascism, like communism, was concerned with the eradication of individuality and creation of a 'mass mind', with the suppression of freedom and imposition of 'slavery': soon 'from the Rhine to the Pacific there will be ... millions who have been trained to be either Bolshevik robots or Nazi robots'. Britain, he declared in a broadcast in March 1934, was 'the last stronghold of freedom, standing like a rock in a tide that is threatening to submerge the world'. Accordingly, British public figures had a duty not just to their own people but to the whole world to maintain 'the torch of freedom'. Baldwin's arguments were not only political but spiritual, the evocation of moral and religious resistance to amoral and atheistic doctrines: 'the recognition of the dignity of man and of his individuality ... as a child of God ... is the unbridgeable gulf between democracy and the isms'. So frequent and prominent was defence of 'ordered liberty' as a theme in Baldwin's public statements that he became a leading international spokesman against fascism and communism, invited twice to North America during 1939 to speak on the causes of freedom and democracy.

Presenting 'dictatorship' as the ideological enemy expressed a belief that the political extremes were linked: that fascism and communism bred upon each other, that more communist activity would provoke more fascist activity and *vice versa*, degenerating into class war, civil breakdown and ending, whichever prevailed, in the destruction of democracy and liberty. Attacking dictatorship in generic terms also had the effect of reducing foreign policy complications. Conservative leaders not only understood the character of Nazism, but also had some knowledge of its practical effects. One instance is that in 1935 Baldwin, Churchill, Cecil, Halifax and Londonderry as university vice-chancellors appealed on behalf of the Academic Assistance Council, assisting Jewish scholars fleeing from Germany; another is the establishment after *Kristallnacht* of the Lord Baldwin Fund for Refugees. But given the horrors of modern warfare, National Government ministers did not want ideological and moral resistance to become a diplomatic and military crusade; and in seeking conciliation with Italy and Germany yet judging Mussolini and Hitler to be dangerously irresponsible and volatile, they sought to minimise provocations. The Cabinet twice accepted that Italian fascist and German Nazi party organisations active in Britain should be proscribed, but then agreed that action was 'inopportune' while agreements were being sought with their governments.[67] During 1938 the Cabinet urged newspapers to avoid excessive criticism or abuse of Hitler.[68] Neville Chamberlain was particularly insistent that foreign policy should not be conducted nor presented in ideological terms. If other countries decided that fascism or communism suited their own conditions, 'I do not see why we should try to impose our ideas upon them so long as they do not try to impose their ideas upon us'; it was 'neither useful nor desirable to criticise others because they prefer systems which would not suit us but do suit them'.[69] The effect was to make anti-fascism less prominent in prime-ministerial speeches and party statements than under Baldwin. The separation of appeasement and ideology could get Chamberlain into difficulties. His defence of the Italian treaty in May 1938 and attempts to prevent war during the Czechoslovakian crisis led to some Labour criticisms that he was 'a Fascist', and 'truckles to the dictators because he likes their principles'.[70] But Chamberlain's point was always that foreign fascisms had no claims and no place within Britain, and in a low-keyed way his public statements upheld 'our democratic conditions, with their insistence on the supreme value of individual liberty' and 'ordered constitutional government based on peace, tolerance, moderation and freedom'. When accused of fascist sympathies in May 1938, he retorted that fascism and communism alike were 'utterly inconsistent with our democratic notions of equality and liberty'.[71] Halifax, his foreign secretary, went further, maintaining a Baldwin-like defence of democracy in moral and spiritual terms.[72]

Appeasement did give succour and encouragement to 'fellow travellers' with Nazism. But this was not the intention of Chamberlain and his ministers. With the end of appeasement in March 1939, ministerial arguments shifted, effortlessly, to the sorts of attack on Nazi dictatorship that Baldwin had been conducting since 1933, which Churchill made more frequently after the *Anschluss* in March 1938, and which Halifax intensified after the Munich settlement. The Second World War and more precisely the war crisis and creation of the Churchill coalition government in May 1940 made anti-fascism into a central British ideology; but the Conservative origins of this lay firmly in the 1930s.

Conclusion

If British fascism had indigenous sources, the same was still more so of British anti-fascism. Resistance to fascism and Nazism had deep and robust resources in British political culture,[73] in a parliamentary and historical ideology and in political practices and arguments that reached across the main political parties. From 1918 to 1939 Conservative-dominated coalitions or Conservative governments pursued economic and social policies which aimed to preserve as much of the established social and political structures as possible against challenges from the Labour movement, seeking a stabilisation that mitigated the effects of economic depression in ways which weakened all 'extremist' political movements. The Conservative Party and more particularly the National Government provided security against radical Left governments in ways which contained serious challenge from the 'Right', and insofar as diehards wanted an alternative government they meant a Conservative government under different Conservative leadership, not any alliance with the BUF. Few Conservative politicians were involved or interested in pro-fascist organisations, and these were much exceeded in number and importance by those Conservatives who participated in cross-party bodies in support of democracy and freedom. In February 1934, for example, John Buchan, Lord Cecil and Lord Eustace Percy joined prominent Liberals in signing the 'Liberty and Democratic Leadership' manifesto. Baldwin became president, other Conservatives were vice-presidents, Halifax and Eden gave addresses to, and the Conservative Party's political education college was a conference venue for the Association for Education in Citizenship.[74] The Conservative Party also mounted a defence of parliamentary institutions and ordered liberty which, while originally directed against a supposed challenge from the Labour Left, was re-directed against British and international fascism from 1933 and – given the shared ground of parliamentary democracy – was expressed in similar terms to the anti-fascism of the Labour and Liberal parties. The Conservative Party's contribution to British political, economic and ideological conditions made it the chief and most effective obstacle to all extremist groups in inter-war Britain, with greater importance for the marginalisation of fascism than the explicitly 'anti-fascist' movements of the political Left.

Notes

1   A. Olechnowicz, 'Liberal Anti-Fascism in the 1930s, the Case of Sir Ernest Barker', *Albion* 36 (2004), 636–60, particularly the discussion of work by David Renton and Nigel Copsey on pp. 636–60; and idem, 'Historians and the Study of Anti-Fascism in Britain', above pp. 1–27.

2   H. McCarthy, 'Parties, Voluntary Associations and Democratic Politics in Interwar Britain', *Historical Journal* 50 (2007), 891–912.

3   See e.g. J. Ramsden, *The Age of Balfour and Baldwin 1902–1940* (London: Longman, 1976), pp. 345–8; B. Coleman, 'The Conservative Party and the Frustration of the Extreme Right', in A. Thorpe (ed.), *The Failure of Political Extremism in Inter-War Britain* (Exeter University Press, 1989), pp. 49–66; J. Stevenson, 'Conservatism and the Failure of Fascism in Interwar Britain', in Martin Blinkhorn (ed.), *Fascists and Conservatives* (London: Unwin Hyman, 1990), pp. 264–82.

4   N. Copsey, *Anti-Fascism in Britain* (Basingstoke: Macmillan, 2000), pp. 3–4, 190–2, in considering the Labour Party, includes in his definition of 'passive anti-fascism' the 'state and the media' and so Labour lobbying in 1936 for what became the Public Order Act, which he describes as 'anti-fascist legislation'. The leading elements in the state and media were of course Conservative ministers or Conservative-inclined newspapers, and the Public Order Act had originated (in 1934) with, and was passed by, the National Government.

5   Given observations in some of the literature on the 'far right', it should be noted that Lords, Viscounts, Earls and Dukes were not necessarily active or weighty in the House of Lords, and that only a few were members of or important for the Conservative Party's leadership. Nor were those with other titles (knight, baronet, lady, even King), with double-barrelled surnames, or with the military or naval ranks of a retired officer thereby politically important, effective or influential, or necessarily representative either of the Conservative Party or the political 'establishment'.

6   E.g. R. Thurlow, *Fascism in Britain. A History 1918–1985* (Oxford: Blackwell, 1987), chs 1–2; T. Linehan, *British Fascism 1918–39* (Manchester: MUP, 2000), chs 1–2; M. Pugh, *'Hurrah for the Blackshirts!'* (London: Jonathan Cape, 2005), chs 1–2; Alan Sykes, *The Radical Right in Britain* (London: Palgrave, 2004), chs 1–2; and for more particular cases, D. Stone, *Responses to Nazism in Britain 1933–1939* (London: Palgrave, 2003), chs 5–6.

7   Best set out in M. Cowling, *The Impact of Labour 1920–1924* (Cambridge: CUP, 1971), and *The Impact of Hitler 1933–1940* (Cambridge: CUP, 1975); E. Green, *Ideologies of Conservatism* (Oxford: OUP, 2002) rightly emphasises Conservative plurality, though his focus was just on economic ideas and he engaged in a dubious search for a Conservative 'minimum', pp. 280–90.

8   These statements were made at or following an *English Review* luncheon addressed by Mosley: Butler to Lord Brabourne, 15 June 1934 (adding, pointedly, that 'my loyalties were naturally with the government') and 20 June 1934, India Office Collections, British Library, Brabourne papers F97/20B. For other Conservatives interested in economic organisation and planning, see L. P. Carpenter, 'Corporatism in Britain 1930–1945', *Journal of Contemporary History* 11 (1976), 3–25, and D. Ritschel, *The Politics of Planning* (Oxford: OUP, 1997), esp. ch. 5, but note the wide interest in such

ideas, on the Left as well as with Mosley. For Elliot and other younger Conservative modernisers, see also below pp. 83, 84.

9 R. Griffiths, *Fellow Travellers of the Right* (1980; Oxford: OUP edn 1983), esp. pp. 21–7, 40–9, 61–8, 233–9. Bryant has received extensive study, in work by Andrew Roberts, Julia Stapleton, Reba Soffer and Richard Griffiths.

10 See e.g. D. Jerrold, *Georgian Adventure* (London: Right Book Club, 1937), for one of their most active journals, the *English Review*, and its luncheon discussion club: its editor records contacts with prominent politicians as 'mere formalities', and its political impact as negligible (pp. 334, 344–5).

11 Pugh, *Blackshirts*, p. 5; see also M. Pugh, *The Making of Modern British Politics 1867–1939* (Oxford: Blackwell 1982), pp. 279–81; 'The British Union of Fascists and the Olympia Debate', *Historical Journal* 41 (1998), 529–42; and 'The National Government, the British Union of Fascists and the Olympia Debate', *Historical Research* 78 (2005), 253–62.

12 Pugh, *Blackshirts*, pp. 58–61. For the anti-Soviet campaign, including Albert Hall meetings, see *Times*, 16 July, 17 Sept. and 16 Oct. 1926: because unofficial, these had no assistance from the party organisation.

13 Cabinet 47(25), 7 Oct. 1925; R. Maguire, '"The Fascists ... are to be Depended Upon": The British Government, Fascists and Strike-Breaking during 1925 and 1926', in N. Copsey and D. Renton (eds), *British Fascism, the Labour Movement and the State* (Basingstoke: Palgrave, 2005), pp. 6–26.

14 British Fascisti Council offer to the Home Secretary, *Times*, 28 March 1924. Generally Thurlow, *Fascism in Britain*, pp. 46–7, 51–4, 57; Linehan, *British Fascism*, pp. 63–6; D. Baker, 'The Extreme Right in the 1920s: Fascism in a Cold Climate, or "Conservatives with Knobs On"?', in M. Cronin (ed.), *The Failure of British Fascism* (Basingstoke: Macmillan, 1996), pp. 19–26; Pugh, *Blackshirts*, pp. 56–7.

15 *Times*, 28 April 1926; Thurlow, *Fascism in Britain*, p. 55 (also noting Joynson-Hicks as vice-president of the National Citizens Union threatening to resign if it allowed Fascists to join *en masse*); Pugh, *Blackshirts*, pp. 66, 98.

16 Gilmour, 'Preservation of Public Order', appendix to Cabinet 24(34), 3 June 1934, and his further memoranda, CP 189(234) 11 July 1934. Compare Pugh, *Blackshirts*, pp. 59, 163–4, using Gilmour's temporising House of Commons statements while awaiting Cabinet decision rather than his private advice to the Cabinet, and Pugh, 'National Government', 254, which mysteriously lists Gilmour as a 'pro-fascist'. Similarly, although Oliver Locker-Lampson used 'fascist' stewards in 1926 (Pugh, *Blackshirts*, p. 61; Pugh, 'National Government', 254), he is correctly listed as an 'anti-fascist' in 1934 in Pugh, 'British Union of Fascists', 532: see *House of Commons Debates [HC Deb]* 290, cols. 1993–4.

17 Thurlow, *Fascism in Britain*, p. 101.

18 Griffiths, *Fellow Travellers*, pp. 49–53.

19 Pugh, 'British Union of Fascists', 532–4, and compare J. Lawrence, 'Fascist Violence and the Politics of Public Order in Inter-War Britain: The Olympia Debate Revisited', *Historical Research* 76 (2003), 250–1. Of Pugh's supposed 'pro-fascists' speaking in *HC Deb* 290, 14 June 1934, Winterton deprecated anything that would help the fascist cause (cols. 1985–6, 1989), Lovat Fraser was not a supporter (2001), Howard had 'no respect or admiration

for [Mosley's] principles' (2009), Dixey had 'no sympathy nor any regard' for him (2028), Macquisten thought the BUF misguided and Mosley a megalomaniac (2038), and Pike did 'not agree with Fascism' (2040).

20   Moore in the *Daily Mail*, 25 April 1934, quoted in Pugh, *Blackshirts*, p. 151; D. S. Lewis, *Illusions of Grandeur* (Manchester: MUP, 1987), pp. 146–7; G. C. Webber, *The Ideology of the British Right 1918–1939* (London: Croom Helm, 1986), pp. 45–6, 86–8, 139.

21   C. Bridge, *Holding India to the Empire* (London: Oriental UP, 1986), pp. 136–7. A Commons debate on an Indian matter on 13 June attracted far more diehard interest than the Olympia debate on the following day.

22   E.g. Howard, Hales and Macquisten in *HC Deb* 290, 14 June 1934, cols. 2011–12, 2032–3, 2036, and Lloyd in July 1934, quoted in Ramsden, *Age of Balfour and Baldwin*, pp. 336–7. For the limited aims (and failure) of the Lloyd 'movement' in late 1933, see Jerrold, *Georgian Adventure*, pp. 341–5.

23   Well explained in N. Smart, *The National Government 1931–1940* (Basingstoke: Macmillan, 1999), pp. 102–4.

24   As claimed in Pugh, *Making of Modern British Politics*, pp. 279–80; Pugh, 'British Union of Fascists', 530–1, 540–1; and Pugh, 'National Government', 259–62. What follows supports the contrary verdicts in Lawrence, 'Fascist violence', p. 249' and J. Lawrence, 'Why Olympia Mattered', *Historical Research* 78 (2005), pp. 265–6. For public order legislation see pp. 85–6 below.

25   For Anti-Waste, see Cowling, *Impact of Labour*, pp. 55–9, 73–5, 120–1, and for the later movements S. Ball, *Baldwin and the Conservative Party 1929–31* (London: Yale UP, 1988), ch. 3, pp. 210–12, 222–3.

26   Grand Council minutes (noting also 'a good number of letters'), 7 June 1934, MSS Primrose League 7/1, Bodleian Library, Oxford: compare M. Pugh, *The Tories and the People 1880–1935* (Oxford: Blackwell, 1988), p. 191.

27   National Union executive committee minutes, 14 March 1934, Conservative Party archives NUA 4/1/5, Bodleian Library, Oxford, and for the Lancashire area, see AREA 3/1/2: compare M. Pugh, 'Lancashire, Cotton and Indian Reform: Conservative Controversies in the 1930s', *Twentieth Century British History* 15 (2004), 147–50.

28   I am very grateful to Stuart Ball for this information, derived from his examination of the inter-war records of some 150 Conservative constituency associations, in all parts of Britain.

29   E.g. *The Diaries and Letters of Robert Bernays 1932–1939*, ed. N. Smart (Lampeter: Edwin Mellen, 1996), p. 87 (32 Oct. 1933); *Parliament and Politics: The Headlam Diaries 1923–1935*, ed. S. Ball (London: The Historians' Press, 1992), pp. 292–3 (13 Feb. 1934). For a similar Liberal view, Lothian reported in Butler to Brabourne, 20 June 1934, Brabourne papers F97/20B.

30   See Olechnowicz, 'Liberal Anti-Fascism', p. 643.

31   *Times*, 21 Jan. 1927, and see R. J. B. Bosworth, 'The British Press, the Conservatives, and Mussolini', *Journal of Contemporary History* 5 (1970), 173–80, and Griffiths, *Fellow Travellers*, pp. 14–15.

32   P. Murphy, *Alan Lennox-Boyd* (London: Tauris, 1999), p. 47 and see pp. 42–6. As an admirer of foreign fascisms and advocate of some fascist notions for domestic purposes, Lennox-Boyd is a key example in Pugh, *Blackshirts*, esp. pp. 9, 58, 146, 148.

33 S. Haxey, *Tory M.P.* (London: Victor Gollancz, 1942), pp. 207–9; E. W. D. Tennant, *True Account* (London: Max Parrish, 1957), p. 194; for pro-Franco numbers and a lower AGF figure (22 MPs and 12 peers), see N. Crowson, *Facing Fascism* (London: Routledge, 1997), pp. 207–9. Though the two peers had been ministers, neither had influence with Conservative leaders after 1935: see I. Kershaw, *Making Friends with Hitler* (London: Allen Lane, 2004).

34 G. Bruce Strang, 'The Spirit of Ulysses? Ideology and British Appeasement in the 1930s', *Diplomacy and Statecraft* 19 (2008), 487.

35 Re-affirmed in *ibid.*, 483–93, but evident in all serious studies of 'appeasement'.

36 Pugh, *Blackshirts*, p. 273, writes of a 'rapprochment', but this was wholly on Mosley's part in that he supported appeasement: ministers had no political interest in him or his campaign.

37 R. Griffiths, *Patriotism Perverted* (London: Constable, 1998), pp. 145–55, 158–60; R. Thurlow, *The Secret State* (Oxford: Blackwell, 1994), pp. 207–8, describes the total membership as 'miniscule'.

38 See speeches in *Times*, 30 April 1923, 23 Feb. 1925, 29 Sept. 1928.

39 E.g. speeches in *ibid.*, 8 Jan. 1934, 10 June 1935.

40 See below p. 90.

41 E.g. Stone, *Responses to Nazism*, pp. 187–8; Pugh, *Blackshirts*, pp. 315–16.

42 See e.g. P. Ghosh, 'Gladstone and Peel', in P. Ghosh and L. Goldman (eds), *Politics and Culture in Victorian Britain* (Oxford: OUP, 2006), pp. 47, 72–3; R. McKibbin, *Ideologies of Class* (Oxford: OUP, 1990), pp. 16–23.

43 For a distinctly hard-headed yet subtle explanation, see Cowling, *Impact of Labour*, pp. 3–12, and see R. Skidelsky, 'Great Britain', in S. J. Woolf, *Fascism in Europe* (London: Methuen, 1981), p. 276: 'the instinctive cleverness of political arrangements which got [Britain] through a dangerous decade is astounding' and 'the sheer *political* competence of the ... parliamentary system ... is remarkable'.

44 Ramsden, *Age of Balfour and Baldwin*, p. 118.

45 See, variously, Cowling, *Impact of Labour*, chs 2–3, and R. McKibbin, *Classes and Cultures* (Oxford: OUP, 1998), pp. 50–8.

46 McKibbin, *Ideologies of Class*, pp. 265–75.

47 P. Williamson, *Stanley Baldwin* (Cambridge: CUP, 1999), pp. 168–73.

48 Cowling, *Impact of Labour*, p. 421, referring to Baldwin's 'function'.

49 H. Nicolson diary, 15 Feb. 1930, Nicolson papers, Balliol College, Oxford. On 'crisis' and Mosley's activities and connections, see P. Williamson, *National Crisis and National Government 1926–1932* (Cambridge: CUP, 1992), ch. 4 (esp. pp. 145–9), pp. 230–1, 276, with further details in M. Worley, 'What was the New Party? Sir Oswald Mosley and Associated Responses to the "Crisis", 1931–1932', *History* 92 (2007), 39–63, and the symposium on the New Party in *Contemporary British History* 23 (2009), 421–542.

50 Williamson, *National Crisis*, pp. 435, 445–6.

51 *Ibid.*, pp. 344–5, ch. 11, pp. 433–54, ch. 14 and conclusion. For economic measures see also A. Booth, 'Britain in the 1930s: A Managed Economy?', *Economic History Review*, 2nd s. 40 (1987), 499–522, and for 'corporative' proposals, Ritschel, *Politics of Planning*, ch. 5.

52 J. Stevenson and C. Cook, *The Slump* (London: Cape, 1977), ch. 2.

53   Cowling, *Impact of Hitler*, p. 16, and see chs 1–3 for the various oppositions and the government's political management.

54   'The National Government ... a Conservative Manifesto', *Times*, 14 June 1934.

55   Cabinets 29 and 31 (34), 18 and 31 July 1934; and for desire to legislate, readiness to ignore any Conservative 'extremist' criticism, but exasperation at non-co-operation from the 'Liberals and Left Wing', see Somervell (Solicitor-General) journal, 15 July 1934, Somervell papers, Bodleian Library, Oxford. Generally, G. Anderson, *Fascists, Communists and the National Government* (Columbia: University of Missouri Press, 1983), pp. 11–18; Thurlow, *Secret State*, pp. 182–97.

56   Lawrence, 'Why Olympia Mattered', pp. 268–9, comments on Mosley's resentment at *Conservative* criticism.

57   P. Williamson, 'The Monarchy and Public Values 1910–1953', in Andrzej Olechnowicz (ed.), *The Monarchy and the British Nation 1780–2000* (Cambridge University Press, 2007), pp. 223–57.

58   For much of this paragraph see Williamson, *Baldwin*, ch. 7, esp. pp. 235–42; material in official Conservative publications readily supports the evidence from Baldwin's speeches. For 'constitutional classes', McKibbin, *Classes and Cultures*, p. 58.

59   J. Lawrence, 'The Transformation of British Public Politics after the First World War', *Past and Present* 190 (2006), 198–201.

60   Aside from numerous Baldwin speeches, see Conservative Party *Hints for Speakers*, *Politics in Review*, and *Election Notes 1935*, pp. 348–53, in the Conservative Party Archive.

61   Thurlow, *Secret State*, p. 182, and see Cabinets 6 and (36), 12 and 19 Feb. 1936, on the BBC being persuaded not to broadcast talks by Mosley and the Communist, Pollitt, as leaders of parties 'advocating the forcible overthrow of the constitution'.

62   T. Jones, *A Diary with Letters 1931–1950* (London: OUP, 1954), p. 130 (12 June 1934).

63   *Times*, 18 June 1934; Pugh, 'National Government', p. 261, and *Blackshirts*, pp. 151–2; and see Lawrence, 'Why Olympia Mattered', pp. 267–8.

64   *Notes for Conservative Canvassers*, Sept. 1933, quoted in C. Bussfeld, *Democracy versus Dictatorship* (Paderborn: Ferdinand Schöningh, 2005), p. 204, and Conservative Party *Election Notes 1935*, pp. 378–85.

65   For this paragraph see Williamson, *Baldwin*, pp. 313–35; P. Williamson, 'Christian Conservatives and the Totalitarian Challenge 1933–40', *English Historical Review* 115 (1999), 615–19, and the commentaries on Conservative Party literature and speeches in Bussfeld, *Democracy versus Dictatorship*, pp. 194–206, 246–71.

66   Jones, *Diary with Letters*, pp. 123–4 (27 Feb. 1934).

67   Cabinets 55 (36) and 182(37), 29 July 1936 and 8 July 1937.

68   Though this did not amount to government 'control', as argued in R. Cockett, *Twilight of Truth* (London: Weidenfeld and Nicolson, 1989). The various newspapers had their own reasons for wanting to avoid war: see M. Meznar, 'The British Government, the Newspapers and the German Problem 1937–39' (Durham PhD thesis, 2005).

69   Speeches in *Times*, 13 May and 14 Dec. 1938.

70 Williamson, 'Christian Conservatives', 640–1.
71 Statements in *Times*, 29 June and 10 Dec. 1937, 7 Jan., 13 May and 14 Dec. 1938.
72 Williamson, 'Christian Conservatives', 623–7, 634–8.
73 Compare Stone, *Responses to Nazism*, p. 9, which asserts the importance of Continental anti-fascist authors. However, the book's focus is on formal political writings, rather than the politics of the politicians and of the political public in general.
74 *Times*, 15 Feb. 1934; E. Simon et al., *Constructive Democracy* (London: Allen and Unwin, 1938), consisting of addresses delivered at an AEC conference at the Bonar Law Memorial College in July 1937. For the AEC generally, see Olechnowicz, 'Liberal Anti-Fascism', 657–9.

Part II
Civil Society and the State

4
Varieties of Feminist Responses to Fascism in Inter-War Britain

Julie Gottlieb

Introduction

The responses of British political women to the rise of fascism had some significant qualitative differences from that of men. Political responses were coloured and conditioned by sex, and during the 1930s there were feminine and feminist interpretations of fascism that contributed to the diverse practice of anti-fascism. Most active feminists understood what fascism represented for the progress of their own political concerns and for the peace of the world more generally. As Storm Jameson commented 'only under Western democracy is it still possible for a feminist movement to exist'.[1] Furthermore, given women's continued political marginality in relation to the parliamentary system, within each party, and in the higher echelons of political journalism, women often resorted to new and more innovative genres to express their fears and their despair at the rise of fascism. Therefore next to publishing articles in newspapers and journals and producing monographs, the novel, and the dystopian novel in particular, became an important feminist anti-fascist genre.[2]

Nonetheless, what is interesting, and no doubt disappointing, is that there was never a unified female response to fascism, either to the home-grown or the Continental model. A range of 'womanist' interpretations of fascism can be seen to have emerged within the Labour Party, the Conservative Party, the Liberal Party, the CPGB, the ILP, the pacifist movement or among women who combined various of these political identities and affiliations. The variety of responses reflected fundamental aspects of British political culture, namely those aspects that most thoroughly negated fascism – the relative freedom of political discourse, the progress British women had made in entering both domestic and international politics in the period, and the multi-party system. Yet the picture is further complicated by the fact that the inter-war period is often and rightly regarded as one of backlash against feminism, a 'return to home and duty', and the hemming in of women's political and domestic status after the major gains of their expanded roles in the labour market during the Great War and their partial enfranchisement in 1918 and their full enfranchisement in 1928. This backlash fuelled fears among feminists that even the demo-cracies were taking examples from fascist states with regard to women's employment, reproductive rights, and position in the family. This chapter is therefore interested in illustrating the diversity of female opinion but especially the variety of tactics applied to anti-fascist initiatives in feminist organisations, eventually coming to focus on a comparison between two British feminist organisations that each func-tioned on the international stage, the Six Point Group (SPG) and the Women's International League (WIL).

If before the First World War political women had agitated to have their voices heard in national affairs and in the domestic sphere writ large (i.e. government), the discernible shift after the war was for now enfranchised women to argue for the importance of their pres-ence, influence and input in international and world affairs. By the 1930s, the novelist Phyllis Bentley could not emphasise enough the significance of current events, and particularly events in the international sphere, for women. 'Most of us are, in fact, at the present time made more conscious than ever before of being members of a world-wide community. We are able to see – and indeed are constantly being made to see – our own little affairs not as an isolated phenom-enon, but as part of great world reactions.'[3] Eleanor Rathbone explained how:

> the sphere of effort into which enfranchised women have thrown themselves in the greatest number and with the greatest intensity of interest is the sphere of internationalism. Even before the vote was won, after the first few months of the Great War, the passionate desire for peace felt by many of the leading feminists caused a split in the ranks of the National Union of Women's Suffrage Societies, which carried off a considerable number of its leading personalities to form a new organization – the Women's International League for Peace and Freedom. This, under the familiar initials WIL, has carried on this fight ever since – first for a negotiated peace, afterwards for disarmament and all that mechanism for the prevention of war and

the peaceful settlement of disputes which we now call collective security.[4]

There could be no doubt then that inter-war feminism was not merely a response to women's issues in the domestic sphere and in domestic politics.

Nonetheless, aside from some very valuable and groundbreaking work by a small number of women's historians,[5] the story of women's history and the history of feminism in inter-war Britain tend to be told from the perspectives of internal affairs and women and children's welfare; the priority of a return to domesticity and 'gender peace' after the fracture of war; and the widespread rejection by the majority of younger women during the 1920s and 1930s of feminist political tactics, aims and styles. If feminist historiography has given short shrift to women's engagement with foreign affairs, the field of international relations has been even more negligent by overlooking women's contributions and by failing to consider the category of gender. Recently, Van Seters has shown that 'in spite of the fact that international relations scholarship concerning British foreign policy in the 1930s is extensive and has acknowledged the insights to be gained from looking beyond a small circle of high-ranking policy makers, recognition of women's activism has remained very limited'.[6] This chapter will demonstrate that the historiography has tended to overlook the prime importance for those women either active in the still vibrant and determined women's movement, or for those in the women's sections of other political parties, of international concerns and worlds beyond Britain's national and imperial borders. It is particularly concerned to examine the ways in which women's organisations interpreted the rise of fascism, at home but mainly abroad, and how they tailored their propaganda and activities in response to this most menacing political phenomena rising in their purview.

It is not quite realised to what a significant extent politicised women argued for and struggled to achieve influence and equality in foreign affairs and international relations during the inter-war years. As the relationship between British women and foreign policy is a very long, involved and complex history, complete with colourful stories of individuals and myriad twists and turns in opinion and tactics, the discussion here will be confined to how a selection of women's organisations reacted to the suddenness and unpredictability of international crises in the late 1930s.

Of particular concern is how a number of individuals and women's organisations made or did not make the intellectual and emotional *conversion* from some variant of pacifism to a position that allowed for the necessity of war as the means to defeat fascism and Nazism. In the context of feminists' abandonment of pacifism in the course of the First World War, Gorham has observed that 'during actual conflict, men and women alike tend to support war, even if they have, beforehand, expressed anti-war sentiments. Understanding why this is so should be of major importance to those interested in non-violence as a political principle and in the history of non-violence as a political program'.[7] Taking perhaps what might at first appear to be the reverse approach, in the context of the build up to the Second World War, the attempt here is to understand why it took so long for some women to abandon their pacifism when confronted by the spectre of Hitler and the mounting evidence of Nazi male supremacy, misogyny and the victimisation of women. Why were so many women actually reluctant anti-fascists, or at least reluctant to give active form to their deeply felt concerns about fascist ambitions throughout Europe?

Coming to terms with international crises and the attendant conversions, or lack thereof, were deeply gendered experiences. While there can be no doubt that men too experienced the anxiety and deep moral, intellectual and personal doubts associated with an unstable world on the brink of world war, these experiences were all the more acute for women. In brief, the female experience came to be differentiated from the male in so far as the whole rhetoric and mindset was dominated by the views that, first, women and their children would be at once the more vulnerable and defenceless in the face of modern warfare, and, secondly, by the commonly held view that women, as the world's natural pacifists, were innately suited as a sex to exercise moral authority and practice feminine diplomacy and commonsense in negotiations between belligerents. As Vera Brittain explained in 1933, the outcome of the Disarmament Conference is one 'which we, as women, can't be indifferent, however great our private preoccupations, for on it depends the safety of the homes in which we work so hard, and the welfare of our children whose future occupies so much of our thoughts'.[8] Brittain's best friend, the prolific 'equalitarian' feminist journalist and novelist Winifred Holtby, explained why she believed women were better equipped for the diplomatic and consular service, especially in the post-Versailles world that had invested so much hope in the structures and new ethos of the League of Nations: 'in 1934 women are not handicapped by a great burden of outworn ritual; they have not learned the elaborations of prestige-hunting, and they care, desperately, earnestly, with an urgency which increases monthly, for peace throughout the world. Let them at least try their hands at this business of diplomacy.'[9] However problematic reliance on these essentialist gender roles may be from our contemporary theoretical viewpoints, there can be little doubt that there was perceived to be a distinct and uniquely feminine response to foreign affairs and, ultimately, to war, in Britain. Of course, the experience was also gendered by the conspicuousness of women's relative powerlessness and subordination at all levels of the political hierarchy – including Parliament, the diplomatic service, extra-parliamentary pressure groups, popular demonstrations and petitioning, and so on – no matter how hard British women tried to secure places for themselves and their sisters in established venues of power or attempted to set up an alternative realm of women-only political organisations.

The proliferation of women-led internationalist and pacifist groups was a notable feature of the first part of the twentieth century, and this certainly put to rest any presumption that women should be denied citizenship because they could not think beyond their limited domestic sphere. These women-led organisations included the Women's International League for Peace and Freedom (founded in 1915), the Women's Peace Crusade (founded 1916), the Women's International Alliance (Mrs Margery Corbett Ashby served as president), the Women's Peace Pilgrimage, the Women's Advisory Committee to the Labour and Socialist International, and the Women Against War and Fascism (established in 1934 as the British branch of the Women's World Committee Against War and Fascism). The Open Door Council (formed in 1926), and its offshoot the Open Door International (formed in 1929), and the Six Point Group, while not formed for the purpose of taking a feminist approach to international affairs, each developed deep concerns with foreign affairs and a variety of anti-fascist campaigns. Women were also very active in the League of Nations Union (founded in 1918), which established early on in its existence a Women's Advisory Council, although women continued to be active in other branches and on other committees of the LNU as well. The records of the Women's Section of the Labour Party also shows how central disarmament, foreign policy, and later rearmament were for the women of the Party, leaving little doubt that international affairs defined the priorities and anxieties in women's politics in the period. For example, during the inter-war years the Standing Joint Committee of Industrial Women's Organisations lent its members support to the Women's Socialist International, the No More

War Movement, the National Council for the Prevention of War, the Peacemakers' Pilgrimage, the League of Nations Union, the British-American Women's Crusade, the Women's Peace Crusade, and the Women's International League, and in October 1936 set up a 'Women's Committee in Aid of Spanish Workers' (in association with the International Solidarity Fund and the Medical Aid Committee). While, at face value, the list of organisations speaks for the mature politicisation of women in their engagement with foreign affairs, what is also striking is the absence of a unified movement that would bring together these like-minded women: the debilitating ideological schisms and the failure to mount a popular or united front in democratic countries against fascism was just as characteristic of women's politics as this was the weakness of inter-war political radicalism more generally.

It is interesting to chart changes of opinion – political conversions – over the course of the second half of the 1930s. For much of the 1920s and well into the 1930s the vast majority of the middle-class, educated, intellectual and elite politicised and political women who had the most opportunity to express their thoughts on national and world events reflected the general mood of the British public, namely that mood that was recorded in the LNU's Peace Ballot of 1935. Few dissented from the view that the priority was to avert war, and it was not until after the Abyssinian crisis that profound disillusionment with the League of Nations began to be expressed. In quick succession, Japanese aggression in Manchuria (1931), Hitler's accession to power (1933), the remilitarisation of the Rhineland, the Abyssinian crisis (1935), the Spanish Civil War (1936), China, the *Anschluss* (1938), the Czechoslovakian crisis and the Munich Agreement (September 1938), *Kristallnacht* (1938), the Nazi occupation of Czechoslovakia, and finally the Nazi invasion of Poland and the allied declaration of war on 3 September 1939, represented the key junctures at which women felt their pacifist resolve tested and their anti-fascism reinforced. I have begun the project of mapping individual women's reversals of opinion, and I would suggest that the later the conversion took place along this timescale, the more intellectually wrenching and psychologically traumatic. The same that can be said for individual women's experience can also be said for that of women's organisations as one after the other struggled to stay true to founding principles while still adapting to the exigencies and emergencies of their times. Rather than focus here on individuals, the above points will be illustrated by comparing and contrasting two feminist organisations that took an abiding interest in peace, diplomacy, the League of Nations, war, fascism, and women's relationship with and the feminist connection to all the above.

The Six Point Group

It is worthwhile to compare and contrast two of these feminist organisations to see how they each came to terms with fascism and with the rapidly changing political situation. The first under examination here is the Six Point Group (SPG), a non-party feminist organisation founded by Lady Margaret Rhondda in 1921, whose campaigns were advertised and publicised in the feminist journal, also founded by Rhondda, *Time and Tide*. It was initially established to agitate for changes in British law in six areas: child assault; widowed mothers; unmarried mothers and their children; equal rights of guardianship for married parents; equal pay for teachers; and equal opportunities for men and women in the civil service. While its concerns were therefore about domestic affairs in both the wider and narrow sense, during the 1920s the SPG was active in trying to have the League of Nations pass an Equal Rights Treaty. The SPG was not principally an internationally-minded group, nor had foreign affairs figured in the original six points of its manifesto. Nonetheless, by the 1930s, from a comparative perspective, it was the SPG that did the most among feminist organisations and had the most to say about the fascist threat, both abroad as well as on the domestic front in the form of Mosley's British Union of Fascists. Indeed, while more attention will be paid to the SPG's response to fascism abroad, it is noteworthy that it demonstrated concern about native fascism. For example, in 1935, at the SPG's Executive Committee meeting, Monica Whately 'read a letter from the British Union of Fascists proposing a debate on Equal Pay for Equal Work with a representative of the SPG but it was decided by the Executive that the BUF were seeking to obtain propaganda by this means, and that it would be best to refuse their offer'.[10] Active opposition was maintained when, only a few months later 'Miss Whately reported that she had attended as an observer on behalf of the National Council of Civil Liberties outside the Mosley Meeting at the Albert Hall.'[11] Later in that same year, 1935, the Group hosted a meeting (in the home of Mrs. Whyte) where Mrs. Carrington Wood, former women's organiser for the British Union of Fascists, 'clearly showed the anti-feminist trend in that movement'.[12]

The Six Point Group's primary motivation for resisting fascism was not its place on the Left/Right political spectrum, nor its position on the whole question of war, but its feminist principles:

> Deeply perturbed by the news that under Fascist and Nazi dictatorships the hard won rights to political recognition as citizens are

being wrested from women, the Group called the first women's meeting in England to consider the situation and attempt to rally feminists to stand together to resist any encroachment of this philosophy and to assist our fellow women under the yoke of these dictatorships. Miss Ellen Wilkinson and Miss Whately addressed a large At Home in the Lyceum Club on 'Women under the Hitler Regime'.[13]

Of all the feminist organisations, the SPG was the most dedicated in its anti-fascism, both in theory and in practice. In theory, the SPG never allowed criticism of fascism to be divorced from criticism of the fascist victimisation of women and the regime's sexist reaction. On the practical side, the SPG did much heroic work on behalf of specific women victims of the Nazi regime, being partly responsible in some cases for the saving of lives. The SPG took a firm stand against Nazism and recognised the suffering of its victims: 'We would remind our members that Hitler's habit of arresting innocent women for alleged crimes of their husbands and brothers is an insult to feminists throughout the world ... it disassociates itself entirely from the school of thought which says such incidents are no concern of English feminists. It holds that the fight for equality involves active opposition to fascism, whether in Germany, or in any part of the world'.[14]

Given this feminist anti-fascist pedigree dating back to 1933, it was no wonder that the organisation was one of the few that did not undergo a heart-wrenching experience when it came to accepting the inevitability of war. But was there something inherent in the SPG's structure and programme that predisposed the Group to such a line? Actually, it would seem that it had far more to do with personal initiatives taken by some of the leaders than with ideology. The Group's vociferous anti-fascism was largely attributable to Miss Monica Whately's (1889–1960) dedication to the cause. Whately had a solid feminist and internationalist pedigree. She had been active in the militant suffragette movement, and in 1912, with her mother, became a founder member of the Catholic Women's Suffrage Society. During the interwar years she was an active member not only of the SPG but also the National Union of Societies for Equal Citizenship, presided over by Eleanor Rathbone; she was involved with international work through Save the Children, and peace work as a member of the Peace Army and No More War Movement, as well as a speaker for the League of Nations Union; she served as honorary treasurer for the Open Door Council, vigorously supporting its resistance to protective legislation for women workers; and she was a member of the Independent Labour Party, standing as an ILP candidate in 1929, 1931 and 1936. While she was unsuccessful at the Parliamentary level, significantly she successfully stood against BUF candidates in Limehouse at the 1937 London County Council elections, thus coming into close contact and direct debate with fascists in her midst. Her varied career as feminist, fighter for civil liberties, Catholic (she had converted with her parents in 1899), ILP member, and anti-fascist has led Linda Walker to see her career as one that 'epitomized the dissipation of energy which fragmented the inter-war women's movement. But it was precisely because she channeled her feminism into many diverse campaigns and issues that she showed its relevance to all the key movements of the twentieth century'.[15]

Indeed, if it was not down to personality and the drive of certain individuals, then the question is why the Open Door Council (ODC) and the Open Door International (ODI), whose papers I have also been examined in light of the concerns of this chapter, did not similarly foreground policies and develop tactics of feminist self-defence against fascism. It is notable that neither the ODC nor even less the ODI had much to say about Fascism or National Socialism. Indeed, these political terms scarcely appeared in their official literature. There are also similarities to be drawn here with other international organisations in which women seemed reluctant to use the term 'fascism', often for the good reason that members feared alienating their affiliates in fascist countries at critical and sensitive times. With the single-minded dedication to the economic emancipation of women, ODC and ODI members certainly did not fail to observe, comment upon and categorically condemn the treatment of women workers in the new Germany. Still, from the outset, from 1933, they tended to take as neutral a stance as possible on the regime in order to substantiate their claim of being non-party. In its ideology, vigilance, and uncompromising dedication to one fundamental component part of women's emancipation – economic emancipation – the ODC represented one of the more radical 'feminist' voices in the 1930s. Unlike so many other feminists and feminist organisations, the ODC never lets its eye off the ball, so to speak, on its central and only object, and the ODI itself expresses pride in its diverging from the more murky legacy of suffrage disunity and schisms with the outbreak of the First World War. Nonetheless, this single-mindedness also leads one to wonder if the focus on a single issue did not become an unrealistic and even irresponsible obsession under the circumstances of the outbreak of World War II and, earlier, in the face of fascism itself. In this respect, the SPG could not differ more from the ODC, even as it shared, among its other objectives, the ODC's concern for the protection of the status of the woman earner.

In terms of direct anti-Nazi action, informed by feminist conviction and priorities, it was the SPG that achieved the most of all the various women's organisations during the 1930s. In September 1934 a Women's Organising Committee was formed to arrange to send a deputation to Germany and the Saar to investigate the case of women held as hostages for their husbands, and to try to secure their release. The deputation was composed of Miss Whately, Mrs. Cooper, a JP, and representative of the Co-operative Women and of Women Weavers. The deputation was unable to secure the release of the women hostages, but this was only the beginning of a consistent campaign to help women political prisoners. The organisation worked to secure the release of the women in the Wuppertal Trial; the cases of Ukrainian women prisoners under savage sentences in Poland; the case of Frau Klaus, a young wife held in German prison merely as a hostage for her husband (later executed); and the case of Anna Pauker, held and tortured in a Romanian prison without trial, and who gave birth to a baby while in prison – by the international agitation of women the child at least was rescued from the fate of being put into a Government orphanage. It was through repeated interviews between Miss Whately and the German Ambassador and his representatives that they sought to apply pressure, bringing to their notice 'the co-operation of world feminist opinion ... in the endeavour to help these unfortunate victims'.[16] Further, the SPG chairman, Miss Betty Archdale, was one of a Delegation who went to Germany in November 1935 in order to try and procure the release of Elsie Evert and Olga Prestes – deported from Brazil and landed in Germany where they had not been since 1928, immediately arrested by the secret police and incarcerated. Whately's work on behalf of women victims continued with her authorship of the pamphlet entitled 'Women Behind Nazi Bars' (1935), printed in the hundreds of thousands and distributed around the country and in many parts of the Continent. In April 1935 wide press publicity was secured when Whately protested at a parade of German fashions organised by the German Embassy, no doubt drawing attention to the Nazi objectification of women.

Due largely to Whately's interest, the SPG worked closely with Women Against War and Fascism. As they enthusiastically described their activities in their annual newsletter:

A great world conference of Women Against Fascism and War was called in Paris on August 4th to 8th. Twelve hundred delegates from 40 nations and all shades of political opinion, colour, religion, race and class were gathered in Conference, which was eagerly followed by a great audience of visitors. Monica Whately and Dorothy Evans attended as representatives of the SPG. Monica Whately made a fine speech before the full conference, urging that women should work for the setting up of definite bulwarks to resist this tyranny wherever it shall raise its head, and asking the Conference to support the Equal Rights Treaty and try to get each country to sign it as an assurance before the evil spreads.[17]

In 1934 the SPG became one of the co-operating organisations of the World Committee of Women Against War and Fascism and 'kept up an agitation against Dictatorships and the whole male minded nationalist philosophy which has wrested from women in other lands their hard won liberties'.[18]Again, it was Whately who was most active in joint action with the above Committee, speaking at many of their meetings, as well as working with the International Non-Sectarian Anti-Nazi Council and the Boycott Committee. However, the SPG's collaboration with the World Committee of Women Against War and Fascism was not an entirely smooth alliance. While Whately had pressed for the association, she was under no illusions about the partisan line taken by the Committee and often had to stress, in the more private documents in the SPG, her disquiet with the direction taken by the Committee:

> Miss Marsh as our representative on the British Committee Against War and Fascism reported that financially the Committee were in great difficulties and it was doubtful whether they would be able to continue to publish their Bulletin. Miss Whately said she was opposed to any grant being made to this organisation until she was convinced that they were pressing the Anti-Fascist side of their work with the same enthusiasm with which they were doing peace propaganda, for it was on the Anti-Fascist not the peace side that the Group were co-operating. She pointed out that whereas we had consented to co-operate in the Demonstration to Trafalgar Square, believing it to be a demonstration against War and Fascism, the handbill took a strong party line in denouncing the National Government in stressing peace, and even the resolution which was originally proposed had nothing in it about the lowered status of women under Fascism, until Miss Whately had rung up the Secretary to point out the omission.[19]

This exemplifies the basis of collaboration but also the fundamental mistrust among women in their anti-fascist efforts, illustrating well the ultimate failure of anti-fascism to become a unifying cause.

The Group co-operated with other feminist organisations in 1935 for the Anti-Nazi exhibition, which included a lecture by Whately. With pride in her public profile, the SPG pointed out that 'our Honourable Secretary [Whately] has been in great demand as a speaker against these tyrannous dictatorships. She was on Spanish soil during the first weeks of the Civil War and her eloquence has been powerful in rousing people to the assistance of those fighting in defence of democracy'.[20] In 1937 'a hundred women shoppers from all parts of London met at the Grosvenor Gardens Club, Victoria ... to discuss a boycott of the aggressor nations. Miss Monica Whately, who presided, said: "We are at a turning point today when democracies must stand together in friendship as the Fascist nations do, and where a boycott of the Fascist nations is the only alternative to the destruction of democracy"'.[21]

While Whately readily collaborated with the Women's World Committee Against War and Fascism, a Communist-sponsored organisation, she was very skeptical about communism herself. She felt compelled to disassociate herself from the CPGB, and emphasise that anti-fascist activism was not always the outgrowth of the opposite extreme. 'I desire to state: I am not and have never been a member of the Communist Party, not could I have affiliation with the Party as long as they deny freedom to any to practice their religious beliefs. As a Catholic with full freedom to practice my religious beliefs in a Protestant country, I realise that only under a Democratic system can such religious freedom exist, and for that reason I am opposed to Dictatorships, Fascist or Communist.'[22] Certainly in the case of Monica Whately we have an excellent example of feminist anti-fascism, in thought and in action. However, such decisive and unswerving political, ideological and moral positioning was far more the exception than the rule.

Given the consistent line of militant feminist anti-fascism, it comes as little surprise that the SPG did not align itself with the peace movement, and therefore with the outbreak of the war could adopt a neutral position that compelled its members to neither resist the war effort or to support it. 'After very careful consideration, the Executive felt it their duty to recommend to the members the importance of keeping together a non-partisan Group without adopting any definite policy in relation to the war, in which matter each individual will act as he or she thinks right.'[23] This flexible line meant that there were few dramatic desertions by members and no obvious schisms in the group as the world crisis accelerated and after war broke out. The transcendence of their anti-fascism over other issues is well illustrated by the following example:

> Miss Whately reported that Miss Maitland had written to her protesting against the Group being officially connected with the Anti-War and Anti-Fascist Demonstration in Trafalgar Square. In replying to Miss Maitland, Miss Whately had pointed out that we were definitely represented on the British Section of the Women's World Committee Against War and Fascism, and it would have been difficult, therefore, for us not to have co-operated with them in their effort. We had, however, made it perfectly clear that we were co-operating only from the Anti-Fascist side as our members were divided on the question of the best peace policy, and we could not, therefore, officially have views on this matter.[24]

Nonetheless, the SPG's non-committal position and implicit support for the war effort did not appeal to all its members. In 1940, 'Miss Hay sent her resignation as she wanted to give all her spare time for Peace work, and was no longer entirely in sympathy with us.'[25]

Women's International League for Peace and Freedom

The story of the Women's International League for Peace and Freedom (the WIL, British Section), tells a different story about British women's engagement with and reaction to foreign policy and international crises. While the SPG opted to remain neutral on the question of pacifism, the WILPF, formed at the Hague in 1915, considered peace work to be at the heart of its mandate. At the dawn of the 1930s, the WIL was busy gathering signatures and organising processions for the Disarmament Declaration Campaign. The WIL's first reaction to the rise of Nazis was hardly welcoming but nonetheless measured, reiterating the pacifist line that 'conditions in Germany are largely the result of unjust treatment since the war by this and other nations,' but still protesting Nazi methods of 'cruelty and terrorism to political opponents' because 'it inevitably creates antagonism in other countries and thus hinders the removal of the admitted grievances of Germany'.[26] Indeed, this was a common understanding of the situation in Germany, and one that was also articulated by Vera Brittain: '[I]t was our Treaty of Versailles with its war guilt clauses and other humiliating provisions, which plunged Germany into despair, and sowed the seeds of Hitlerism that we know to-day.'[27] Note that there was no interest in the special case of women under dictatorship, the first indication of the transcendence of pacifism over feminism, and even pacifism over anti-fascism.

However, over the course of the next few years, the WIL's interpretation of fascism, while never fully articulated or worked out, differed from the Communist line, with an emphasis instead on safeguarding democratic principles as a bulwark against fascism. Their 'Statement of Fascism' is illuminating in this regard, as well as worthy of contrast with the afore-quoted resolution passed by the SPG at around the same time:

> This Committee views with grave alarm the growing movements in the world to-day especially in Central Europe contrary to liberty and democracy, together with the growth of violence, and resolves to study what steps can best be taken to combat this menace from whatever quarter it may come, to give support to freedom and democratic institutions.[28]

With regard to home-grown fascists, Miss Courtney felt that 'the best method of counteracting them would be by definite propaganda for democratic ideals',[29] rather than anything more interventionist or offensive. Indeed, I have not come across any evidence of the presence or representation of the WIL in anti-BUF activity. Like so many other women's organisations, they responded to the fall out of fascism in Europe on a case-by-case basis, seeking to help women and cohorts of women in need, beginning with those members of the WILPF who were being persecuted under the new regime, and sending women among their own number to observe the situation for themselves (Miss Edith Pye visited Germany in the spring of 1933 under the auspices of the WIL). When, also in 1933, a German Relief Committee, soon to be renamed the Relief Committee for Victims of German Fascism, was appointed (with Dorothy Woodman and Isabel Brown as secretaries) to raise funds and give assistance to victims of fascist terror, rather than for the purpose 'to undertake propaganda against fascism as such', the WIL declined the invitation to join the Committee as 'it is our rule not to undertake relief work, but we would be glad to be kept informed of their activities'.[30] Indeed, the WIL seemed very reluctant to do more than observe events as they unfolded.

There was little friction within the WIL British Section before the war itself, but by 1934 it did come into conflict with the WILPF. It is very interesting that the WIL differed from the French Section of the WILPF on the grounds that it felt that the later was adopting a militant anti-fascism that fundamentally threatened to undermine the international movement's pacifist credentials. The WIL seemed ready to stand virtually alone in its unswerving determination to pacifism at all costs, and supported the WILPF's new 'Statement of Aims' of 1934 that read as follows: 'The WILPF aims at bringing together women of different political and philosophical tendencies united in their determination to study, make known, and abolish the political, social, economic and psychological causes of war, and to work for a constructive peace.'[31] Although members of the British Section of the WIL attended the first meeting of the Women's World Committee Against War and Fascism in Paris in August, 1934, unlike the Six Point Group, they warned their members against the new movement, and advised that 'the greatest care should be used in any dealings with this organisation and that judging from the Paris Congress the impression is gained that it is a strong Communist body. Their pledge is: "I pledge myself to oppose capitalist war and Fascism and to support all united actions against these menaces." The WIL is opposed to all war and to all violence.'[32] Further, when Monica Whately sent a letter to the WIL in April 1935 'regarding the condition of women in Germany, and inviting the WIL to send a delegate to an informal meeting to discuss the possibility of some massed protest by the women of England, against the debasement and persecution of their sisters in Germany',[33] the WIL voted against sending anyone.

If this was the WIL's position by the mid-1930s, even as women members were in possession of a great deal of evidence of Fascist and Nazi terror, sexism and anti-semitism, and when many had witnessed such things for themselves in their visits abroad, where did the WIL stand by the end of the 1930s? Did its pacifist stand withstand further revelations of Nazi atrocities, and did members all agree that a pacifist stand was still the only appropriate response? In March 1938 the WIL spoke of the desirability of 'moving towards general appeasement',[34] and during the war itself they maintained faith in arbitration and refused to support the war effort as such. Of course such a stand invited dissent within the WIL's ranks. Starting in April, 1938, Mrs. Helena Swanwick was one of the first to resign from the WIL because she thought the group's position naïve, and argued that 'a political organisation should not overlook all the immense difficulties and complexities of the situation as it is'.[35] In July 1940 Dr Clark, a long-standing WIL Executive Committee member, acknowledged that 'it seemed no longer possible to evade an attitude to the resistance of the German attack. She believed a world settlement in our day was dependent on defeating the German armed forces and the possibility of that defeat rested on the general morale of the people. ... [W]e cannot stay neutral'.[36] While Clark thought that 'absolute pacifism was never the basis of the WIL', her fellow committee members begged to differ, and in November she resigned, stating that she believed that 'the WIL must be based on agreement on such an essential and vital issue as that of resistance to Nazi aggression. Failing this agreement, she felt that we can neither influence our fellow men and women to maintain the ideals of democracy nor take our share in any positive policy for the reconstruction which we hope to see'.[37] Clark's resignation from the Committee was followed by that of Mrs. Thornycroft's, on similar grounds, the next month. Perhaps the question is not why some WIL members resigned by this juncture, but why so many still remained throughout the war. However, what is clear is that, unlike the Six Point Group, issues quite divorced from ideological feminism dominated debates within the WIL, and while it is clear that it emerged as a pacifist organisation, it is unclear if it deserved to be called a feminist one, and even less an anti-fascist one.

Conclusion

In conclusion, this chapter has compared the response to fascism by two British women's organisations during the 1930s in order to make a start at charting female engagement with issues of foreign policy and reactions to international crises. It is something of a paradox that while the Six Point Group had its origins as a domestic/national feminist organisation, it was to take a far more interventionist and far more sophisticated feminist anti-fascist stance than the British Section of the Women's International League, itself a branch of an international women's organisation with direct links to the women victims of Nazi oppression. The WIL maintained the integrity of its *pacifist* principles throughout the 1930s and right through the war years, although it ceased to have much to say about feminist issues as such. In contrast, the Six Point Group made no claim to represent either pacifism or patriotism but, likewise, was able to maintain the integrity of its *feminist* work well into the war years. Nigel Copsey proposes that anti-fascism should be 'defined as a thought, an attitude of feeling of hostility towards fascist ideology and its propagators which may or may not be acted upon. It other words, anti-fascism can be both active and passive'.[38] In this comparative study of these two feminist organisations we see the wide range of politicised women's responses to fascism, and the great gulf between those who sought to actively oppose fascism, on the behalf of women and in defence of democracy, and those who were willing to take a passive approach. Ultimately it would only be those who gave active form to their conviction that could own the label feminist anti-fascist.

Notes

1 Quoted in Ethel Mannin, *Women and the Revolution* (London: Secker & Warburg, 1938), pp. 201–2.
2 See Julie Gottlieb, 'Feminist and Anti-Fascism in Britain: Militancy Revived?', in Nigel Copsey and David Renton (eds), *British Fascism, the Labour Movement and the State* (Basingstoke: Palgrave-Macmillan, 2005), pp. 68–94.
3 Vera Brittain Papers, McMaster University: F10, 30 November 1932, 'Why Current Events Matter to Us', Halifax Luncheon Club.
4 Eleanor Rathbone, 'Changes in Public Life', in Ray Strachey (ed.), *Our Freedom and Its Results* (London: Hogarth, 1936), p. 40.
5 Johanna Alberti, 'British Feminists and Anti-Fascism in the 1930s', in Sybil Oldfield (ed.), *This Working-Day World: Women's Lives and Culture(s) in Britain 1914–1945* (London: Taylor & Francis, 1994) pp. 111–22; Sandi E. Cooper, 'Peace as a Human Right: The Invasion of Women into the World of High International Politics', *Journal of Women's History* 14, 2 (Summer 2002); Helen Jones, *Women in British Public Life, 1914–50: Gender, Power and Social Policy* (London: Longman, 2000), especially chapter 5, 'The European Stage'; Christine Bolt, *Sisterhood Questioned: Race, Class and Internationalism in the American and British Women's Movements* (London: Routledge, 2004); Leila Rupp, *Worlds of Women: The Making of an International Women's Movement* (NJ: Princeton: Princeton University Press, 1997); Carol Miller, 'Lobbying the League: Women's International Organisations and the League of Nations' (D.Phil Thesis, University of Oxford, 1992); Jill Liddington, *The Road to Greenham Common: Feminism and Anti-Militarism in Britain since 1820* (Syracuse: Syracuse University Press, 1989); Sybil Oldfield, *Women Against the Iron First* (London: Basil Blackwell, 1989); and Julie Gottlieb, 'Feminism and Anti-Fascism in Britain: Militancy Revived?', in Nigel Copsey and David Renton (eds), *British Fascism, the Labour Movement and the State.*
6 Deborah E. Van Seters, *Women's Foreign Policy Advocacy in 1930s Britain* (PhD Thesis, University of Toronto, 1999), p. ii.
7 Deborah Gorham, 'Vera Brittain, Flora MacDonald Denison and the Great War: The Failure of Non-Violence', in Ruth Roach Pierson (ed.), *Women and Peace: Theoretical, Historical and Practical Perspectives* (London: Croom Helm, 1989), pp. 137–48.
8 Vera Brittain Papers: H281, 'Politics and League of Nations', BBC News from Abroad, 30 September 1933.
9 Winifred Holtby, 'Where We Could Excel: From a Woman's Angle', *News Chronicle*, 22 January 1934. The Open Door Council regarded it as a priority to place pressure on the government to admit women to the Consular and Diplomatic Services. See [W]omen's [L]ibrary, London: 5/ODC/A7 Open Door Council, Eighth Annual Report, March 1934.
10 WL SPG A1–9, Executive Committee of the Six Point Group, 12 December 1935.

11 WL SPG A1–9, Executive Committee of the Six Point Group, 28 April 1936.
12 WL SPG/B1–5, Annual Report of the Six Point Group, Nov. 1934–Nov. 1935.
13 WL SPG/B1–5, Six Point Group, Annual Report, Nov. 1933–Nov. 1934.
14 WL SPG/B6–13, Annual Report of Six Point Group, 1937–1938.
15 Linda Walker, '(Mary) Monica Whately', *Dictionary of National Biography*.
16 WL SPG/B6–13, Annual Report of the Six Point Group, Nov. 1935–Nov. 1936.
17 WL SPG/B1–5, Six Point Group, Annual Report, Nov. 1933–Nov. 1934.
18 WL SPG/B1–5, Annual Report of the Six Point Group, Nov. 1934–Nov. 1935.
19 WL SPG A1–9, Executive Committee of the Six Point Group, 23 June 1936.
20 WL SPG/B6–13, Annual Report of the Six Point Group, Nov. 1935–Nov. 1936.
21 'Women's War on Fascism', *News Chronicle*, 17 December 1937.
22 Labour History Archive Study Centre: CP/CENT/SUBJ/04/04, 27 February 1937.
23 WL SPG/B6–13, Annual Report of the Six Point Group, 1938–1939.
24 WL SPG A1–9, Executive Committee of the Six Point Group, 18 May 1936.
25 WL SPG/A29–39, Executive Committee of the Six Point Group, 15 January 1940.
26 [L]ondon [S]chool of [E]economics Library: WILPF 1/9, Minutes of the Executive Committee, 14 March 1933.
27 Vera Brittain Papers: F14, 'Relief Committee for Victims of German Fascism', 13 October 1933.
28 LSE WILPF 1/9, Minutes of Executive Committee Meeting, 9 May 1933.
29 LSE WILPF 1/9, Minutes of Executive Committee, 13 June 1933.
30 LSE WILPF 1/9, Minutes of Executive Committee Meeting, 11 April 1933.
31 LSE WILPF 1/10, Minutes of Executive Committee, 25 September 1934.
32 LSE WILPF 1/10, Minutes of the Executive Committee, 16 October 1934.
33 LSE WILPF 1/11, Minutes of Executive Committee, 9 April 1935.
34 LSE WILPF 1/14, Minutes of the Executive Committee, 8 March 1938.
35 LSE WILPF1/14, Minutes of the Executive Committee, 12 April 1938.
36 LSE WILPF, Minutes of the Executive Committee, 3 July 1940.
37 LSE WILPF, Minutes of the Executive Committee, November 1940.
38 Nigel Copsey, *Anti-Fascism in Britain* (Basingstoke: Macmillan, 2000), p. 4.

5
'I was following the lead of Jesus Christ': Christian Anti-Fascism in 1930s England

Tom Lawson

Introduction

Religion has recently re-emerged from the shadow cast by the idea that the history of modernity and post-modernity could only be sought in secular terms. There has been a flurry of publications reasserting the centrality of religion, especially Christianity, in twentieth-century Britain.[1] The study of political extremism has also been reinvigorated using the concept of 'political religion'.[2] However the role of Christians and their churches in the history of British political extremism, both in terms of support and opposition, remains – despite notable exceptions – underexplored.[3] This chapter attempts to fill a small part of that gap by exploring Christian anti-fascism in Britain. In doing so it will further assert the importance of Christian discourse in the history of modern Britain by demonstrating that Christians – especially the Church of England – provided both a language of opposition to fascism and inspired anti-fascist action. But it will also be noted how Christian faith could also underpin fascist politics too. I will thus seek also to problematise the history of anti-fascism by exploring its discursive basis in order to demonstrate how far fascism and anti-fascism could *share* a vocabulary. As such the history of Christian anti-fascism might occasion some recasting of the binary opposition between fascism and anti-fascism which has characterised historiography thus far.

The chapter begins with analysis of the lacuna surrounding the role of Christians and Christianity in the histories of both British fascism and anti-fascism. In order to demonstrate that this omission is a serious one I then investigate the vocabulary of opposition to fascism provided by the mainstream of the Church of England, as revealed by the

Christian press. But there is, of course, not just one Christian discourse about either fascism or anti-fascism and the chapter therefore considers the sharp differences between Anglican and Roman Catholic appraisals of fascist politics, albeit often seen through the prism of European developments. But Christian anti-fascism did not simply provide the rhetorical tools for opposing the fascist worldview, some anti-fascist *activism* can be broadly considered Christian too. As such the penulti-mate section considers individuals, most notably Fr. John Groser, who were involved in direct physical and ideological clashes with fascists especially in the mid-to-late 1930s and assesses the degree to which such activism was religiously, as opposed to politically, inspired. Yet even overt and active anti-fascists such as Groser appeared to succumb to a vocabulary that was closer to fascism than anti-fascism at times, espe-cially with regard to Jews and Judaism, and as such the chapter concludes by investigating where the language of Christian anti-fascism overlapped with the language of fascism itself – pointing to the ultimate ambivalence of this variety of anti-fascism.

For the most part this chapter concentrates on Christian opposition to the most developed form of British fascism in the shape of the BUF in the 1930s. There simply is not enough evidence of institutional engagement with nascent fascism in the 1920s, movements such as the British Fascisti, to produce a thorough analysis. However, where 1930s opposition does have its roots in the previous decade, or where indi-vidual engagement with fascism in the 1920s can be identified, I have attempted to do so. Christian engagement with British fascism must also be considered as inseparable from interpretations of, and attitudes to, Continental fascism, and in particular National Socialism. Christian attitudes to Nazism are well-documented, and complex, but they appear only in the background here as the canvas upon which opposition to *British* fascism was painted.

It is worth beginning with a brief word on the status of Christianity and Christian institutions in inter-war Britain in order to establish some context. As the focus of this chapter will be the institutions and communicants of the Church of England and the Roman Catholic Church I will confine my observations to them. The inter-war Church of England suffered from a political and theological identity crisis between the wars. It was in many ways still the stereotypical 'Tory party at prayer'. Cosmo Lang, who was Archbishop of Canterbury between 1928 and 1942, was, for example, a very close associate of leading Conservative politicians. But at the same time it was a church whose clergy was increasingly dominated by a social radicalism concerned to transform the lives of ordinary people in Britain, and not with the vested interests which the Church might traditionally be seen as representing. The concern that the Church develop a wider social relevance was accompanied, perhaps paradoxically, by a sense within the hierarchy at least, that the Church played an increasingly marginal role in the life of the nation. The Lord Bishops may still have sat in the House of Lords, but less and less people went to Mass on a Sunday and this at the time when increasingly the leaders of the Church, such as George Bell (who was Bishop of Chichester) and William Temple (who was Archbishop of York and then after 1942 of Canterbury), sought a concrete social relevance for the Church. As such by the end of the 1930s the Church needed to seek again the 'Conversion of England', and to demonstrate its importance in this world – something its leaders did by identifying themselves with the kind of politics that ultimately came to underpin the post-war consensus.

As such the Church of England was politically engaged during the inter-war period, something which should have and indeed did bring it into contact with British fascism as a form of politics. This is not to say that the Church of England's political engagement was all in one direction. Prominent figures offered starkly different appraisals of European politics – ranging from the Bishop of Gloucester, Arthur Headlam's, open support for Nazism, to the so-called 'Red' Dean of Canterbury, Hewlett Johnson's, admiration of Stalin's Soviet Union.

The Roman Catholic Church was both similarly politically focused – and perhaps to an even greater degree this was passed through the prism of European politics, and especially the Spanish Civil War. Its leaders helped to paint that conflict as a Manichean struggle between Good and Evil, between the Catholic and Godly nationalist and the satanic and Communist Republicans. But the Catholic community was also sharply divided. Depending on to whom one listened, it was a home for intellectuals of the political Right (as symbolised by a number of high profile conversions such as Geoffrey Dawson's); or it was the home of an Irish immigrant community which in Liverpool and London for example formed a significant support base for the labour movement.

The European focus of the Church of England was in part a result of the increasing importance of ecumenism in inter-war Christianity. However the focus of this rapprochement was much more likely to be the European churches than with other denominations in Britain. Indeed despite the growing importance of the Anglo-Catholic movement within the Church of England, inter-denominational relationships were increasingly fractious. Callum Brown has recently commented on the sharpened edges of British inter-war Christian culture,[4] in which perhaps the perception of crisis heightened the passions of doctrinal dispute. Indeed, one arena where in the 1930s one could certainly witness clashes between the Anglican and Roman Catholic communities of faith was over attitudes to both domestic and European fascism.

Overall then we are not going to be able distinguish either a single Christian attitude towards anti-fascism, or even a single attitude within each denomination – although the Roman Catholic hierarchy did undoubtedly offer unambiguous support for Franco's Spanish fascists. The communities of faith of inter-war Britain were sharply divided, and the multivalent responses to both fascism and anti-fascism reflect that.

Christianity, fascism and anti-fascism: an absent historiography

History and memory records little role for the churches, churchmen or Christianity in the history of anti-fascism, or indeed fascism itself. The historiography of anti-fascism in particular is so dominated by the idea of class that only socio-economic or political identities seem to have been allowed. David Renton's histories of anti-fascism are typical here, in that he only defines anti-fascism in terms of grass roots political activism, emanating from the labour movement.[5]

This omission can in part be traced back even to the original appraisals of anti-fascist action by British security forces. The Special Branch report of what has become known as the 'Battle of Cable Street' simply labelled the anti-fascist activists of 4 October 1936 as 'Jewish' and 'Communist'.[6] The original historiography also sought the identity of anti-fascists in only political terms. Mullally wrote in his *Fascism Inside England* that 'though it suited Mosley to label them [his anti-fascist antagonists] all "Reds", they were made up of Communists, Socialists, trade-unionists, Liberals and, to their credit, a sprinkling of honest anti-fascist Tories'.[7] No religious identity was allowed. Local memory projects which seek to document the history of anti-fascist action also ignore religion.[8] Although the Church does feature for example in an account of anti-fascism in Tyne and Wear, it is only as part of the community under attack from the fascists, which is then delivered by representatives of working-class politics.[9]

Even where historians have considered individual clergy who did actively oppose fascist politics in the 1930s, it is not, by implication, their Christianity that has been found to define their opposition. Fr. John Groser, an East End prelate who physically 'fought' fascism, is invariably referred to as a 'Labour' activist. This is not to say that Christianity is denied, but it is denied priority. Tom Buchanan's history of British reactions to the Spanish Civil War is typical when it includes reference to 'a Marxist clergyman' in Islington who opposed the fascists.

Churches and churchmen play only a very marginal role in the memory of anti-fascism too. Consider the iconic moment of anti-fascist action at Cable Street, which is investigated here as symbolic rather than representative. Although Joe Jacobs remembers the involvement of Irish Catholics in his account of the battle – he does so only in the context of their socio-economic identity as dockers neglecting any creative role for their Catholicism in opposing Mosley's Blackshirts.[10] Bill Fishman similarly recalls 'Jews and Irish Catholic dockers standing up to stop Mosley. I shall never forget that as long as I live, how *working-class people* could get together to oppose the evil of racism'.[11] There is no place for identifiable Christian symbols in the Cable Street mural commemorating the battle and unveiled in the 1980s either. And although Fr. John Groser, who took part in the battle, does appear in Simon Blumenfeld's play about the 'Battle', he features only as an adjunct to the main, Communist, protagonists. Indeed in the play's only discussion about Groser he is warmly declared not to be a 'real Priest', who 'you can't tell from rent collectors'.[12]

Christianity also plays little or no role in the historiography of British fascism itself, despite the evident Christianity of some fellow travellers. I do not mean by this that the Christian beliefs of General Fuller or Nesta Webster are not discussed, it is just that they rarely seem to be investigated as important for their own sakes – as if their Christianity and their fascism might have drawn from the same inspiration. Tom Linehan has perhaps gone further than most in attempting to delineate the BUF as a political religion but his work is typical when it understands the Christian contribution to fascist discourse only as situated on top of more fundamental socio-economic grievances in the minds of fascist supporters. For example in Hackney and Stoke Newington Linehan informs us that Christian anti-semitism was a part of fascist politics because of the economic impact of Jewish immigration into the area.[13] Martin Pugh's *Hurrah for the Blackshirts* is keen to explore the links between the conservatism of prominent fascists and their fascist politics, as a way of domesticating their extremism, but neglects entirely the interaction between their politics and faith.[14]

Church historiography is no different. Adrian Hastings' *History of English Christianity* just records that Christian engagement with Mosley (presumably either positive or negative) was 'slight'.[15] Edward Norman dismissed the possibility of Christian support for fascism, declaring that the clergy felt it 'alien' but gives no details of clerical opposition to fascism other than this in his history of modern church and society.[16] Even Callum Brown, who has done so much to assert the importance of Christianity in Modern Britain, in his history of twentieth-century British religion only remembers anti-fascism and particularly Cable Street as significant in terms of British *Jewish* history. It has no role in the history of Christian institutions and communities that he outlines.[17]

As such Christianity and fascism seem by implication to be opposites in these historiographies; it is therefore ironic that faith has been absent from the history of opposition to fascism. The churches and their followers do exist in such historiographies but only as a part of an unexplored backdrop, the canvas on which the events are played out, but seemingly without a creative influence. This chapter now seeks to correct this.

The Church of England and the language of opposition to fascism

If anti-fascism is more than just action, then the Church of England deserves a place in its history. Elements of the Anglican community articulated a consistent opposition to fascist politics across the 1930s using a Christian vocabulary.[18] Especially prior to the disturbances at the Olympia meeting of the BUF in June 1934, the Church's press for example gave voice to a principled opposition to fascism as the unambiguous enemy of Christianity. After Lord Rothermere had declared 'Hurrah for the Blackshirts' in January 1934, the *Church Times* instructed its readers that 'everywhere Fascism is necessarily a danger to the Christian religion'.[19] At the time leading figures in the Church of England were also increasingly troubled by the treatment of some clergy in Nazi Germany.

Why did the opinion formers of the Church of England regard fascist politics as a danger to Christianity? After all in Italy and indeed in National Socialist Germany many churchmen had adopted precisely the opposite view, as would some in the English Christian community. Ironically some of the assumptions that led German Christians to either identify with or at the very least tolerate their own fascist regime actually underpinned the language of English Christian opposition. At issue was the status of the individual and her relationship with God. For German Catholics, for example, agreements between the Vatican and the Nazi regime appeared to protect the sacred space occupied by the church and thus safeguarded the individual and her faith. But for the English Christian community the promotion of the state as all powerful appeared to necessarily undermine the role of the churches as the guardians of individual salvation because it denied the very existence of the individual and her conscience through the repression of free speech. Accordingly the *Church Times* declared that under fascist regimes 'the individual has become the slave of the state, this is the very antithesis of catholic sociology'.[20]

Fascist anti-semitism was also important in shaping Anglican opposition to domestic fascism. Indeed Anglicans seemed to see the anti-semitism of Mosley et al. rather more clearly than they did Nazi anti-Jewish intent. Nazism was consistently portrayed as primarily a threat to the *Christian* world.[21] Anglican concern at BUF anti-semitism appears to pre-date what has been traditionally regarded as the time when British fascism was converted, wholeheartedly, to the anti-semitic cause. Nigel Copsey has identified a second wave of anti-fascism following the 'forcible injection of militant anti-Semitism into the BUF's campaign towards the end of 1935'.[22] But as early as January 1934 the *Church Times* was warning that Mosley intended to 'launch an anti-Semitic campaign', something gleaned from his attacks on 'alien forces in the City of London'.[23] Unsurprisingly little changed in the Anglican appraisal of the fascist menace when that anti-semitism became less ambiguous. Both before and after the Cable Street disturbances in 1936 Anglicans again publicly opposed fascism on the grounds of its anti-Jewish rhetoric. George Bell warned that anti-semitism was spreading to England, through the BUF, like a 'contagious disease' in September 1936 and the following month his counterpart in Southwark identified fascist 'Jew-baiting' as a symptom of the decline of 'civilisation' into 'cruelty'.[24]

Bell's construction of anti-semitism as a contagion imported into Britain by the BUF betrayed one of the central tropes of Anglican opposition to domestic fascism – that it represented a rather alien and foreign form of politics. The church publication *The Guardian* for example praised Stanley Baldwin's attack on the BUF as having introduced the 'foreign notion' of force into British politics in June 1934. The *Church Times* agreed that 'fascism is alien to the traditions of this country'.[25] Two years later the Bishop of London referred to the attempted march of Mosleyites through the East End as 'monstrous' precisely because they were 'outsiders' attempting to sow discord.[26] *The Church Times* articulated its anger at the Cable Street disturbances as a form of 'political blackguardism utterly opposed to the English tradition and the English character'.[27]

For Anglicans, the idea that BUF was alien, perversely, rather under-mined the case for *actively* countering the fascist menace, because its very foreignness ensured it was unlikely to succeed. As such one of the premises of opposition dictated that Anglicans, while clear in that opposition, at times did not perceive *British* fascism as something they need take tremendously seriously. George Bell is a case in point here – while he dedicated his life to opposing *German* fascism his engage-ment with British right-wing extremism was very limited. Indeed his papers preserve no correspondence on the matter, and in the aftermath of war Bell could find common cause with former members of the BUF in their shared opposition to the trial of German war criminals.[28] As *The Guardian* put it 'we do not think Oswald Mosley is a real danger. He is too unstable and theatrical'.[29]

The clarity of the Anglican communities' anti-fascism was also obscured by the associations made between fascism and communism as forms of anti-Christian alien politics. At times Anglican objections to fascism became lost within this wider objection to 'totalitarian' politics – as the *Church Times* proclaimed in February 1934 'there is no difference between Bolshevism and Fascism. Both are equally the enemy'.[30] In part this also explains the omission of any serious engagement with Christian anti-fascism from the historiography of the modern English churches – Adrian Hastings argued in his *History of English Christianity* that communists and fascists were close together in terms of 'funda-mental ideology' and therefore necessarily reviled by the Christian community. In making such a statement Hastings was echoing the language used by inter-war Anglicans. When churchmen made these associations in the 1930s it inevitably meant that their appraisal of *anti-fascist* action itself became bound up with the appraisal of fascism, and thus a clear Christian perspective became difficult to delineate or disentangle.

After all anti-fascist action was to an extent bound up with organised communism. When the Bishop of Southwark opined against 'cruelty in the modern world' in the aftermath of the Cable Street disturbances for example, his objections to 'Jew baiting' became generalised objections to any effort to 'organise society' in ways that have led to 'cruelty and suf-fering'.[31] Such a view was typical of an Anglican imagination during the 1930s that conceived of the world as engaged in general battle for the future between the 'pagan ideals' of communism and fascism and the 'ideals of Christ, which are responsible for all that is best and noblest in our life'.[32] This was a forerunner of what Bishop of Chichester would deter-mine as the 'thirty years war of the twentieth century' for the future.[33]

This tendency to consider anti-fascism and fascism as emerging from the same alien wellspring was most evident in Anglican appraisals of the disturbances at Olympia. Some rejected the fascist appraisal that the violence accompanying Mosley's rally had been the result of *communist* agitation, for example the Bishop of Durham Hensley Henson recorded in his diary that he could not 'set aside' fascist involvement in the violence.[34] However, most Anglican readings of Olympia saw a concerted 'totalitarian' attack on democracy – 'the freedom for which our ancestors fought' considered the *Church Times* 'is being ground out of existence between the upper and nether millstones of Fascism and Communism'.[35] *The Guardian* agreed that both communism and fascism had demonstrated at the meeting that they had 'fell designs upon what our democratic bureaucracy leaves us of our liberties ... The Communists would have interfered with the right of free meeting and speaking. The Fascists interfered with the freedom of opinion'.[36]

At times the Anglican understanding of fascism did escape these interpretative shackles. Such was the shock of Cable Street, it was represented as a purely fascist menace. In the Church press the 'battle' was portrayed almost entirely as a struggle between the law abiding community and alien invaders attempting to import hatred and violence. The idea that those blocking Mosley's path were Communists was rejected as the 'pretence of a political adventurer'.[37] Cable Street could be much more simply explained – the 'community' which Blackshirts were attempting to destabilise simply 'would not have it'.[38]

However, Cable Street proved the exception and the idea of totalitarianism *did* continue to shape Anglican engagement with fascism. By the time Mosley attempted to march through Bermondsey a year on from Cable Street both he and his opponents were 'represent[ed] as not native but alien conceptions'.[39] This seems to have been the result of the increased tendency to consider the politics of extremism in a European context. Political violence like that which took place in Bermondsey in Autumn 1937 were then cast as part of the wider struggle, encapsulated most clearly in the Spanish Civil War, in which both 'fascism and Bolshevism' were seen as 'anti-Christian.'[40]

Of course Communists themselves attempted to relate their own anti-fascism to a more universal struggle against right-wing politics, as such we cannot be surprised if the Christian community believed them. This was particularly the case after the beginning of the Spanish Civil War.[41] The conflict in Spain was particularly problematic for Christians, in that any identification with active opposition to fascism was challenged by the anti-clerical outrages of the Republicans. The majority of

Anglicans did not support Franco's 'fascists' but they could not unambiguously support their opponents either. Archbishop of Canterbury Cosmo Lang's close relationship with the government perhaps made his support for non-intervention inevitable, but he was supported by the majority of the Christian press and indeed in the Church Assembly where, for example, Hewlett Johnson was upbraided for his support for the Republican cause.[42]

Anglican support of non-intervention remained more sympathetic to republican anti-fascism than Franco's forces. The Anglican community was scathing of those who chose to support Franco as fighting with God on his side, although there were notable exceptions like Dean Inge. Again the *Church Times* provides a useful example here, where Roman Catholic support for Franco on those terms was mocked precisely because supporters of Franco could not understand that communism and fascism were both the opponents of Christianity. Interpretations of the Spanish Civil War were thus cast inside a domestic denominational conflict in which it was declared that 'Rome [stood] for slavery, Canterbury for Liberty'.[43]

Overall then the Anglican community steadfastly provided a language of opposition to fascism, both home and abroad. This was an opposition that means that Anglican Churchmen can be rightly considered anti-fascist. However the terms of that opposition, and the consistent deployment of the idea of totalitarianism within it meant that the Anglican appraisal of anti-fascism itself could be more ambiguous. Often the Church appeared to wish to place itself between fascism and anti-fascist action, especially when this was considered in a European context.

English Roman Catholicism and anti-fascism

The English Roman Catholic Church was much more likely to harbour sympathies with European fascists – especially those in the Mediterranean. Are there therefore *any* terms on which the Catholic Church and community can be considered as contributing to the discourse of domestic anti-fascism?

Church historiography suggests not. Adrian Hastings argues that the majority of Roman Catholics supported the nationalist cause in Spain, and even goes so far as to describe English Catholics as sympathising with fascism. Certainly Catholic intellectuals flirted with fascist discourse, Hilaire Belloc for example had 'long preached about the phoney quality of western democracy'.[44] Members of the hierarchy were also drawn to some Continental fascist leaders. Cardinal Hinsley, Archbishop of

Westminster, famously kept a photograph of Franco on his desk and the Catholic press, such as *The Tablet* certainly endorsed the nationalist cause as a struggle between Christianity and Communism.[45] In domestic terms it seems less clear cut however.

Tom Linehan has found evidence of working-class Catholics being drawn towards fascism because of events in Spain.[46] But at the same time, memories of anti-fascist action commonly refer to the involvement of Irish Catholic working class. It may be that this is just a case of their class winning out over their religion, and thus evidence of the irrelevance of religious narratives in the history of anti-fascism. After all the English Roman Catholic Church hierarchy could brook no compromise whatsoever with the Communist anti-fascists that they believed were competing for the souls of the faithful. As the Archbishop of Liverpool wrote in 1937 of the struggle between communists and fascists: 'it is the communists who are the enemies of the poor, for with false promises they rob the worker of his dignity and immortal hopes'.[47]

However there is some evidence of an elongated engagement within the Catholic community with British fascism that was more sceptical than their engagement with the likes of Franco and Mussolini.[48] It is certainly not the case that support for fascists abroad led directly to support for domestic fascism. In fact there may be some role for Catholics and Catholicism in this history of anti-fascism too. Despite the mocking tones of the *Church Times* in their dismissal of Catholic fascism, there was in fact a good deal in common between Catholic and Anglican appraisals of British fascism, especially prior to the outrages in Spain. Again it is possible to argue that Catholics attempted to articulate an oppositional language to fascism, which placed Christianity between fascism and communism. But again this meant that anti-fascist *action* was considered to represent a similar danger to fascist politics itself.

First, it seems clear from the Catholic press that British fascists went some way to attempt to recruit Catholics and Catholicism to their cause and thus that they identified the Catholic community as a potential support base. Efforts were made, largely through letter writers to highlight the similarities between BUF and 'Catholic ethics' for example. During the early part of 1935 the BUF went to some lengths to make clear its support for denominational education. But these overtures were rebuffed and, for example, *The Tablet* maintained a consistent opposition to Mosley in the early-to-mid 1930s. Again Catholic opposition to British fascism appeared to be based upon the fascist conception of the individual and her relationship with the state, and the idea that by promoting the sanctity of the state, fascist politics denied the church.[49]

This was not precisely the same as Anglican evaluations of the BUF. There seemed to be little fear of anti-semitism for example. Indeed the Catholic press was in part anguished at the prospect that the BUF might split the support for the political Right in Britain, and thus open the door to the Godless Left.[50] But there seemed as little enthusiasm for the political tactics of Mosley's men in the Catholic Church as there was in the Church of England. The Blackshirts were declared to be an 'intolerable danger to the state', because their embrace of violence was an effort to usurp constitutional order.[51] There is also little doubt too that the danger of fascism was considered in relation to the Communist menace. *The Tablet's* long leader article on Olympia was titled 'Six and Six Make Twelve' which is an apt summary of the analysis offered. Communism and Fascism, and crucially the interaction between the two, threatened the present order. Their dynamic relationship meant that in reality the two creeds were constituents of a totalitarian whole.

This said, an analysis of the language of the Catholic appraisal of Olympia suggests that it was the shadow cast by Communism that Catholics found most terrifying. The Olympia meeting had been wrecked by Communists, which suggested that it was they that inspired and indeed caused the fascist turn to violence. It was also Communists that were constructed as the most alien force. Communist women used language that one observer had, for example, never heard coming from the mouth of a women before.[52] While *The Tablet* considered that Mosley might be able to explain the violence, it was not possible that the inherently alien communists might be able to do the same. As such it seems that while Roman Catholics did employ a similar totalitarian model in their appraisal of British fascism to the Church of England, it was more decisively motivated by anti-communism. Indeed one of the objections raised by a correspondent to *The Tablet* about Mosley was that he was, when all was said and done, too 'Bolshevik'.[53]

Christianity and anti-fascist action

Despite fears of anti-fascist action and its relationship to Communism, it is not the case that there was no Christian involvement in such activism. Churches featured prominently in the built environment in which the battle with fascism was enacted, and individual clergy took prominent roles in the active opposition to both fascists and fascist politics. The following section of this chapter explores the contribution of prominent Christians to the anti-fascist crusade and considers the role that their faith played in motivating such politics. This analysis is, because of the vagaries of source material, confined to the clergy of the Church of England.

I will begin with a discussion of John Groser, Vicar of Christ Church Watney Street in the East End, who is certainly the most famous Christian opponent of fascism. But he was not alone. Those clergy and laity involved in the formation and sustaining of the Council for Civil Liberties, whose first meeting took place in the basement of St Martins in the Fields in February 1934 can certainly be counted amongst the number of active Christian anti-fascists.[54] These included the peace activist Dick Sheppard (despite the obvious ambivalence of his relationship with Mosley) who had direct experience of fascist violence at Olympia and the Reverend Leonard Schiff who was addressing the crowd at an anti-fascist demonstration in Thurloe Square in March 1936 when they were charged by police.[55] There are other examples too, but Groser provides us with the opportunity for the most systematic analysis of Christian active opposition.

Groser, by necessity operated outside of the Anglican mainstream. He was a committed opponent of the monarchy, which was unsurprisingly an unusual position in the Church of England. He tolerated active communism in a way that few in his communion would allow. Indeed in the early part of his career he clashed with both his parish and his diocesan authorities over a set of political beliefs which included the claim that the Marxist view of religion as a constituent of the 'superstructure' was '90% just'.[56] This politics led him directly to involvement in local activism, from rent strikes committees in the 1930s to campaigning against racial prejudice in the 1950s.

Groser's activism began with involvement in the General Strike which left him with a permanent injury to his hand, sustained it appears in a clash with the police.[57] When Groser turned down the chance to be appointed a Missioner in the diocese of Hereford in 1928 he did so because it would have taken him away from this kind of political activism. 'I am known as a socialist of a very advanced type' Groser wrote to the Bishop of Hereford, 'I took a very active part in the General Strike and would do so again'. This commitment to activism was Groser argued not 'political in a narrow sense' but was part of his religious calling. He was he claimed simply 'following the lead of Jesus'.[58]

Groser's opposition to fascism was thus sustained and active. He spoke to counter fascist propaganda in his Watney Street parish and therefore directly confronted both Blackshirts and the police who sought to prevent him getting to them.[59] He marched ahead of anti-fascists demonstrations carrying the 'crucifix and other Christian symbols'.[60] When addressing either the local community, the fascists or the police it is clear that Groser attempted to articulate a distinctively Christian opposition to fascism. Ken Leech used the memory of Groser's activism in his criticism of churchmen in the 1970s who failed to actively oppose the growth of fascism in the National Front. Leech quoted at length an address that Groser made to a crowd in July of 1936, precisely because it articulated an eternal Christian opposition to the politics of fascism:

> Chief Inspector, we wanted our meeting at that corner, you made us come here instead. If we had called it here, you would have made us go there. It does not matter to us whether we are here or there, but it does matter to you that where we speak shall be a matter for your decision, not ours. Comrades, I am saying this in your hearing, because I want you to realise what is happening, you won't let it break your spirit and that is what matters most. They don't want you to feel that you are persons with the right to make decisions for yourselves. They want you to feel that you have no will of your own, for they are afraid of what will happen if you begin to act as persons. Don't let any of these things destroy your self-respect and the knowledge that each one of you matters because you are a child of God. If you lose that, you lose everything. If you retain that, one day you will win through, and people will treat you again as men and women who matter.[61]

Groser's language of opposition is typically Anglican – in that he emphasises the value of the individual as a child of God. His anti-fascism was also, it appears motivated by a commitment to Jewish-Christian relations, which was another feature of more mainstream Anglican critiques of fascism. Groser believed that the rent strikes that he led during the 1930s were a practical example of positive Jewish-Christian relations and co-operation.[62] Indeed Sir Israel Brodie, who was Chief Rabbi after 1948 and had been an associate of Groser's in the rent strikes of the 1930s agreed. Brodie described Groser as having 'embodied the characteristics of a saint'.[63]

Despite his atypicality, Groser's own narrative of anti-fascism was peculiarly Anglican too. His analysis of the disturbances at Cable Street evoked the image of Mosley's aliens attempting to invade the East End and cause 'rupture' between the peacefully coexistent population.[64] In his autobiography Groser explained that 'whatever his personal feelings the East Ender was not going to allow an outsider to exploit our internal difficulties for political advantage', and thus the population spontaneously united to expel the alien Mosley.[65] The British working man, Groser went on, 'instinctively distrusts dictatorship' while he personally rejected fascism because of its promotion of the state as a potential barrier between man and God.[66]

The only other extended Christian account of anti-fascist opposition that I have found comes from Leslie Allen Paul the teacher and journalist who founded the 'Woodcraft folk' and whose conversion to Christianity and particularly to the Anglican Church post-dated his involvement in the politics of repelling Mosley. Although raised as a Christian, Paul deserted his faith in the 1920s and only returned to the Church of England during the Second World War. Yet his involvement in anti-fascist activism involved the Church, he co-operated with a Reverend William Dick for example who was the Vicar of Trinity Church on the East India Dock Road. Paul used Church buildings to provide classes for men, in part to attempt to educate them away from fascist politics. Intriguingly Paul's account differs markedly from Groser's in some of its evaluations of fascism and the nature of its threat. Paul declares that fascism was a part of the political culture of the East End, thus the rejection of the Blackshirts was not about a community preventing the passage of an alien contagion but about fighting the cancer within. Perhaps Paul's memories were less subject to the overarching Anglican narrative of fascism because he was, at the point he was remembering at least, outside of the church.[67]

So what then is the role of Christianity, of faith in the activism of individuals like Groser and Paul? Although self-evidently a committed socialist, Groser was, in his own estimation, a Christian first and foremost. His socialism was a consequence of his Christianity, of his desire to follow the lead of Jesus Christ. Socialism was simply the 'application of the values of Christ' to the modern world.[68] According to David Platt, Groser's thought was 'completely integrated', 'what makes his thought remarkable is the total interdependence between theology and politics'.[69] As such there was no division in his mind between his socialism and his faith – Groser urged that all Christians agree with the 'essential Marxist position' which rejected a classless society.[70] Indeed he went so far as to argue that all working-class protest was Christian, even if its protagonists failed to understand that they were doing the work of Christ.[71] Leslie Allen Paul made a very similar claim, in that he found protest to be essentially Christian when the protagonists were themselves unbelievers.[72]

Groser's anti-fascism could, therefore, be argued, even when mediated through his political thought to be at root Christian and come from the well-spring of his Christianity. It was certainly, as has already been noted, phrased using a Christian semantic. Fascism underestimated the value of man, and denied that all were equal children of God accordingly, essentially in the same way that class-based suffering did.[73] According to Paul, the attempt to materially improve the lives of the poor, to reject the divisions promoted by the BUF were all part of a single Christian project – to achieve the redemption of the East End.[74]

However, it is clear that if Groser's anti-fascism was the result of his faith, of his Christianity then his interpretation of that faith was outside of the mainstream. Ultimately what led Groser to anti-fascist action, where his fellow Anglicans could only oppose fascism more ambiguously and became caught *between* fascism and anti-fascism, was his attitude to communism. Groser's anti-fascism required the rejection of the idea that Christians could be opposed to the twin totalitarian devils in equal measure, and indeed required the view that Marxism was, in essence, also a doctrine with fundamental Christian principles. Might it be then that Groser's anti-fascism was more *politically* determined? This is ultimately a judgement for theologians rather than historians, but when Groser marched against Mosley under the cross of Christ he did not do so because he was a Marxist.

Christianity and the language of fascism

Perhaps surprisingly however John Groser's opposition to fascism also flirted with a language which at times came close to fascist politics itself. The final section of this chapter briefly discusses this ambivalence, where the language of Christian anti-fascism used the very vocabulary of fascism itself . While Groser's anti-fascism was on the surface motivated by a commitment to Jewish-Christian co-operation, at times his attitudes to Judaism were mired in negative stereotypes. As Tom Linehan has observed Groser was more than prepared to perpetuate the idea that it was Jews that were responsible for exploiting local labour in Stepney during 1936, a charge which came close to those made by the Blackshirts.[75] Although in his memoir he denied that the rental problem was the result of exploitation by Jewish landlords, Groser's characterisation of the East End in the 1930s certainly implied that there was an objective problem regarding the role of Jews in the local economy.[76] Might the Christian role in the history of anti-fascism have been obscured by the essential ambivalence of this discourse?

As we have already seen there was a similarity between Anglican and Roman Catholic objections to fascism, as a force that threatened to obscure the relationship between the individual and God. However this similarity also reveals a further ambivalence, in that in the Anglican community it led to a reluctant support of non-intervention in the Spanish Civil War and in the Catholic community to ultimately whole-hearted support for Franco's nationalists. *The Tablet* declared on 1 May 1937, using precisely this formulation, that 'the fascism of Spain, resting on the age-old and ingrained individualism of the Spaniard will be something new in Europe'.[77]

Of course all Christian communities provided fellow travellers of fascism too. The original British fascists grouped around Nesta Webster used an unambiguous Christian semantic especially in *The Patriot*.[78] For all the objections to Mosley in the Christian press, both denominations had correspondents who were prepared to argue in favour of fascism, often using the kind of discourse that was also used in opposition – for example when a 'communicant of the Church of England' wrote to the *Tablet* that fascism sought to protect the relationship between the individual, church and God. Rev. Pierce-Butler wrote to the *Church Times* in January 1934 in order to correct the assertion that fascism was a necessary contradiction of Christianity because it encouraged the kind of self sacrifice that churches sought to inculcate.[79] Lincolnshire Vicar, H. E. B Nye would have agreed. He described fascism as 'the modern Saint George', the 'killer of the dragon of communism' and thus saviour of religion and civilisation.[80]

Although Tom Linehan has argued that the religiosity of the BUF, and its Christian supporters, was fundamentally different to that of the mainstream Churches because it was so 'this worldly', it is certainly possible to argue that such rhetoric came close to Anglican efforts to build a new Jerusalem.[81] The generation of Anglicans who rose to prominence in the inter-war period were committed to the transformation of society, to the social relevance of their faith. When one adds to this the pervasive sense of crisis within the 1930s Church of England, both in terms of its own role and the future direction of society and the role of religion within it, then it is not surprising that some Christians were drawn to fascist answers.

Towards the end of the 1930s the languages of particularly the Church of England and Mosleyite British fascism converged even further, with Mosley's conversion to peace campaigner. The Church of England's own attitudes to the prospect of war with Germany were although diverse, largely committed to peace at any cost throughout the 1930s. Amongst mainstream Anglicans the idea that most German action was justified by the criminal injustices of Versailles was prominent as it was in the peace community in general.[82] As such the basis of Christian opposition to Mosley became fundamentally more ambiguous as the reality of war approached. The Christian press could offer no critique of Mosley's peace rallies in the summer of 1939 because essentially they were offering the same arguments against war.

Ultimately the similarities between Anglican and fascist appraisals of the coming war with Germany revealed a similarity between certain aspects of the British Christian and British fascist world view. A similarity, of course, which also included a fear of communism. These overlaps ultimately would allow fascists and Christian anti-fascists to find common cause – especially in the aftermath of war. George Bell, who more than any other member of the Church of England was the author of the Anglican discourse of opposition against European fascism but also against the way in which war was fought, would for example, share a platform with General Fuller of the BUF in their opposition to trials of accused German war criminals in the later 1940s. Again this is not the place to consider this at length, however in large part it was because Fuller and Bell could both recognise the understanding of the world as a European civil war for the future in which communism was now the primary enemy. When European fascism disappeared then the Communists became the unambiguous enemy. For the Christian community we must remember it was a vision of the world caught in a struggle for the future between Christianity, fascism and communism that had defined their anti-fascism and its limits. Perhaps nothing symbolises more the extent of those limitations than Bell's post-war rapprochement with fascists and fascist ideals.

Conclusion

Ultimately then it is clear there was no single Christian anti-fascism. The two largest Christian communities did attempt to articulate a Christian opposition to fascist politics – although it is clear that the Church of England did this more successfully than the Roman Catholic Church. Yet at the same time both communities carried with them fellow travellers of the Right too. But it is not this that defined the ambivalence of both communities to anti-fascist action. Because Christian anti-fascism was so frequently anti-totalitarianism, it was difficult for Christians to find common cause with communism. Only those who could accommodate communism within their faith, most notably John Groser, seemed fully able to become active opponents of domestic fascism. Within the mainstream Christian anti-fascism seemed to attempt to steer a course between fascism and activism, and thus became caught between the two. Indeed such was the ambivalence of Christian anti-fascism that ultimately Christians and former fascists could find common cause in their opposition to communism. Yet Christian discourses do deserve a place in the historiography of anti-fascism. Indeed the shades of grey in which such a history must be painted should help nuance the very idea of anti-fascism itself.

Notes

1 Most notably Callum Brown, *Religion and Society in Twentieth-Century Britain* (London: Longman, 2006).

2 See for example Michael Burleigh, *Sacred Causes: Religion and Politics From the European Dictators to Al Qaeda* (London: HarperCollins, 2006).

3 See for example Thomas Linehan, 'The British Union of Fascists as a Totalitarian Movement and Political Religion', *Totalitarian Movements and Political Religions* 5, 3 (2004), 397–418; *idem*, 'On the Side of Christ: Fascist Clerics in 1930s Britain', *Totalitarian Movements and Political Religions* 8, 2 (2007), 287–301. See also Lydia Sheldon, 'Fascist Christians/Christian Fascists', BA Dissertation, University of Winchester, 2008. Thanks to Tom and to Lydia for providing me with some of the references that informed this chapter.

4 Brown, *Religion and Society in Twentieth Century Britain*, p. 124.

5 See David Renton, *Fascism, Anti-Fascism and Britain in the 1940s* (Basingstoke: Palgrave-Macmillan, 2000).

6 Tony Kushner, 'Long May its Memory Live! Writing and Re-Writing the Battle of Cable Street', in Tony Kushner & Nadia Valman (eds), *Fascism and Anti-Fascism in British Society* (London: Vallentine Mitchell, 2000), p. 123.

7 Cited in Nigel Copsey, *Anti-Fascism in Britain* (London: Macmillan, 2000), p. 19.

8 See for example 'The Struggle Against Fascism in the Thirties', *North East Labour History Society Bulletin* 17 (1983), 21–3.

9 Nigel Todd, *In Excited Times: The People Against the Blackshirts* (Whitley Bay: Bewick Press, 1995), p. 12.

10 Joe Jacobs, *Out of the Ghetto* (London: Phoenix Press, 1978), accessed on-line at http://libcom.org/library/battle-cable-st-1936-joe-jacobs

11 Emphasis added. Cited in Audrey Gillan, 'Day the East End said "No Pasaran" to Blackshirts', *The Guardian*, 30 September 2006.

12 See Simon Blumenfeld, 'The Battle of Cable Street', in Kushner & Valman (eds), *Fascism and Anti-Fascism*, p. 235.

13 Thomas P. Linehan, *East London for Mosley: The British Union of Fascists in East London and South-West Essex* (London: Frank Cass, 1996), pp. 27–8.

14 Martin Pugh, *Hurrah for the Blackshirts: Fascists and Fascism in Britain Between the Wars* (London: Johnathan Cape, 2006).

15 Adrian Hastings, *A History of English Christianity* (London: Collins, 1986), p. 314.

16 E. R. Norman, *Church and Society in England, 1770–1970: A Historical Study* (Oxford: Clarendon, 1976), p. 360.

17 Brown, *Religion and Society*, p. 135.

18 Copsey, *Anti-Fascism in Britain*, p. 4.
19 *Church Times*, 'Editorial', 19 January 1934.
20 *Church Times*, 16 February 1934.
21 See Tom Lawson, *The Church of England and the Holocaust* (Woodbridge: Boydell, 2006), pp. 31–80.
22 Copsey, *Anti-Fascism in Britain*, p. 42.
23 *Church Times*, 26 January 1934.
24 George Bell quoted in *The Guardian*, 11 September 1936; Bishop of Southwark in *The Guardian*, 23 October 1936.
25 *The Guardian*, 22 June 1934, *Church Times*, 22 June 1934.
26 *The Guardian*, 30 October 1936.
27 *Church Times*, 16 October 1936.
28 For details see Tom Lawson, 'Bishop Bell and the Trial of German War Criminals: A Moral History', *Kirchliche Zeitgeschichte/Contemporary Church History*, forthcoming.
29 *The Guardian*, 14 September 1934.
30 *Church Times*, 16 February 1934.
31 *Southwark Diocesan Gazette*, November 1936.
32 *Church Times*, 13 April 1934.
33 Bell, *Hansard* (HL), Vol. 154 (349), 3 March 1948.
34 Hensley Henson, *Retrospect of an Unimportant Life Vol. II* (Oxford: Oxford University Press, 1944), p. 330.
35 *Church Times*, 22 June 1934.
36 *The Guardian*, 15 June 1934.
37 *Church Times*, 16 October 1936.
38 *The Guardian*, 9 October 1936.
39 *The Guardian*, 8 October 1937.
40 *Church Times*, 8 October 1937.
41 Kushner, 'Long May its Memory Live!', p. 117.
42 Tom Buchanan, *Britain and the Spanish Civil War* (Cambridge: Cambridge University Press, 1997), p. 173.
43 *Church Times*, 2 October 1936.
44 Hastings, *History of English Christianity*, p. 324.
45 Buchanan, *Britain and the Spanish Civil War*, p. 180.
46 Linehan, *East London for Mosley*, p. 85.
47 Brown, *Religion and Society in Twentieth-Century Britain*, p. 150.
48 Thanks to Sue O'Brien for some of the references in this section of the chapter.
49 See exchange of letters *The Tablet*, 12 January and 19 January 1935.
50 Editors Note, *The Tablet*, 19 January 1935.
51 *The Tablet*, 16 June 1934.
52 *The Tablet*, 16 June 1934.
53 *The Tablet*, 26 May 1934.
54 Sylvia Scaffardi, *Fire Under the Carpet: Working for Civil Liberties in the Thirties* (London: Lawrence and Wishart, 1986), p. 43.
55 Scaffardi, *Fire Under the Carpet*, p. 127.
56 *Watford Observer*, 20 October 1934 – this extract can be found in the Groser Papers, [L]ambeth [P]alace [L]ibrary, MS3562, f.90.
57 Jim Desormeaux, 'Poplar Days', in Kenneth Brill (ed.), *John Groser: East London Priest* (Oxford: Mowbrays, 1971), pp. 35–6.

58 LPL: Groser Papers, MS3562, f. 59.

59 Scaffardi, *Fire Under the Carpet*, p. 140.

60 Groser, *Politics and Persons*, p. 38.

61 Kenneth Leech, *Struggle in Babylon: Racism in the Cities and the Churches of Britain* (London: SPCK, 1988), p. 96.

62 LPL: Groser Papers, MS3772, ff. 409–11.

63 Kenneth Brill, 'The World his Parish', Brill (ed.), *John Groser*, p. 102.

64 LPL: Groser Papers, MS3772, ff. 409–11.

65 John Groser, *Politics and Persons* (London: SCM Press, 1949), p. 54.

66 Groser, *Politics and Persons*, pp. 100, 136.

67 See Paul, *Angry Young Man*, p. 232.

68 Groser, *Politics and Persons*, p. 28.

69 David Platt, 'Socialist Because Christian', Brill (ed.), *John Groser*, p. 160.

70 Groser, 'On Communism', talk given to the 1933 World Student Christian Federation, LPL: Groser Papers, MS3562, ff 194–201.

71 Groser, *Politics and Persons*, p. 75.

72 Paul, *Angry Young Man*, p. 222.

73 Groser, *Politics and Persons*, p. 167.

74 Paul, *Angry Young Man*, p. 222.

75 Linehan, *East London for Mosley*, p. 80.

76 Groser, *Politics and Persons*, pp. 54, 72.

77 Buchanan, *Britain and the Spanish Civil War*, p. 186.

78 Tom Linehan, *British Fascism 1918–39: Parties, Ideology and Culture* (Manchester: Manchester University Press, 2000), p. 156.

79 *Church Times*, 26 January 1934.

80 H. E. B. Nye (ed.), 'Fascism versus Democracy', Erminio Turcottie (ed.), *Fascist Europe: Europa Fascista* (Milano, 1939), p. 79.

81 Linehan, 'The British Union of Fascists as a Totalitarian Movement', p. 414.

82 See for example *Church Times*, 29 October 1937. For a discussion of Anglican attitudes to war see Lawson, *The Church of England and the Holocaust*, pp. 55–80.

6

'It certainly isn't cricket!'[1] – Media Responses to Mosley and the BUF

Janet Dack

Introduction

The response of the mainstream press to British fascism has attracted little analysis and there is no definitive assessment of the extent to which the British media could be described as anti-fascist. The response of the British mainstream media to fascism was complex and varied, and for some elements of the media there was a dichotomy in their attitudes to fascism that makes the categorisation of their stance in terms of anti-fascism problematic. This was particularly noticeable in the Tory press where the expression of tolerance for, and in the popular press admiration for, the fascist regimes in Italy and Germany were initially commonplace. Even when these papers began to voice their opposition to Mosley and the BUF their criticism did not necessarily extend to other forms of fascism, though criticism of the policies of the Nazi regime became increasingly frequent as the 1930s progressed. It is beyond the remit of this chapter to discuss the response to Continental fascism, which will concentrate on the mainstream media's reaction to the BUF. The expression of opposition to British fascism came in three distinct forms: firstly, the dismissal or ridicule of the organisations and individuals concerned; secondly, the provision of a platform for those articulating anti-fascist opinions; and, thirdly, the encouragement of the confrontation of fascism and the advocation of a popular front against it. Only in the case of the *News Chronicle* can all three forms be found.

During the inter-war period there were three major sources of news and opinion: the press, BBC radio broadcasts, and cinema newsreels. The newspapers consulted during the course of this chapter can be classified in a variety of ways. Here they will be grouped in terms of both their political leanings and the size of their readership. During the 1930s the *Times*, the *Daily Telegraph*, the *Daily Express*, the *Daily Mail*, and, at the beginning of the decade, the *Daily Mirror* were allied to the Conservative Party, though they often took issue with it on matters of policy. The *Manchester Guardian* and the *News Chronicle* espoused Liberal principles, while the Labour Party/Trades Union Congress had control of the *Daily Herald*. The popular press, including the *Daily Express*, the *Daily Herald*, the *Daily Mail*, and the *Daily Mirror*, were mass circulation papers. In the early 1930s the *Daily Express* and the *Daily Herald* each had more than two million readers. The circulation of the *Daily Mail* (1.6 million) and the *Daily Mirror* (800,000), both owned by Lord Rothermere, was falling, yet after Rothermere relinquished control of the *Daily Mirror*, it implemented a successful long-term strategy to attract working-class readers and during the mid-1930s sales improved, reaching 1.5 million by 1939. The quality press, papers such as the *Times* (187,000), the *Daily Telegraph* (200,000), the *Observer* (201,000), the *Manchester Guardian* (45,000), and to a lesser extent, *News Chronicle* (1.4 million), had a smaller circulation but carried more political weight than the popular press. Their editors were more independent and suffered less interference from their proprietors than tended to be the case among the popular press. Many of the editors of the quality papers had close ties with members of the establishment and the Government, for example, Geoffrey Dawson, the editor of the *Times*, was a close friend of Lord Halifax, a confidante of Neville Chamberlain and, along with H. A. Gwyne, of the *Morning Post* and J. L. Garvin of the *Observer*, encouraged and supported Chamberlain's policy of appeasement.[2]

Often the reports and editorials referred to in this chapter do not have a by-line, and due to the constraints of time and space the chapter will generally concentrate on giving a reflection of the voice of the paper concerned rather than that of its individual contributors. However, there are some significant instances where the views being expressed are clearly stated as being those of an individual, rather than the paper, or where they depart noticeably from the paper's usual stance, that warrant particular attention.

When considering the mainstream media, academic attention has concentrated on the support given to the BUF by the Rothermere press during the period January to July 1934.[3] The element of the historiography most relevant to this chapter is the debate between Martin Pugh and Jon Lawrence, concerning their differing interpretations of the significance of Olympia.[4] Although the main focus of their analysis is the response of the Conservative Party, they both consider the reaction of the mainstream press in the lead up to and the aftermath of Mosley's meeting at Olympia in June 1934. Pugh maintains that Olympia was not a propaganda disaster for the BUF as it attracted more press attention thereafter, and reports in the Tory press were not hostile. On the other hand, Lawrence argues that revulsion at fascist violence at Olympia alienated the Conservative press and political opinion and was a significant factor in the failure of British fascism. Of the two, Lawrence's reading of the Conservative press sources is more convincing, though his assessment of the *News Chronical* is questionable. Pugh offers a more cursory survey of press attitudes. Pugh points out that following Rothermere's withdrawal of support the *Daily Mail*, the *Times*, and the *Daily Telegraph* continued to report Mosley's speeches, and the *News Chronicle*, the *Daily Express*, the *Manchester Guardian*, and the *Daily Herald* were hostile to the BUF.[5] This is a very broad-brush approach, not entirely consistent with his earlier analysis, and appears to categorise the papers as either covertly for or openly against the BUF.[6] Pugh's division of the press into two camps suggests that the reporting of BUF meetings provided encouragement to the fascist cause. This chapter challenges that approach and, for the first time, clearly differentiates the range of stances taken by individual newspapers.[7] By examining the degree to which reporting of the BUF was influenced by an anti-fascist perspective, and considering what shaped that perspective, it is possible to assess the extent to which mainstream reporting of the BUF constituted a variety of anti-fascism.

From the founding of the BUF to Olympia: A minor excitement

Initially, the response of the mainstream media to Mosley and the BUF was not hostile. This was consistent with attitudes to fascism in Italy and Germany during the early 1930s. The mainstream press generally regarded both with a degree of complacency, despite reservations regarding the methods used to suppress opposition.[8] The popular press appeared particularly approving when commenting on Hitler and Mussolini.[9] Despite the expressions of tolerance, and in some cases enthusiasm, for fascism outside of Britain there was a distinct lack of interest in the home-grown variety. From the beginning fascist organisations in Britain had rarely attracted press attention, and the occasional reports of their activities were not supportive. The British Fascists were widely regarded as insignificant, and the more extreme National Fascisti, despite being described by the *Manchester Guardian* as 'Dangerous Play-Boys', were also seen as being of no consequence.[10] Apart from the trial of Arnold Leese for seditious libel in 1936, the Imperial Fascist League was only mentioned in the mainstream press when they caused a disturbance, for example, when they courted controversy by flying a union flag embellished with a swastika from prominent buildings or when their meetings were disrupted.[11] Disappointingly, from Mosley's point of view, reports in the mainstream press of the BUF's early meetings were similar in tone to reports of other fascist organisations in Britain and, while the BUF generated more coverage than the others, it was not generally encouraging.

Mosley had been a figure of interest to the press for some time before the founding of the BUF and he provided a touch of glamour that earlier manifestations of British fascism lacked. Indeed, Julie Gottlieb has described him as the 'Rudolph Valentino of Fascism'.[12] He was the youngest member of the House when he was first elected as a Conservative MP. His wife was a noted society heiress, and their joint defection to the Labour Party fuelled many column inches in the national press. His decision to leave the Labour Party and set up the New Party, also attracted press interest, though this was not as enthusiastic as he had hoped. The founding of the BUF roused little interest in the mainstream press and the emphasis was often on Mosley's 'society' life rather than his political ambitions.[13] A portrait photograph of Mosley, seated at his desk, published in the *Sketch*, was typical of his representation in the popular press. Mosley was described as 'looking the complete British Fascist', but there was no mention of the BUF's policies or activities.[14]

The indifference shown by the British press is more marked when compared with coverage from the USA. In part this was a continuation of American society's fascination with Mosley as an international political and sporting figure, whose allure was heightened by his marriage to the granddaughter of the American millionaire Levi Zeigler Leiter. The US press interest in Mosley's fascist activities reflected a significant interest in the growth of fascism in Europe. Some articles, while not recommending Mosley's policies, lauded what was seen as his success in attracting growing numbers of young men into the BUF.[15] However, opinion was divided and whilst the *Washington Post* declared that Mosley was no longer a political joke, the *New York Times* averred that he was.[16]

A notable exception to the general indifference shown by the British press to Mosley's political aspirations was an article by G. Ward Price in the *Daily Mail*, which appeared immediately prior to the official launch of the BUF in October 1932 and coincided with the publication of

Mosley's book *The Greater Britain*. Ward Price, an admirer of Mussolini and Hitler, praised Mosley's courage and ability, promoted *The Greater Britain*, and agreed with Mosley's claim that fascism was a 'world-wide modern creed'.[17]

According to Nicholas Mosley, press reports of his father's speeches during the first six months of the BUF's existence concentrated on the presence of Mosley's family, references to Jews and incidents of violence.[18] There is ample evidence to endorse this reading of press reaction to the launch of the BUF.[19] As the mainstream press viewed British fascism as part of the political margins, it was rare for Mosley to find mainstream papers willing to publish his propaganda. Seizing one such opportunity, offered by the *Daily Mirror*, Mosley complained that the ideology and philosophy of the BUF were dismissed or ignored while trivial incidents of violence were misrepresented as fascist brutality. Although aggrieved at the lack of press interest in the BUF's political programme, Mosley was adamant that the BUF neither needed nor desired the 'hothouse of a sudden and artificial publicity'.[20] All this was to change when the Rothermere press swung its considerable weight behind the 'Blackshirts' in January 1934.

Pugh has suggested that Rothermere's support for the 'Blackshirts' was based not on any appreciation of the virtues of fascism, but on a desire to use the movement to pressure the Conservative Party into adopting policies more in line with Rothermere's own views.[21] Comparison of reports of BUF meetings from the *Daily Mail* and the *Blackshirt* supports this argument. Coverage in the *Daily Mail* focused on issues dear to Rothermere's heart, particularly the Empire. *Blackshirt* reports of the same meetings said little about the Empire and concentrated on Mosley's ability to hold an audience, local issues and the failures of the 'old gang'. In keeping with the fascist tendency to deification of the leader, other speakers were given less coverage in the *Blackshirt* and what was reported generally bore little resemblance to what appeared in the *Daily Mail*. A clear example of this vastly different perspective can be seen in the reports of a speech given by William Joyce at Chiswick on 18 January 1934. For the *Daily Mail* the most significant aspect of Joyce's speech was his condemnation of the Government's India White Paper proposals. Also prominent was an expression of gratitude for the support of Rothermere and his 'influential papers'. There was no reference to Hitler or Germany.[22] The *Blackshirt*, on the other hand, reported Joyce as giving a brief history of the growth of fascism, describing developments in Germany, and explaining that Hitler was not a tyrant. Class unity, a condemnation of the system of party politics, and the need for rearmament were the other issues reported.[23] From the way that his papers represented the Blackshirts, it is clear that Rothermere had a limited understanding of the fascist agenda and that he did not fully endorse its revolutionary potential.

The support of the Rothermere papers, particularly that of the *Daily Mail*, led to a rapid increase in membership of the BUF and forced other British papers to take note. It also attracted increased press interest further afield, with articles on Mosley and the BUF appearing in US papers such as the *Los Angeles Times*, the *Wall Street Journal*, the *Christian Science Monitor*, and the *Hartford Courant*, in addition to those already mentioned.[24] Coverage included interviews with Mosley; articles reporting the rapid growth of the BUF, with some describing growing concern in Britain at the potential threat to democracy; reports of disorder, arrests, and court cases; and editorials concerned at the international impact of the spread of fascism.[25] The *Hartford Courant* and the *Christian Science Monitor* both regarded the British Labour movement as likely to provide the most effective block to Mosley's prospects.[26] However, despite several expressions of concern, the overall tone was one of detached interest.

In Britain the reaction to Rothermere's announcement and the consequent surge in BUF membership was more pronounced. Although the *Daily Express* and the *Daily Mirror* shared the *Daily Mail*'s generally positive attitude to the Continental dictators, the popular press was divided in its response to the rapidly increasing presence of the BUF. Rothermere and Beaverbrook continued to cooperate on campaigns to save the British Empire and to defeat the perceived threat of the Coops, but Beaverbrook did not share Rothermere's enthusiasm for the Blackshirts. In the *Daily Express*, Beaverbrook was quick to defend democratic principles as essential to the continuation of the Empire.[27] He also allowed Tom Driberg who penned the 'William Hickey' column 'These Names Make News', an unusual degree of latitude in his attacks on Mosley.[28] Apart from reporting occasional court cases, the *Daily Express* ignored the BUF's activities, advising its readers not to worry about 'Shirts' as if it became necessary to save the country it would be decided, as previously, by 'grown-up citizens ... through legitimately elected representatives'.[29] In the *Evening Standard*, Beaverbrook gave the cartoonist David Low free reign to produce a number of cartoons that highlighted Mosley's arrogance and the Blackshirts' brutality.[30]

Another major element of the popular press, the *Daily Mirror*, had a tendency to blow hot and cold when it came to the Blackshirts. The reports of court proceedings in cases such as the tithe dispute, the castor oil allegations, and charges of violence were couched in the neutral tones adopted by the rest of the mainstream press.[31] However, in January 1934 the *Daily Mirror* reprinted an appeal by Rothermere for recruits for the Blackshirts that had originally been published in the *Sunday Pictorial*.[32] Subsequent coverage did not reflect the patriotic, disciplined and tolerant movement that Rothermere had described. On occasion the *Mirror*'s reports treated Mosley's meetings as a spectacle and were full of colourful details, but failed to mention the content of the speeches.[33] Other reports concentrated solely on the BUF's policy.[34] While some reports took a light-hearted tone, others suggested a darker side to the BUF.[35]

Uniquely, among the mainstream popular press, the *Daily Herald* concentrated its energies on opposing Continental fascism. This was consistent with Labour Party policy, which was predicated on an understanding of fascism that correlated the rise of fascism with the growth of communism, and saw violent confrontation as counter-productive. With only a couple of notable exceptions, the *Daily Herald* did not actively campaign against British varieties of fascism and urged readers to avoid confrontation with the BUF.[36] One exception was the printing of Oliver Baldwin's fierce rejection of fascism on behalf of British youth during which he savaged Rothermere's arguments for supporting the Blackshirts.[37] There was also an editorial pointing out the fallacy of Rothermere's claim that the BUF was not anti-semitic.[38] Hannen Swaffer, the *Daily Herald*'s gossip columnist, frequently mocked Mosley and the Blackshirts and was threatened by fascists who objected to his column.[39] Interestingly, Lawrence notes that, prior to Olympia, the Communist Party's response to British fascism was very similar in practice to that of the Labour Party, viewing fascism as a Continental problem. Like much of the mainstream media the *Daily Worker*'s attitude towards the BUF swung between indifference and ridicule. However, in the days before the Olympia meeting readers were encouraged to take a more confrontational approach.[40]

The quality Conservative papers, the *Times* and the *Daily Telegraph*, remained largely unimpressed. They did not trouble their readers with polemics for or against the movement, although the *Times* reminded its readers that while the electorate required constructive action this should not be misconstrued as a desire for dictatorship.[41] Both the *Times* and the *Daily Telegraph* continued to report incidents of violence, Mosley's court cases and other occurrences involving the police or the courts.[42] The reporting of Mosley's speeches should not be taken as giving tacit support, for example, the *Times* recorded that the people of Birmingham were uninspired by Mosley's creed of action.[43] Other speeches were reported in a more neutral manner.[44]

Surprisingly, although they would prove to be the most dedicatedly anti-fascist of all the mainstream press, some of the liberal papers were initially more accommodating. The *Observer* justified publishing an article on the BUF on the grounds of the movement's rapid growth and Rothermere's support. Mosley was described as a sincere speaker who argued his case well, though the *Observer* passed no judgement on the merits of that argument.[45] The *Observer* also gave publicity to the creation of a BUF branch in Berlin, and to a speech by Mosley in which he attacked Conservative leaders who criticised the 'British Blackshirts as foreign imports while they worshipped at the shrine of an Italian Jew'.[46]

It was the *News Chronicle* that campaigned most strongly against fascism, yet prior to Rothermere's involvement some of its articles appeared to flirt with the ideology and the leaders of fascism. Disparagement of the National Government and of Parliament was frequent. A. J. Cummings was critical of the ineffectiveness of both the Government and the Opposition and claimed that there were 'no young politicians in any party with a glimmer of promise'.[47] A week later Cummings developed this theme, claiming that young men in Britain 'have gone flabby' and that generally speaking the British Parliament was 'a collection of nonentities' incapable of challenging the 'old gang'. The only politician Cummings saw as having any potential was Oswald Mosley.[48] The tone of reports relating to fascist activities appears to have been one of amused tolerance, for example, descriptions of athletic or picturesque young men giving fascist salutes, but unable to answer questions.[49] However, the *News Chronicle*'s editor, Aylmer Vallance, made clear his personal political stance: 'Against fascism in this country I would fight to my last breath.'[50]

Following Rothermere's announcement of support for the Blackshirts the *News Chronicle* began to take a more robust attitude to British fascism. The next day, while maintaining that the British electorate would not be 'seduced from their faith in democracy' by dubious promises of 'Action' and 'discipline', its editorial cautioned that, with Rothermere promoting the possibility of a continental style dictatorship, 'farce takes on a more sinister complexion'.[51] The paper also printed the views of politicians, trade union leaders and other public figures opposed to fascism.[52] The *News Chronicle* continued to ridicule Rothermere's enthusiasm for the Blackshirts, while acknowledging Mosley as a more serious concern, albeit one that was unlikely to develop into a

serious threat to democracy.[53] Reports of Mosley's speeches concentrated on expressions of dissent from the crowd and Mosley's
plans to ensure a fascist government had complete power of action,
untrammelled by parliamentary procedure.[54]

From the beginning, the *Manchester Guardian* regarded the BUF as a
paper tiger and Mosley as a pinchbeck candidate for dictatorship.[55] Its
attitude to Mosley was clearly expressed; it did not matter what Mosley
said or where he said it.[56] The paper was scornful of Rothermere's
promotion of the BUF, referring to his previous ill-fated political
ventures.[57] Reports of Mosley's speeches were neutral in tone, but
headlines highlighted disorder and violence and large audiences were
attributed to contingents of Blackshirts from outside the local area.[58]
Opportunities to mock were regularly taken advantage of.[59]

Although Rothermere's support had gained the BUF increased press
coverage it is evident from its content that, except for Rothermere's
own papers, particularly the *Daily Mail* and the *Sunday Dispatch*, the
British mainstream press regarded Mosley and the BUF as little more
than a sideshow, of no real political significance. However, the BUF
meeting at Olympia in June 1934 and the subsequent public reaction,
coupled with growing distaste at developments in Germany, upped the
political stakes.

Post Olympia: Confrontation or dismissal?

In his earlier article Pugh recognised the variety and complexity of
press responses to the violence at Olympia, and there is considerable
common ground between his evaluation of the Rothermere and
Beaverbrook papers and that of Lawrence.[60] However, some elements
of his analysis are open to a different interpretation. His assessment of
the Rothermere press from initial enthusiasm to polite disengagement
fits well with the available evidence, as do his conclusions as to the
reasons for Rothermere's withdrawal of support, but his suggestion that as
the *Daily Mail* continued to report Mosley's speeches it was simply not
promoting the BUF as blatantly as before could be more convincing.[61] As
part of their coverage of current events, most of the mainstream press
continued, intermittently, to report Mosley's speeches. This cannot be
construed as even covertly promoting the BUF. However, the *Daily Mail*,
without ever mentioning the BUF, continued to criticise the Government
for talking instead of taking action and on one occasion, in relation to
increased aeroplane construction, demanded: 'When will the country discover some leader or organised party that will see things as they really

are?'[62] Readers would possibly be aware that the BUF shared the *Daily Mail*'s belief that the British Air Force needed to be greatly expanded.

From the start the Rothermere press had reported clashes between fascists and anti-fascists as a Manichean struggle between fascism and communism, and this pattern continued throughout the 1930s. In October 1936 the *Daily Mail*'s headline over a report of the Battle of Cable Street read 'REDS ATTACK BLACKSHIRTS – Girls Among Injured.'[63] The report of Mosley's 'consultation' with Sir Philip Game, the Commissioner of Police, suggests that Mosley was a party to the decision to cancel the march.[64] Throughout the report, anti-fascists are referred to as 'Communists'. Similarly, in October 1937, following disorder in Bermondsey during the BUF's fifth anniversary march the *Daily Mail* report referred to 'Reds' and 'Communists' and claimed that many of those who clashed with police appeared to be foreigners of 'swarthy complexion, some wearing clothes of obviously foreign origin'.[65]

Although Rothermere had publicly distanced himself from the BUF in July 1934 he continued to meet Mosley socially, and as late as June 1939 he hosted a dinner party at which Mosley was encouraged to speak about how a national leader is found.[66] Nor did he cut all his political links to Mosley.[67] Rothermere used Ward Price as a conduit between Mosley and himself, and also introduced his protégée and confidante, Collin Brooks, to Mosley. Brooks kept in touch with Mosley and BUF officials, and his journal shows that in March 1938 he met Mosley for lunch to discuss the future of British fascism, during the course of which Mosley complained that nobody would report his meetings.[68] This was untrue, but his meetings were not reported as often as he thought they should be, possibly because the same issues were addressed at different locations and the speeches would have appeared repetitive to readers.

Pugh's assessment of the position of the Beaverbrook press is largely consistent with the evidence. The reports relating to Olympia and the subsequent debate were complete, factual and neutral in tone.[69] The lack of any editorial comment was in keeping with the previously expressed advice that those wearing coloured shirts, of any hue, were not a serious concern. However, he neglects to mention that Low, in the *Evening Standard*, continued to produce anti-fascist cartoons, the most telling of which, *The Other Test Match*, showed a cricket pitch on which a heavily outnumbered team dressed in whites was being brutally assaulted by Blackshirts while Mosley looked on, giving the fascist salute. A John Bull figure in the stands exclaims: 'I don't know what you think you're playing at, young man, but it certainly isn't cricket!'[70]

Following the Battle of Cable Street the *Daily Express* praised the police and reiterated its commitment to democracy.[71] A week later it reported a largely peaceful march by communists and the attack of Jewish shops and passers-by by a 'gang of hooligans' shouting pro-Mosley slogans.[72] The editorial column criticised 'Redshirt-Blackshirt tomfoolery' for diverting police resources every Sunday afternoon.[73] The *Daily Express* reacted in similar fashion to the riots in Bermondsey a year later, claiming that communist opposition to Mosley's fascists generated publicity for the fascists and incurred heavy police costs.[74]

Unfortunately, the *Daily Mirror* does not figure in the analysis of either Pugh or Lawrence. Its reports of the Olympia meeting are sketchy and vaguely pro-Blackshirt. There is little mention of violence. Unlike most other mainstream papers the *Daily Mirror*, when reporting the Home Secretary's response to events, concentrated on alleged communist violence.[75] The paper continued to report Mosley's speeches and there was no editorial comment on either Olympia or the ending of Rothermere's support for the BUF.[76] Reports of meetings included photographs of a smiling Mosley, huge crowds, and female fascist marchers.[77] The tenor of the paper's response to Mosley and the Blackshirts swung between factual reporting and presenting a slightly exotic and possibly dangerous entertainment. In March 1935, as part of a series entitled 'If I was Dictator', the *Mirror* published an article by Mosley setting out the issues he regarded as needing prompt action. It advised readers to: 'Decide if you like him, because you can't be sure you won't have to.'[78] By 1936 the *Daily Mirror* was less inclined to drape all Mosley's opponents in the red flag, reports of disorder in the East End and in Bermondsey were phrased in terms of 'fascist' and 'anti-fascist' – there were no references to 'Reds' or 'Communists'.[79] The only editorial comment followed Mosley's injury in Liverpool; readers were advised to avoid violence, which could create martyrs, and recommended to: 'Kill by silence and absence.'[80]

Both Pugh and Lawrence pay scant attention to the *Daily Herald*, grouping it with the Liberal press. Pugh argues that Olympia merely confirmed the left-wing press in their hostility to the BUF, while Lawrence concludes that although the *Daily Herald* was surprisingly even-handed in its initial reports, like other left-wing papers, it took advantage of the controversy to mount an anti-fascist propaganda campaign. Certainly, post Olympia, reports of BUF meetings and court cases in the *Daily Herald* were more frequent, and concentrated on the hostility of the crowds, the Blackshirts' need for police protection, and violence allegedly committed by fascists.[81] However, editorial comment, again in line with Labour Party policy, advised readers to keep away from fascist meetings and marches, as aggressive opposition generated more publicity and sympathy for fascism.[82] Following the Battle of Cable Street the *Daily Herald's* leader writer argued that while the fascists had no chance of success they provoked disorder and it was the duty of the Government to 'rid the country of this menace to the King's peace'.[83] After the violence in Bermondsey and Mosley's injury in Liverpool the editorial column stressed again that using physical violence to fight fascism advertised fascism and allowed Mosley to appeal to public sympathy.[84]

Pugh provides only a brief assessment of the Liberal press' response to Olympia, though he does note the strong anti-Blackshirt bias in the *News Chronicle* report of the meeting. In contrast, Lawrence sees little difference in the coverage provided by the left-wing papers and, surprisingly, describes the *News Chronicle* as adopting a low-key approach. While there is some similarity between the line taken by the *Manchester Guardian* following Olympia and that of the *Daily Herald*, there were distinct differences in the tone of reports and in the editorial attitudes of the other liberal papers. An *Observer* editorial, while critical of 'organised attempts' to disrupt meetings, also firmly rejected 'the Nazi technique' and 'the Nazi temper'.[85] A week later the *Observer* reported a speech by Herbert Morrison in which he dismissed Mosley and the BUF on the grounds that the British public would not be fooled by 'spotlight, film star swank'.[86] There was no editorial comment on Rothermere's decision to part-company with Mosley. The paper remained opposed to fascism, although its claim that the people of the East End were not hostile to BUF meetings suggests a limited perception of the East End's population.[87] As the 1930s progressed the *Observer* expressed concern that Mosley's anti-semitic tactics would lead to serious consequences in the East End.[88]

The *Manchester Guardian* did cover the disturbances at Olympia, but its initial reports were reluctant to apportion blame.[89] The following day, however, the leader column criticised Mosley's methods.[90] A week later concern was expressed regarding the BUF's semi-military character and there was also support for the Government's decision to consult the leaders of the major political parties regarding fascist disorder.[91] The paper applauded Rothermere's reasons for breaking with Mosley, but pointed to inconsistencies in his argument and criticised his judgment in attempting to turn the BUF into a Tory 'ginger group'.[92] Reports of BUF meetings continued to focus on disorder and violence, although some did include details of Mosley's speeches or policies.[93] In the days prior to the Battle of Cable Street the *Manchester Guardian's* London correspondent noted an increasing sense of tension as preparations to oppose the march were made.[94] There was no editorial enthusiasm for resistance, and reports of the disturbances were low-key.[95] The leader column praised the police action and stressed that ignoring Mosley's meetings and marches was more effective than disrupting them.[96] However, the report of the disturbances in Bermondsey, a year later, conceded that forcing a change of route represented a moral victory for Mosley's more militant opponents.[97]

The *News Chronicle* remained steadfast in its opposition to fascism, and was by far the most anti-fascist of the mainstream publications. The paper's leader-writers took every opportunity to remind readers that the British did not require or desire Continental methods of government.[98] The paper's coverage was not totally one sided: it did report attacks on fascists.[99] However, its reporting of the Olympia meeting was notably different from other papers surveyed, it was clearly anti-fascist, and there was no mention of 'Communists'. Instead the Special Correspondent praised the interrupters, who 'showed both courage and resource'. Mosley's big meeting 'had been killed dead by the carefully organised demonstration of English men and women who hate Fascism and all its works'.[100] The following day's editorial was forthright in its condemnation of the brutality, and rejected Mosley's assertion that the Blackshirt Defence Force was needed to secure free speech in Britain.[101] Following Olympia, the *News Chronicle*'s attitude to the BUF hardened and by the end of the month the delegation of TUC and Labour Party representatives to Sir John Gilmour was said by their industrial correspondent to have carried the 'fight against Fascist terrorism' to the Home Office.[102]

References to acts of fascist terrorism increased in the aftermath of the Battle of Cable Street.[103] So concerned was the *News Chronicle*, that it published calls by James Maxton, and by A. A. H. Findlay, chairman of the TUC, for a popular front against fascism.[104] The leader column was also used to urge a popular front. Fascism was not perceived as a present threat to democracy but had the potential to develop into one if left unchecked.[105] However, by October 1937 the *News Chronicle* was more sanguine and argued that the best way to defeat Mosley was to ignore him as violent opposition garnered publicity and, if they were injured, public sympathy for the fascists.[106]

Pugh's analysis of the quality press concluded that Olympia had a positive result for the BUF as afterwards their meetings were more frequently reported. He also claims that the *Daily Telegraph*'s reporting of the event was sympathetic to the Blackshirts; this is strongly disputed by Lawrence who maintains that the *Daily Telegraph*'s stance was unequivocally anti-

BUF.[107] The evidence supports Lawrence's interpretation. The report published by the *Daily Telegraph* was a neutral, factual account of the meeting, interruptions and ejections. It is not surprising that, being a Tory paper, it also reported the disturbances prior to the meeting and attributed them to communists, nor is it an indication of sympathy for the Blackshirts. That the report of the meeting was immediately followed by eyewitness testimony of Blackshirt violence suggests that the paper was not predisposed to the fascist cause.[108] For the *Daily Telegraph* fascism was as much to be deplored as communism and in an editorial the paper insisted that 'British political tradition must combine without thought of party to fight the spirit of the new violence from whichever side it comes'.[109] Only days later another editorial stressed that there was no doubt that the use of reasonable force had been gravely exceeded at Olympia and encouraged the Government to suppress any attempt to usurp Government functions, such as the preservation of order.[110] The *Daily Telegraph* continued to provide its readers with factual reports of disturbances, including the Battle of Cable Street in 1936 and the barricading of streets in Bermondsey in 1937.[111]

Pugh and Lawrence agree that the *Times* continued to adopt a lofty, almost supercilious, tone in its editorial comment on Olympia, though Pugh does not pay enough regard to the editorial's content which stressed that there was no place for fascism in Britain.[112] Additionally, Pugh's argument that in defending the principle of free speech the paper had softened its attitude to the Blackshirts is not convincing.[113] Like the *Daily Telegraph*, the *Times* regarded both fascism and communism as undesirable. Following the Battle of Cable Street the *Times* described the activities of both fascists and communists as 'a tedious and rather pitiable burlesque'.[114] The increased level of public violence was said to be a public nuisance that required Government intervention, 'without violating the traditional canons of British Liberty'.[115] As far as the *Times* was concerned the only place for the Blackshirt was in Madame Tussaud's.[116]

That the Olympia debacle had not benefited the BUF is further illustrated by the reaction of the BBC. Previously Mosley had taken part in a radio debate on fascism, and immediately after Olympia he had been given the opportunity to defend the actions of the BUF.[117] There were also plans for him to take part in a series of broadcasts on constitutional issues. However, following debates on the violence at Olympia in Parliament and in the press, these were shelved and Mosley would not take part in a BBC radio broadcast again until 1968.[118] Francis Hawkins did attempt to get Mosley included in a series of debates in 1939, but the BBC declined on the grounds that the debates were restricted to MPs from the main political parties.[119] Later that year Mosley protested at what he called 'silly lies' broadcast internationally by the BBC that included suggestions that the BUF was less successful than the Communist Party and that they were holding fewer meetings than previously.[120]

In contrast to the souring of relations with the BBC there was little change in the way that cinema newsreels reported BUF activity. Although the BUF had claimed that Jewish pressure had resulted in film of their meetings being cut from cinema programmes, reports continued in a neutral and detached style, and, as can be seen from footage shot in 1936 during the Battle of Cable Street, did not imply any criticism of Mosley and the BUF.[121] The US press also retained its interest in Mosley, but was dismissive of his political significance. He was regarded as being dogmatic and bombastic, opposed by the majority of the British people, more of a nuisance than a threat, and only newsworthy because of the opposition he generated.[122]

Conclusion: A variety of anti-fascism?

Although the mainstream press continued to print factual reports of BUF meetings, editorial comments were generally critical of the BUF and its methods. Mosley and the BUF frequently complained that the mainstream press was against them and there were repeated allegations that the press was under Jewish influence.[123] Despite the BUF's assertions of conspiracy, Britain's mainstream press did not present a united front against fascism, each paper had a slightly different stance, and there were different gradations of anti-fascism. Broadly speaking, the quality press was opposed to Mosley and the BUF and was the most clearly anti-fascist. For some papers, particularly the *Daily Telegraph*, and the *Times*, participating in a popular front against fascism, as advocated by the *News Chronicle* at the height of its anti-fascist campaign, would have given British fascism a prominence it did not deserve and might also have had implications for Britain's foreign affairs. If papers known to be closely allied to the Government's political aims had actively pursued an anti-fascist agenda it would have made Britain's already fraught diplomatic relations with Italy and Germany even more difficult. Certainly, those advocating a popular front did not suggest the inclusion of the Conservatives.[124] The Tory papers regarded the BUF with disdain, seeing it as a nuisance rather than a threat, and had no objection to fascism as a Continental phenomenon. The government of other countries was seen as no concern of Britain's, unless they posed a threat to international stability.[125] The response of the Tory press to events such as Italy's invasion of Abyssinia, the persecution of Jews and other minority groups in Germany, the annexation of Austria, and the invasion of Czechoslovakia show that, although some Tory papers expressed regret, they were all opposed to any confrontation with the fascist regimes. Despite this tolerance of fascism beyond the Channel, its imposition in Britain was implacably opposed. The liberal papers perceived the fascist movement as more of a threat and were correspondingly more vocal in their opposition, with the *News Chronicle* being the most outspoken in this regard. Their antifascism was more ideologically based and extended to Continental varieties. The *Daily Herald* shared this opposition to fascism in all its forms, but, for tactical reasons, as Nigel Copsey's chapter in this volume shows, was less vocal in its opposition to the British variety.

The popular press, with its tendency to embrace new trends, gimmicks and 'stunts' was more receptive to the novelty of fascism. However, the *Daily Express* regarded British fascism as a potential, though unlikely, threat to the Empire and, while against it in principle, generally ignored it. The *Daily Mirror*, while not promoting fascism, could not, initially, be regarded as anti-fascist and was opposed to 'fronts' in Britain.[126] However, by 1937 its opposition was clear and the paper can be counted amongst those anti-fascist papers that regarded violent opposition as counter productive. Only the Rothermere press actively promoted fascism for a short period, an error of judgement based on Rothermere's misreading of the situation and his misunderstanding of fascism's revolutionary nature. It was not long before economic and political realities encouraged Rothermere to direct his papers to take a more neutral stance, although this did not extend to any criticism of, or opposition to, the BUF. The political violence and increasing antisemitism of the BUF appeared to mimic the European fascist movements and, as the 1930s drew to a close, this, coupled with the growing political tension in Europe, ensured that the British mainstream press, including the *Daily Mail*, put aside any earlier misgivings regarding the efficacy of the parliamentary system and reinforced the message that there was no place in the mainstream social or political spectrum for British fascism. While it would be overstating the case to describe this as a 'united' or 'popular' front against fascism it could be seen as a *de facto* front for British democracy that contained distinct strands of anti-fascism within it.

Notes

1   David Low, 'The Other Test Match', *Evening Standard* 13 June 1934.
2   James Curran & Jean Seaton, *Power Without Responsibility* (Glasgow: Fontana, 1981), pp. 55, 82–4; Sally J. Taylor, *The Great Outsiders: Northcliffe, Rothermere and The Daily Mail* (London: Weidenfeld & Nicolson, 1996), pp. 140, 227, 285 & 313–14; Paul W. Doerr, *British Foreign Policy 1919–1939* (Manchester: Manchester University Press, 1998), p. 151; Lord Burnham, *Peterborough Court: The Story of the Daily Telegraph* (London: Cassell & Company Ltd, 1955), p. 178; John Evelyn Wrench, *Geoffrey Dawson and Our Times* (London: Hutchinson, 1955), p. 373.
3   Thomas Linehan, *British Fascism 1918–39* (Manchester: Manchester University Press, 2000), pp. 98, 160 & 187; Martin Pugh, *Hurrah for the Blackshirts* (London: Jonathon Cape, 2005), pp. 149–50 & 167–9; Richard Thurlow, *Fascism in Britain* (London: I. B. Tauris, 1998), pp. 69 & 72.
4   Jon Lawrence, 'Fascist Violence and the Politics of Public Order in Inter-War Britain: The Olympia Debate Revisited', *Historical Research* 76, 192 (May 2003), 232–67; *idem* 'Why Olympia mattered', *Historical Research* 78, 200 (May 2005), 263–72; Martin Pugh, 'The British Union of Fascists and the Olympia Debate', *The Historical Journal* xli (1998), 592–642; *idem* 'The National Government, the British Union of Fascists and the Olympia Debate', *Historical Research* 78, 200 (May 2005), 253–62.
5   Pugh, *Hurrah for the Blackshirts*, p. 169.
6   Pugh, 'The British Union of Fascists and the Olympia Debate', pp. 534–8.
7   All the British newspapers referred to in this chapter are held in the British Library Newspaper Collection at Colindale, or are available online from the following digital archives: The *Times* Digital Archive, 1785–1985 at http://www.gale.cengage.com/DigitalCollections/products/Times/; the *Daily Mirror* Digital Archive at http://www.arcitext.com/arcitext/index.html; the *Guardian* Digital Archive at http://archive.guardian.co.uk. The US newspapers are from the ProQuest Historical Newspapers Digital Archive at http://www.proquest.com.
8   For examples relating to fascist Italy see: *Observer* 19 May 1929; *Manchester Guardian* 20 May 1930 & 21 May 1930; *Times* 15 March 1933; & *Daily Telegraph* 18 March 1933. For Nazi Germany see: *Times* 31 January 1933; 3 February 1933; 17 February 1933; *Observer* 23 July 1933; & *Manchester Guardian* 19 September 1933.
9   For examples see: *Daily Express* 3 May 1932; 6 June 1932; 17 July 1932; 25 February 1933; 11 April 1933; 3 May 1933; & 26 April 1934. *Daily Mail* 3 August 1934; 6 August 1934; 7 August 1934; & 20 August 1934.
10 *Manchester Guardian* 15 June 1925; & 31 July 1925. Other examples can be found at *Manchester Guardian* 27 April 1925; 25 May 1925; 29 July 1925; 12 October 1927; & *Times* 16 June 1925; 1 September 1925; 24 April 1926; & 1 March 1934.
11 *Manchester Guardian* 7 November 1931; 15 September 1936; & 19 September 1936. *Times* 25 November 1933; 27 November 1933; 15 August 1936; 22 August 1936; & 19 September 1936. *Daily Mirror* 8 June 1932; 7 November 1932; 19 October 1933; 25 November 1933; 25 May 1934; 22 September 1936; & 7 April 1937.

12 Julie V. Gottlieb, 'Britain's New Fascist Men: The Aestheticization of Brutality in British Fascist Propaganda', in Julie Gottlieb and Thomas Linehan (eds), *The Culture of Fascism* (London: I. B. Tauris, 2004), p. 85.

13 Examples include reports of Mosley's fencing prowess and speeches unrelated to the BUF. *Times* 14 November 1932; 5 December 1932; & 8 December 1932. *Daily Mirror* 11 February 1933. The Mosleys also continued to feature in gossip and 'Court & Society' pages. *Times* 21 December 1932. *Daily Mirror* 21 December 1932; 29 December 1932 & 26 January 1933. Cynthia Mosley generated a substantial amount of positive press coverage and her final illness and untimely death were treated with great sympathy. *Daily Express* 15 May 1933; & May 1933.

14 *Sketch* 11 January 1933.

15 *Chicago Daily Tribune* 6 November 1932; 3 April 1933; *Washington Post* 15 May 1933; & *New York Times* 26 November 1933.

16 *Washington Post* 17 June 1933; & *New York Times* 22 October 1933.

17 *Daily Mail* 30 September 1932. S. J. Taylor describes Price as a close friend of Mosley, see Taylor *The Great Outsiders: Northcliffe, Rothermere and The Daily Mail*, p. 281.

18 See Nicholas Mosley, *Rules of the Game/Beyond the Pale* (London: Pimlico, 1998), pp. 230, 233, 275.

19 For examples see, *Times* 25 October 1932. *Daily Mirror* 13 March 1933.

20 *Daily Mirror* 25 August 1933.

21 Pugh, *Hurrah for the Blackshirts*, pp. 48 & 168.

22 *Daily Mail* 19 January 1934.

23 *Blackshirt* 26 January–1 February 1934.

24 *Harford Courant* 15 January 1934; 17 January 1934; 24 April 1934; & 20 May 1934. *Wall Street Journal* 16 January 1934. *Los Angeles Times* 1 February 1934. *Christian Science Monitor* 7 February 1934; 21 April 1934; & 26 April 1934.

25 For examples see *New York Times* 24 April 1934; 18 February 1934; 21 February 1934; & 24 June 1934. *Christian Science Monitor* 7 February 1934; 19 February 1934; & 21 April 1934. *Chicago Daily Tribune* 18 February 1934; 25 February 1934; 23 April 1934; & 13 May 1934.

26 *Hartford Courant*, 24 April 1934; & *Christian Science Monitor* 26 April 1934.

27 *Daily Express* 17 January 1934.

28 Anne Chisholm and Michael Davie, *Lord Beaverbrook a life* (New York: Alfred A Knopf, 1992), p. 366.

29 *Daily Express* 22 February 1934. See also 13 March 1934 for similar editorial comments. For examples of reports of court cases see 3 March 1934; 12 March 1934; & 15 March.

30 See the British Cartoon Archive at http://opal.ukc.ac.uk/cartoonx-cgi/ccc.py.

31 *Daily Mirror* 3 March 1934; 27 March 1934.

32 *Daily Mirror* 22 January 1934.

33 *Daily Mirror* 23 April 1934.

34 *Daily Mirror* 13 July 1934.

35 The gossip column treated with levity the possibility of a Blackshirt candidate in the North Hammersmith by-election and a Blackshirt wedding was reported as an interesting oddity. *Daily Mirror* 8 March 1934; 15 March

1934. News that the BUF had taken delivery of six armoured vans produced a bustle of activity by the *Daily Mirror*, including interviews with the manufacturer of the vehicles and other experts. Details were sent to Scotland Yard. The tone of the report implied that the vans were possibly illegal, and if they were not, then they should be. *Daily Mirror* 9 January 1934.

36　See Nigel Copsey's chapter in this volume for an outline of the rationale underpinning the Labour Party's policy.

37　*Daily Herald* 17 January 1934, p. 8. Oliver Baldwin had been a supporter of Mosley's New Party, see Pugh, *Hurrah for the Blackshirts*, p. 118.

38　*Daily Herald* 25 January 1934.

39　*Daily Herald* 1 January 1934; 20 January 1934; & 25 January 1934. For an example of fascist response to Swaffer see *Blackshirt*, 11–17 November 1933.

40　Lawrence, 'Fascist Violence', p. 25.

41　*Times* 19 January 1934. See also editorial 26 January 1934, that refers to Mosley and Cripps as 'germs of an infection that may easily spread if not immediately suppressed'.

42　*Daily Telegraph* 19 February 1934. *Times* 7 April 1934; 20 January 1934.

43　*Times* 22 January 1934.

44　*Times* 7 February 1934; 9 April 1934; & 23 April 1934.

45　*Observer* 21 January 1934.

46　*Observer* 28 January 1934; & 13 May 1934. See also, *Times*, 14 May 1934.

47　*News Chronicle* 2 January 1934.

48　*News Chronicle* 9 January 1934.

49　*News Chronicle* 11 January 1934.

50　*News Chronicle* 11 January 1934.

51　*News Chronicle* 16 January 1934. On the same page, A. J. Cummings 'Political Peep-Show' also refers to the 'singularly unattractive phenomenon' offered by Rothermere.

52　*News Chronicle* 17 January 1934; & 18 January 1934. Letters from readers opposed to Rothermere's espousement of fascism were also printed, see 18 January 1934.

53　*News Chronicle* 23 January 1934; & 27 January 1934.

54　*News Chronicle* 22 January 1934.

55　*Manchester Guardian* 30 September 1932; & 14 March 1933.

56　*Manchester Guardian* 27 April 1933.

57　*Manchester Guardian* 16 January 1934. See also 18 January 1934, which compares Rothermere unfavourably to Beaverbrook.

58　*Manchester Guardian* 22 January 1934; 19 March 1934; 9 April 1934; 16 April 1934; 23 April 1934; & 27 April 1934. For court cases relating to BUF members see, 21 February 1934; 27 February 1934; 3 March 1934; 15 March 1934; 27 March 1934; & 10 April 1934.

59　*Manchester Guardian* 23 January 1934; 25 January 1934; 10 April 1934; 9 June 1934; & 13 June 1934. The satirical magazine *Punch* also found Mosley an easy target, see *Punch* 2 November 1932; & 27 December 1933.

60　Pugh, 'The British Union of Fascists and the Olympia Debate', pp. 534–8.

61　*Ibid.*, pp. 535–6.

62　*Daily Mail* 24 July 1934.

63 *Daily Mail* 5 October 1936.
64 *Daily Mail* 5 October 1936; Reports in other papers shows this was not the case, see *Daily Mirror*, 5 October 1936; *Daily Telegraph* 5 October 1936; *News Chronicle* 9 October 1936; *Daily Express* 4 October 1937; *Manchester Guardian* 5 October 1936; & *Times* 5 October 1936.
65 *Daily Mail* 4 October 1937.
66 N. J. Crowson (ed.), *Fleet Street, Press Barons and Politics The Journals of Collin Brooks* (Cambridge: Press Syndicate of the University of Cambridge, 1998), p. 250.
67 Stephen Dorril, *Blackshirt: Sir Oswald Mosley and British Fascism* (London: Viking, 2006), p. 329.
68 Dorril, *Blackshirt*, pp. 353, 397, & 431. Crowson, pp. 81, 122–3, 190, 199–200, & 234–5.
69 *Daily Express* 8 June 1934; 9 June 1934; & 12 June 1934.
70 *Evening Standard* 13 June 1934.
71 *Daily Express* 5 October 1936.
72 *Daily Express* 12 October 1936.
73 *Daily Express* 12 October 1936.
74 *Daily Express* 4 October 1937.
75 *Daily Mirror* 15 June 1934.
76 *Daily Mirror* 13 June 1934; & 13 July 1934.
77 *Daily Mirror* 10 September 1934.
78 *Daily Mirror* 11 March 1935.
79 *Daily Mirror* 5 October 1936; & 4 October 1937.
80 *Daily Mirror* 13 October 1937.
81 Except for the fascists, the reports do not mention the political or religious affiliations of those involve in fighting. *Daily Herald* 12 June 1934; 15 June 1934; 18 June 1924; 22 June 1934; 28 June 1934; 29 June 1934; 13 July 1934; & 19 July 1934.
82 *Daily Herald* 1 October 1936; & 11 October 1937.
83 *Daily Herald* 15 October 1936.
84 *Daily Herald* 11 October 1937.
85 *Observer* 17 June 1934. The same issue also included a report of Stanley Baldwin's description of Fascism as 'ultramontane Conservatism'; pushing the tenets of Conservatism to their limits and combining them with an alien, Continental desire 'to suppress opposition and to proceed by dictatorial methods'.
86 *Observer* 24 June 1934.
87 *Observer* 4 October 1936.
88 *Observer* 18 October 1936. The paper's special correspondent was a little too ready to accept the reasoning that one cause of Mosley's anti-semitism was the Jews' suspicion of the BUF.
89 *Manchester Guardian* 8 June 1934.
90 *Manchester Guardian* 9 June 1934.
91 *Manchester Guardian* 15 June 1934.
92 *Manchester Guardian* 20 July 1934.
93 *Manchester Guardian* 11 June 1934; 15 June 1934; 22 June 1934; 23 June 1934; 28 June 1934; 12 July 1934; 13 July 1934; 21 July 1934; & 30 July 1934.

94   *Manchester Guardian* 3 October 1936.
95   *Manchester Guardian* 5 October 1936.
96   *Manchester Guardian* 5 October 1936.
97   *Manchester Guardian* 4 October 1937.
98   *News Chronicle* 4 June 1934; & 6 June 1934. A. J. Cummings also continued to nip at Rothermere's heels, suggesting, just before the meeting at Olympia, that his Lordship 'could easily be frightened out of his support of the Blackshirts if he thought the game would not pay'. *News Chronicle* 5 June 1934.
99   *News Chronicle* 4 June 1934; 11 June 1934. There is no condemnation of those hostile to the fascists, and the merest hint of satisfaction in the tenor of the report describing fascists having to seek the protection of park-keepers and the police.
100 *News Chronicle* 8 June 1934.
101 *News Chronicle* 9 June 1934.
102 *News Chronicle* 21 June 1934. Readers' accounts of violence at Olympia appeared under the headline 'BLACKSHIRT TERRORISM' see 12 June 1934.
103 *News Chronicle* 9 October 1936; 12 October 1936, & 17 October 1936.
104 *News Chronicle* 8 September 1936.
105 *News Chronicle* 12 September 1936.
106 *News Chronicle* 12 October 1937.
107 Pugh, 'British Union of Fascists', p. 537. See also Pugh, 'The National Government', p. 256.
108 *Daily Telegraph* 8 June 1934. Further eyewitness accounts were published on 9 June 1934; & 11 June 1934.
109 *Daily Telegraph* 12 June 1934. The previous day's editorial had made clear that there was no room in Britain for 'Private Armies'.
110 *Daily Telegraph* 15 June 1934.
111 *Daily Telegraph* 5 October 1936; & 4 October 1937.
112 *Times* 8 June 1934.
113 Pugh, 'British Union of Fascists', pp. 537–8. See also Pugh, 'The National Government', p. 256.
114 *Times* 5 October 1936. See also 8 October 1936.
115 *Times* 12 November 1936.
116 *Times* 12 November 1936.
117 *Manchester Guardian* 16 March 1933; & 9 June 1934.
118 *Manchester Guardian* 15 March 1933; & 16 March 1933. *News Chronicle* 9 June 1934. See also Robert Skidelsky, *Oswald Mosley* (London: Macmillan, 1990, 3ʳᵈ edn), pp. 370–1.
119 *Manchester Guardian* 17 February 1939; & 21 February 1939.
120 *Manchester Guardian* 22 July 1939.
121 *Blackshirt* 4–10 November 1933.
122 *Los Angeles Times* 7 August 1937; 5 October 1937. *Washington Post* 9 October 1937. *New York Times* 17 October 1937.
123 *Blackshirt* May 1933; 16 June 1933; 4–10 November 1933; 2 November 1934; & 5 October 1934. *Action* 12 December 1936; 6 March 1936; 19 March 1936; 2 April 1936; & 9 April 1936.
124 A *News Chronicle* editorial had proposed an alliance between the Liberal Party and the Labour Party in a popular front against fascism. *News*

Chronicle 12 September 1936. Others, including Findlay, Maxton and Eleanor Rathbone had called for a broader based common front encompassing the ILP, the Labour Party, the Liberals and the Communists. *Manchester Guardian* 4 August 1936; 8 September 1936; & 5 November 1936. *News Chronicle* 8 September 1936.

125   *Times* 20 February 1933; & 22 March 1933.
126   *Daily Mirror* 24 September 1936.

7
Passive and Active Anti-Fascism: The State and National Security, 1923–45

Richard Thurlow

Introduction

This chapter will argue that although there were significant divisions within the state on how British fascism should be managed, the preferred formal and informal methods of control can basically be described as a passive form of anti-fascism. While the threatened invasion and imagined 'fifth column' crisis of 1940 marks a significant turning point between passive (political surveillance and tinkering with common law) and active (internment and proscription) state anti-fascism, the reversion to less draconian methods after the emergency suggests that the authorities were concerned, as with the Communist Party of Great Britain (CP or CPGB), not to drive alleged political extremism underground.[1] While the sledgehammer response was understandable in the context of 1940, and although some plausible evidence was later discovered about actual or potential treasonable behaviour by a miniscule minority of British fascists (e.g. William Joyce), the British Union of Fascists (BUF) maintained its opposition to the war within the law. Although Mosley's refusal to play the rules of the political game eventually led him to go beyond the pale, thus making his political behaviour unacceptable to most Conservative and Labour politicians in the inter-war period, there was a more complex response to international fascism. Many right-wing politicians, including Winston Churchill, saw Mussolini's foreign policy as not threatening British interests in the 1920s, and although his domestic policies were perceived as undesirable, they at least brought stability and social peace to Italy. Similarly, during the 1930s most of the Conservative Party was more concerned about appeasing rather than opposing Hitler. While Labour was vehemently anti-fascist and anti-Nazi, for much of the 1930s it supported policies that prevented a coherent or effective military response to aggression, given the failure of the League of Nations and Collective Security to check German or Italian expansionism.

In domestic politics there was near consensus within the parliamentary political spectrum that held the BUF as primarily responsible for the threats to civil liberties and public order, and the growth of political anti-semitism in the East End of London during the 1930s.[2] Other fascist organisations, such as the British Fascists, National Fascisti, British Empire Fascists, or the Imperial Fascist League, were mainly seen, in so far as they were considered at all, as crackpot organisations viewed with derision or contempt by most politicians after 1926.

Passive anti-fascism differed from active forms in that its function was to isolate and marginalise the BUF through denying it the oxygen of publicity and to control its behaviour through changes in the law, rather than confrontation on the streets. A wide spectrum of opinion viewed Mosley, in personal and political terms as a 'cad and a wrong un' (Stanley Baldwin).[3] Most of the police authorities wanted the BUF banned and the Metropolitan Police Commissioners argued that Mosley deliberately threatened public order by provoking anti-fascists and the Jewish community.[4] Only when the problem threatened to get out of control after the Olympia demonstration (7 June, 1934) and the Battle of Cable Street (4 October, 1936) was marginal tinkering with the law allowed after the passing of the Public Order Act in December 1936, which was to apply to all political groups not just the BUF.[5] The Home Office argued that unless Mosley challenged the law, which he was very careful not to transgress, the maximum degree of civil liberty should be allowed to enable the BUF to put their case, that was mainly falling on deaf ears anyway, outside limited regional enclaves, such as the East End of London. This policy was advocated even after the outbreak of war in 1939.

It took the collapse of much of Western Europe following the Nazi blitzkrieg in 1940 for the resistance of the Home Office to stronger measures to change. Until then, the fear of driving the fascists underground, or turning them into martyrs, outweighed the political nuisance and the potential threat to national security that the BUF represented.[6] This led to a move from a policy of political surveillance to one of *agent provocateur* tactics by the Security Service, and to some alleged dubious behaviour by Special Branch and MI5 agents. As I have written previously on public order and civil liberties with relation to British fascism and anti-fascism, this chapter will concentrate on passive anti-fascism and national security issues.

British fascism and the secret agencies of government in the inter-war period

Although the rise to power of Mussolini in Italy in 1922 made little impact on British domestic politics and in Whitehall, it proved to have some significance for the secret agencies of government. This related to the bitter 'turf wars' between the various secret agencies, the draconian cuts in public expenditure after the First World War, the replacement of the 'Hun' by the 'Beastly Bolshevik' as the main threat to national security, and the outsourcing of agent penetration of alleged extremist movements to right-wing private detective agencies.[7] In 1931 two years after the discovery of Soviet moles in Special Branch, who had compromised British civil security policy for much of the 1920s, MI5 was made the lead agency in the newly formed Security Service. Whereas the police authorities were mainly concerned with public order, secret policemen monitored the threat to public security.[8] This implied political surveillance of organisations deemed subversive by the authorities, or to have primary allegiance to a foreign power. In the inter-war period this meant the CPGB and the BUF. This also involved security aspects of the work of SIS and the Government Code and Cypher School (GCCS).

As MI5 had no executive powers, such as the ability to arrest suspects or the preparation of the case for trial, these measures were delegated to Special Branch (SB), usually disguised as 'Scotland Yard'. In fact there was considerable scope for both cooperation and conflict between the relevant security agencies, a situation exacerbated by the severe under-funding of the intelligence and security communities during the inter-war years.[9] Resource constraints had significant consequences for British security. This affected both the quality and quantity of personnel in MI5. The number of officers was pruned back to a skeleton staff, with never more than 30 officers during the inter-war period. As a result HUMINT (human intelligence) was mainly outsourced to private detective agencies, which organised agent running, in the 1920s. Officers were expected to live primarily off a private income or military or service pension and were recruited through personal recommendation rather than by advertisement. This tended to reinforce the right-wing prejudices and preconceptions of the leadership, the conservatism of tradecraft, and the tunnel vision and conspiratorial mindset, primarily with Comintern and the CPGB.[10]

In spite of these limitations some of the pre-war professionals, such as Guy Liddell, T. A. Robertson, Dick White and Roger Hollis proved to be significant appointments. Recruited in the 1930s they avoided the administrative failings and unimaginative approach to counter-intelligence of the Director (1909–40), Vernon Kell, his deputy since 1912, Eric Holt Wilson, and the head of B division O. A. 'Jasper' Harker.[11] Maxwell Knight, the head of the agent running B5b (later M section), a key figure in the evolution of MI5 and the move from 'collusion' to passive and active anti-fascism straddled both groups, being imbued with many of the administrative and political prejudices of the Kell generation, but also with more advanced views on tradecraft and agent running. In the 1920s Maxwell Knight was the most significant figure in the private detective agencies, becoming the Director of Intelligence in the British Fascists (BF), a key organiser in the Industrial Intelligence Board (IIB) agent network, and an associate of the anti-semitic con-spiracy theorist, Nesta Webster, who introduced him to both Kell and Desmond Morton (SIS). He was also connected to the more dubious counter-intelligence tradition of the *agent provocateur*. Knight was a close associate of James Mcguirk Hughes, and was involved in anti-communist baiting and burglary organised by him in the 1920s.[12]

A sizable third group was drafted in from the business and academic professions during the Second World War. These included such gifted amateur security officers as John Masterman, Victor Rothschild and the Soviet Intelligence agent, Anthony Blunt. Unlike the relations of Hugh Trevor-Roper with his superior officers in Section V of SIS, the pre-war professionals and wartime recruits in MI5 developed a successful anti-Nazi and anti-fascist counter-intelligence strategy, under Guy Liddell.[13]

Passive anti-fascism began when the BUF was placed under political surveillance in November 1933.[14] After satisfying themselves that the activities of the BUF did not pose a significant threat to the British constitution MI5 concern diminished in December 1936 after eight reports, and surveillance was downgraded to SB sources, relating mainly to public order problems. Kell, after consultation with the Home Office, did not target the Nazi party in London, which was limited to somewhat desultory SB investigations of its activities.[15] Before 1938 Knight was not given the resources to target HUMINT agents at Anglo-German friend-ship organisations. It was perhaps fortunate that Hitler reciprocated such lack of interest in possible Nazi permeation of British society. In fact the best counter-intelligence information on Nazism derived from Sir Robert Vansittart's private detective agency and his sources in Ribbentrop's German embassy, particularly Wolfgang zu Putlitz and the ex-press officer, Jona 'Klop' Ustinov, recruited by Dick White to become MI5 agent 'U 35'. He was the father of Sir Peter Ustinov.[16]

MI5 obsession with communism meant the Security Service was ill prepared for the Second World War. By 1939 there was only one officer investigating the BUF and when over 750 British fascists were interned no personal files, which had to be hurriedly concocted. Anti-fascism in the 1930s was perceived primarily as a CPGB front. Counter-intelligence against Nazi Germany in the 1930s was in an even worse state. In September 1939 MI5, like SIS, did not even know the name of the principal German intelligence organisation, the Abwehr, nor its chief, Admiral Wilhelm Canaris.[17]

'Collusion' in the 1920s

The interest of the Security Services in the radical Right after the First World War had nothing to do with the threat to national security or public order posed by British fascism. It was seen instead as a cheap source of information about the activities of Comintern and the CPGB, on the principle that the enemy of our enemy is our friend. Although SB and MI5 rapidly became sceptical of much of the information they received, there was sufficient unease posed by labour unrest and mass unemployment to maintain indirect surveillance of 'subversives'. These concerns proved a mixed blessing producing much alarmist intelligence from dubious confidence tricksters and right-wing citizens with vivid imaginations. This represented what John Hope has called 'collusion' between state and independent security agencies.[18]

Patriotic middle-class groups were organised by the ex-Director of Naval Intelligence and Unionist MP, Sir Reginald 'Blinker' Hall, to establish a network collated by 'National Propaganda'. This provided a conduit for intelligence on Comintern and the CPGB, collected by organisations such as the British Empire Union (BEU) and the BF to pass to the authorities. The Industrial Intelligence Board (IIB), organised by Sir George Makgill until his death in 1926, the Federation of Liverpool Ship owners, notably Sir Vincent Caillard of Cunard, and the Economic League run by John Baker White in the 1930s, had links to either MI5, SB, the Supply and Transport Organisation, BEU or BF.[19] Through some of these groups, the most dynamic of these operatives, Maxwell Knight and James Mcguirk Hughes, were placed on the payroll of the security services. Knight, a key figure in the IIB and BF, was recruited by Desmond Morton for SIS in 1929, and transferred to MI5 in the 1931 reorganisation.[20] The operational head of SB, Colonel J. F. Carter employed the private intelligence agent and most active infiltrator and *agent provocateur*, Hughes, as an anti-communist source in the 1920s, and he was to become the main informant, using the pseudonym 'Captain P. G. Taylor', as a salaried official of the BUF, in charge of Labour policy and intelligence and security operations.[21] In the 1920s, however, MI5 were suspicious of Hughes methods, and his alleged inability to be trusted with secret information. He was criticised as the 'biggest windbag in Asia'.[22]

'Collusion' was not a smooth process. Necessitated by the effect of draconian financial cuts it was exacerbated by 'turf wars' amongst the intelligence and security agencies. Gill Bennett argued that SIS became highly critical of SB management of civil security, and the second 'C', Sir Hugh 'Quex' Sinclair, began a sustained campaign after 1923 to unify British intelligence and security under his leadership.[23] After this failed, he created the new counter-intelligence section V in 1925 led by Valentine Vivian, and the head of Production, Desmond Morton, made independent arrangements to monitor domestic subversion in Great Britain, despite the agreement that SIS should operate only outside territorial waters and the British Empire. Morton subcontracted this out in 1929 to Maxwell Knight and his 'casuals', a network of up to 100 national and international sources.[24]

The belief that SIS was using agents in Britain infuriated Carter and he stopped cooperating with SSI, the liaison section with SIS based at Scotland House. This forced the intervention of the Secret Service Committee in 1931. SB, however, had been weakened in 1929 by the discovery that two of its most highly regarded officers, Inspector Hubert Ginhoven and Sergeant Charles Jane, had acted as Soviet moles since at least 1922, thus given the former access to the Registry, compromising civil security throughout the 1920s. Ginhoven and Jane were dismissed, but not prosecuted.[25] The creation of the Security Service in 1931 increased efficiency and reduced costs as a response to financial crisis. The responsibility for civil security was transferred from SB to MI5.[26] Although the scandal was quietly buried the Secret Service Committee re-organised British counter-intelligence in the aftermath of the bitter dispute over Maxwell Knight and the leakage from Scotland Yard.[27] The research sections at Scotland House, SS1, including Guy Liddell, the link between SB and SIS, and SS2, which monitored domestic subversion, together with their records were also moved to MI5. Guy Liddell told Sir Findlater Stewart, the head of the Security Executive in 1945, he was moved to MI5 in 1931 because Sir John Anderson had finally ruled that SB should be denied access to the Registry following the espionage of Ginhoven and Jane.[28] The Secret Service Committee placed much of the blame for the ongoing feud between SS1 and SB/SS2, and SIS and SB on Carter.[29]

Passive to active anti-fascism, 1933–40

The creation of the Security Service in 1931 and the political surveil-lance of the BUF in the 1930s led to new perceptions. The MI5 reports on the BUF mainly reflected the information, most of it vague, col-lected by Chief Constables and SB and forwarded to Kell, and a synthesis of media reports.[30] There were some secret sources but con-clusions drawn from them were guarded. MI5 perceived the BUF, not inaccurately, as a volatile and contradictory mix of right-wing Con-servatives, and revolutionary nationalists to whom Mosley inclined. MI5 was interested in the size and nature of the membership, the attempts to influence the establishment and the armed forces, its res-ponsibility for provoking political violence and anti-semitism, and its links with foreign movements, particularly Fascist Italy and Nazi Germany.[31] This included both the influence of ideology, propaganda, style and finance, and whether members could be seen as agents of a foreign power. Hence the need for political surveillance, but resource limitations, advice from the Home Office and the perceived failure of the BUF in the 1930s meant the 'red menace' and the activities of the CPGB were always given a much higher priority.

During the second half of the 1930s there was a slow drift to a more aggressive form of passive anti-fascism. This had nothing to do with any sympathy for the anti-fascist movement, rather the reverse. As far as the Security Service was concerned the danger of British fascism was that it encouraged the growth of a much larger anti-fascist movement under the alleged influence and control of Comintern/CPGB, as demon-strated by the Olympia demonstration on 7 June 1934 and the Battle of Cable Street on 4 October 1936.[32] The deterioration in international rela-tions with the fascist powers after 1934 was closely followed by changes in the behaviour of the BUF according to the Security Service. MI5 noted the failure of Mosley and the BUF to criticise any of the actions of Hitler, Mussolini or Franco during the 1930s. Mosley became the British cheer-leader in support of Mussolini's invasion of Ethiopia in 1935–36 in the 'Mind Britain's Business' campaign. The change of name to become the 'British Union of Fascists and National Socialists' in April 1936 and the development of political anti-semitism, particularly in the East End of London in 1935–36, was perceived, whatever Mosley might say, as evid-ence of increased Italian Fascist or German Nazi influence on the ideas and behaviour of the BUF. When the movement was re-branded as British Union in 1937, this was interpreted as the perceived failure of the imitation of Continental fascism.[33]

The declassified Home Office and MI5 files from the 1930s show that despite the circumstantial evidence, few of these suspicions could be proved. The authorities were aware that the BUF survived in the 1930s largely as a consequence of the overseas funding of Mussolini, and possibly the Nazis, but neither MI5 nor SIS could provide much more than anecdotal evidence from many of the ex-officials who had fallen out with Mosley. It was not until the Second World War that more substantial proof was provided with the testimony of a solicitor, Cecil Lewis, the discovery by SB of a secret bank account and the laundering of £220,000 in foreign currencies at a BUF bank account in the Westminster bank at Charing Cross.[34] Some of the labyrinthine complexity of these arrangements was explained, together with an interesting account of Mosley's attempts to finance the BUF by wireless advertising revenue, including a deal with Hitler to build him a transmitter, by W. E. D. Allen in two interviews with MI5 in 1942.[35] Stephen Dorril has also discovered interesting sources, including Goebbels diaries, which suggests a degree of Nazi funding as well.[36] The 'Mussolini monies' were highlighted when James Chuter Ede, the Labour Home Secretary read out excerpts, to much laughter, from Italian foreign office files to the House of Commons in 1946.[37]

The patchy nature of contemporary evidence about BUF secret activities in the 1930s suggests that the political surveillance of the BUF was not considered a priority between 1936 and the collapse of the Munich agreement in the spring of 1939. We do not know much about the details of MI5 agent running under Maxwell Knight with regard to British fascism, as personal files on agents have been withheld under Sections 3.4 and 5.1 of the Public Record Act of 1958.[38] Some information has been provided by Knight on tradecraft and his most successful cases during the Second World War.[39] As far as we know, the nearest equivalent of 'Miss X' (Olga Gray) and the passive roles she played as an MI5 mole in the CPGB, and countering espionage in the 1930s, in the BUF, was the SB source/agent, 'Captain P. G. Taylor', James Mcguirk Hughes. Although not directly run by Knight, he had collaborated with him since joining the BEU, in the murky underworld of anti-communist activity during the 1920s.[40] In the 1930s Hughes was BUF industrial adviser, head of BUF secret operations, and the liaison between Mosley and Maule Ramsay in the phoney war period, where his role changed from that of a passive mole to that of *agent provocateur,* who actively fomented coup d'etat plots and subversive behaviour, according to members of the BUF.[41]

As the war clouds loomed with continuing Nazi aggression in 1939, MI5 received valuable new information on British fascism and anti-semitism from a significant and reputable private detective agency, that of the Secretary of the Board of Deputies of British Jews, Neville Laski. Laski's source, an ex-SB Inspector called Pavey, acted as a passive mole in the co-ordinating committee of the Nordic League, an umbrella organisation of the most extreme fascist and pro-Nazi groups.[42] He provided a valuable insight into the increasingly erratic behaviour of the Conservative MP, Archibald Maule Ramsay, and his role in the organisation that confirmed SB reports on its meetings.

From active to passive anti-fascism, 1940–45

The Second World War, or at least the political and military crisis in 1940, marked the transition by the security authorities from passive to active anti-fascism. In the week before the outbreak of war, new Defence Regulations, based on the Defence of the Realm Act in the First World War, were rushed through parliament and enacted.[43] Although there were amendments, and the process was watered down during the Phoney War, it became the legal basis, with the King's prerogative, for the internment of aliens and more than 750 British fascists in the spring and summer of 1940 under DR 18b (1A). This enabled the Executive to issue Orders in Council without the necessity for parliamentary approval during proclaimed periods of emergency, such as war. Such powers were justified in terms of alleged 'hostile associations' and actual or potential ability to commit 'acts prejudicial'.[44] The process was carefully planned, with three successive periods of arrest, which removed the national leadership and the alleged most dangerous fascists, the regional leadership, and their replacements, in May–June 1940. With the leadership and organisation destroyed, the BUF was proscribed on 10 July 1940. There were also restrictions on movement and powers to direct labour of those whose internment orders were rescinded after release. The judiciary acquiesced in these new executive powers, provided that the authorities acted in good faith on the information received.[45]

This implied both the suspension of habeas corpus for the duration of emergency powers and the reliability of the intelligence on which the authorities based their actions. The latter proved to be a grey area, as the Advisory Committee on Internment disagreed with MI5 on the criteria that justified internment. These divisions were deepened by the suspicion that some of the information received from Knight's agents about the alleged secret activities of fascists was manufactured, manipulated or encouraged by *agents provocateurs*. Interned British fascists also suspected dubious behaviour by MI5. The Home Office became increasingly concerned when agent reliability was undermined by the Ben Greene case in 1941, when his solicitor obtained a confession from one of Knight's agents, Harald Kurtz, that the accusations about the disloyalty of Greene were false.[46] Knight himself, it has plausibly been suggested, masterminded the entrapment of Anna Wolkoff, by encouraging her to send an innocuous message of support to William Joyce in Berlin in 1940, through a letter provided by 'P. G. Taylor'. Knight also planned the setting up of Norah Briscoe and Molly Hiscox, with the recording of a meeting between Kurtz, posing as a Gestapo agent, and the two women.[47] They both pleaded guilty to the charges and were sentenced to five years imprisonment, thus avoiding awkward questions by the defence probing the *agent provocateur* operation. Similarly John Bingham was used to entrap foreign agents, although the Home Office criticised the attempt to compromise the 'fascist rector', George Dymock, by M/Y (Marjorie Amor).[48]

As well as pro-active measures to encourage the breaking of defence regulations, MI5 provided much of the evidence, such as it was, which orchestrated the 'fifth column' scare in 1940. The alleged activities of the 'fifth column' made neutralising the BUF a top priority for British security.[49] Although there were some reports of 'acts prejudicial' by a small minority of British fascists, it was the radio propaganda of 'Lord Haw-Haw (William Joyce and others), the use of material from British fascist and communist publications by Nazi secret broadcasting stations, the 'secret' meetings between fascist organisations during the 'phoney war' supposedly to plot a fascist revolution or a coup d'etat, and the alleged role of the fascist 'fifth column' in Norway, Holland and Belgium during the Nazi blitzkrieg in the spring of 1940 which enabled the military authorities, through the Imperial Defence and the Joint Intelligence Committees to press for blanket internment of aliens, fascists, communists and other perceived security risks during the developing crisis.[50] This was opposed by the Home Office on practical and ideological grounds. The lack of suitable accommodation and infringement of personal liberty concerned the Home Office mandarins. MI5 pressure, together with the logic of events, proved the deciding factor.

The 'evidence' that justified internment of the alleged fifth column was mainly provided by public opinion, and comprised of unsubstantiated gossip and innuendo. Some of the more serious accusations derived from the dubious methods of Knight's agents. Guy Liddell justified the use of *agent provocateur* methods in his diary as the only way in which individuals who wished to do harm to the country could be apprehended.[51] Knight's agents in the Right Club (RC) discovered that Maule Ramsay had seen secret correspondence between Winston Churchill and the American President, Franklin D. Roosevelt, and that there were potential chains of leakage to the enemy, both via RC connections in Belgium, and the Italian embassy.[52] The Tyler Kent affair proved to be the trigger mechanism that helped justify and orchestrate the internment of British fascists, even though BUF members were not involved. The tenuous links between Mosley and Ramsay were used to justify state reactions to the 'fifth column' scare. Using material from declassified MI5 files Bryan Clough has argued that Maxwell Knight, with the help of a friend at Bletchley Park managed a sting operation that incriminated Anna Wolkoff and Tyler Kent, through the activities of agents M/Y (Marjorie Mackie, known in the RC by her maiden name, Marjorie Amor) and M/I (Helene Louise de Munck) and 'Captain P. G. Taylor' (James McGuirk Hughes), and to a lesser extent, Joan Miller.[53]

Internment and the Tyler Kent affair demonstrated how civil liberties became subordinate to security considerations during the war. Individuals were interned on little or no evidence, as Home Office and MI5 personal files were not opened until after individuals were interned. The trial was held *in camera*, with significant evidence being given by Marjorie Amor and Helene Louise de Munck. Hughes, although summoned, failed to appear.[54] Defence counsel failed to make use of the inadequate presentation of the case and Wolkoff was sentenced to 10 years and Kent to 7 years imprisonment. The outcome was to provide the green light for further *agent provocateur* operations in 1940–41.

The 'fifth column' crisis and the resultant security revolution led to the restructuring of MI5 through the Home Defence (Security) Executive and the new Director-General, appointed in April 1941, Sir David Petrie. The simmering row over internment between the Home Office and MI5 was defused gradually, through closer co-operation, good personal relations between Petrie and the Home Office Permanent Under-Secretary, Sir Alexander Maxwell, and the indoctrination of a Home Office official, Miss Nunn, into MI5 operations and procedures.[55] Disputes slowly diminished after Home Office disquiet over the Dymock case when Sir Frank Newsam complained about the blatant provocation and the use of 'Gestapo' tactics in the attempt to incriminate.[56]

Although public opinion approved of the necessity for heightened security consciousness during the Second World War, and the emergence of anti-fascism as a significant feature of British political culture, there were limits to the perceived decline of civil liberties. Thus the decision to prosecute Christabel Nicholson in 1941 following the Kent/Wolkoff trials, backfired. Although she photocopied one of Kent's more sensitive documents, she was found not guilty by the jury, when she was prosecuted for breaking the Official Secrets Act. According to Sir William Jowett, the Solicitor-General, this represented one of the most flagrant miscarriages of justice in British legal history. Allegedly the jury could not believe that the wife of an admiral could endanger national security. Such a verdict did not benefit Mrs. Nicholson. She was immediately re-interned for the next two years. It was, perhaps, not surprising that she did not harbour pleasant memories of the actions of MI5. She complained in a letter to a friend, 'It is confirmed that they (MI5) are the flotsam and jetsam failures in their professions reduced to the level of the "narks" they employ.'[57]

If the Tyler Kent affair saw the peak of Knight's influence in MI5 it also sowed the seeds of his decline. The dubious methods of active anti-fascism were replaced by blanket political surveillance organised mainly by the new F division, created in Petrie's reorganisation. This presaged a move back to passive anti-fascism as both aliens and British fascists were progressively released from internment between 1941 and 1944, as the 'fifth column' threat and the fear of invasion declined. Guy Liddell decided on the use of *agents provocateurs* for deception and surveillance purposes rather than for providing evidence in criminal prosecutions.[58] Although the use of *agents provocateurs* was not entirely stopped after the Tyler Kent affair and the trials of Molly Hiscox and Norah Briscoe, the fall out from the Ben Greene case led to the gradual transfer of M section officers and agents to F division and other branches. Friedl Gartner, for example, who was then the sister-in-law of Stewart Menzies brother, was recruited in 1938 by Knight to infiltrate the Anglo-German Fellowship and was transferred to B1a, the double agent branch and became 'GELATINE'.[59] Knight's deputy, John 'Jack' Bingham, was loaned to the counter-sabotage section, B18 (later B1C) to make contact with the supposed 'fifth column' in England in 1940 and his work as a fake agent of the Gestapo led to the arrest of Irma Stapleton and Rogeiro de Menezes.[60] As well as personnel there was also cross fertilisation of ideas in MI5. Thus deception, a crucial element in double agent operations was also employed in domestic counter-intelligence. The most audacious use of this resulted from Victor Rothschild's scheme to manipulate the 'fifth column'.

The British Gestapo: organising the 'Fifth Column'

Knight, despite the relapse to the *agent provocateur* methods of his work in the private detective agencies of the 1920s during the war, had always preferred the use of passive surveillance by agents for counter-intelligence work. His summary of the work of M section during the war for the in-house history of MI5 compiled by Jack Curry in 1945, puts emphasis on both the nature and training of tradecraft for agent work, the role of officers, the qualities of women agents and the use of moles. This is illustrated by a number of case studies, particularly the success of a key agent Olga Gray, as a secretary in the CPGB between 1931 and 1935, and as a counter-intelligence agent in monitoring the Glading spy ring in 1937–38. Although a very interesting document it has to be regarded more as an 'ideal type' history than what actually happened in M section during the war.[61] Knight also laid emphasis on the necessity for patience. An agent should never take the initiative, but be the passive recipient of offers to advance his career. In this way the agent would escape suspicion. Although Knight had never had a monopoly of agent running in MI5, he also argued that agent training and operation should be administered centrally (and by implication through himself) rather than by the divisions and branches who employed them. In this he was to fight a losing battle, and the assets of M section were to be incorporated into other divisions, Knight himself being transferred to F division after the war.

By 1941 it was becoming clear that Nazi Germany had made little attempt to organise either an intelligence network or a 'stay behind' subversion organisation amongst German citizens or Anglo-Germans in Britain. The 'fifth column' was a myth.[62] MI5, SB, the Security Intelligence Centre and the Regional Security Liaison Officers could find no credible evidence of its activities. The appointment of Victor Rothschild as MI5 scientific expert and head of counter sabotage, included the investigation of the 'fifth column'.

Knight, acting as a talent spotter, supplied him with Jack Bingham as an officer to organise the study.[63] Beginning with the branch of the firm of Siemens established in Britain, the potential for German 'fifth column' activity was researched. This soon developed during 1942 into a broad ranging investigation involving aliens, British fascists and those of dual nationality. Rothschild's investigations led to direct or indirect contact between Bingham and up to 500 individuals in London who, allegedly, were willing to help the enemy.[64] The 'Marita Case' was cleverly organised and manipulated by Rothschild, with Theresa Clay of B1c and Jack Bingham. Posing as the 'chief Gestapo agent in Britain' Bingham brought the potential for the formation of a 'fifth column' under MI5 control.

This operation, as well as remaining one of the most secret activities during the war, was significant for other reasons. It represented the domestic equivalent of the 'Double Cross' deception. No trace was ever discovered of Bingham's informants ever having contact with the real Abwehr or SD, or of any organised British 'fifth column'. Guy Liddell justified such methods as the best way of flushing out those individuals who wished to help the enemy or to collaborate with a Nazi puppet government in Britain. In November 1942 Guy Liddell noted that, whilst the evidence could not be used in court, two individuals could have been prosecuted under the Treachery Act, there were several DR 18b cases, and at least 20 could be added to the invasion or suspects list.[65] Liddell argued this was a mild form of provocation. Its purpose was to investigate the extent of fascist collaboration and support in a future crisis.[66] The invasion or suspects list was not abandoned until September 1944.

Needless to say the so-called Marita case caused significant contro-versy in MI5. Liddell and Rothschild were its most enthusiastic sup-porters. Dick White (B1b) and Roger Hollis (F3) were more critical. White argued the Marita case should be closed down, with a prosecution of the leading miscreants as a warning to others. Hollis was equally sceptical and disapproved of the *agent provocateur* on liberal grounds. He accepted that a very small minority wished to harm the war effort. They, however should be left to rot in obscurity, rather than be given unwanted publicity that a court case would bring. Maxwell Knight, who had successfully pioneered passive penetration to the centre of CPGB secret activities with 'Miss X' (Olga Gray), and had lent Jack Bingham to B1c, thought that the agent running section (i.e. himself) should be responsible for training and operating agents.[67] Liddell argued the case could do no harm. Continued political surveillance of Hitler's supporters in Britain should be maintained, as it provided a focus for the rapid internment of individuals if that ever became necessary. This also provided the opportunity for moles, particularly women agents, to be infiltrated into extremist movements. This would be useful in the imme-diate post-war period when both right- and left-wing movements would have the potential to cause trouble. Sleeper agents would then prove their worth.

For Liddell, the policy of passive anti-fascism proved successful with the inclusion of a 'Mrs Leach' into the 'ruling council' of the supposedly defunct Imperial Fascist League (IFL) in 1944.[68] Although fascist intern-ment was aimed at the BUF, and there was no evidence of the Mosley movement making contact with Bingham, the IFL had caused prob-lems for the authorities since the outbreak of war. Arnold Leese, the Director-General had proved particularly obstreperous, and MI5 were aware of his eccentric, if principled, opposition to the 'Jewish War of Survival'. This was one of several issues that led one of his senior officers, Jimmie Dickson, to become critical of Knight's operation of M section. Dickson, a personal friend of Knight, and a civil servant on loan from the Department of Labour, investigated both the financing of the BUF, became increasingly critical of the reason for the continued internment of fascists, and organised a secret operation, with Mrs Gladstone, that with the connivance of a reputable domestic agency was successful in infiltrating agents into neutral embassies. Dickson argued that the racism and conspiratorial anti-semitism of Leese,[69] however obnoxious, were sincerely held.[70] His opinions, that included criticism of Hitler for invading 'Nordic' Norway and threatening the integrity of the British Empire, should not have led to his internment, particularly as he threatened to expel pro-German members of the IFL.[71] Indeed internment alienated Leese further, and on principle he refused to appeal to the Advisory Commission. Several of the more extreme anti-Semites in the IFL became involved with Rothschild's British Gestapo, and it was this connection that probably led to the termination of the Marita case at the end of the war. This was when evidence from 'secret sources' with surviving documents from B1c, suggested that members of the IFL, now including Leese, assisted two escaped Dutch prisoners of war, who had joined the SS, in an attempt to flee to South America, via a 'rat line'. Although it took several months for SB to discover Herman Meijer and Hendrik Tiecken, their confessions enabled the authorities to prosecute the ex-IFL members without compromising secret sources. Leese and his fellow conspirators were jailed for a year.[72]

Both a Home Office investigation and a Cabinet Committee on Fascism in 1946 concluded that British fascism was a dead duck, a political dodo, almost as extinct as Nazi Germany or Fascist Italy. Although Mosley's Union Movement and Leese's virulently racist and anti-semitic propaganda were to create a 'new fascism', full employment and economic growth were to ensure that this was to remain on the margins of British society for the next sixty years, even if it was to exert a bee sting effect on the issue of immigration in parliamentary politics.[73] The authorities were to continue a policy of passive anti-fascism based on political surveillance and moles during the post-war era. This contrasted with the more complex developments of the inter-war period. Then, there was a changing pattern from 1923–1938, with fascism viewed with a mixture of contempt, an unnecessary foreign import alien to British cultural and political traditions, a cause of public disorder, and on the radical Right, an ally against the overstated communist threat and socialist 'menace'. With the deterioration of international relations with the fascist powers, and the perceived threat to British interests after Munich, and the failure of the BUF to criticise any of the actions of the dictators before the Second World War, a more active anti-fascism developed out of political surveillance and developing passive anti-fascism from 1934. The radical state measures of 1940, which effectively snuffed out inter-war British fascism, were slowly downgraded to a more passive anti-fascism that was to be continued as extensive political surveillance up until well after the cessation of hostilities in 1945. Both in the inter-war and post-war periods fascism was seen as a minor problem. The most dangerous threat posed by political extremism as far as the British state was concerned, derived from the activities of Comintern, Cominform and the CPGB. It was only during the Second World War that the threat posed by the fascist powers and the fictitious 'fifth column' caused the authorities to move beyond general legislation, its preferred method of managing political extremism and threats to public order, to specifics, in this case closing down the remnants of inter-war British fascism.

Notes

1 David S. Lewis, *Illusions of Grandeur: Mosley, Fascism and British Society* (Manchester: Manchester University Press, 1987); Gerald D. Anderson, *Fascists, Communists and the National Government. Civil Liberties in Great Britain, 1931–37* (Columbia: University of Missouri Press, 1983).

2 Richard Thurlow, *The Secret State: British Internal Security in the Twentieth Century* (Oxford: Blackwell, 1994), pp. 107–72.

3 Thomas Jones, *Whitehall Diary Volume 2* (London: Routledge and Kegan Paul, 1969), p. 195.

4 Richard Thurlow, *Fascism in Britain: From Oswald Mosley's Blackshirts to the National Front*, revised and updated edition (London: I. B. Tauris, 1998), pp. 188–9.

5 Thurlow, *The Secret State*, pp. 182–203; Paul Cohen, 'The Police, the Home Office and the Surveillance of the British Union of Fascists', *Intelligence and National Security* 1, 3 (1986), 416–39.

6 Richard Thurlow 'Blaming the Blackshirts: The Authorities and the Anti-Semitic Disturbances in the 1930s', in Panikos Panayi (ed.), *Racial Violence in Britain in the Nineteenth and Twentieth Centuries* (Leicester: Leicester University Press, 1996), pp. 112–30.

7 Christopher Andrew, *Her Majesty's Secret Service: The Making of the British Intelligence Community* (New York: Elizabeth Sifton Books, Viking, 1985), pp. 224–45. This was published in England as Christopher Andrew, *Secret Service* (London: Heinemann, 1985).

8 Jane Morgan, *Conflict and Order* (Oxford: Oxford University Press, 1987); Richard Thurlow, 'The Security Service, the Communist Party of Great Britain and British Fascism 1932–51', in Nigel Copsey and David Renton (eds), *British Fascism, the Labour Movement and the State* (Basingstoke: Palgrave-Macmillan, 2005), pp. 27–45.

9 Andrew, *Her Majesty's Secret Service*, pp. 112–30.

10 Thurlow, *The Secret State*, pp. 107–22.
11 John Curry, *The Security Service* (Kew: Public Record Office, 1999), pp. 65–8.
12 John Hope 'Fascism, the Security Service and the Curious Careers of Maxwell Knight and James Mcguirk Hughes', *Lobster* 22, 1–5 (n.d.).
13 P. R. J. Winter, 'A Higher Form of Intelligence: Hugh Trevor Roper and Wartime British Secret Service', *Intelligence and National Security* 22, 6 (2007), 847–80.
14 [T]he [N]ational [A]rchives: HO 45/25386/54–59.
15 James J. and Patience. Barnes, *Nazis in Pre-war London: The Fate and Role of German Party Members and British Sympathisers* (Brighton: Sussex Academic Press, 2005), pp. 177–98.
16 TNA: KV4/170 'MI5 note on the aggressive policy of Hitler and Ribbentrop and consequent instructions to the Abwehr', n.d.
17 Andrew 'Introduction' in Curry, *The Security Service*, p. 9.
18 John Hope, 'Surveillance or Collusion? Maxwell Knight and the British Fascisti', *Intelligence and National Security* 9, 4 (1994), 651–75.
19 John Hope, 'British Fascism and the State 1917–27: A Re-examination of the Documentary Evidence', *Labour History Review* 57, 3 (1992), 72–83.
20 John Hope, 'Fascism and the State in Britain: The Case of the British Fascisti 1923–31', *Australian Journal of Politics and History* 39, 3 (1993), 367–80; Gill Bennett, *Churchill's Man of Mystery: Desmond Morton and the World of Intelligence* (London: Routledge, 2007), pp. 127–34.
21 Bryan Clough, *State Secrets: The Kent-Wolkoff Affair* (Hove: Hideaway Publications, 2005); Bennett, *Churchill's Man of Mystery*, pp. 120–4.
22 TNA: KV 2/997 Walter Dale, 'James Mcguirk Hughes', n.d., KV 2/1016/598b William Norman Ewer, 'Note for O.A. (Jasper) Harker, 23/4/1929.
23 Bennett, *Churchill's Man of Mystery*, pp. 87–94.
24 *Ibid.*, pp. 127–34.
25 Victor Madeira, 'Moscow's Interwar Infiltration of British Intelligence 1919–29', *The Historical Journal* 39, 4 (2003), 915–33.
26 Curry, *The Security Service*, pp. 101–3; Bennett, *Churchill's Man of Mystery*, pp. 133–4.
27 Bennett, *Churchill's Man of Mystery*, pp. 122–6, NA FO 1093/74, 'Minutes of the Prime Minister's Secret Service Committee', 27 April, 11 June, 22 June 1931.
28 TNA: KV 4/196 Guy Liddell diary, 29 May 1945.
29 Bennett, *Churchill's Man of Mystery*, pp. 127–34.
30 The surviving reports are to be found in TNA: HO 144/20141-4, HO 144/21068, and HO 45/25385.
31 *Ibid.*
32 Richard Thurlow, 'The Straw that Broke the Camel's Back: Public Order, Civil Liberties and the Battle of Cable Street', in Tony Kushner and Nadia Valman (eds), *Remembering Cable Street: Fascism and Anti-Fascism in British Society* (London: Valentine Mitchell, 2000) pp. 74–94.
33 Thurlow, *Fascism in Britain*, pp. 132–56.
34 TNA: HO 283/10/9 'BUF Secret Bank Account'.
35 Stephen Dorril, *Blackshirt: Sir Oswald Mosley and British Fascism* (London: Viking, 2006) pp. 437–8, TNA: KV 2/880/129a, Interrogation of W. E. D. Allen, 27.3.42, KV 2/880 Second Interrogation of W. E. D. Allen, 7.4.42.

36 *Ibid.*, pp. 376–7.
37 Thurlow, *Fascism in Britain*, p. 105.
38 Anthony Masters, *The Man who was M: The Life of Maxwell Knight* (Oxford: Blackwell, 1984) is a useful biography, but needs to be handled with care as some of the details of Knight's intelligence career need revision.
39 TNA: KV 4/227 'History of the Operations of M. S. during the War, 1939–45'.
40 See the cited articles by John Hope in footnotes 18–20.
41 Thurlow, *The Secret State*, pp. 208–9.
42 Board of Deputies of British Jews: C6/10/29, letter N. Laski to Inspector Keeble, n.d.
43 Thurlow, *Fascism in Britain*, p. 159.
44 *Ibid.*, pp. 157–62.
45 A. W. Brian Simpson, *In the Highest Degree Odious: Detention without Trial in Wartime Britain* (Oxford: Clarendon Press, 1992).
46 Masters, *The Man who was M*, pp. 141–67, TNA: KV 2/489/91a, Sir David Petrie to Sir Alexander Maxwell, 23 October 1941.
47 TNA: KV 2/898/44b,45a,45b, Maxwell Knight and M/H reports on arrest of Norah Briscoe and Molly Hiscox n.d.
48 TNA: KV 4/189 Guy Liddell diaries, 18 January 1942.
49 Richard Thurlow, 'The Evolution of the Mythical British Fifth Column, 1939–46', *Twentieth Century British History* 10, 4 (1999), 477–98.
50 Thurlow, *The Secret State*, pp. 218–36.
51 TNA: KV 4/193 4 February 1944.
52 Masters, *The Man who was M*, pp. 76–106.
53 Clough, *State Secrets*.
54 TNA: KV 2/543/413a Rex v Kent and Wolkoff, 11 November 1940.
55 TNA: KV 4/192, Guy Liddell diaries, 7 January 1944.
56 TNA: KV 4/189, Guy Liddell diaries, 18 January 1942.
57 TNA: KV 2/904/186b, Christabel Nicholson to Mrs Whinfield, 17 February 1942.
58 TNA: KV 4/192, Guy Liddell diaries, 24 August 1943.
59 Joan Miller, *One Girl's War* (Dublin: Brandon Press, 1986), pp. 86–90.
60 TNA: KV 4/227, Knight, 'History', p. 30, KV 4/189 Guy Liddell Diaries, 18 November 1941, KV 4/190 Guy Liddell Diaries, 14 November 1942.
61 TNA: KV 4/227, Knight, 'History of the Operations of M.S. during the War 1939–45'.
62 Thurlow, 'The Evolution of the Mythical Fifth Column, 1939–46'.
63 TNA: KV 4/189, Guy Liddell diaries, 25 March 1942.
64 Curry, *The Security Service*, p. 312.
65 TNA: KV 4/170, Comment by D. B. (Liddell) on Dick White's Note 7.11.42.
66 TNA: KV 4/192, Guy Liddell's diaries, 4 October 1943.
67 TNA: KV 4/227, Knight 'History', pp. 24–7, KV 4/331, 'Policy re Study and Investigation of Fascism and Right Wing or Kindred Movements and Activities, 1933–45', Paper by T.M. Shelford, Minutes 7 and 9 by Victor Rothschild and Maxwell Knight, TNA: KV 4/192, Guy Liddell diaries, 24 August, 4 October 1943.
68 TNA: KV 4/193 Guy Liddell diaries, 26 January 1944.
69 TNA: KV 2/1365/3a, J. G. Dickson, 'Note on Arnold Leese', 1.8.40, KV 4/192 Guy Liddell diaries, 20 October 1943.

70   TNA: HO 45/24967/105, MI5 report on the Imperial Fascist League, 8.3.42.
71   TNA: KV 2/1365/25b, B1c report on Arnold Leese, 31.5.45, KV 2/1366/444b, B1d report on Arnold Leese, 30.9.46, KV 3/62, Information from secret sources for the Prime Minister on trial of Arnold Leese, 13.1.47.
72   TNA: KV 3/38/65a, Rex v Leese et al., March 27–March 31 1947.
73   Graham Macklin, *Very Deeply Dyed in Black: Sir Oswald Mosley and the Resurrection of British Fascism after 1945* (London: I. B. Tauris, 2007).

Part III
Intellectual Responses

8
Anti-Fascist Europe Comes to Britain: Theorising Fascism as a Contribution to Defeating It

Dan Stone

> The democracies ... lead their people not to defeat but to collapse without fighting. In a word, it is not war but peace which seals the doom of liberal civilization.
>
> Aurel Kolnai, 1939

Introduction

Anti-fascism is, in a sense, a Continental European idea and not a British one. The urgency of the fascist threat was never felt as keenly in Britain as on the Continental mainland between the Wars, and the instrumentalised ideology of anti-fascism as it informed the post-war communist republics was of course not experienced by the British people, even if pride in defeating Hitler became central to post-1945 British national identity. Thus, without overlooking the very real commitment to anti-fascism made by many in Britain – as Nigel Copsey points out, 'far more people supported the anti-fascist cause than ever supported fascist organisations'[1] – I want here to advance the argument that towards the end of the 1930s anti-fascist exiles contributed a theoretical seriousness, if not necessarily a practical pugnacity, to inter-war anti-fascism in Britain. The British manifestation of what David Kettler refers to as 'the legacy of Antifascism as total ideology' was certainly driven, as David Renton reminds us, by the activities of anti-fascists (as opposed to those who were not fascist but did nothing to combat fascism), but the writings of these exiles, I submit here, were also forms of anti-fascist activity, and ones that made no little contribution to bringing about an urgent realisation of what fascism meant.[2] Furthermore, 'anti-fascist culture', as Enzo Traverso notes, was 'to a very great extent, a culture of exile'.[3] Its proponents were people who knew whereof they spoke and urgently felt a need to transmit their views to as wide an audience as possible in the hope of persuading the supposedly stolid and cynical British to take seriously what, from the editorial office of the *Times*, looked rather too ridiculous to warrant much attention other than to be praised occasionally for having supposedly saved Italy (and later, Germany) from left-wing militancy. This urgency was felt even more keenly in Britain given the relatively small number of exiles from Nazi Germany that settled in the UK, in comparison with France, Czechoslovakia or, especially, the US.[4] The chapter does not seek to call into question the historical significance of anti-fascist activity in the struggle against fascism. But I do argue that the attempt to understand fascism (especially Nazism) and the spreading of an émigré-driven intellectual anti-fascist literature should be seen not merely as a middle-class or academic anti-fascism (that is, one that ultimately *does* nothing), but as a key part of the anti-fascist movement.

The history of anti-fascism in Britain needs to be internationalised. A number of studies have examined German exiles in Britain, their networks, their difficulties and their aspirations for their homeland.[5] Others have investigated exiles' plans for the restructuring of Germany after the war or their active participation in the war effort, especially on the part of the representatives of suppressed left-wing political parties and their links (or lack of) with the British authorities.[6] But few scholars have looked at the exiles from the perspective of their attempts to influence the outlook of their adopted country, although Werner Röder claims that 'Press services, announcements, speeches, contributions by émigré journalists to the press and radio of their countries of exile, books published by prominent politicians and well-known authors, as well as reports on the experiences of persecuted persons influenced international political opinion on National-Socialist Germany.'[7] Certainly their propaganda output riled the Nazis, who revoked their German citizenship and did all that they could to discredit them.[8]

In this chapter I seek to show that at the level of ideas anti-fascist theory had developed a highly sophisticated critique of the nature of fascism by the late 1930s. This went far beyond the orthodox Marxist understanding of fascism as a form of capitalist crisis-management (fascism as the tool of big business) – although this was not without its merits – to include studies that somewhat dangerously sought to understand the appeal of fascism to its adherents, in order to be better able to combat it. The writings of Aurel Kolnai, Franz Borkenau and Sebastian Haffner that I examine in this chapter are especially important, for their writings exemplify the claims made for anti-fascism by

Kettler and Traverso. What is noteworthy about these three authors is that none was British, although they published their major studies of Spain and Germany in English with British publishers (Gollancz, Penguin, Secker and Warburg). All were from central Europe, the first two of Jewish origin – though their Jewishness was of little significance to them as youngsters – and the third engaged to a Jewish woman; and the first two were both, for a time, communists. What is significant in their analyses of fascism is that they probed more deeply into the fascist mindset than did most studies of the period. Indeed, they explicitly referred, almost in terms of admiration, to the 'energy' that drove fascist movements, and did so in order to stress how serious the threat posed by fascism was to the staid, and soon to be superannuated democracies. In a sense their writings gave intellectual credence to the response of active British anti-fascists, for whom, as Nigel Copsey notes, 'evaluations of foreign fascism were important in shaping responses to domestic fascism'.[9]

These three were of course not the only émigrés involved in anti-Nazi activities; others included pacifist and writer Otto Lehmann-Russbüldt, playwright Ernst Toller, journalist and former SPD member of the Reichstag Gerhart Seger, who spent a short time in the UK, sociologist Franz Neumann, who also soon moved to the US, publisher and associate of Willi Münzenberg, Babette Gross, and businessman David Yaskiel, who was involved in the publication of the *Brown Book* of the Reichstag fire in 1934.[10] Among interned 'enemy aliens', Heinrich Fraenkel's book *Help Us Germans to Beat the Nazis!* (1941), which was published shortly before his release from internment, 'served to familiarise the British with the aims of the refugee anti-fascists, and to promote their common struggle against National Socialist Germany'.[11]

This chapter will focus on these written critiques as a particular manifestation of this wider sphere of action. I draw out the main themes of their critique and will argue that it was no coincidence that it took central Europeans writing about Nazism rather than about Italian Fascism to produce a really insightful anti-fascist theory that challenged the British tendency to downplay the seriousness with which fascist movements took their own ideas. Italian anti-fascists did of course contribute to the attack, and had done so for longer, most notably Luigi Sturzo, formerly head of the now banned Italian People's Party, and Gaetano Salvemini, whose *Under the Axe of Fascism* (1936) and *Italian Fascism* (1938) were published by the Left Book Club. But Salvemini referred dismissively to 'Fascist "thinkers"' and dismissed the idea of the corporate state as a 'corporative fairy-tale'.[12] In general, whilst he spoke of the threat of 'Fascist totalitarianism', Salvemini regarded Italian Fascism as engaged in a battle with big business whose future was uncertain, though the thrust of his analysis made it clear that Fascism was by no means sure to win out. In other words, and as the title of George Seldes's book on Mussolini, *Sawdust Caesar*, implied, there was little here that would make the average British reader feel that something that concerned them was at stake.[13] Nazism, in the writings of the German émigrés, was presented as more imminently dangerous, not just for its internal enemies, but for the wider world.

Franz Borkenau

George Orwell, reviewing Franz Borkenau's *The Totalitarian Enemy* (1940) wrote: 'We cannot struggle against Fascism unless we are willing to understand it, a thing which both left-wingers and right-wingers have conspicuously failed to do – basically, of course, because they dared not.'[14] Borkenau, then, 'one of the most valuable gifts that Hitler has made to England',[15] was conspicuous as one of the rare analysts of Nazism who were neither sympathetic nor, in the manner of many British commentators, opposed primarily because they saw Nazism as the inheritor and most recent manifestation of Prussian militarism.

Nigel Copsey notes that the only people in Britain really to take the threat of fascism seriously in the 1920s were the Communists (especially after the kidnapping of Harry Pollitt in 1925). It is therefore more than coincidence that Borkenau (1900–1957) was originally a member of the KPD who broke with the party in 1929, going on to become, especially after World War II, a vigorous Cold Warrior and advocate of the progressive mission of the west. In the 1930s, following his departure from Germany, he lived in Paris, Panama and then London, but is remembered primarily for his trips to Spain during the Civil War, trips which resulted in his still-in-print classic work *The Spanish Cockpit* (1937). Indeed, the fact that Borkenau had experienced communism from within but then rejected it – he was actually arrested by the communists whilst in Spain – is the key to understanding his fierce anti-fascism and his attempt to go beyond the orthodox Marxist analysis of its origins and potential. In the British context, clearly the communists' understanding of fascism drove the anti-fascist movement in terms of its action at street level – and there are many texts (again, mostly by émigrés such as Erckner or Henri, but also by officially non-aligned leftists like John Strachey) that equally slavishly follow the same analysis, both before and after Dimitrov's famous definition – but here I want to suggest that Borkenau's writings provided a level of sophistication that went beyond this communist analysis. Borkenau himself was of course vilified by the communists but the significance of his writings lies in the fact that he sought to reach out beyond the circles of communists and others who had concerned themselves with fascism since the 1920s and to mobilise a broader section of opinion, especially in terms of the threat posed specifically by Nazi Germany.

Borkenau made a name for himself, then, with his studies of communism, *The Communist International* (1938) and *The Totalitarian Enemy* (1940). But in between those two publications he published a book, number 33 in the Penguin Specials series, which was one of the more combative analyses of the Third Reich that had appeared at that point. *The New German Empire*, published just before the outbreak of war, looks at first glance like many of the books about the Third Reich that appeared at this time: a general discussion of the 'Nazi crusade' followed by an analysis of the regime's approach to foreign policy that pointed to the Third Reich's dream of acquiring first, a European empire and second, world domination. Yet the book is different in several important respects.

First, Borkenau rejected out of hand any sense of 'liberal' compromise with the Nazi regime, arguing that British 'reasonableness' had thus far led only to capitulation and, if continued, would result in catastrophe. In an earlier book he had already condemned the policy of appeasement by noting that the British were 'far too greatly imbued with the soft and reasonable atmosphere of compromise prevailing in democratic countries, and instinctively expect the revolutionaries beyond the Rhine to come over, given only sufficient time and a willingness to grant concessions, to their own approach to politics'.[16] Now he extended this critique, noting that, after the occupation of Prague, he had been proven correct and stressed the urgency of the situation. Rather than just condemn the softly-softly approach of the democracies, Borkenau contrasted this style of politics with that of the Nazis:

> The query is not whether Germany will now continue her course of indeterminate aggression or not. There can be no doubt that she will. The problem, and a very important one at that, is whether Germany is simply carrying out well-thought-out plans or is driven into limitless adventures by developments over which she herself is not the master. In the one case, we must still reckon with some rational plan on the part of Germany which it would be important to discover. In the second case, we are faced with an outburst of

incalculable instincts which cannot but end in disaster, both for Germany and for others.[17]

Borkenau, then, rejected any sense of compromise with Nazism and made it his task to demonstrate that the regime was driven by an unstoppable dynamic towards war that neither internal nor external influences could hinder. In other words, trying to establish a Nazi 'programme' was pointless since the regime was consumed by 'quasi-mystical fanaticism' (21) and the idea of it settling down to some sort of 'normalcy' was 'quite meaningless' (22). Nazism could not be understood using the conventional tools of diplomacy or scholarship since it was ultimately driven by a 'supernatural urge' (26).

We see here an analysis of Nazism that went way beyond the conventional idea that the democracies in general and Britain in particular were faced with an unusual political movement but one which could in the end be understood and brought to participate in the ordinary machinations of great power politics. Furthermore, with its focus on Germany ('The Nazi disease ... must be crushed, or it will crush civilization'[18]) it superseded any anti-fascist action that was driven by the need to keep fascists off the streets of East London, Birmingham or Liverpool. But it also provided fuel for the latter, ultimately backing it in its assessment that no compromise could be brooked with fascism and that the only way to tackle it was through violence.

Aurel Kolnai

If Borkenau became a critic of communism and, after the war, one of its most vigorous opponents, he nevertheless did not match the Cold Warrior credentials of Aurel Kolnai. Kolnai (1900–1973), was brought up in Budapest, converted from Judaism to Catholicism and, after leaving central Europe shortly before war broke out, ended up after a convoluted passage, in London, where he taught philosophy at Bedford College. Before the war, and whilst still in Vienna, he wrote – in English in a Nazi café – one of the most powerful analyses of Nazi ideology of the pre-1945 period, *The War Against the West* (1938). Yet after the war, Kolnai regretted spending so much time on Nazism, seeing communism as a greater threat to world peace and security.

Nevertheless, *The War Against the West* should be judged neither in the light of Kolnai's subsequent Cold war activities nor by the fact that it was published by Victor Gollancz's Left Book Club. For it neither discussed communism (or comparative 'totalitarianism') nor was it a standard, orthodox Labour socialist LBC work. Gollancz himself claimed that the book was 'without exception, the most important book that the Club has yet published' and referred to it as 'the bible of anti-fascism',[19] quite a remarkable appraisal when one sees the extent to which it departs from the standard leftist analysis of fascism as 'crisis capitalism with a cudgel', what Orwell called the 'Strachey-Blimp thesis' in which 'Hitler was a dummy with Thyssen pulling the strings.'[20] Whilst Kolnai shared with Gollancz a variety of Christian Socialism, nevertheless Kolnai's understanding of Nazism went way beyond that ordinarily associated with the LBC, and his personalist Christian conservatism – he sympathised, for example, with Hilaire Belloc's description of the 'servile state' and the Distributist argument that freedom depended on the widest distribution possible of private property – would have been anathema to Strachey and Laski.[21] His task, as he saw it, was to educate the British reader, making him realise the real meaning of Nazism: 'English public opinion will have to learn that the mere removal of "injustices" and discriminations is far from touching on the core of the German problem, and the farthest possible from unseating National Socialism.'[22] It should come as no surprise then, that whilst the *Manchester Guardian* praised the book, other reviewers were less impressed. The *Sunday Times* noted that the book sounded like Churchill, but that 'its idiom was un-English', and the *TLS* reserved its praise for Kolnai's grammar. Many reviewers seemed to prefer Hermann Rauschning's *Germany's Revolution of Destruction*, also published in 1938 (in German as *Die Revolution des Nihilismus*, then in English in June 1939), a book whose emphasis was more on the Third Reich destroying itself than having to be destroyed from without.[23]

Still, Kolnai understood Nazism in the same way that he later understood communism – as a 'fall away from Christianity'[24] – and fought it for its atheism and its rejection of reason. Nazism, he argued even before it came to power in Germany, represented no mere counter-revolution but an 'overturning of values' (*Umsturz der Werte*).[25] Hence, like Borkenau he argued that there was no point in trying to compromise with Nazism; rather, one must understand it in order the better to combat it. Whilst this meant undertaking the distasteful task of entering into the thought-processes of Nazis, this was, he maintained, the only way of really getting to grips with the phenomenon.

This methodology led to some potentially rather dangerous exercises in proximity. Kolnai sought, in a way that must have seemed quite shocking to British readers – for whom Kolnai explicitly wrote, in English – to elucidate the appeal of fascism to its adherents. English writers, such as

R. G. Collingwood, who had previously tried this sort of approach found themselves isolated as intellectual renegades, but Kolnai did not face Collingwood's problem of uppity Oxford colleagues, and picked up where Collingwood left off: 'The National Socialist doctrines', he argued, 'though ultimately false and immoral, and liable to degenerate into comic vulgarity, are at their highest endowed with spiritual grandeur and relevancy' (18). Outside of the descriptions of the Nuremberg rallies offered by fellow travellers of fascism, this sort of statement was not commonly heard, least of all in the LBC's publications; they bespeak Kolnai's intellectual bravery and his attempt to infuse anti-fascism with the sort of energy that drove the fascists themselves.

In an article of January 1939 Kolnai wrote:

> We ... are hugging the complacent belief that the essence of demo-cracy is compromise; so we brook 'compromise' with the fascists, of the Munich type for instance, as a triumph not only of peace but even of democracy. We only forget that there is a marked difference between compromise within democracy, which presupposes the common ground of democracy accepted by all the various compet-ing groups of the people, and compromise with the convinced and uncompromising mortal enemies of democracy. We are extremely afraid of tarnishing the immaculate beauty of our democracy by any use of violence or display of intolerance; not, however, of compro-mising democracy in its integrity.[26]

Or, as he put it in his talk to the Left Book Club summer school in 1939:

> The naïve people who in March 1939 accused the Germans of having committed a 'breach of faith', 'deceived' Mr. Ch[amberlain] at Munich, could have been spared their surprise and deception if they had *not* refused dogmatically to attach an importance to Nazi ideologies.[27]

Thus, like Borkenau, Kolnai's basic message was that attempting to under-stand Nazism through the tools of diplomacy, analysis of leaders' speeches or Nazi legislation was fruitless. Rather, he argued that one had to grasp the will that drove the Nazi dynamic towards war and catastrophe: fas-cism, he argued, would make war not to placate its supporters or to counter popular discontent but 'to save its soul: to stave off the revelation of its inner barrenness, the vacuum of despair at its core' (637). Whilst this analysis necessarily took Kolnai – and his readers – too close to the core of Nazism for comfort, this was precisely the point; for treating Nazism as a difficult but otherwise ordinary political movement was, in his estimation, to set off down the road to ruin. Nowhere is this clearer than in his LBC summer school talk, for here he spoke of the 'freedom' of the fascist system, even if this was 'the extreme opposite of what we are accustomed to understand by freedom.' What he meant was that fascism generated a 'sense of an unlimited Power in which the subject is supposed to "participate" in a mystical way, as it were: through patriotic loyalty, kinship of "kind" as contrasted to "alien kind", through the very fact of his absolute, total subjection' (1). In order then to understand the appeal of fascism there was little point merely condemning it. Every sane person would do so, but this was insufficient to combat fascism. 'We must have the courage,' Kolnai went on, 'to fight an enemy, – or rather, to reject a creed – of which we recognise the grandeur, the positive implications, the creative power. Evil may be "ultimately" destructive, but no great evil is merely and altogether destructive. Else, it could not even be really, effectually destructive' (3).

Nigel Copsey has written of the LBC that it 'became an important vehicle for promoting anti-fascism'. He then goes on to note that by 'important' he means that it assisted in the promotion of political activity: 'Indeed, Club members would often use the "discussion groups" to organise concrete political agitation rather than merely discussing abstract ideas raised from current volumes.'[28] My discussion of Kolnai is meant to suggest that it is not so easy to separate the 'merely' abstract ideas contained within the books from the political action; indeed, Kolnai's important talk at the LBC's summer school, along with Gollancz's (and others') estimation of *The War Against the West* indicates that the contribution of the uncompromising stance towards fascism taken by the émigrés was indispensable. Kolnai – remember, no friend of communism, was open about the nature of the west and why it had to work harder than the Soviet Union to resist fascism:

> Berlin has incomparably more hope of engineering an ideological deception of the capitalist West, with its pacifist sentimentalism and its anti-proletarian instincts, than to allay the astute rulers of Russia, untrammelled by inhibitions prevailing in the West, into a common action against the Liberal world – whose downfall would immediately throw the Soviet Union upon the mercy of triumphant Central European Fascism. [561]

Kolnai's writings – which are inseparable from anti-fascism activity, as his LBC work shows – reveal that a theory proclaiming the need to crush fascism, not compromise with it, had, by the start of the war, extended beyond the radical Left and contributed to the hardening of resolve required to end rightist appeasement, leftist pacifism and armchair anti-fascism, and to take on the Third Reich in the only way possible. As Kolnai noted in his memoirs, 'With the birth of the Third Reich, the Second World War had virtually begun, and anti-Nazi action came forthwith under the heading, not of domestic politics but of War operations.'[29]

Sebastian Haffner

By the time of his death in 1999 at the age of ninety-one, Sebastian Haffner (the pen-name of Raimund Pretzel) had become famous as the author of *The Meaning of Hitler* and various other works in German history, and for his journalism in West Germany, to which he returned from Britain in 1954.[30] He has since become even better known as the author of a memoir that he wrote as an émigré lawyer in London in 1939 and then put aside as events, he felt, had rendered it irrelevant or, at least, necessitated a new analysis. The memoir, published in 2002 as *Defying Hitler*, and the second study, *Germany Jekyll and Hyde* (1940), republished in 2005, are, taken together, among the more remarkable contemporary analyses of Nazism and the Third Reich. Here I will suggest that the latter work should be seen a key contribution to the anti-fascist struggle, to be set alongside the works of Borkenau and Kolnai, as well as other, more famous works by German exiles such as Konrad Heiden and the former Nazi Hermann Rauschning.

Germany Jekyll and Hyde was first published in June 1940, and its analysis of events – which was based on the circumstances of 1939 – rapidly became outdated with the end of the Phoney War, the Nazi invasion of Norway, Denmark and France and, not long after, the invasion of the USSR and the US entry into the war. This was most unfortunate for Haffner, since the unfolding of events, though it destroyed much of the book's timeliness and left it more or less forgotten, by no means contradicted the analysis of Hitler and Nazism that underpinned it. Haffner's combative and felicitous turns of phrase are deliciously citable, but it is also necessary to point to the limits of Haffner's vision, and to show where others have developed his claims.

The book is split into eight simple units of analysis: Hitler, the Nazi leaders, the Nazis, the loyal population, the disloyal population, the opposition, and the émigrés. The final chapter, 'Possibilities', contains some extraordinarily powerful assessments, and is written in a dramatic prose that gives those of us who did not live through those days a sense of the urgency that characterised them. The way Haffner divides the book up may seem simplistic, but it actually reveals a very clear understanding of the nature of German society under the Third Reich.[31]

First, Hitler. In many ways, this is the most important chapter. Not because Haffner overestimates Hitler as a thinker or leader – far from it. Rather, Haffner shows the way in which the Third Reich is inseparable from Hitler's person. It does not suffice, in Haffner's opinion, to historicise Hitler, to try and understand him, as so many Allied propagandists did, as part of a German tradition:

> to tabulate Hitler, as it were, in the History of Ideas and degrade him to an historical episode is a hopeless undertaking, and can only lead to perilous miscalculations. Much more progress towards an accurate estimation of the man can be made if one takes exactly the opposite course and considers German and European history as a part of Hitler's private life.[32]

Although it runs against commonsense to equate Nazism with Hitlerism, as Ian Kershaw has recently reminded us,[33] the logic of Haffner's claim is that the only way to deal with Hitler – and here Haffner sounds pleasingly un-English – is to eliminate him. This is not a question of being for or against appeasement; rather, it is a simple necessity: 'There is sufficient reason to destroy the man as a mad dog' (10). Hitler cannot be treated as an extreme variant of the statesman; he is, rather, 'a swindler in a statesman's mask' (9). And the only answer to this swindle is to kill it three times: as institution (the position of Führer), as a man (he must be killed), and as a legend (21). So far, so clear. There is thus no danger of misunderstanding Haffner when he attempts to rescue the German majority from being tarred with the same brush, an all-too common phenomenon in the middle of the war.

Haffner next turns to the Nazi leaders. Although he condemns them individually as philistines, thugs, and arrivistes (in the manner of Arendt's claim that Nazism came 'from the gutter'), this does not mean that Haffner underestimates their strength as a group. He is impressed by their 'boundless corruption, boundless efficiency, and boundless cynicism' (25), and dismisses any notion that Nazism as an ideology is worth considering:

> "What about the National Socialist world-conception?" To which we must answer that, save for the title, it does not exist. Behind the

ostentatious name there is nothing; or, at most, the doctrine that it is permitted and even commanded to rob, torment, and kill Jews. Somewhat scanty contents for a world-conception! ... In fact, this world-conception is rubbish if not an impudent fraud. Moreover, none of the Nazi leaders take it seriously. The National Socialists are a reality, but their world-conception is not. [33–34]

Most historians today – not to mention Kolnai and many Nazi theorists at the time – bristle at the claim that Nazi ideology was unimportant, but Haffner at least has the virtue of clarity. Besides, the fact that the Third Reich was 'organised' as a bandit kleptocracy is increasingly being revealed by historians such as Jonathan Petropoulos and Frank Bajohr in ways that echo the 1940s' Frankfurt School analysis of Nazism as a 'racket'.[34] When Haffner goes on to claim that 'The Nazi leaders aim at converting Germany into a gigantic sports club which is always winning "victories" – and thereby losing its happiness, character, and national identity' (34) he provides a vision of the Third Reich akin to Georges Perec's dystopian society in *W*,[35] and, more importantly, explains why, in his view, ideology is not the Nazi elite's driving force.

How then does Haffner explain anti-semitism? He sees it as a kind of shibboleth, as a quasi-ritualistic way of binding the Nazis together: 'The chief aim of anti-semitism is to serve, firstly, as a kind of secret sign and binding mystery among Nazis, like a continuous ritual murder; and, secondly, as the conscience-killing course in the education of the second generation of Nazis' (45). He thus concludes that it is mistaken to understand Nazism as one political position among others. Rather, it is an existential choice: *'Nazism is no ideology but a magic formula which attracts a definite type of men. It is a form of "characterology" not ideology. To be a Nazi means to be a type of human being'* (46).

The following chapters provide equally acerbic and penetrating insights into the various strata of German society. Along the way Haffner makes plain how unlikely it will be that Nazism will be overthrown from within (103); that the plan to force Germany to become a democratic state is doomed to failure ('To wish to make a democratic power out of Germany is to look for apples on a rose-bush. There are none. There never will be' (104)); that Nazism can be explained neither by Marxist or liberal frameworks ('Nazism a "first" (original and new) form of radical nihilism, that equally denies *all* values, capitalist and bourgeois as well as proletarian' (136)); and that the Allies are to blame for failing to recruit in large numbers potential émigrés (147) and for providing succour to the Nazis' ambitions when they believed themselves to be doing the opposite ('every agreement intended by the Allies to be a treaty of peace must appear to the Nazis, by reason of their inborn and unalterable mental outlook, as a tactical measure of war' (170)). In other words, each of these brief quotations reveals that Haffner was an unusually hard-headed and unsentimental observer. His argument that only war can pacify a regime like Nazi Germany (159) and that the war should not be brought to too speedy a conclusion merely to save lives if doing so jeopardises 'the very cause at stake' – for example, by making a premature peace with the German Army – was remarkably prescient given the post-war efforts by many to defend the 'honourable Wehrmacht' and make plain that Haffner knew how deep the rot had got.

Haffner's vision, however, does not seem so convincing today, when Germany has become a parliamentary democracy. Haffner may have railed unequivocally against the Nazis but, like Kolnai and Borkenau, he was no orthodox leftist. His alternative vision for Germany is a conservative, aristocratic one. Seeing Nazism (here more conventionally than Borkenau or Kolnai) as a logical successor to Prussianism, Haffner believed that a period of conservatism would be the only way to restore Germany to peaceful neighbourliness. In one sense he was right: the Adenauer epoch in the Federal Republic was indeed a conservative one, politically, socially and culturally. Whether it also saw a restoration of worthwhile older values is another matter:

> It seems clear that for Germany, as for Europe at large, a conservative epoch is 'due' to follow the present crisis, such as succeeded the reign of Napoleon; a rehabilitation of the old and the oldest cultural values, a period of preservation, restoration, and healing. [129]

Yet the way in which he saw this state of affairs being realised was through a political realignment that today seems fantastical: a return to the pre-unification world of German states:

> [I]f a real peace is possible, the spell must be broken, Which means: *the German Reich must disappear, and the last seventy-five years of German history must be erased. The Germans must retrace their steps to the point where they took the wrong path – to the year 1866. No peace is conceivable with the Prussian Reich which was born at that time, and whose last logical expression is no other than Nazi Germany. And no vital*

"other" Germany is anywhere to be found but that which in that year was worsted by the caprice of war – without ever totally succumbing. [183]

Here events overtook Haffner. Yet, in pugnacious prose, the analysis of Nazism itself and Haffner's level-headed assertions that no appeasement was possible with the Nazis make *Germany Jekyll and Hyde* far more than just a fascinating document. As Lothar Kettenacker notes, 'it was precisely his reservations about a compromise peace with the old ruling classes which distinguished his position from that of Rauschning and gave his liberal views weight in official circles.'[36] It remains an analysis of Nazism that merits serious attention and that, even in the context of war, will have seemed terribly outré to British readers accustomed to the idea that diplomatic channels were still possible or that a separate peace with the Axis might save the Empire.

Since *Defying Hitler* was unpublished in his lifetime one cannot argue that it contributed directly to the development of British anti-fascism. The book is worth reading in its own right as one of the more remarkable analyses of Hitler's rise to power, and in this context it helps explain how those who had direct experience of fascism arrived at conclusions that few British authors came to independently. Although Haffner and the other émigrés were prevented from entering into real partnership with the British government where consultation on postwar Germany was concerned, Churchill certainly borrowed ideas from Haffner and others to feed his own prejudices.[37]

Conclusion

Anti-fascism is more than just an ideology, it is a meta-narrative of the twentieth century, albeit one that has suffered since the end of the Cold War at the hands of competing narratives based on nationalism and in the wake of the anti-communist backlash. As David Kettler says, 'there is unfinished business with regard to the costs of treating Antifascism as nothing but an obsolete instrument of political manipulation'.[38] Or, even more starkly, in Traverso's words, 'Anti-fascism cannot be reduced to a simple variation of Soviet Communism.'[39] Borkenau, Kolnai and Haffner show the truth of these claims, and analysing their contribution to the anti-fascist struggle of the late 1930s makes clear how unjust the contemporary revisionist account of anti-fascism that does reduce it to a variant of Soviet communism is to the complex reality of the anti-fascist movement.[40] All three men, but Kolnai in particular, went on after 1945 to become anti-communist Cold

Warriors,[41] but even during the fight against Nazism none subscribed (or, in Borkenau's case, not for long) to the version of anti-fascism that some commentators would have us believe was the only one – the communist variant. Kolnai later wrote with some regret of his pre-war activities, stating not only that his belief that '"anti-Fascism" must imply a resolute Leftism (short of Communism) as its foundation and operational frame' had been an illusion but that 'not only was there greater moral weight in combating Fascism on conservative grounds, even "anti-Fascism" as such made us miss the special edge of *Naziism*'.[42] But even such claims – which today's anti-fascists might find disagreeable – reveal that holding an anti-communist position should not automatically lead one to reject anti-fascism, and that the tendency for the former (anti-communism) to lead to the latter (rejecting anti-fascism) can potentially take one in the direction of apologies for fascism.

In the context of Britain in the 1930s, the basic position of the émigré anti-fascists – that there could and should be no compromise with fascism – was a shock to the appeasers, fellow travellers and opponents of fascism (whether pacifist or not) alike, with the exception of the active anti-fascist militants. For them, the writings of the exiles, if they read them at all, would have confirmed their belief that only street action was the answer, and heightened their distaste for what they saw as the inability of 'liberal' opponents to organise or to offer an alternative political vision. But the émigrés' critique of 'English' liberalism, regarding its desire for conversation and diplomacy as inappropriate when faced with Nazism, brought a new seriousness to the understanding of what the Third Reich and, by extension, British fascism, was all about, for they could not simply be lumped together with the communists and the small militant ultra-leftist anti-fascist groups that could so easily be discredited by the mainstream, middle-class press. The émigrés may have been regarded as extreme, but by the late 1930s a position that had been confined to the Far Left was now shown to be compatible with all shades of political opinion short of the extreme Right. It is important to remember here that the books I have discussed were all published in the late 1930s, long after both the BUF's success had peaked and the British anti-fascist movement, with all its strands and feuds, had developed, in the context of a wider acceptance of the need for rearmament and a deepening sense of the inevitability of war with Germany. Although the political émigrés tended to be overlooked by the Foreign Office,[43] anti-fascist intellectuals had a greater impact in the public sphere. Where in the 1920s and early 1930s British anti-fascism had, understandably, been a response to the emergence of British fascism, the émigrés helped to prepare active anti-fascists and the politically inactive alike for the magnitude of the European and worldwide task that lay ahead.

Notes

1 Nigel Copsey, *Anti-Fascism in Britain* (Basingstoke: Macmillan, 2000), p. 2. See also Nigel Copsey and David Renton (eds), *British Fascism, the Labour Movement and the State* (Basingstoke: Palgrave Macmillan, 2005).

2 David Kettler, 'Antifascism as Ideology: Review and Introduction', p. 16. Online at www.bard.edu/contestedlegacies/lib/kettler_articles.php?action=getfile&id=362394 (accessed 14 March 2008); David Renton, 'A Provisional History of Anti-Fascism in Britain: The Forties', paper given to Northern Marxist Historians Group, 18 September 1996. Online at http://members. lycos. co.uk/mere_pseud_mag_ed/History/Renton1.htm (accessed 25 March 2008). See also, for a case study, Neil Barrett, 'The Anti-Fascist Movement in South-East Lancashire, 1933–1940: The Divergent Experiences of Manchester and Nelson', in Tim Kirk and Anthony McElligott (eds), *Opposing Fascism: Community, Authority and Resistance in Europe* (Cambridge: Cambridge University Press, 1999), pp. 48–62.

3 Enzo Traverso, 'Intellectuals and Anti-Fascism: For a Critical Historization', *New Politics* 9, 4 (2004), online at: www.wpunj.edu/~newpol/issue36/Traverso 36.htm (accessed 14 March 2008).

4 See for example, Francis L. Carsten, 'German Refugees in Great Britain 1933–1945: A Survey', in Gerhard Hirschfeld (ed.), *Exile in Great Britain: Refugees from Hitler's Germany* (Leamington Spa: Berg Publishers, 1984), p. 11; Ludwig Eiber, 'Verschwiegene Bündnispartner: Die Union deutscher sozialistischer Organisationen in Großbritannien und die britische Nachrichtendienste', *Exilforschung: Ein internationales Jahrbuch* 15 (1997), 68.

5 For example, Herbert Loebl, 'Das Refugee Industries Committee: Eine wenig bekannte britische Hilfsorganisation', *Exilforschung: Ein internationales Jahrbuch* 8 (1990), 220–41; Hirschfeld (ed.), *Exile in Great Britain*; Daniel Snowman, *The Hitler Emigrés: The Cultural Impact of Refugees from Nazism* (London: Chatto & Windus, 2002); Marion Berghahn, *Continental Britons: German-Jewish Refugees from Nazi Germany*, rev edn (New York: Berghahn Books, 2006).

6 Werner Röder, 'The Political Exiles: Their Policies and Their Contribution to Post-War Reconstruction', in Herbert Strauss and Werner Röder (eds), pp. xxvii–xl *International Biographical Dictionary of Central European Emigrés 1933–1945, Volume II Part 1: A–K. The Arts, Sciences, and Literature* (Munich: K. G. Saur, 1983); Andreas Klugescheid, '"His Majesty's Most Loyal Enemy Aliens": Der Kampf deutsch-jüdischer Emigranten in den britischen Streitkräften 1939–1945', *Exilforschung: Ein internationales Jahrbuch* 19 (2001), 106–27; Helga Grebing, 'Was wird aus Deutschland nach dem Krieg? Perspektiven linkssozialistischer Emigration für den Neuaufbau Deutschlands nach dem Zusammenbruch der nationalsozialistischen Diktatur', *Exilforschung: Ein internationales Jahrbuch* 3 (1985), 43–58; Jan Foitzik, 'Revolution und Demokratie: Zu den sofort- und Übergangsplanungen des sozialdemokratischen Exils für Deutschland 1943–1945', *Internationale wissenschaftliche*

Korrespondenz zur Geschichte der deutschen Arbeiterbewegung 24, 3 (1988), 308–42; Isabelle Tombs, 'Socialists Debate Their History from the First World War to the Third Reich: German Exiles and the British Labour Party', in Stefan Berger, Peter Lambert and Peter Schuman (eds), *Historikerdialoge: Geschichte, Mythos und Gedächtnis im deutsch-britischen kulturellen Austausch 1750–2000* (Göttingen: Vandenhoeck & Ruprecht, 2003), pp. 361–81; Marjorie Lamberti, 'German Antifascist Refugees in America and the Public Debate on "What Should be Done with Germany after Hitler," 1941–1945', *Central European History* 40 (2007), 279–305.

7 Röder, 'The Political Exiles', p. xxxv.
8 John P. Fox, 'Nazi Germany and German Emigration to Great Britain', in *Exile in Great Britain*, Hirschfeld (ed.), *Exile in Great Britain*, pp. 38f.
9 Copsey, *Anti-Fascism in Britain*, p. 6.
10 Fox, 'Nazi Germany and German Emigration', p. 61, n70. Among their most relevant publications, see Ernst Toller, *I Was a German* (London: John Lane, 1934); Otto Lehmann Russbüldt, *Germany's Air Force* (London, G. Allen & Unwin, 1935); Gerhart Seger, *A Nation Terrorised* (Chicago: Reilly & Lee Co., 1935); Franz Neumann, *Behemoth: The Structure and Practice of National Socialism* (London: Victor Gollancz, 1943). See also Charmian Brinson, 'The Gestapo and the German Political Exiles in Britain during the 1930s: The Case of Hans Wesemann – and Others', *German Life and Letters* 51, 1 (1998), 43–64; James J. Barnes and Patience P. Barnes, *Nazi Refugee Turned Spy: The Life of Hans Wesemann, 1895–1971* (Westport, CT: Greenwood Press, 2001), pp. 32–5; Andrea Reiter, *Narrating the Holocaust* (London: Continuum, 2000), on Seger's internment in Oranienburg; Anson Rabinbach, 'Staging Antifascism: The Brown Book of the Reichstag Fire and Hitler Terror', *New German Critique* 103 (2008), 97–126.
11 Michael Seyfert, '"His Majesty's Most Loyal Internees". The Internment and Deportation of German and Austrian Refugees as "Enemy Aliens": Historical, Cultural and Literary Aspects', in Hirschfeld (ed.), *Exile in Great Britain*, p. 185.
12 Gaetano Salvemini, *Under the Axe of Fascism* (London: Victor Gollancz, 1936), pp. 119, 156. Luigi Sturzo, 'Fascism and Nazism', *Quarterly Review* 261 (1933), 162–76.
13 George Seldes, *Sawdust Caesar: The Untold History of Mussolini and Fascism* (London: Arthur Baker, 1936). Seldes was an American radical journalist. See also R. J. B. Bosworth, *The Italian Dictatorship: Problems and Perspectives in the Interpretation of Mussolini and Fascism* (London: Arnold, 1998), ch. 2.
14 George Orwell, 'Review of *The Totalitarian Enemy*', in Sonia Orwell and Ian Angus (eds), *The Collected Essays, Journalism and Letters of George Orwell. Vol. 2: My Country Right or Left, 1940–1943* (Harmondsworth: Penguin, 1970), p. 40. Carsten too described Borkenau as 'the eminent anti-Nazi publicist and writer'; 'German Refugees in Britain', p. 22.
15 Orwell, 'Review of *The Totalitarian Enemy*', p. 42.
16 Franz Borkenau, *Austria and After* (London: Faber and Faber, 1938), p. 15.
17 Franz Borkenau, *The New German Empire* (Harmondsworth: Penguin, 1939), p. 11. Further references in the text.
18 Franz Borkenau, 'The German Problem', *Dublin Review* 209 (October 1941), 196.

19 Victor Gollancz, 'The Most Important Book the Club Has Issued', *Left News* 25 (May 1938), 790–1.
20 Orwell, 'Review of *The Totalitarian Enemy*', p. 40.
21 On Personalism see John Hellman, 'From the Söhlbergkreis to Vichy's Elite Schools: The Rise of the Personalists', in Zeev Sternhell (ed.), *The Intellectual Revolt Against Liberal Democracy 1870–1945* (Jerusalem: Israel Academy of Sciences and Humanities, 1996), pp. 252–65.
22 Aurel Kolnai, *The War Against the West* (London: Victor Gollancz, 1938), p. 518. Further references in the text.
23 Reviews cited by Kolnai in *Twentieth-Century Memoirs* (1952–55), VII, p. 84. Kings College London, Archives, MV29/8.
24 Francis Dunlop, *The Life and Thought of Aurel Kolnai* (Aldershot: Ashgate, 2002), p. 137.
25 Aurel Kolnai, 'Die Credo der neuen Barbaren', *Oesterreichische Volkswirt* 24 (3 September 1932), p. 1174.
26 Aurel Kolnai, 'Pacifism Means Suicide', *The Nation* (21 January 1939), p. 88.
27 Aurel Kolnai, *The Pivotal Principles of NS Ideology* (handwritten ms, 1939), p. 3, in possession of Francis Dunlop, University of East Anglia.
28 Copsey, *Anti-Fascism in Britain*, p. 46.
29 Kolnai, *Twentieth-Century Memoirs*, VII, p. 10. Kings College London, Archives, MV29/8.
30 On Haffner in the context of the German exiles in Britain see Werner Röder, *Die deutschen sozialistischen Exilgruppen in Großbritannien 1940–1945: Ein Beitrag zur Geschichte des Widerstandes gegen den Nationalsozialismus*, rev. edn (Bonn-Bad Godesberg: Verlag Neue Gesellschaft, 1973), pp. 132–4.
31 For other appraisals of *Germany Jekyll and Hyde*, see Jörg Thunecke, '"Characterology", not "Ideology": Sebastian Haffner's Refutation of Daniel Goldhagen in *Germany: Jekyll and Hyde* (1940)', in Ian Wallace (ed.), *German-Speaking Exiles in Great Britain, Yearbook of the Research Centre for German and Austrian Exile Studies* 1 (1999), 75–93; Nick Hubble, 'Franz Borkenau, Sebastian Haffner and George Orwell: Depoliticisation and Cultural Exchange', in Edward Timms and Jon Hughes (eds), *Intellectual Migration and Cultural Transformation: Refugees from National Socialism in the English-Speaking World* (Vienna: Springer, 2003), pp. 109–27.
32 Sebastian Haffner, *Germany Jekyll and Hyde: An Eyewitness Analysis of Nazi Germany* (London: Libris, 2005), p. 5. Further references in the text. [Orig. London: Secker and Warburg, 1940.]
33 Ian Kershaw, 'Hitler and the Uniqueness of Nazism', *Journal of Contemporary History* 39, 2 (2004), 242.
34 Jonathan Petropoulos, 'The Nazi Kleptocracy: Reflections on Avarice and the Holocaust', and Frank Bajohr, 'Cliques, Corruption, and Organised Self-Pity: The Nazi Movement and the Property of the Jews', both in Dagmar Herzog (ed.), *Lessons and Legacies, Vol. VII: The Holocaust in International Perspective* (Evanston: Northwestern University Press, 2006), pp. 29–38 and 39–49. On the Frankfurt School, especially Friedrich Pollock's view of Nazism as a 'racket', see Martin Jay, *The Dialectical Imagination: A History of the Frankfurt School and the Institute of Social Research, 1923–1950* (Berkeley: University of California Press, 1996 [1973]), pp. 156–7.

35 Georges Perec, *W, or the Memory of Childhood*, trans. David Bellos (London: The Harvill Press, 1996).

36 Lothar Kettenacker, 'The Influence of German Refugees on British War Aims', in Hirschfeld (ed.), *Exile in Great Britain*, p. 106.

37 Neal Ascherson, 'Introduction' to *Germany Jekyll and Hyde*, p. xviii; Kettenacker, 'The Influence of German Refugees', pp. 108–9.

38 Kettler, 'Antifascism as Ideology', p. 5.

39 Traverso, 'Intellectuals and Anti-Fascism', p. 6. See Andrzej Olechnowicz, 'Liberal Anti-Fascism in the 1930s: The Case of Sir Ernest Barker', *Albion* 36, 4 (2004), 636–60 for an example from Britain, and Peter Monteath, 'A Day to Remember: East Germany's Day of Remembrance for the Victims of Fascism', *German History* 26, 2 (2008), 195–218 for the ways in which the GDR's official ceremony has been taken over and developed by grassroots movements since the demise of the regime.

40 See also George L. Mosse, *Confronting History: A Memoir* (Madison: University of Wisconsin Press, 2000), pp. 100–12 for an interesting consideration of this point.

41 See Jeffrey C. Isaac, 'Critics of Totalitarianism', in *The Cambridge History of Twentieth-Century Political Thought*, in Terence Ball and Richard Bellamy (eds) (Cambridge: Cambridge University Press, 2003), p. 192 for broader context.

42 Aurel Kolnai, *Twentieth-Century Memoirs*, Kings College London Archives, MV29/8, pp. 72–3, 77.

43 Anthony Glees, 'The German Political Exile in London 1939–1945: The SPD and the British Labour Party', in Hirschfeld (ed.), *Exile in Great Britain*, p. 98.

9
Labour Theorises Fascism: A. D. Lindsay and Harold Laski

Andrzej Olechnowicz

> But we are all students – enforced students – today, in the debate and clash of doctrines which whirls around us and affects all our lives. ... Forty years ago I could keep abreast of the political literature which concerned my times: today it is a hopeless task.[1]

Introduction

This chapter engages with three strands of recent historiography. The first is David Renton's distinction between 'anti-fascists' and 'non-fascists' whereby only organised, active resistance counts as 'anti-fascism'.[2] The second is the common view that Continental labour parties failed to prevent the rise to power of fascism because they were 'ideological' and subservient to the Comintern's reckless and opportunistic manipulation of 'Marxism'.[3] In the most crass hands this becomes a wholesale condemnation of Marxism as an intellectual project,[4] even a wholesale denigration of the 'entire anti-fascist tradition'.[5]

The third is Dan Stone's contention that 'anti-fascism' was a Continental not an indigenous phenomenon, the creation of émigré scholars such as Borkenau and Kolnai, some of whose writings were available in English. Although 'many books were published that subjected Nazism to tough-minded analysis, and almost every issue of a "quality" journal dealt with the subject in one way or another', Stone maintains 'that it took a handful of continental writers to alert the British to the seriousness of Nazism'. British writers expressed moral outrage, but did not produce perceptive and detailed analyses.[6] The reason why conservative and liberal understandings of fascism, which were 'based on arguing logically against fascist ideas', or vulgar Marxist ones did not apprehend the 'seriousness of Nazism' was because they failed to 'understand the force of its attraction'. This was based on the quest for 'power as an end in itself, not power as the means for implementing a particular social programme; power as an affective force, an inherent aggression that permanently needed an outlet'. Compared to this elemental 'energy of nihilism', 'the ideas of fascism are of secondary concern'.[7] The only exceptions to this British failing were, according to Stone, 'a few lesser studies', and most notably R. G. Collingwood, who recognised that fascists and Nazis were successful in annihilating liberal-democratic opposition because they had 'the power of arousing emotion in their support', making it '"think with their blood", as the Nazis say'.[8] The explanation for this lies not in the existence of 'a kind of common-sense empiricism in Britain' which was insensitive to the role of passions in politics; rather 'it makes more sense historically to suggest that the reasons why British authors failed to take Nazism seriously were that their own circumstances – political and social contexts, and intellectual frameworks – did not permit it to be understood'.[9]

This chapter will examine the activities of two prominent Labour public intellectuals – A. D. Lindsay and Harold Laski – in order to challenge each of these three strands. Firstly, both combined the active and contemplative life, engaging in courageous political action as well as lecturing and publishing extensively, in a way that makes a nonsense of Renton's position. Moreover, although both were in certain respects involved in government service, neither thereby surrendered the responsibility of the intellectual to be 'the author of a language that tries to speak the truth to power'.[10] Secondly, both found certain aspects of Marx's thought attractive. In the case of Lindsay this did not inform his rather shallow and superficial understanding of fascism; but in the case of Laski it did, with Laski coming close in the mid-thirties to the Comintern line. Both, however, remained attached to the value of political discussion and Britain's liberal freedoms; and 'Marxism' did not oblige Laski to surrender individual conscience in a way that many critical of left-wing anti-fascism have believed inevitable.

Thirdly, Stone's is a more partial account than he allows. His critique is certainly valid in the case of Lindsay, who did little more than warn against the menace of fascism and showed no awareness of Continental writers: his chief contribution was to re-state the essentials of democracy. Laski, however, as his thinking about fascism evolved, came to endorse by 1943 a view of fascism as a *'condottiere'* or 'gangster' regime rooted not in a systematic political philosophy but an expansionist, destructive quest for arbitrary power. Moreover, Laski was well aware of Continental writing and far less sanguine about the improbability of fascism in Britain. Still, the analyses of Laski and Lindsay are less impressive in some respects than those of many European émigrés writers working in much less comfortable circumstances. To some extent these shortcomings were a consequence of Lindsay's and Laski's many other commitments;[11] but they also reflected weaknesses in the academic study of politics in Britain. But this is a different charge from that of a lack of awareness of 'the seriousness of Nazism' which Stone makes. To privilege exclusively a recognition of the nihilistic energy of Nazism is to foreclose understanding in a way that Lindsay and Laski would have found intolerant. It thereby pays scant regard to others ways of characterising fascism which many contemporary as well as later writers have considered important. For some the connection between a particular personality type and fascism was critical.[12] For a 'surprising number of socialists' the 'socialistic' elements of fascism proved attractive enough to cause them to move from the Left to the Right in the thirties.[13] For yet others the critical relationship was between liberalism and fascism (and communism) since the former was 'the parent of these ungracious children', though 'so great is its influence over them that each finds it necessary to make some compromise': fascism claimed that it was 'the truest and most genuine democracy'.[14] Both Lindsay and Laski were preoccupied (in different ways) with fascism's connection with liberalism.

Finally, this chapter continues the recent re-evaluation of Laski's status as a Labour thinker.[15] While Lindsay's political thought has received a largely favourable verdict as being 'wise and admirable',[16] Laski's was for a long time denigrated. Deane in particular argued that the role Laski accorded to noneconomic factors in his wartime view of fascism meant that his Marxist 'doctrine' of the state 'finally collapses'; but Laski continued to repeat the 'familiar and persuasive' Marxist phrases causing reality to recede 'farther and farther from his grasp' until he had 'to a large extent, substituted a world of fiction and shadows for the world of facts'.[17] With regard to fascism, however, it is Lindsay who demonstrated little or no intellectual curiosity in analysing its precise character while Laski continually struggled to do so and arrived at an understanding which views such as Deane's misrepresent or misunderstand.

Action

A. D. Lindsay was Master of Balliol College from 1924 to 1949 and a key figure in the Oxford Labour Club, who embodied the centrist instincts of a broad Oxford liberalism.[18] He thought Labour in 1939 'a party with no leaders worth mentioning' but the Liberals 'leaders with no party worth mentioning';[19] and he admired the working-class movement as 'the most democratic thing in the world and democracy is bred in the bone of its members'.[20] He was an adviser on education to the party and his commitment was recognised by the offer of a peerage in 1945. Laski became Professor of Political Science at the London School of Economics in 1926. He had joined the Fabian Society executive committee in 1921 and was elected to the Labour Party national executive committee in 1937. From November 1934 to 1945 he was an alderman on Fulham borough council and played an active role on three committees.[21] While Lindsay was probably in broad agreement with Labour's anti-fascist stance in *Democracy versus Dictatorship*,[22] Laski was not, and did not accept that fascism and communism were equivalent forms of 'totalitarian dictatorship' (until his disillusionment with the Communist Party's policy of 'revolutionary defeatism' in October 1939).[23] While it seems they moved in different circles, there is evidence of some contact.[24] Both, moreover, published sympathetic popular studies of Marxism, with Lindsay's *Karl Marx's Capital* condemned as a 'subtly poisonous book'.[25] While Laski acknowledged the value of Lindsay's book in the preface to *Communism* (1927),[26] Lindsay believed, in the title of an address to the Glasgow I.L.P. in 1923, 'We are not the Prey of Blind Economic Forces, but are the Masters of our Social Fate', a view he found confirmed by Marx himself,[27] whereas Laski was less sanguine about the malleability of economic forces. Nonetheless, at the level of theory, both undertook to 'demolish the foundations of individualistic society'.[28]

Both recognised the menace of fascism; but while for Lindsay this was primarily a matter of resisting the external threat of Continental fascism, for Laski it was equally about meeting the genuine internal threat posed by the British Union of Fascists and the National Government in the face of capitalist crisis. By September 1935 Lindsay believed that both Britain and 'much more strikingly' America had shown that 'a democratic government can survive [an economic] crisis' and any 'democratic crisis' was also manageable since democracy 'just because it is alive is always in crisis'. Since democratic politics remained intact, the task was to ensure 'no compromise between the totalitarian state and democracy' in the face of 'the challenge of National Socialism'.[29] Laski's tone was altogether darker and more desperate. Already towards the end of 1933 Laski was noting the 'fascistic' tendencies of the National Government;[30] and Conservative ministers were in turn condemning

'Professor Laski and his friends, the Communists'.[31] He wrote to Justice Holmes at the same time that the British government was 'completely supine' in the face of the 'new Germany' which was 'brutal, beastly, and belligerent':

> The whole thing, not least the Reichstag trial, is a perpetual nightmare; and the sense of helplessness one has as chaos comes ever more near is a grim experience. I have never seen a whole continent before drift with open eyes into a dark age.

The following year he feared that 'we are in for an iron age in which the chances of decency will be small; and it is not going to be easy for those of us who think that the claims of reason against passion are paramount'; and that it could not 'seriously be denied that Fascism grows'.[32] Laski had appreciated Mosley's 'rhetorical gifts' and 'great gifts of leadership' in May 1930 when he had still been a Labour MP, and now saw them in the service of the BUF, which attacked him personally as the 'little Jewish professor'. In 1934 the fascist ideologist William Allen characterised fascist leaders as 'natural aristocrats' and Laski as one who 'wails against these new men'.[33] Dystopian fantasies of a fascist takeover in Britain circulated,[34] and even in the period 1936–39 some progressive opinion was not willing to discount entirely the possibility of a fascist revival in Britain.[35] In 1937 Laski could see 'no logical reason' why Britain should be free of fascism and feared that the beliefs that 'such an experience is wholly alien from our character, or that democratic institutions are here too firmly rooted to be overthrown' were unconvincing responses.[36]

Lindsay and Laski responded by taking action against fascism. It may not have been the street fighting stipulated by Renton (though Laski did monitor the policing of street demonstrations for the National Council for Civil Liberties, of which he was a founder member);[37] but it was purposeful and courageous action none the less. Both were involved in a large number of press campaigns.[38] Laski was involved in organisations such as the Relief Committee for the Victims of German and Austrian Fascism and in the international support for the four Communists charged with the Reichstag fire in 1934.[39] He played an important role in creating the LSE's Academic Assistance Council and was tireless in finding employment for émigré scholars,[40] including Gaetano Salvemini, who dedicated his study of the origins of Italy's fascist dictatorship to 'English friends who have caused me to realize that I have two countries',[41] and Franz Neumann, whose doctorate he supervised at the LSE.[42] In May 1936 he joined Victor Gollancz and John Strachey in launching the Left Book Club, and encouraging the formation of local discussion groups which often became 'centres of active and energetic work for a "Popular Front" in their localities'.[43] Laski worked tirelessly as a writer and a speaker in the Socialist League from 1932 until its dissolution in 1937 to unite first left-wing forces in a United Front and then all progressive forces in a Popular Front.[44] Lindsay's contribution to the Popular Front campaign was even more dramatic: he stood as an 'Independent Progressive' in the Oxford by-election in October 1938, arguing that 'only a profound sense of our destiny and purpose as a great democratic people can unite us in the efforts required of us'.[45]

Beside these partisan actions, both also participated in 'non-party' (that is, all-party) initiatives to strengthen British democracy. Lindsay was chairman of the Unemployment Committee of the National Council of Social Service throughout the 1930s, in which role he fostered the growth of local schemes to provide a 'varied range of opportunities open by day to those who are without work, and to their friends as well after working hours'.[46] Their object was to dispel 'the curse of all the days that have somehow got to be spent', which had a 'deteriorating effect' on character and made the unemployed potentially vulnerable to the appeal of fascist demagoguery.[47] This was crucial work, for Lindsay believed that when recovery came, there would still be 'a fairly large section of the unemployed that it will not reabsorb'.[48] As well as this practical task, the N.C.S.S. regarded its work as demonstrating the value of 'Diversity, Local Autonomy and Cooperation' and that 'a self-imposed unity is no less effective than a super-imposed uniformity'.[49] The fullest defence of social service in the face of fascism (and communism) came in 1938:

> Two kinds of all-controlling State are functioning in Europe to-day; ours might be a third kind, tempered by democratic processes and traditions. But it may be questioned how far and how long those processes and traditions would survive; for they have been continuously moulded and strengthened by the free criticism and constructive public effort of the community expressing itself outside, as well as through the formal machinery of government. ... Social service is a name, perhaps an inadequate name, for the thinking and acting which the community has got to do for itself outside, but often in partnership with, the machinery of State, if it is to get the kind of social evolution it wants.[50]

Laski too endorsed the value of voluntary action, not only in his long-standing commitment to educational settlements,[51] but in his membership of the Association for Education in Citizenship, founded by the Liberal Sir Ernest Simon in 1934 to promote 'training in the moral qualities necessary for the citizens of a democracy', and including Conservatives such as Arthur Bryant.[52]

Although they had different conceptions of fascism and of the Labour Party, the anti-fascist activism of Lindsay and Laski was broadly identical. Laski's Marxist analyses did not prevent him co-operating with supporters of the National Government; and he certainly enjoyed socialising with and gossiping about the political and social elites.[53] This combination has exercised some commentators. For Noël Annan it represented a personal failing on Laski's part: there was a contradiction between 'the sober suit of a constitutionalist' corresponding with Justice Holmes and 'the tweed coat and flannel bags of the ardent revolutionary and use of language of class warfare'. Annan appears to believe that National Government figures discounted this contradiction because of 'the Establishment belief that in high politics statesmen all talk the same language', making them 'insensitive' to ideology.[54] For the Marxist Dmitri Mirsky in 1935, Laski was 'most typical' of the 'labourist intelligentsia' which, finding itself 'a "responsible" part of "his majesty's opposition", which meant that at any moment it might be called upon to take over the command', played the role of 'defence corps to protect the extant social system from the working class'.[55] Neither view is wholly convincing; and Laski's instincts were more complex.

Laski understood and deplored the force of 'English snobbery'. He agreed with Bagehot that the English were deferential, affected by 'even the remotest members of the Royal Family'; and this included the Labour Party, 'many of whose members assume that the battle of social justice has been won because they dine at the great houses'. Laski rejected as superficial the idea that this demonstrated the absence of 'a democratic spirit' in England; rather it reflected 'a collective inferiority complex'. For two centuries people had been taught that 'only the gentleman is fit to govern' and gentlemen had 'inherited unquestioned leadership'. The gentleman was now a 'public danger' since 'he has never encouraged himself to use his imagination; and for our problems imaginative leadership is above all essential' and because opposition to his superiority 'tends, by its surprise, to embitter him'. And yet, wrote Laski, no one would see his passing 'without a brief annotation of regret'. The gentleman had tolerated the 'open mind', clemency and 'difference of opinion'; the plutocrats of the new ruling class would govern by 'hewing' their way to their goal.[56] Laski consistently praised these 'bourgeois' values. While working on *Communism*, he wrote to

Justice Holmes that he found its dogmatism 'unlovely' and that 'I emerge also with the conviction that toleration and good will, bourgeois as they are, outweigh in virtue all the other qualities in the world'. In 1933 he praised a speech on intolerance by H. G. Wells as 'one of the ablest pleas for free discussion I have ever heard'.[57] Moreover, he retained some aspects of his early pluralism as his thought developed: the emphasis on active citizenship and the idea that individual fulfilment consisted of developing an 'active mind' through 'personal experimentation'.[58] One aspect of Mirsky's criticism was that Laski's commitment to 'the absolute value and rights of the individual' was incompatible with attacking the *status quo*; in truth there was a tension in Laski's thought in the 1930s, but the war resolved this by enabling him to believe that the strengthened position of labour made possible 'revolution by consent'.[59]

Perhaps of greater importance was that both Laski and Lindsay were, in a real sense, part of the governing institutions – examples of Nairn's general thesis that the British intelligentsia is 'much more part of the state ... than in any other bourgeois society'.[60] As chairman of the Unemployment Committee Lindsay was in regular contact with ministers and negotiated and administered government grants; and Brian Harrison maintains that Oxford generally had 'a taste for the practical' which made it 'alert to governmental concerns'.[61] Laski was a member of the Donoughmore Committee on Ministers' Powers between 1929 and 1932, the Departmental Committee on Local Government Officers between 1930 and 1934, and the Lord Chancellor's Committee on Legal Education between 1932 and 1934. For fifteen years from 1926 he was a member of the Industrial Court, maintaining the confidence of both the Treasury and the Civil Service.[62] Lindsay and Laski were insiders who understood the consequences of *action* based on an 'ethic of intentions'.[63]

Lindsay: Mass society, German nationalism and British democracy

Christopher Hill wrote that Lindsay 'gave a lead where few others in university circles did ... in opposing Nazism earlier than was fashionable'.[64] What is striking is that he did not produce a *theory* of fascism; and the political theory that he did produce was woolly and vague. There are a number of possible explanations for this. One might be the fact that he meant to but did not get round to it in the midst of many other commitments. At the end of *The Modern Democratic State* (1943) he wrote that 'in the next volume we examine the modern challenges to democracy', the greatest being totalitarianism which succeeded by 'the suppression of discussion';[65] but a second volume did not appear. Even if it had, however, it is unlikely that it would have presented a theory of *fascism*. There were two reasons for this.

First, Lindsay believed that fascism (like communism but unlike liberal democracy) was an 'ideology' the characteristic of which was its 'obvious irrationality', the inability to 'reason and think out honestly' its doctrines. A fifth-form boy 'would have the sense to know what nonsense those theories are' and therefore 'they do not bear thinking out' – a fact 'very obvious to people ... who have spent large portions of their lives teaching political theory'. Instead Nazi doctrines were 'meant to make everyone frightfully excited' and were exercises in 'mass psychology'.[66]

Second, 'mass society' was the fundamental challenge to liberal democracies. As Karl Mannheim wrote to Lindsay in 1940:

> I am delighted to know that we are working on such similar lines. It is amazing that you should have seen as early as 1934 trends of which the meaning is only becoming evident to us today. The Crisis of Democracy in mass society, the necessity for growing state interference in an industrial society, the standardisation of life through the application of science, the antagonism, capitalism versus socialism becoming a minor issue versus these trends, and so many other things.[67]

Lindsay was deeply influenced by Ortega y Gasset's 'remarkable book', *The Revolt of the Masses*, published in English in 1932, and by Adolph Löwe's 'beautiful and penetrating study', *The Price of Liberty*.[68] Ortega's themes of the purposelessness of the mass-man, who 'simply goes drifting along', 'the political dominance of the masses', 'the barbarism of specialisation', the novelty of fascism as 'the right not to be reasonable, the "reason of unreason"', the mass-man's determination 'to have done with discussion', 'the absorption of all spontaneous social effort by the State' at the behest of the masses and the view that 'all nationalisms are so many blind alleys' are all prominent in his work.[69] Löwe argued, said Lindsay, that 'if for any reason you allow Society to become dissolved into isolated, suspicious units, if the ordinary close, small, complex texture of social life goes to pieces, it has got to be forcibly united for purposes of government'.[70] Lindsay's own view was that:

> Modern industrialism has taken away from the great mass of men in an industrialized community their independence. It has condemned

very many of them to specialized and narrow lives. ... How can we keep a modern industrial society from becoming not a community but a mob, not a society of persons capable of judging for themselves, discussing and criticizing from their experience of life the proposals put before them, but a mass played upon by the clever people at the top? These, nowadays armed with new psychological techniques, claim to be able to manipulate those masses to their will, make them believe what the rulers want, hate what the rulers want, and even fight and die for what the rulers want.[71]

It was not capitalism as such but any economic system based on mass production which centralised planning and control in a 'scientific' business administration which anticipated 'totalitarian government'.[72] Nazi Germany demonstrated that it was possible for a government 'to get such control over the minds and wills of a people and to have imposed such discipline upon them' as to make them 'ready to undergo almost any sacrifices'.[73]

What was distinctive about Lindsay's version of mass society was the significance he attached to the 'powerful and malignant theory' of scientific individualism and its most acute exponent Hobbes. It was a theory of society which 'denies the possibility of a will for the common good' since its fundamental unit is the mechanistic 'Economic Man' invented by Hobbes; and:

Hobbes himself was acute enough to see that if men are really isolated, equipollent units, united only by relations external to their nature, they can only be held together by a power external to them. He had no illusions that such men could make a working democracy. He wanted Hitler and a totalitarian state.

Modern society not only faced the same 'theoretical desire' to see society in this way as in Hobbes's day; but there were now also 'much more potent practical forces working in the same direction'.[74]

Fascism then represented only one variant of mass society for Lindsay. In one respect, Germany was peculiarly vulnerable. Lindsay emphasised the authoritarian characteristics of the historic Prussian state and of German nationalism – themes he had first developed in 1914.[75] He wrote that the Prussian state had enforced 'the absolutist doctrine of the state ... absorbing in itself the activities of its members'.[76] He distinguished between 'nationality' – 'a sense of belonging together', with democratic states ones in which 'differences are recognized and maintained alongside of the unity' – and 'nationalism' – 'a collective or mass emotion'. Germany did not have a democratic nationality and was left with nationalism, which 'as a mass emotion ... discourages criticism and discussion and is so far naturally anti-democratic'.[77]

In another respect, Germany was *typical* in experiencing 'the distraction of the War', and an 'economic crisis' which 'put a severe strain upon post-war democracy'.[78] Lindsay ascribed great importance to the collapse of the German labour movement 'largely because of the failure of German democracy to grapple with wide scale unemployment'. Unemployment was 'the danger sign of an industrial democracy', creating 'a fatal division between employed and unemployed workers', and leaving workers with no economic security and 'prepared to follow anyone who would promise and give them security'.[79] Moreover, his work for the N.C.S.S. notwithstanding, Lindsay realised that for the unemployed their increased leisure was 'a burden' which 'education for leisure' could not easily compensate since they had lost 'the ordinary social structure of their lives and were isolated and disillusioned units.[80] Investigations found that German youth was 'disillusioned, cynical, indifferent' and therefore 'ready to welcome the devils who came'. Yet Lindsay believed that 'the German conditions were reproduced in faithfulness' in South Wales. There the young unemployed were also 'completely hopeless and completely cynical'. He concluded: 'We were, it was clear, preparing for another Hitler.'[81]

In sum these were largely commonplace observations – they hardly constituted a theory of fascism to compare with Neumann's or indeed Laski's. Lindsay rather concentrated on producing and spreading a *theory of democracy* which he believed was an antidote to mass society. He summarised its main features in 1935:

> The main thesis ... is that discussion is fundamental to democracy: that the purpose of democratic machinery is to represent differences: that democracy requires an official and encouraged opposition: that the principle of toleration is essential to it, and that finally democratic politics can only be successful in a democratic society – and that that means a society of democratic non-political associations. It is pointed out that one implication of all this is that in a democracy politics are a secondary matter, for the purpose of the compulsory machinery of the state is to safeguard and harmonize a common life which has its inspiration in voluntary non-political activities. There can therefore be no compromise between the totalitarian state and democracy.[82]

Lindsay repeatedly emphasised that in a democracy 'the work of developing the meaning of the good life' and overcoming sectional interests had to be left to 'individuals and voluntary associations' while the reach of the state was limited to maintaining 'a certain minimum of moral behaviour'.[83] Lindsay looked to his own Free Church background and found in Cromwell's position and in the Puritan meeting the models for the theory and the practice of a democracy of toleration and 'open discussion'.[84] The modern equivalents were the churches and, *above all*, 'the thoroughly democratic organization of the working-class movement' which created 'innumerable centres of discussion' in union branches, co-operative guilds, WEA classes and many other groups.[85] In this sense the labour *movement* was a more powerful anti-fascist force than the National *Government*: it made democracy a vibrant, daily reality.

Laski: Gangsters, socialists and appeasers

Laski did eventually arrive at a theory of fascism in *Reflections on the Revolution of Our Time* (1943) which drew upon the work of a number of Continental writers and can stand comparison with those singled out by Stone (and also with G. D. H. Cole's who, according to Tony Wright, 'provided a richer and more convincing (indeed, more accurate) account of fascism than many of his contemporaries on the left').[86] Even so, the theory is rather sketchy, poorly presented and largely without supporting evidence; and it took Laski longer than some others to move away from an over-simplified identification of fascism with the interests of a capitalist class in crisis and decline.[87]

In 1931 Laski saw the state as advancing 'the interests of the rich' and consequently fascism as 'a deliberate alteration of the whole constitutional arrangements of the state, encouraged and supported by the employers' class because it would involve, among much else, the destruction of trade-union organisation'.[88] In 1935 he argued that fascism rescued capitalism in a phase of contraction from having to concede the democratically validated economic demands of the masses by entrusting 'unlimited political power to those who own and control the means of production' which they used to destroy the labour movement and to impose wage reductions. He noted, however, that fascist state had 'built their authority in part upon an agreement with the armed forces of the society ... and, in part, by arming the forces of its own partisans'. Doctrines were designed to hide 'the sacrifice of the ordinary worker to the capitalist need to make profit' and were therefore 'nothing more than an ill-assorted rag-bag in which all kinds of remnants from the most diverse philosophies seek, as best they may, to find a place'. Laski was clear that there was nothing 'socialistic' about fascism: Hitler had explained to a 'capitalist subscriber' that 'we must talk the language of the embittered socialist workmen … or else they wouldn't feel at home with us'; but policies with 'a socialist emphasis' were abandoned to avoid any threat to private profit. He also observed that Labour's move to a 'thorough-going socialism' after 1931 caused 'members of the Conservative Party [to] show a significant tendency to question the assumptions upon which the British Constitution has long rested'.[89] Laski held to this theory for the rest of the thirties.[90]

By 1940 Laski was advancing a significantly different and more complex theory which had its most complete expression in 1943.[91] There was now an equivocation over Marxist analyses which defined fascism as 'simply the expression of monopoly-capitalism in decay': there was 'real truth in this analysis' but it was 'not, I think, rigorous enough in character to cover all the facts involved'. It gave 'inadequate attention' to two key features. The first was the fact that fascism created a mass movement of 'the disinherited' and of women through 'a skilful exploitation of nationalist sentiment' and by offering 'the prospect of a career with the right to command to those who joined it'. The second was that in power fascism was 'driven by its own inner logic to the destruction of capitalism in its historic liberal form' since the scale of public works required to absorb the unemployed could not be carried out under a capitalist economy and big business was subordinated to the needs of rearmament, which was essential in order to 'draw attention away from domestic grievance' by the restoration of national prestige.[92] Big business, the civil administration and the heads of the army had put fascist leaders in power in order to advance their own interests; but they found that they 'had put themselves under masters whose sole care was the perpetuation of their own power'. Laski now compared fascist leaders to Capone and 'Dutch Schultz' and described them as '*condottiere*' or 'outlaws' who attracted a retinue of 'mercenaries' or 'gangster-elements in society'. He looked to a psychological explanation to understand their drive: they came from those social elements which had not been able to attain success within existing society. Since their objective was 'simply to remain in power' the test of what was good was 'the purely pragmatic test of success'.[93] Success was to be ensured by a system of terror and a policy of 'conquest without in order to maintain its conquests within' – a policy which made war certain at some point.[94]

Laski continued to believe, like Lindsay, that it was a 'waste of effort' to try to find a 'philosophy of Fascism': doctrines were solely 'propaganda expedients which have no meaning except their power to bolster up the particular regime'. Fascism 'in any of its forms' was 'at bottom a doctrine-less nihilism'. He saw nothing distinctive in Nazi anti-Semitism: they deployed it as did 'every ruler who needs an enemy to exploit and property to distribute'.[95] What took the place of a body of ideas was 'worship of, and utter surrender to, the leader', who was simultaneously 'godlike' and 'of common clay'.[96] In the same way as Kolnai and countless others both before and during the war,[97] Laski saw fascism as 'the enemy of civilization': by denying 'the power of reason' and the role of 'settled legal principles' it made man 'the slave of his ugliest passions'. Without invoking the role of classes, he believed fascism was only possible in an epoch when 'men no longer have the great ends of life in common' and there was therefore 'no longer a common faith in the purposes of the law'. Resorting to the most determinist Marxist notion, Laski saw this breakdown as evidence that society had reached the point 'when its relations of production are in contradiction with its forces of production'. A new equilibrium between relations and forces of production would generate a state-power 'deemed to be devoted to purposes which command a general approval'. In these terms, fascism was 'a contradiction of the objective movement of history' because it combined 'all the elements adverse to productive capacity'. There was, however, a second reason why fascism was a passing phenomenon which demonstrated Laski's growing emphasis on psychological explanations and his acceptance of the totalitarian model: 'Psychologically, men cannot live continuously in the strain and at the tempo that totalitarian systems require. Fascism throws them too grimly out of the private routine in which most of them wish to pass their existence.'[98]

While the fascist conquest of Italy was 'not surprising', its success in Germany was, given her educated population and strong labour movement. But the Left in both countries made two fundamental errors. First, it divided the workers, 'above all by the divisions which sympathy for, and reaction against, the Communist International had created'. Second, it played at revolution, 'terrifying its bourgeoisie without ever having the material power to subdue it'; but 'refused to be the state' when it was essential for its own and democracy's survival – as in Prussia in 1932.[99] Laski also apportioned blame to the appeasers in the liberal democracies who failed to see that 'a peace-economy' was impossible for the fascist powers since it would have meant that 'attention was withdrawn from foreign adventure to domestic grievance', and who sought to avoid the 're-definition of class-relations' and the loss of their own 'time-honoured privileges' that war would inevitably entail.[100]

Conclusion: The British way

It is clear that both Lindsay and Laski took fascism seriously. Both were active anti-fascists whose choice of action was determined to some extent by the fact that they operated from within the 'governing class'. As a general proposition, the claim that Continental writers produced more impressive analyses of fascism than British ones is indefensible. Lindsay did not produce a theory of fascism. Laski did, and by 1943 it included two key insights which Stone commends in Continental writers, namely, a recognition of the energy of the 'gangster' regime, and a recognition that it was a threat to civilisation. Nonetheless, there are also weaknesses in both authors. The most striking theoretical weakness is perhaps that neither gave sustained consideration to Nazi racial thinking or policies.[101] While Lindsay's work is very lucid, it is also very general, devoid of detail and referencing, and often recycled.[102] There is no evidence in his published work or his papers that he had read a great deal about fascism. Laski's work is less vague and his occasional footnotes indicate that he kept up with Continental and American writing on fascism.[103] However, his expression is sometimes clumsy and there is often a good deal of repetition both within a book and between books.[104] As Barker said of him in 1935, 'Professor Laski ... is somewhat a plagiarist – from himself'.[105]

How, finally, should these faults be explained? Reviewers and biographers have often emphasised that both were writing under pressure of myriad other commitments and to address a wide public; and this obviously played a part. But each wrote as he did because of the way he conceived of his vocation. Laski felt that 'Oxford breeds elegant learning rather than real profundity';[106] but this waspish aside did capture something of Lindsay's outlook. For Lindsay stood out against specialisation and the danger of a division between the theoretical and practical: he regarded research 'as a form of self-indulgence'.[107] Moreover, the academic study of politics in Britain could not easily proceed towards an empirical, scientific discipline in the manner of American political science because it continued to 'rub shoulders with older accounts of the subject as a branch of moral philosophy and of history'.[108] Where the former encouraged precision, the latter encouraged speculation; and the tension is evident throughout much of Laski's work. If Lindsay and Laski acted as they did because of their position in the British political community, then they theorised fascism as they did because of their position in the British academic community.

Notes

1   Ernest Barker, 'Foreword' [5 November 1938], in Michael Oakeshott, *The Social and Political Doctrines of Contemporary Europe* (Cambridge: CUP, 1939), p. vi.

2   Dave Renton, 'The Attempted Revival of British Fascism', quoted in Nigel Copsey, *Anti-Fascism in Britain* (Basingstoke: Macmillan, 2000), p. 4; Dave Renton, *This Rough Game: Fascism and Anti-Fascism* (Stroud: Sutton, 2001), pp. xiii–xiv, 149–51.

3   For a detailed account of the resulting analyses of fascism – but one still highly critical of the Comintern, David Beetham, 'Introduction', in *Marxists in Face of Fascism: Writings by Marxists on Fascism from the Inter-war Period* (Manchester: MUP, 1983), pp. 2–62. For a more charitable view, Eric Hobsbawm, *Politics for a Rational Left: Political Writing 1977–1988* (London: Verso, 1989), pp. 105–16.

4   E.g. A. James Gregor, *The Faces of Janus: Marxism and Fascism in the Twentieth Century* (New Haven: Yale University Press, 2000).

5   Enzo Traverso, 'Intellectuals and Anti-Fascism: For a Critical Historization', *New Politics* 9 (2004), www.wpunj.edu/newpol/issue36/Traverso36.htm.

6   Dan Stone, *Responses to Nazism in Britain, 1933–1939: Before War and Holocaust* (Basingstoke: Palgrave Macmillan, 2003), pp. 9, 18, 191–2.

7   *Ibid.*, p. 18.

8   *Ibid.*, p. 9; R. G. Collingwood, 'Fascism and Nazism', *Philosophy* 15 (1940), 172.

9   Stone, *Responses*, p. 10.

10   Edward Said, *Representations of the Intellectual* (London: Vintage, 1994), p. xiv.

11   *Holmes-Laski Letters: The Correspondence of Mr. Justice Holmes and Harold J. Laski 1916–1935*, ed. by Mark DeWolfe Howe (London: Cumberlege/ OUP, 1953), p. 1458 'I have only just been able to meet the problem of time' (17 Dec. 1933). Laski often worked fifteen or sixteen hours a day: Michael Newman, *Harold Laski: A Political Biography* (Basingstoke: Macmillan, 1993), 180.

12   Beetham, *Marxists*, pp. 58–9; David McLellan, *Marxism After Marx* (Basingstoke: Macmillan), pp. 303–6.

13   Sheri Berman, *The Primacy of Politics: Social Democracy and the Making of Europe's Twentieth Century* (New York: CUP, 2006), pp. 125–51; Tony Wright, *G. D. H. Cole and Socialist Democracy* (Oxford: Clarendon Press, 1979), pp. 108–9. Stone notes that in Britain there were relatively few 'artless enthusiasts' of the Left: Stone, *Responses*, p. 8.

14   Michael Oakeshott, 'Introduction', in Oakeshott, *Social and Political Doctrines*, p. xvii; Tom Linehan, *British Fascism 1918–39: Parties, Ideology and Culture* (Manchester: MUP, 2000), pp. 1–3.

15   For the most complete rehabilitation of Laski's thought, Michael Newman, 'Harold Laski Today', *Political Quarterly* 67 (1996), 229–38; Newman, *Laski*, esp. chs 7–9; and see also Kinglsey Martin, *Harold Laski (1893–1950): A Biographical Memoir* (London: Gollancz, 1953); Granville Eastwood, *Harold Laski* (London: Mowbrays, 1977); Kenneth O. Morgan, 'Harold Laski', in *Labour People* (Oxford: OUP, 1987), p. 93; Isaac Kramnick and Barry Sheerman, *Harold Laski: A Life on the Left* (London: Hamilton, 1993).

16 W. T. Jones, 'Review: *The Modern Democratic State* by A. D. Lindsay', *Annals of the American Academy of Political and Social Science* 257 (1948), 205; Harry A. Holloway, 'A. D. Lindsay and the Problems of Mass Democracy', *Western Political Quarterly* 16 (1963), 798–813; Graham Maddox, 'The Christian Democracy of A. D. Lindsay', *Political Studies* 34 (1986), 441–55 and 'Skirmishers in Advance: A. D. Lindsay and Modern Democratic Theory', *Balliol College Annual Record 1997* (Oxford: Balliol College, 1997), pp. 11–18.

17 Herbert A. Deane, *The Political Ideas of Harold Laski* (New York: Columbia University Press, 1955), pp. 237–9. In a long review of this book, the Conservative politician Viscount Hailsham not only endorsed Deane's criticisms but stated that he had 'always refused to take Laski seriously as a political writer' and accused him of being a liar: *Yale Law Journal* 65 (1955), 281–8. His critics make much of the claim that he was an 'inveterate romancer' – with little serious evidence to substantiate it: e.g. 'Man of the Depression', *Economist*, 17 Jan. 1953.

18 Brian Harrison (ed.), *The History of the University of Oxford, Vol. 8 the Twentieth Century* (Oxford: Clarendon Press, 1994), pp. 395, 404.

19 Gary McCulloch, 'A. D. Lindsay', *Oxford Dictionary of National Biography* (online edition).

20 Lindsay of Birker, 'The New Labour Government in Britain' [n.d. 1946–49?], Lindsay Papers, LIN 158, Keele University.

21 Kramnick and Sheerman, *Laski*, pp. 338–9.

22 Michael Newman, 'Democracy versus Dictatorship: Labour's Role in the Struggle against British Fascism, 1933–1936', *History Workshop Journal* Issue 5 (1978), 68–75.

23 Harold J. Laski, 'Preface', in Victor Gollancz (ed.), *The Betrayal of the* (London: Gollancz, 1941), pp. xi–xvii.

24 E.g. Harold J. Laski to A. D. Lindsay, 27 Nov. 1948, Lindsay Papers, LIN 158.

25 *Morning Post*, 12 Feb. 1926, quoted in Harrison, *Oxford*, p. 395.

26 Harold J. Laski, *Communism* (London: Williams & Norgate, 1927), p. vii.

27 A. D. Lindsay, 'Historic Materialism', *Forward*, 10 Feb. 1923, Lindsay Papers, LIN 159.

28 Stuart Macintyre, *A Proletarian Science: Marxism in Britain 1917–1933* (Cambridge: CUP, 1980), p. 166.

29 A. D. Lindsay, *The Essentials of Democracy* (London: Cumberlege/OUP, second edition 1935), p. 1.

30 *New Clarion*, 23 Sep. 1933, quoted in Paul Corthorn, *In the Shadow of the Dictators: The British Left in the 1930s* (London: Tauris, 2006), p. 36.

31 *The Times*, 6 Oct. 1933 (Walter Elliot).

32 *Holmes-Laski Letters*, pp. 1452, 1459, 1468, 1469 (9 Sep. 1933, 17 Dec. 1933, 16 Dec. 1934).

33 Robert Skidelsky, *Oswald Mosley* (London: Macmillan, 1975), pp. 210, 313.

34 E.g. Storm Jameson's *In the Second Year* (1936), reviewed in 'In England, Too', *Time Magazine*, 17 Feb. 1936.

35 Martin Pugh, 'The Liberal Party and the Popular Front', *English Historical Review* 121 (2006), 1333.

36 Harold J. Laski, 'Foreword', in Robert A. Brady, *The Spirit and Structure of German Fascism* (London: Gollancz, 1937), p. 12.

37 Kramnick and Sheerman, *Laski*, p. 341; Mark Lilly, *The National Council for Civil Liberties: The First Fifty Years* (London: Macmillan, 1984), pp. 1–19.

38 E.g. Lindsay signed the 'Liberty and Democratic Leadership' manifesto which condemned the 'intimidating behaviour and mobilization at meetings' of the Fascist Blackshirts and the militant language of the Communists: *The Times*, 15 Feb. 1934; Laski signed a letter against the Incitement to Disaffection Bill which allowed homes to be searched 'on a warrant issued on mere suspicion': *The Times*, 27 Apr. 1934; both Lindsay and Laski signed a protest against the bombing of towns in Spain: *The Times*, 10 Feb. 1938.

39 *The Times*, 27 Feb. 1934; 2 Oct. 1934; World Committee for the Relief of the Victims of German Fascism, *The Reichstag Fire Trial: The Second Brown Book of the Hitler Terror* (London: Allen Lane/Bodley Head, 1934).

40 Ralf Dahrendorf, *LSE: A History of the London School of Economics and Political Science 1895–1995* (Oxford: OUP, 1995), pp. 286–90, 293; *Holmes-Laski Letters*, p. 1114 'I had also a very moving interview with a young Italian exile ... nearly beaten to death in his own house by a gang of Fascist ruffians' (20 Nov. 1928).

41 Gaetano Salvemini, *The Fascist Dictatorship in Italy, Vol. I, Origins and Practice* (London: Jonathan Cape, 1928). However, Salvemini considered the British government to be sympathetic to fascism: Claudia Baldoli, *Exporting Fascism: Italian Fascists and Britain's Italians in the 1930s* (Oxford: Berg, 2003), p. 10.

42 Martin Jay, *The Dialectical Imagination: A History of the Frankfurt School and the Institute of Social Research 1923–1950* (London: Heinemann, 1973), p. 144. Neumann's doctoral work was the basis of his classic book *Behemoth: The Structure and Practice of National Socialism*, published in 1942 by Gollancz as a Left Book Club choice.

43 Ben Pimlott, *Labour and the Left in the 1930s* (Cambridge: CUP, 1977), pp. 156–7. Pimlott considers that the Club's work may have been a 'crucial factor' in Vernon Bartlett's success as a Popular Front candidate in the Bridgewater by-election in November 1938.

44 Newman, *Laski*, ch. 9; David Blaazer, *The Popular Front and the Progressive Tradition: Socialists, Liberals, and the Quest for Unity, 1884–1939* (Cambridge: CUP, 1992), chs 5 & 6; Pimlott, *Labour*, chs 5, 8, 9 & 10 for a more critical assessment.

45 Drusilla Scott, *A. D. Lindsay: A Biography* (Oxford: Blackwell, 1971), p. 248. Lindsay lost but the turnout increased and the Conservative majority was reduced. For an argument that the tactic was misjudged in the case of Oxford, Pugh, 'Liberal Party', 1342.

46 *Voluntary Service: Thirteenth Annual Report of the N.C.S.S. 1932–3*, p. 20.

47 Master of Balliol, 'Time to Spare! Voluntary Work by Ordinary People', *The Listener*, 4 Jul. 1934, 7–8; 'The Lincoln Club for Unemployed Men', *Public Opinion*, 20 Jul. 1934, 56; Andrzej Olechnowicz, 'Unemployed Workers, "Enforced Leisure" and Education for "The Right Use of Leisure" in Britain, c. 1930–1952', *Labour History Review* 70 (2004), 31–7.

48 A. D. Lindsay to Lionel Ellis (secretary of the N.C.S.S.), 21 Feb. 1933, Lindsay Papers, LIN 170.

49 Wyndham Deedes, 'The Aims and Objects of the National Council of Social Service'. *The London Head Teacher* (May 1934), 14; *Voluntary Service: Seventeenth Annual Report of the N.C.S.S. 1936–7*, p. 80.

50 *Partnership in Social Effort: Eighteenth Annual Report of the N.C.S.S. 1937–8*, p. 15.

51 *The Times*, 6 Jul. 1922; 16 Jun. 1924.

52 Ernest Simon et al., *Education for Citizenship in Secondary Schools* (Oxford, 1936) n. p. 'Object'. 'Education and Citizenship', *New Statesman and Nation*, 14 Jul. 1934, 61–73.

53 *Holmes-Laski Letters*, p. 827 (6 Feb. 1926); p. 963 (18 Jul. 1927); p. 1004 (12 Nov. 1927); p. 1229 (22 Nov. 1930); p. 1270 (26 Jul. 1930). For Laski's attendance at the St. Paul's School Chesterton Society debate dinner in the company of the National Government M.P. Commander Robert Bower: *The Times*, 2 Jul. 1937.

54 Noël Annan, *Our Age: The Generation that Made Post-War Britain* (London: Fontana, 1991), pp. 246, 174.

55 Dmitri Mirsky, *The Intelligentsia of Great Britain* (London: Gollancz, 1935), p. 70.

56 Harold J. Laski, 'The Danger of Being A Gentleman: Reflections on the Ruling Class in England [1932]', in *The Danger of Being A Gentleman and Other Essays* (London: Allen & Unwin, 1939), pp. 26–30; Stefan Collini, *Absent Minds: Intellectuals in Britain* (Oxford: OUP, 2006), p. 133 observes that on many matters Laski had 'the tastes of the average educated Englishman of the period'.

57 *Holmes-Laski Letters*, p. 883 (9 Oct. 1926); p. 1453 (24 Sep. 1933).

58 Newman, 'Laski Today', 232–3; Edmund Neill, 'Review Article: Conceptions of Citizenship in Twentieth Century Britain', *Twentieth Century British History* 17 (2006), 430. Laski also, of course, published *Liberty in the Modern State* in 1930, reissued in 1937 – 'a hymn to civil liberties in highly traditional Millite terms' (K. O. Morgan).

59 Newman, *Laski*, pp. 178, 208–9.

60 Tom Nairn, *The Break-up of Britain* (London: NLB, 1977), p. 36.

61 Harrison, *Oxford*, p. 386.

62 Michael Newman, 'H. J. Laski', *ODNBO*; Eastwood, *Laski*, p. 67; *Holmes-Laski Letters*, p. 1007 (28 Dec. 1927); p. 1458 'I have had a vast and difficult report to write for a government committee to which I belong' (17 Dec. 1933).

63 Max Weber, 'Politics as a Vocation', in *Weber: Selections in Translation*, ed. by W. G. Runciman (Cambridge: CUP, 1978), pp. 219–20. This adherence to an 'ethic of responsibility' was also evident in Laski's acceptance of the need for rearmament by Feb. 1938: Newman, *Laski*, pp. 190–203.

64 Christopher Hill, 'Lindsay, A. D.', in *Dictionary of National Biography, 1951–60*, ed. by Edgar Williams & Helen Palmer (Oxford: OUP, 1972), p. 644.

65 A. D. Lindsay, *The Modern Democratic State, Volume One* (London: OUP, 1943), p. 281. Some notes possibly towards this second volume have survived: Lindsay Papers, LIN 158.

66 Ernest Barker, 'The Conflict of Ideologies', *International Affairs* 16 (1937), 354–5 (Summary of discussion).

67   Karl Mannheim to A. D. Lindsay, 21 Jun. 1940, Lindsay Papers, LIN 154.
68   Lindsay, *State*, p. 261 where he also cites Tocqueville as 'the prophet of the machine age'; Barker, 'Ideologies', p. 355.
69   José Ortega y Gasset, *The Revolt of the Masses* (London: Allen & Unwin, 1932), pp. 17, 53, 80, 81, 132, 136, 197 & ch. XII; Salvador Giner, *Mass Society* (London: Robertson, 1976), pp. 75–9.
70   Barker, 'Ideologies', p. 355. For a fuller exposition, Matthew Forstater, 'Adolph Löwe on Freedom, Education and Socialization', *Review of Social Economy* 58 (2000), 225–39.
71   Lindsay, *State*, p. 280.
72   Lindsay, *Essentials*, p. 3. This was a long-standing theme in Lindsay's thinking and presented to many different kinds of audiences: e.g. 'Democracy and Socialism – an Historical Analogy' (c. 1922), Lindsay Papers, LIN 157; 'What the Churches Can Do to Save Democracy', *Public Opinion*, 17 Aug. 1934, 158.
73   Lindsay, *State*, p. 274; Lindsay, *Essentials*, p. 4.
74   Lindsay, 'Political Theory', p. 168; Lindsay, 'Essentials', pp. 2–3; A. D. Lindsay, *Religion, Science and Society in the Modern World* (London: Milford/OUP, 1943), pp. 23, 40–2. See also, A. D. Lindsay, 'Review of *The Open Society and Its Enemies* by Karl Popper', *Guardian*, 5 Dec. 1945.
75   Matthew Grimley, *Citizenship, Community, and the Church of England: Liberal Anglican Theories of the State between the Wars* (Oxford: Clarendon Press, 2004), pp. 570–8, 173, 198.
76   A. D. Lindsay, 'Political Theory', in Francis S. Marvin (ed.), *Recent Developments in European Thought* (London: OUP, 1920), p. 175. Laski, by contrast, had been impressed during a visit in 1930 by the 'communal virtues' of the German people: *Holmes-Laski Letters*, p. 1276 (9 Aug. 1930).
77   Lindsay, *Essentials*, p. 45; Lindsay, *State*, pp. 16–17. For the context of such distinctions, Julia Stapleton, 'Citizenship versus Patriotism in Twentieth-Century England', *Historical Journal* 48 (2005), 151–66.
78   Barker, 'Ideologies', p. 355; Lindsay, *Essentials*, p. 1.
79   A. D. Lindsay, 'The faith of a democrat. The challenge of Industrialism' (n.d. [1946–9?]), Lindsay Papers, LIN 158.
80   A. D. Lindsay, 'Unemployment and Education', *New Era* (Sep.–Oct. 1935), Lindsay Papers, LIN 170. Cf. for a more positive assessment of the People's Service Club at Lincoln: A. D. Lindsay, 'Time to Spare! Voluntary Work by Ordinary People', *The Listener*, 4 Jul. 1934, 7–8.
81   Lindsay, *Religion*, pp. 37–8. The 'terrible report' Lindsay read was probably Carnegie Trust, *Disinherited Youth* (1943).
82   Lindsay, *Essentials*, p. 1.
83   Lindsay, 'Political Theory', p. 176; Lindsay, *Essentials*, p. 4. See also Lindsay, *State*, pp. 23–4; Grimley, *Citizenship*, pp. 70–91.
84   Lindsay, *Essentials*, pp. 33–4; Lindsay, *State*, ch. XI; Maddox, 'Skirmishers', pp. 14–15. See also Matthew Grimley, 'The Religion of Englishness: Puritanism, Providentialism and "National Character", 1918–1945', *Journal of British Studies* 46 (2007), 890–8 for the significance of the Putney Debates and Puritanism in inter-war constructions of 'national character'.
85   'What the Churches Can Do', 158; Lindsay, *State*, pp. 191, 281. During the war Lindsay welcomed the spread of discussion 'in the Army, in A.R.P. posts, in shelters, in all kinds of places where people come together'.

86 Wright, *Cole*, pp. 166, 208–20. Wright notes Cole's recognition of the existence of large middle classes in his critique of Marxism, and fascism as rooted in the middle class and driven forward by the new, technical *petite bourgeoisie*.

87 Cf. Beetham, *Marxists*, pp. 2–62.

88 Harold J. Laski, *An Introduction to Politics* ((London: Allen & Unwin, 1931, rev. ed. 1951), pp. 39–40. See also Laski, 'Nationalism and the Future of Civilization [1932]', in *Danger*, p. 214.

89 Harold J. Laski, *The State in Theory and Practice* (London: Allen & Unwin, 1935), pp. 130–4, 147, 193–5, 298–9; Newman, *Laski*, 155–8. See also Harold J. Laski, *Democracy in Crisis* (London: Allen & Unwin, 1933), pp. 38–41, 51–5.

90 Harold J. Laski, *The Rise of European Liberalism* (London: Allen & Unwin, 1936), p. 248 fascism was 'the institutional technique of capitalism in its phase of contraction' (p. 248); Laski 'Foreword', p. 11 fascism was 'nothing but monopoly-capitalism imposing its will on those masses whom it has deliberately transformed into its slaves'. Cf. John Strachey, *The Coming Struggle for Power* (London: Gollancz, fourth edition 1934), pp. 261–9.

91 Harold J. Laski, 'What Fascism Is', in *Where Do We Go From Here?* (Harmondsworth: Penguin, 1940); Laski, 'The Meaning of Fascism', in *Reflections*. There is a final shift in Laski's presentation of fascism to be found in the posthumously published *The Dilemma of Our Times* (London: Allen & Unwin, 1952). There the emphasis is on the individual's existential dilemmas in 'the great society' facing 'the torture of an unattained freedom'. It is 'the sense of impotence, or loneliness, or frustration, at the root of all of which lies fear' of these individuals which 'make possible the maintenance of authority by men like Hitler or Mussolini' (pp. 82–3). This is, of course, very similar to Lindsay's view of 'mass society'.

92 Laski, 'Meaning', pp. 88–93. Cf. Paul Einzig, *The Economic Foundations of Fascism* (London: Macmillan, 1933), esp. pp. 118–21; 'V', 'The Destruction of Capitalism in Germany', *Foreign Affairs* 15 (1936–37), 595–607; Gaetano Salvemini, *Under the Axe of Fascism* (London: Gollancz, 1937), pp. 419–29; Werner F. Bruck, *Social and Economic History of Germany from William II to Hitler 1888–1938* (Cardiff: University Press Board/London: OUP, 1938), pp. 204–10; Frank Munk, *The Legacy of Nazism: The Economic and Social Consequences of Totalitarianism* (New York: Macmillan, 1943).

93 Laski, 'What', p. 50; Laski, 'Meaning', pp. 93–4, 105, 108, 111, 113, 120–4. The view of fascists as gangsters was common on the Left and beyond – e.g. Eden thought Mussolini was a total gangster and by March 1939 Lord Lothian came to see Hitler as 'a fanatical gangster': Jay, *Dialectical*, p. 157; D. R. Thorpe, 'Anthony Eden', *ODNBO*; Alex May, 'Philip Kerr', *ODNBO*. Mosley too attracted the term: e.g. *Guardian*, 8 Jun. 1934. It is striking that nowhere does Laski refer to his LSE colleague Herman Finer, who in a meticulously documented book had a more appreciative view of Mussolini: *Mussolini's Italy* (London: Gollancz, 1935), chs II & XVIII.

94 Laski, 'Meaning', pp. 86–112.

95 *Ibid.*, pp. 96, 107; cf. Finer, *Mussolini's Italy*, pp. 14–17; Richard Crossman, *Government and the Governed: A History of Political Ideas and Political Practice* (London: Christophers, 1939), ch. IX; Serge Chakotin *The Rape of the Masses:*

The Psychology of Totalitarian Political Propaganda (Paris, 1939; English trans. 1940). Laski did not address the question of whether fascism and National Socialism were identical: cf. Oakeshott, 'Introduction', p. xxii. Or that Mussolini at any rate 'in his heart of hearts remained a Socialist': Salvemini, *Under*, pp. 405–10.

96 Laski, 'Meaning', pp. 118–19; cf. Collingwood, 'Fascism', pp. 172–3.

97 E.g. Ernest Simon, *The Smaller Democracies* (London: Gollancz, 1939), p. 11. Contrary to the view expressed here, Stone found a 'widespread reluctance to see Nazism as a threat to civilization', which made Aurel Kolnai's insistence on this 'key insight' in *The War Against the West* in 1938 striking and novel: Stone, *Responses*, p. 44.

98 Laski, 'Meaning', pp. 105–7, 110–14, 124–5.

99 *Ibid.*, pp. 89–91, 98–101.

100 *Ibid.*, pp. 94, 116. For a similar argument regarding appeasement, see Ross McKibbin, 'Class and Conventional Wisdom: The Conservative Party and the "Public" in Inter-war Britain', in *The Ideologies of Class: Social Relations in Britain 1880–1960* (Oxford: Clarendon Press, 1990), pp. 290–1.

101 On some possible reasons for this in Laski's case, see Newman, *Laski*, pp. 157–8.

102 See e.g. W. T. Jones, 'Review of *The Modern Democratic State*', *Annals of the American Academy of Political and Social Science* 257 (1948), 204–5.

103 E.g. Laski referred to Benito Mussolini, 'The Political and Social Doctrine of Fascism', *Political Quarterly* 4 (1933), 341–56; Harold D. Lasswell, 'The Psychology of Hitlerism', *Political Quarterly* 4 (1933), 373–84; Hans Gerth, 'The Nazi Party: Its Leadership and Composition', *American Journal of Sociology* 45 (1940), 517–40; Gaetano Salvemini, *The Fascist Dictatorship* (1928); Edgar A. Mowrer, *Germany Puts the Clock Back* (Harmondsworth: Penguin Books, 1933); Ernst Henri, *Hitler Over Europe?* (London: Dent, 1934); Ignazio Silone, *The School for Dictators* (London: Jonathan Cape, 1939).

104 See e.g. Martin, *Laski*, p. 261.

105 Ernest Barker, 'Review of *The State in Theory and Practice*', *International Affairs* 14 (1935), 859.

106 *Holmes-Laski Letters*, p. 1380 (1 May 1932). Laski had been an undergraduate at New College, Oxford.

107 Collini, *Absent*, pp. 460–2; Norman Chester, *Economics, Politics and Social Studies in Oxford, 1900–85* (Basingstoke: Macmillan, 1986), pp. 70–1; McCulloch, 'Lindsay'.

108 Nevil Johnson, *The Limits of Political Science* (Oxford: Clarendon Press, 1989), pp. 19–24; Dahrendorf, *LSE*, pp. 226–8.

10
The Limits of Pro-Fascism and Anti-Fascism: G. K. Chesterton and Arthur Bryant[1]

Julia Stapleton

Introduction

This chapter explores the equivocation that could mark sympathy with fascism in Britain, the contingent nature of a good deal of the support it received and the repudiation of certain forms of fascism while others were tolerated, even extolled. The degree of opposition that fascism encountered at this level was variable, as were the grounds. Nevertheless, the qualms experienced by some who showed early goodwill towards fascism merits close attention, especially when distancing themselves from it subsequently. What were the circumstances in which such retreats took place and the underlying motivations? A number of figures might serve to illustrate this highly problematic 'variety of anti-fascism', for example the historians Herbert Butterfield and Charles Petrie and the writers, Philip Gibbs and Evelyn Waugh. But the chapter confines its attention to the novelist, poet and journalist, Gilbert Keith Chesterton (1874–1936) and the popular historian, Arthur Bryant (1899–1985). They have been chosen because they well capture the ambivalence that was typical of many who welcomed fascism; in addition, they emphasise that receptivity to fascism often owed as much to political conflict at home as admiration for the achievements of fascism abroad. Chesterton's hesitancy never evolved fully into anti-fascism, as might be expected had he not died suddenly in June 1936; as an ideological weapon against domestic foes, his refusal to condemn Italian fascism unambiguously had already become a blunt instrument at the time of his death. But Bryant witnessed another world war, this time engendered by fascism, and changed his stance accordingly, if belatedly.

As writers whose pro-fascism was less than wholehearted, Chesterton and Bryant were linked by *The Illustrated London News*. Their connection with the journal certainly ensured tension between their formative political beliefs focused on the English-British *patria* and their attraction to fascism. Since 1900 the journal had been edited by Bruce Ingram, the grandson of Herbert Ingram who had founded it in 1842. Bruce Ingram maintained a strong though unstated pride in all things English and British, a sensibility formed on the cusp of the Victorian age.[2] He thus sustained the tradition of *The Illustrated London News* as a major focus of patriotism and national unity through news features that ranged from the daily round of royal engagements – it held monarchy in high regard – to developments in transport, industry, religion and society. It was in the flagship column 'Our Note Book' that first Chesterton up until his death in 1936 and then Bryant thereafter sought to influence responses to fascism among a readership dispersed throughout Britain and the empire. Both served other audiences in the inter-war period too. Bryant wrote for a range of newspapers, both national and provincial, and was at the centre of a network of Conservative activists and politicians at Ashridge, former Bonar Law College in Northamptonshire. Similarly, Chesterton edited his own journal *G.K.'s Weekly*, organ of the Distributist movement which sought wide diffusion of property ownership, particularly in land. Nevertheless, *The Illustrated London News* was a primary influence in their lives, and had been since childhood;[3] it was also a leading source of their cultural authority.

The difference of perspective between Chesterton and Bryant on the one hand and more committed pro-fascists on the other is conditioned by the ambiguous influence of Edwardian patriotism. Dan Stone has rightly emphasised the lines of descent linking the fringe movements of inter-war fascism in Britain to the reactionary trends within Edwardian patriotism: the Diehard movement in support of an unreformed House of Lords and aristocratic revolt against democracy more generally.[4] For the members of these movements, there was considerable continuity between patriotism and fascism. But a more diffuse and popular patriotism also existed in the Edwardian years, not just in the Leagues for enhancing Britain's military strength but in a vibrant pageant movement and associated activities at local level which were widely reported in *The Illustrated London News* and elsewhere in the national press.[5] Where the influence of this broader current of patriotism had been felt, it helped to rein in fascist sympathies, at least in the cases of the two figures considered here.[6] Fervent patriotism of an Edwardian kind certainly did succeed in obscuring the evils of fascism; but this was not always sparked by disregard for democracy.

Chesterton and the radical Right

As a leading Edwardian radical, Chesterton's politics were forged out of disillusion with Liberalism and the Liberal Party that came into office in 1906. His animus was directed at the role the Liberal Government had played in the corruption of parliament through the 'secret fund', the sale of honours, inter-Party conferences, and the subordination of the private member to the executive. In addition, he attacked what he regarded as the curtailment of individual liberty through social legislation aimed directly at the control of working-class families by the state. The National Insurance Act of 1911 particularly emphasised the divorce of Parliament from the people it was supposed to represent. He regarded the collusion of the Liberal Press in silencing dissidents such as himself as further evidence of the responsibility of Liberalism for the breakdown of democracy. From his columns in mainstream newspapers such as *The Daily News*, *The Illustrated London News*, and *The Daily Herald* before the First World War, Chesterton defended his understanding of the principles of democracy and liberty against their betrayal not just by a Liberalism that had lost its way but by a plutocratic class that cut across party lines. His populist critique of parliamentary democracy was underpinned by a patriotism that was focused on England as a nation in its own right, distinct from the empire and the United Kingdom.[7] His *English* patriotism was strengthened by sympathy with the Irish and the Boers under the oppression of *British* rule. No patriotism could ever be too local for Chesterton, as he made clear in his first novel, *The Napoleon of Notting Hill* (1904). The book's hero, Adam Wayne, mounted a stalwart defence of his beloved Notting Hill against the imperialist designs of other London boroughs.

Nowhere did Chesterton denounce parliamentary government as the subversion of democracy more vehemently than in the papers founded by his brother, Cecil Chesterton, and Hilaire Belloc: the short-lived *The Eye Witness* (1911–12) and its successor, *The New Witness* (1912–1922). These papers, together with their campaigning organisation, the National League for Clean Government, achieved notoriety for their role in the Marconi scandal. Cecil Chesterton was successfully prosecuted in 1912 for criminal libel in alleging that three ministers of the Crown had misled parliament about the purchase of shares in the Marconi wireless company on the basis of insider knowledge. However, this did not alter Gilbert Chesterton's belief that honesty and integrity were at a severe discount in modern parliamentary government. Nor did his brother's conviction have any impact on the anti-semitism that fuelled the agitation against the 'Marconi ministers', the attorney-general Rufus Isaacs and his brother, Godfrey being the chief targets.

Chesterton's 'anti-parliamentary' stance and exclusive views of nationhood have provided the basis on which he has been considered part of a distinctive *avant-garde* movement in politics before 1914, one that prefigured fascism in inter-war Britain, no less than in Europe.[8] But how complete was Chesterton's alignment with this movement, as measured by his capacity to resist as well as defend fascism?

As a product of Latin Europe fascism was something to which Chesterton – a convert to Roman Catholicism since 1922 but a long-term sympathiser – was instantly drawn. His receptiveness to all things Latin reflected the influence of Belloc before the First World War which regarded the Roman Empire as both the crucible of English nationhood and the 'white civilisation' of Europe.[9] In much the same way he defended the First World War as an attempt to rid Europe of the scourge of Prussia, an upstart nation of the north which, for a while, other countries had taken at its own estimation. During the war and throughout the 1920s he inveighed against the pro-German bias of English history books – a legacy of nineteenth-century Teutonism – particularly those used in schools. It irked him that these continued to be written after the defeat of Germany, although with a shifting emphasis from 'Anglo-Saxon' to 'Nordic' superiority over the Mediterranean nations.[10] The rise of Italy after the war gave the lie to that notion: old nations and empires – not least in the south – were far from 'moribund'.[11] Just before the March on Rome, he was greatly impressed by the degree of contention and division in Italian politics; it was so much preferable, he wrote – with more than a hint of contempt – to the calm of political life in Britain.[12]

Two years later Chesterton denounced those who supported fascism only because of its opposition to Bolshevism. The real lesson to be learned from fascism was the need to 'save democracy from Parliaments, or Parliaments from politicians'.[13] In February 1929, Chesterton turned on those who criticised Mussolini 'as if he were a bloodthirsty organ-grinder'.[14] He remained convinced that fascism had done good work in forcing democracy onto the defensive. He argued that the onus was now on the democrat to pursue economic and political reform simultaneously, achieving equality of citizenship through peasant proprietorship. Only then, he wrote in May of that year, could politicians be confident that the people would defend them against a rush of the mob from the street.[15]

Chesterton's determination here was to expose democracy to what he saw as the full force of fascist critique; but unlike other 'anti-modern' critics of democracy, his intention was to strengthen not weaken it further. He distanced himself from such critics, often inspired by Nietzsche, for example the maverick Jewish writer, Oscar Levy. In 1926 he was urged by a correspondent in *G.K.s Weekly* to respond to Levy who had claimed Mussolini for the Nietzscheans; for the implication was that Chesterton himself was now a Nietzschean, given his defence of Mussolini.[16] Taking up the challenge, Chesterton insisted that he remained wedded to the 'high and heroic' ideal of democracy he had set out in *The Napoleon of Notting Hill*; but given that it was a remote possibility for the present, he preferred that the machinery of the modern state was worked by an 'impatient patriot rather than an unpatriotic conspirator'.[17]

The 'unpatriotic conspirator' was a euphemism for the Jewish industrialist and financier who in Chesterton's eyes bore much responsibility for the powerlessness of democracy against a new aristocracy of wealth. But although this was an indication of the anti-semitism that continued to drive his politics and in a fascist direction, he could not go all the way towards fascism. While he hailed Mussolini for stabilising popular institutions such as the Church in Italy – despite Levy's claims otherwise – and peasant proprietorship against the threat of Bolshevism and capitalism, he was sharply critical of Italian fascism, especially once he had witnessed it at first hand. He concluded an account of his visit to Italy in the autumn of 1929, in which he met Mussolini personally, with a critique of the dictatorship of a minority within the fascist state. The best that could be said of it was that at least it was open, unlike the 'secret' nature of minority rule in Britain.[18]

Chesterton was certainly opposed to fascism in Britain. In 1925 he echoed Baldwin's remark of that year that 'England will never tolerate a Dictator'. The reason was that a dictatorship was fundamentally at odds with the 'tradition of tolerance and the good humour and the geniality of England' consequent upon centuries of rule by aristocracy. As a covert power, the aristocracy had ensured much serenity and security that could easily be lost in a fascist revolution, but without any net gain. This was because there was so little consensus in Britain on alternatives to parliamentary rule, unlike in Italy which could look back to a rich republican past preventing the 'complete destruction of the citizen by capitalism'. Moreover, the danger was that English fascists would aim too low rather than too high in their endeavour to root out treason within the state. This was suggested by their engagement in pointless street muggings rather than assailing the tyrant on the 'throne aloft', a clear reference to the 'wire-pullers', usually of Jewish descent, who undermined democracy.[19]

These fears were confirmed in the light of events at Olympia in 1934 which left Mosley and his Blackshirts completely discredited as far as Chesterton was concerned. The brutal tactics of Mosley's henchmen, he wrote in *G.K.'s Weekly*, were 'peculiar to those who invest the state – an abstract conception – with the dignity that a rational philosophy must reserve for the individual'.[20] The corporatist policies put forward by fascist pamphleteers in Britain also left Chesterton cold; they only seemed to entrench rather than challenge the interests that currently controlled the state and, what was worse, British agriculture.[21] Even before Olympia, the attempt by fascists to curry favour with British Catholics was suspect as far as Chesterton was concerned, suffused as their social policies were with *dirigisme*.[22] In the previous year, he had ridiculed Mosley for attempting to save the aristocratic state in Britain while stoking the fires of anti-semitism. To Chesterton, Mosley's failure to appreciate the extent of Jewish assimilation in aristocratic circles – both Whig and Tory – was striking.[23]

At the same time and in much the same paradoxical way of *opposing* (British) fascism on anti-semitic grounds, Chesterton stressed the dependence of Nazism on Judaism; it was thus a corruption not a variant of fascism. This dependence was due to the strength of Protestantism in Germany courtesy of the Jews. Unable to think for themselves, the 'Nordic Men' turned to the Jews to fill the void once 'the old idea of purposeful fellowship in a Faith open to all' was abandoned. The Jews, ever ready to scheme against Christianity, ensured that by 'concentrating on the ancient story of the Covenant with Israel, and losing the counterweight of the universal Church of Christendom, [the more Nordic sort of German] grew more and more into the mood of seeing their religion as a mystical religion of Race'. Chesterton by no means discounted a noble Jewish genius abroad in German culture exemplified in Heine and Lessing and Mendelssohn, far removed from what he evidently regarded as specious religious interests.[24] But in his eyes this was overshadowed by the anti-Christian culture of Judaism in Germany more generally.

Yet if Chesterton could not resist settling old anti-semitic scores in his dispute with Nazism, especially in *G.K.'s Weekly*, the wider ground of his hostility cannot be gainsaid. He expressed alarm concerning the 'herd-hatred' of Jews in Germany, so different, he maintained, from the targeting of rich Jews only among members of his own circle.[25] Villis concedes the extent of Chesterton's opposition to Hitler's anti-Jewish policy but leaves the impression that this was in spite of his wider *avant-garde* credentials.[26] It can be argued, however, that his opposition to Nazism was a measure of his distance from that movement, a distance that enabled him to distinguish Nazism from fascism, however wrong-headedly, and identify its evils outright. There were certainly other aspects of Nazism besides its indiscriminate anti-semitism that Chesterton could not abide, for example, the manipulation of public opinion. In a clear denunciation of Hitler in 1933, he exposed the lies the Nazi leader had propagated about Germany by framing what would be their English equivalent. In doing so he harked back to the note of humility he had attempted to strike in Edwardian patriotism, against the bombast of imperialists, especially.[27] If he were to appeal to patriotism, Nazi style, in saving his country from ruin, he would have to brag about (dubious) national successes rather than address obvious national weaknesses and moral failings. He would have to counsel brutality in dealing with civil strife rather than recognising the claims of justice. The implication was that Hitler's style as well as his message was acutely un-English; it was also the antithesis of 'true patriotism'. As he concluded a spoof Hitler speech, 'If I flatter all that is most false in England, shall I find an England ready and eager to listen to all that is most painful and true?'[28]

In the light of Hitler, he began to warm to Mussolini again. He certainly found Mussolini a more honest patriot. Writing in *The Illustrated London News* he portrayed Mussolini as a saviour of his country, someone who had re-made it in an entirely new mould and who was beyond the reach of the forces governing the old Italy. By contrast, Hitler was simply the latest prisoner of the Prussian military system, rising to power by 'flattering and inflaming the praise of Blood and Iron and the traditions of Bismarck and the Prussian Kings'. This 'haughty and heathen' spirit once again set Nazism apart from fascism.[29] Hitler exploited what Chesterton regarded as the peculiar vulnerability of the German people to mythology; while there was nothing wrong with mythology in itself, there was certainly something wrong with mythology that always glorified one people, the German people, at the expense of others.[30] Apropos the Aryan myth, it was 'wearisome' to reflect that 'a truth that was so dubious in the school-room of his youth should now be taken seriously as something 'new'.[31]

Just before his death in June 1936, Chesterton witnessed the beginnings of fascism as a source of international aggression as well as domestic upheaval in the countries concerned. Again, Italy got off lightly when Chesterton turned his attention to that country during the Abyssinian crisis in July1935. His response was to reiterate his long-standing conviction that imperialism was a misplaced path of European development in whichever country it took place, including – indeed especially – his own. While not exonerating Italy, this served to turn the spotlight elsewhere.[32] Readers of *G.K.'s Weekly* – he did not comment on Abyssinia in *The Illustrated London News* – were unimpressed. Chesterton tried to quell the dissent – particularly among supporters of the League of Nations – by pleading that the integrity of his own country's patriotism was at stake;[33] this was vulnerable, he maintained, to exploitation by plutocrats posing as champions of 'freedom' by condemning Italy's action.[34] But his efforts were in vain. One of his critics, an Italian ex-patriot and Deputy Chairman of the Distributist League, Conrad Bonacina, did not disagree that patriotism could be used to 'whitewash' capitalism. But he also pointed out that Italians were no strangers to the systematic distortion of patriotism. Moreover, he believed that peace, justice and security trumped concerns about the health of patriotism at home in shaping responses to Abyssinia.[35]

When Germany occupied the Rhineland in March 1936, Chesterton condemned the move unreservedly. He pointed the finger of blame not so much at Hitler but the Prussian system and the unfathomable 'interior' of Germany it commanded. Such a rupturing of the peace could be comprehended solely in terms of a new *Pax Germanica* masquerading as *Pax Romana*.[36] However, there was a major difference between the two forms of empire, as Chesterton implied when contrasting German expansionism in Europe with Italian expansion in Abyssinia: whereas Italy was following a well trodden path of civilised nations subduing non-civilised nations, Germany was like a 'cancer', killing the superior organism (of Christendom) it inhabited.[37] In this, as he so often pointed out, Germany was on a par with Bolshevik Russia. Against the recrudescence of barbarism in both countries, he vehemently defended Catholic Poland throughout the inter-war period. Upholding the territorial integrity of Poland was also vital in combating the 'hatred of Christendom' that motivated Poland's many enemies in England, no less than Germany and Russia themselves.[38]

Chesterton by no means excused Italy's behaviour; he merely meant to show up Nazism as by far the worst scourge of mankind. But if he ever thought that this would silence his critics, he was proved wrong. Once again he was attacked in the columns of *G.K's Weekly* for vilifying German but not Italian aggression.[39] This favouritism Chesterton denied. He proceeded to follow what were by now his usual diversionary tactics, this time focusing on the bombing of civilians from the air in Abyssinia. He believed that this was directly attributable to the destruction of chivalry in war by Germany in the First World War through the use of poison gas. He recalled that he had condemned such inhumanity at the time in *The London Illustrated News* and enjoined restraint against retaliating in kind.

But he merely sparked fresh controversy centring on the contempt he continued to heap on Nazism alone.[40] His exasperated reply, which he had intended to deliver in two parts, was cut short by his death: only the first part appeared.[41] Had he lived to witness Munich, there can be no doubt that he would have excoriated Mussolini for his role in an agreement which gave Nazi annexation the seal of Great Power approval.

Arthur Bryant and the fascist fringe

Notwithstanding Chesterton's failure to condemn Italy unequivocally, his critique of fascism certainly succeeded in leading one young man away from its snares.[42] On the other hand, his denunciation of Nazi Germany made little impact on those committed to a peaceful accord with that country, so sympathetic were they to its 'grievances'. Chesterton's posthumously published *The End of the Armistice* (1940), which drew together articles from *G.K.'s Weekly* and *The Illustrated London News*, was reviewed by Arthur Bryant in *The Observer*. Bryant owed a substantial debt to Chesterton – alongside other Edwardian patriots such as Kipling – for shaping his patriotic turn of mind early on in his life. But he had been an avid supporter of Chamberlain's policy of appeasement.[43] As late as the spring of 1940 and against the trenchant opposition to Nazism of both Chesterton and Kipling,[44] Bryant was still counselling the placation of Germany. Astonishingly, he set out the key solution to the evils of Prussianism, now 'Hitlerism', as 'conversion', not 'extermination'. However, to be effective, he maintained, this strategy had to be backed up by a strong military capability such as had been absent at the time of the Munich agreement. Bryant had been a ceaseless advocate of rearmament since the late 1920s. He had also fought in the First World War as an eighteen-year old, seeing action on the French front in 1917–18 as a bomber pilot in the Royal Flying Corps. The loss of some of his closest friends left a lasting impression.[45] Six months into the Second World War he remained convinced that Nazi Germany was best approached with 'love and understanding' so as to render it 'permanently harmless'. He evaded the serious differences between this approach and that of Chesterton, while giving Chesterton all due credit for predicting a second world war.[46]

In January 1940, Bryant had published a book which he had been writing for the last twelve months and with which he was determined to go ahead, despite the outbreak of the war. *Unfinished Victory* argued that Nazism was a legitimate response to the resentment of Germany at the harshness of the Treaty of Versailles. While expressing regret for the excesses of Nazi policy against the Jews and praising highly their contribution to western civilisation, it repeated uncritically the Nazi claim that the Jews were responsible for the corruption of German nationhood.[47] One anti-war peer with whom he sought peace with Germany, Lord Lymington, was much encouraged by his book.[48] In a letter to Bryant, Lymington denounced the 'wet blanket' review it had received in *The Observer*. The author of the review was Ernest Barker, a respected scholar and Liberal who had confessed himself 'puzzled, and on the whole, saddened' by the appearance of the book at such a time. A supporter of appeasement right up until the invasion of Czechoslovakia, Barker now believed fervently that it was better 'to cultivate our ideals than to cultivate memories of our past defects', that is, in supporting the Treaty of Versailles.[49] Lymington's response was scathing: '...let us always keep a little Liberal sand pit where little Liberal ostriches can bury their little Liberal heads, while all the best blood in Europe is poured out in other places for the comfort of the Liberal ostriches.'[50]

But to what extent did Bryant share the sympathies with Nazism and fascism more generally that were typical of Lymington and the circles he inhabited? Dan Stone has brought to light the extent of Lymington's connections with the fascist movement in Britain and also the virulence of his anti-semitism. Much influenced by a leading English disciple of Nietzsche, Anthony Ludovici, Lymington endorsed the elitist and eugenicist assumptions that nourished certain strands of British fascism. He was actively involved in the attempt to reinvigorate what he saw as a decaying national stock through combating the flight to the towns and away from the soil and the hierarchical relationships it essentially sustained.[51] In this he was linked to groups and individuals who poured all their energy into reviving British agriculture and the 'national' values with which it was deemed to be associated.

One such individual was Rolf Gardiner, who met Bryant towards the end of 1938 through their mutual links with Dorset and Wiltshire. Gardiner owned the Springhead estate near Shaftsbury, Dorset which became the focus of work camps or 'Land Service' intended to enhance the spiritual vitality of Britain's urbanised youth. Bryant had been a regular visitor since childhood to Wincombe, the home of his aunt, in St. Mary Donhead on the Wiltshire-Dorset border. Gardiner visited Bryant at Wincombe in December 1938, and was delighted to have met what he regarded as a kindred spirit.[52] In 1941 Bryant became one of the original members of Gardiner's 'Kinship in Husbandry', an organisation established to promote close links between nation and soil not least through organic methods of farming and land cultivation and the raising of the status of the agricultural worker.[53] Family connections with Germany made Gardiner fully disposed towards the work of national revivalism taking place in that country and across central Europe after 1918 through a network of youth groups linked to the land; it was first-hand experience of this that inspired his work at Springhead.[54] He was much impressed by the work of the Nazis in building on this momentum.[55] Later, he blamed the lack of a 'chivalrous war-generation' in Britain – spearheaded by Baldwin and Halifax – for ensuring that all the idealism of Weimar Germany was supplanted by 'opportunism'.[56] Both Lymington and Gardiner held democracy and the materialist and urban culture in which it was entrenched in considerable contempt.[57]

Bryant, like Gardiner, had urged greater ties of friendship with Germany during the inter-war period, becoming a pillar of the Anglo-German Fellowship which sought to bring together the youth of the two countries. He had no links with the British Union of Fascists, to which he gave little serious attention. In his early *Illustrated London News* columns he counselled respect for Germany and championed its achievements.[58] On this account readers could not have been unaware of the major shift of attitudes towards Germany in the journal following the death of Chesterton. In the same way he urged that credit be given to fascist Italy for turning the fortunes of that country around, and argued that the invasion of Abyssinia was fully warranted given its subjection previously to 'the rule of a race of braggart warriors'.[59] He supported Franco against the Republican forces in Spain, denouncing the divisions and violence they had wrought in the country.[60]

Underlying this invective was a concern to trounce the Left in Britain for cultivating internationalism, pacifism, and solidarity with foreign *patrias* such as the Soviet Union and Republican Spain at the expense of domestic patriotism. In contrast, Bryant embraced fascism abroad as a way of enhancing, not undermining, patriotism at home. He found a focus for the latter in the Crown together with – like other conservatives in this period – a land and countryside steeped in tradition.[61] Dismayed by overcrowded towns and cities and suburban sprawl, he appealed to his compatriots to reconnect with the countryside and their ancestral and national inheritance as a result. As a byword for localities, the countryside was for Bryant the cornerstone of democracy in England through the independence of mind and spirit it had fostered and the communities it had once strengthened, not least the parish.[62] While parliament was not to be dismissed lightly, uniquely English remedies for the abuse of power such as the writ of Habeas Corpus were more important to his mind. This accorded with what he regarded as the greater vitality of democracy in

England at local than national level, and its success in preserving a seam-less web of individual freedom, local liberties and strength of national feeling.[63]

However idealistic an account of 'historic' English democracy this represented and however much it was targeted at the Left in cham-pioning 'democracy' elsewhere, it was bound to clash with his defence of Continental fascism. Indeed, Bryant had growing doubts about Nazism which he expressed in *The Illustrated London News*, particularly after *Kristallnacht* in November 1938. Before then, he had defended the reoccupation of the Rhineland, the *Anschluss*, the Munich agreement, and the occupation of the Sudetenland. But he wrote that *Kristallnacht* could not but alienate 'those with whom a great people would most wish to be on friendly terms'. He was clearly troubled by the invasion of Czechoslovakia in March 1939 and supported the guarantee of inde-pendence that Chamberlain extended to Poland.[64] In April 1940, in recalling a Nazi rally he had attended before the outbreak of war, he gave thanks for the philistinism of England which would have nipped any romantic longings for a heroic leader firmly in the bud.[65]

None of this alters the fact that Bryant was still actively seeking a *modus vivendi* with Nazi Germany. In the first place there were his peace mis-sions, beginning in April 1939 in which he met Ribbentrop and again in July of that year when he met a high-placed Nazi official. His efforts to secure peace with Germany continued after the outbreak of war. While outwardly supporting Britain and denouncing Germany in his *Illustrated London News* columns, he wrote memorandums for 'Rab' Butler, under-secretary of state for foreign affairs, urging a rapprochement. With the full knowledge of Lord Halifax, foreign secretary, he was involved in the efforts of Lord Brocket to forge 'peace without destruction' in the spring of 1940. As Reba Soffer comments, Bryant's *Illustrated London News* audience was oblivious to this effort on Bryant's part.[66] His determination to press ahead with the publication of *Unfinished Victory* – against the better instinct of his publisher, Harold Macmillan – rested as much on a misguided attempt to court Germany's favour as an equally misplaced determination not to waste the effort he had invested in the work throughout the previous year.[67]

Unlike Lymington, however, Bryant was not merely using anti-war arguments to ensure the survival of Nazi ideals. It is true that he was more enthusiastic about Nazism than prominent Conservatives who had also opposed war with Germany at the time of Munich – Baldwin and Halifax, for example.[68] But if his unease about Nazism was more easily suppressed than those of fellow appeasers on the Right, he studiously upheld the integrity of the historic nation-state of England-Britain that sustained both their patriotism and his own. In the context of British fascism, this commitment was decisive in ensuring that his fascist sympathies did not absorb his patriotism entirely. For example, he steered well clear of the pan-Saxon/Aryan enthusiasm of Lymington and the eugenicist policies that accompanied it.[69] In this he was also distinct from Gardiner. Since the mid-1920s, Gardiner's sights had been fixed firmly on a federation of north European nations rooted in a common Protestant religion in which regionalism would receive pride of place; not least, this was to ward off the threat of Soviet Russia.[70] Gardiner shared this federal ideal with a stalwart of the vehemently anti-semitic Imperial Fascist League, the architect and historian John Harvey Hooper. The latter remained unrepentant in his fascist convictions up until his death in 1997. Gardiner was never tempted by Quislingism, unlike Hooper who believed that Hitler's invasion of England would at least be preferable to the sustained rule of Jewish finance.[71] Yet Gardiner too continued to seek the revival of England's flagging national spirit through cultivating the 'organic' ties of geography, culture, history and race across the national borders of Northern Europe, war with fascist Germany notwithstanding.

This difference between Bryant and Gardiner was at the root of the quarrel that led Bryant to resign from the Kinship in Husbandry in 1943. The immediate source was Bryant's growing exasperation with Gardiner's inefficiency as Secretary of the Kinship. But Bryant also worried about the maintenance of Gardiner's pro-German sympathies well into the war. This was something that he shared with another member and fellow writer H. J. Massingham and which cut both men off from the Kinship's 'inner circle' comprising Gardiner, Lymington and Lord Northbourne – a landowner in Kent and previous Secretary of the Kinship with known fascist sympathies.[72] In late July 1943, Gardiner circulated to the original members of the Kinship his poem, 'Totentanz', lamenting the bombing of the Hansa towns in 1942. At the same time he denounced the destruction of the Eder valley following the 'Dambusters' raid in May 1943 as a 'crime against history and eternity'. His 'explanation' for raising these issues was the need – as he saw it – for recognising the urgency of mutual repentance of 'wrongs' done to 'past, present and future' on both sides; also, a more sensitive projection of England's 'voice' in Europe than that of Lord Vansittart, Anthony Eden, and Noel Coward. (Gardiner was not amused by Coward's satirical patriotic song, 'Don't let's be beastly to the Germans'.)[73] Even before this latest intervention, Bryant had been on the point of resignation from the Kinship; but he had held off, hoping that a pompous and verbose memorandum by Gardiner in early July in response to some of Bryant's criticisms of the organisation might be a 'last fling' before a new Secretary took over.[74] However, Gardiner's subsequent suggestion that Britain should humble herself before Germany was obviously the last straw and Bryant duly tendered his resignation. In a draft letter to Northbourne, Bryant expressed his view that Gardiner had gone wide of the Kinship mark. This was merely to 'prepare the ground' for the effective Husbandry association that would be needed after the war. By contrast, Gardiner had taken to 'exhorting us, and in the most intemperate language, to support his own views on matters which have nothing to do with the object for which we were brought together...'[75] The letter was not sent because Northbourne had been unsympathetic to the reason that Bryant had given for his resignation: Gardiner's 'appalling mania for laying down the law on subjects about which he merely feels and has never thought and on which he seems to me to be childishly illogical, intemperate and wrong.'[76] Bryant clearly realised the futility of any further correspondence with Northbourne.

Gardiner saw things differently to Bryant. In an acrimonious response to an emollient letter from Bryant in the autumn of 1943, advising him to stick to husbandry where his real talents lay, Gardiner referred indignantly to his status as an 'instrument of destiny' and of the need to 'obey "my voices" and do bravely what they tell me', despite the discomfort associated with such a role and the 'dangers' of his 'foreignness'. He would not be silenced simply because Bryant and others feared that his influence would 'colour the character of the Kinship' and compromise them as a result, should the organisation attract adverse publicity. This addressed Bryant's concern that a more 'humdrum' secretary than Gardiner should be appointed, one 'less involved than you or I have been in past controversies', a reference to their pro-Nazi past which Bryant was now keen to excise.[77]

Clearly, there was more than a mere personality clash at work here. For without being explicit, Gardiner was still cleaving to Germany in a way that now filled Bryant with revulsion. What could have prompted such obtuseness on Gardiner's part? The fact was that deep antipathy towards the Slavic races in general and the Soviet Union in particular as outposts of Asiatic barbarism against the civilisation epitomised in northern Europe continued to grip Gardiner's mind. Bryant's praise of the Soviet Union in *The Illustrated London News* in July 1941[78] following that country's entrance into the war on the Allied side prompted Gardiner to denounce his 'inconsistency' in joining other 'publicists' in 'whitewashing' Russian idealism. Gardiner looked to an outcome of the war in which there might be 'some Prussian-Slav symbiosis', with

Germany spearheading the 'containment' and 'canalization' of the Slavic peoples by an 'older Europe'.[79] The postwar settlement only deepened Gardiner's hatred of Russia. Once again he took issue with Bryant's more flexible stand in *The Illustrated London News* as the Cold War intensified. Control over the Danube arising out of the Belgrade Conference in July 1948 was a key issue, specifically the withdrawal of Britain and other western powers from the international Commission set up in 1921.[80] After drawing Bryant's attention to what he saw as a few fundamental facts about the divergent course of historical development in northern Europe and its 'Asiatic' counterpart in the Eastern part of the continent, Gardiner continued: 'Sometimes, I wonder if the ghost of that gallant but wordy old GKC [G. K. Chesterton] sits upon your neck as you write your weekly column. For in respect of Eastern Europe, particularly Poland, his knowledge became corrupted by romantic or propagandist misjudgements'.[81]

Here was a major impetus sustaining sympathy with fascism in Britain and with the nations in which it had taken root, despite the Second World War: the sense that Eastern European countries were merely 'upstart' democracies which had impeded the exercise of Germany's talent for 'organisation and colonization'.[82] Gardiner's retention of his pro-German – and clearly pro-Nazi – convictions well into the war and beyond throws Bryant's abandonment of his into sharp relief. Writing in 1967, Gardiner lamented Bryant's retreat since *Unfinished Victory* into a 'rather crabbed view of England's duty towards Europe', a reference to Bryant's role in leading the campaign against Britain's entry into the Common Market in favour of the Commonwealth.[83] Bryant opposed Britain's entry into the Common Market, not least because Continental Europe had proved so prone to authoritarianism, Germany in the recent past being a signal example.[84]

But how exactly did Bryant seek to straighten out the rough edges of his pro-Nazi past? After the war, he continued to defend the Chamberlain legacy in foreign affairs. But he did so in terms of a conception of England's mission – akin to that of ancient Greece – to 'make gentle the life of the world'. He wrote openly and unashamedly of *Unfinished Victory*, but as an attempt to 'prevent us from repeating in victory the mistakes we had made before', that is, of allowing 'a profoundly provoked anger to sway for a time our actions and to obscure our finer sense of humanity'. Ignoring the book's indulgence of Nazi Germany and the critical reviews it had received on this account, he focused instead on the importance it had attached to being 'merciful and forbearing' and 'just even in individual cases'; happily, these standpoints became 'a little easier' with every year of peace.[85] Some such conception of cultivating, not alienating

Britain's enemies clearly informed his response to the Danube issue several months previously.

But Bryant was also contrite. Looking back on the inter-war period towards the end of 1940, he stressed its hallmarks of 'bitterness and discontent', its 'internecine conflict between Englishman and Englishman'.[86] Several months earlier he acknowledged his personal role in fanning the flames of a conflict in which partisan feeling had run far too high. Even more interestingly, he admitted his culpability in 'having failed to see the real enemy and ... hav[ing] often imagined him in our own camp'.[87] This was a reference to the British Left which he had pursued remorselessly in preference to the nation's external foes. In later years he also recognised that 'nothing but a craven surrender to [Hitler's] dictates could avert war' in 1939, conceding that he 'thought differently at the time' and admitting that he had misjudged the German people in their support for war.[88]

This concern to distance himself from his former positions hardly makes an anti-fascist of Bryant. It certainly stopped well short of agreeing to material being placed the public domain that might damage his thriving career and hence livelihood.[89] But it well emphasises the limits of his pro-fascism and his readiness to acknowledge the errors of his earlier political ways, however fleetingly. No such public profession of guilt was forthcoming from his associates on the Right in the inter-war period during and after the war. There was more than a grain of truth in Gardiner's suggestion that the ghost of Chesterton hovered over Bryant, influencing his apparent desertion of Germany and all the – in Gardiner's eyes – fine, 'Nordic' ideals for which that nation stood, regardless of Nazism. Like Kipling, his antagonist in all other respects, Chesterton had carried forward a brand of patriotism from the Edwardian period with which fascism and Nazism proved fundamentally incompatible. This was something which Chesterton himself well recognised, despite the clear attraction he felt towards Italian fascism. It is undeniable that other, more intolerant and elitist strands of Edwardian patriotism also appealed to Bryant, pulling him in the opposite, fascist direction. But like Chesterton his doubts about fascism emphasise the diverse and complex nature of that legacy as a source of opposition to, as well as support for the far Right in Britain.

Notes

1 I am extremely grateful to Reba Soffer for her helpful comments on an earlier draft of this chapter. I would also like to thank staff at the Liddell Hart Centre for Military Archives in making available material from the

Bryant Papers and granting permission on behalf of the Trustees to publish extracts from manuscript documents.

2   See Bryant's eulogy for Ingram on the latter's death, heavily emphasising his patriotism, in *The Illustrated London News* (hereafter, *ILN*), 19 January 1963, p. 72; see also *ILN* 6 May 1950, p. 688 and 2 January 1960, p. 4.

3   For Chesterton's recollections, see *ILN*, 25 May 1912, p. 795; for Bryant's, see *ILN*, 16 May 1942, p. 566.

4   Dan Stone, *Responses to Nazism in Britain, 1933–1939: Before War and Holocaust* (Basingstoke: Palgrave, 2003), pp. 114, 159–60, 186.

5   For this reporting, see Paul Readman, 'The Place of the Past in English Culture c. 1890–1914', *Past and Present* 186 (February 2005), 169; Robert Withington, *English Pageantry: An Historical Outline*, 2 Vols. (London: Harvard University Press, 1918), II, pp. 163, 204, 227–8. For the pageant movement and related patriotic activities more widely, see Readman, *op. cit*, pp. 176–9, 193–5, 197–8.

6   For the influence of this broader current of patriotism on Chesterton, see Julia Stapleton, *Christianity, Patriotism and Nationhood: The England of G. K. Chesterton* (Lanham, Md., Lexington Books, 2008), pp. 23–5. For Bryant's interest in pageantry in the inter-war period, see Julia Stapleton, *Sir Arthur Bryant and National History in Twentieth-Century Britain* (Lanham, Md., Lexington Books, 2005), pp. 51–4.

7   For an account of the 'moment' of English nationalism in the late nineteenth century in response to challenges to *British* industrial and imperial hegemony – albeit with little reference to Chesterton – see Krishan Kumar, *The Making of English National Identity* (Cambridge: Cambridge University Press, 2002), Ch. 7.

8   Tom Villis, *Reaction and Avant-Garde: The Revolt against Liberal Democracy in Early Twentieth-Century Britain* (London: I. B. Tauris, 2006).

9   Stapleton, *Christianity, Patriotism and Nationhood*, pp. 40, 156.

10 *ILN*, 16 July 1927, p. 90. On the 'Nordic' twist in English historiography after the First World War that was central to certain strands of English Fascism, see Richard Thurlow, 'The Developing Fascist Interpretation of Race, Culture and Evolution', in Julie Gottlieb and Thomas P. Linehan (eds), *The Culture of Fascism: Visions of the Far Right in Britain* (London: I. B. Tauris, 2004), pp. 68–70.

11 *ILN*, 13 May 1922, p. 688; 17 July 1926, p. 100.

12 *ILN*, 7 October 1922, p. 528. For the more hard-hitting editorial in *The New Witness* on events in Rome, undoubtedly written by Chesterton, see Villis, *Reaction and Avant-Garde*, pp. 104–5.

13 *ILN*, 7 June 1924, p. 1052.

14 *ILN*, 2 February 1929, p. 170.

15 *ILN*, 25 May 1929, p. 890.

16 Letter from W.N. Smith, *G.K.'s Weekly* (hereafter *GKW*) 3, 73, 7 August 1926, 376. Chesterton otherwise admired Levy as a 'cosmopolitan Jew' of an admirable kind, that is, unconnected with international finance: see Villis, *Reaction and Avant-Garde*, p. 162.

17 'The Napoleon of Nonsense City', *GKW*, 3, 74, 14 August 1926, 388–9.

18 G. K. Chesterton, *The Resurrection of Rome* (London: Hodder & Stoughton, 1930), in *The Collected Works of G. K. Chesterton*, 21 (San Francisco: Ignatius Press, 1990), pp. 429, 436–7.

19 'The Black Peril', *GKW*, Vol. 2, no. 32, 24 October 1925, pp. 129–30.
20 'The Goose Step', *GKW*, Vol. 19, no. 483, 14 June 1934, pp. 225–6.
21 'Queries on Fascism', GKW, Vol. 19, no. 489, 26 July 1934, pp. 328–9.
22 'A Fascist Explanation', *GKW*, Vol. 19, no. 478, 10 May 1934, pp. 145–6.
23 'The British Fascist', *GKW*, Vol. 17, no. 440, 17 August 1933, pp. 375–6.
24 'The Judaism of Hitler', *GKW*, Vol. 17, no. 436, 20 July 1933, pp. 311–12.
25 'The Horse and the Hedge', *GKW*, Vol. 17, no. 420, 30 March 1933, pp. 55–6.
26 Villis, *Reaction and Avant-Garde*, p. 15.
27 Stapleton, *Christianity, Patriotism and Nationhood*, pp. 64–5.
28 'If it were England', *GKW*, Vol. 17, no. 428, 25 May 1933, p. 183.
29 *ILN*, 27 May 1933, p. 718.
30 *ILN*, 26 May 1934, p. 808.
31 *ILN*, 27 July 1935, p. 154.
32 'Abyssinia', *GKW*, Vol. 21, no. 540, 18 July 1935, pp. 297–8.
33 Jay P. Corrin wrongly places these League supporters alongside Chesterton against the Right in the dispute within the paper over Abyssinia: 'Catholic Writers on the Right', *The Chesterton Review*, Vol. 25, nos. 1 & 2 (February & May 1999), pp. 81–101 at p. 87. Their quarrel was *with* Chesterton.
34 'Prussian and Plutocrat', *GKW*, Vol. 22, no. 551, 3 October 1935, pp. 5–6.
35 Conrad Bonacina, *GKW*, Vol. 22, no. 552, 10 October 1935, p. 37; and Vol. 22, no. 548, 12 September 1935, p. 437.
36 'Why did he do it?', *GKW*, Vol. 23, no. 576, 26 March 1936, pp. 17–18.
37 'Hitler versus History', *GKW*, Vol. 23, no. 575, 19 March 1936, pp. 1–2.
38 'The Enemy of Poland', *GKW*, Vol. 5, no. 121, 9 July 1927, p. 491.
39 See A. H. Lee, *GKW*, Vol. 23, no. 579, 16 April 1936, p. 86; A. M. C. Field, *GKW*, Vol. 23, no. 585, 28 May 1936, p. 182; L. Collier, *GKW*, Vol. 23, no. 587, 11 June 1936, p. 213.
40 'Apologia', *GKW*, Vol. 23, no. 583, 14 May 1936, pp. 137–8; *ILN*, 5 June 1915.
41 'In Reply to Critics', *GKW*, Vol. 23, no. 587, 11 June 1936, pp. 201–2.
42 Joseph Pearce, 'Fascism and Chesterton', *The Chesterton Review*, Vol. 25, nos 1–2 (1999), pp. 69–79 at p. 79.
43 Stapleton, *Sir Arthur Bryant and National History*, pp. 129–30, 134–5.
44 In one of Kipling's last addresses in May 1935, at the time of George V's Jubilee, Kipling spoke darkly and directly of 'an opponent whose national life and ideals were based on a cult – a religion as it now appears – of War': quoted in Andrew Lycett, *Rudyard Kipling* (London: Weidenfeld & Nicholson, 1999), p. 580. There was little accord between Bryant's views on Germany and those expressed by Kipling, although Bryant confessed in 1967 that it had been 'impossible to listen to him without being brought up sharp'. *ILN*, 3 June 1967, p. 18.
45 Stapleton, *Sir Arthur Bryant and National History*, p. 22.
46 'Looking Before and After: G. K. Chesterton and the War', *The Observer*, 10 March 1940, p. 4.
47 Arthur Bryant, *Unfinished Victory* (London: Macmillan, 1940), pp. 140, 144, 145, 150.
48 The other peers were Lords Queenborough and Brocket and the Dukes of Buccleuch and Westminster: see Richard Griffiths, *Patriotism Perverted: Captain Ramsay, the Right Club and British Anti-Semitism, 1939–1940* (London: Constable, 1998), pp. 206–8.

49   Ernest Barker, 'The Other Side: Peace with Understanding', *The Observer*, 28 January 1940, Review Section, p. 3. For Barker's previous support for appeasement, see Stapleton, *Sir Arthur Bryant and National History*, pp. 132–4.
50   [L]iddell [H]art [C]entre for [M]ilitary [A]rchives Bryant Papers, E/60, Lymington to Bryant, 29 January 1940,
51   Stone, *Responses to Nazism*, p. 155.
52   LHCMA: Bryant Papers, E/19, Gardiner to Bryant, 27 January 1939.
53   Richard J. Moore-Colyer, 'Back to Basics: Rolf Gardiner, H. J. Massingham and "A Kinship in Husbandry"', *Rural History* 12, 1 (2001), 85–108 at pp. 95–6.
54   Rolf Gardiner, *England Herself: Ventures in Rural Restoration* (London: Faber & Faber, 1943), p. 63.
55   Frank Trentmann, 'Gardiner, (Henry) Rolf (1902–1971)', *Oxford Dictionary of National Biography*, vol. 24 (Oxford: Oxford University Press, 2004), pp. 427–9 at p. 428.
56   LHCMA: Bryant Papers, E/19, Gardiner to Bryant, 2 January 1940; 28 February 1940; and 17 August 1941.
57   Stone, *Responses to Nazism*, p. 181; Moore-Colyer, 'Back to Basics', pp. 91–3; and for an illuminating contrast between British anti-urbanism along these lines and its German counterpart see Bernhard Dietz, 'Countryside-versus-City in European Thought: German and British Anti-Urbanism between the Wars', *The European Legacy* 13, 7 (2008), 801–14.
58   'Doing in Rome as Rome Does', *ILN*, 15 August 1936, in Arthur Bryant, *Humanity in Politics* (London: Hutchinson, 1938), pp. 296–9.
59   'On Understanding Foreigners', *Manchester Evening News*, 23 October 1936, in Bryant, *Humanity in Politics*, pp. 291–5.
60   See his articles in *The Observer*, June–September 1937, in Bryant, *Humanity in Politics*, pp. 322–46.
61   David Matless, *Landscape and Englishness* (London: Reaktion Books, 1998), chs 3 & 4.
62   Bryant, *ILN*, 5 February 938, p. 198; 'The Foundations of Democracy', *The Highway* 30 (December 1937), 45, reprinted in Bryant, *Humanity in Politics*, pp. 75–95.
63   *ILN*, 24 June 1939, p. 1146. The example he used in this article of protest by a local community in Buckinghamshire against the dictates of the Stuart state during the English Civil War, although without any real commitment to the Parliamentary cause, reinforces recent historiography on the 'unacknowledged republic' that was at the centre of seventeenth-century Radicalism: see J. C. Davis, 'Reassessing Radicalism in a Traditional Society: Two Questions', in Glenn Burgess & Matthew Festenstein (eds), *English Radicalism, 1550–1850* (Cambridge: Cambridge University Press, 2007), pp. 344–50.
64   Stapleton, *Sir Arthur Bryant and National History*, pp. 129–31.
65   *ILN*, 13 April 1940, p. 472.
66   Reba Soffer, 'Political Ideas and Audiences: The Case of Arthur Bryant and the *Illustrated London News*, 1936–1945', *The Parliamentary History Yearbook Trust* 27, 2 (January 2008), 156–67 at p. 166; see also Reba Soffer, *History, Historians and Conservatism in Britain and America: From the Great War to Thatcher and Reagan* (Oxford: Oxford University Press, 2009), pp. 156–63.

67 Stapleton, *Sir Arthur Bryant and National History*, pp. 146–53.

68 Philip Williamson, 'Christian Conservatives and the Totalitarian Challenge, 1933–40', *English Historical Review* 115, 462 (June 2000), 607–42.

69 Stone, *Responses to Nazism*, p. 158.

70 Trentmann, 'Gardiner, (Henry) Rolf (1902–1971)', p. 428; Matless, *Landscape and Englishness*, p. 122; Richard Moore-Colyer, 'A Northern Federation? Henry Rolf Gardiner and British and European Youth', *Paedagogica Historica* 39, 3 (2003), 305–24.

71 Even so, Graham Macklin suggests that Hooper was no 'fringe' figure but was closer to mainstream thinking than is often imagined, not least on account of his similarities with Bryant: 'The Two Lives of John Hooper Harvey', *Patterns of Prejudice* 42 (2008), 167–90 at pp. 176–7, 185. But this parallel is only at the expense of exaggerating Bryant's anti-semitism.

72 For the split within the Kinship between its 'patrician leaders' on the one hand and 'literary men' on the other, see Richard Moore-Colyer and Philip Conford, 'A "Secret Society"? The Internal and External Relations of the Kinship in Husbandry, 1941–52', *Rural History* 15, 2 (2004), 189–206. The authors regard Bryant's siding with Massingham against 'the squires' as 'somewhat anomalous', given that he shared many of their political views (p. 201). However, it is clear that Bryant was distancing himself from those views in 1943.

73 'A communication to the original members of *A Kinship in Husbandry*' from Rolf Gardiner, dated 'End of July 1943', among Bryant's correspondence with Northbourne, LHCMA: Bryant Papers, E/60.

74 LHCMA: Bryant Papers, E/60, Bryant to Lord Northbourne, 7 August 1943. Gardiner's memorandum, dated 7 July 1943 and entitled 'Kinship in Husbandry' contained the sentence, 'I think the most important thing is that the Kinship should have its own free rich life in time and space: Lebensraum and Lebenszeiten'. Bryant scribbled in the margin, 'Horrible German words'.

75 LHCMA: Bryant Papers, E/60, Bryant to Northbourne, 15 August 1943, headed 'not sent'.

76 LHCMA: Bryant Papers, E/60, Bryant to Northbourne, 7 August 1943; and Northbourne to Bryant, 12 August 1943.

77 LHCMA: Bryant Papers, E/19, Gardiner to Bryant, 8 October 1943, responding to an undated, typed letter from Bryant beginning, 'I had a letter from John Massingham this morning...'. Gardiner resumed correspondence with Bryant a year later, with no mention of their earlier rift.

78 *ILN*, 5 July 1941, p. 5. Bryant argued that Russia had now become 'our partner in the crusade' against the belief of Nazi Germany that 'anything can justify the destruction of the national liberty of one nation by another'. He acknowledged that 'we too in a less enlightened age' shared that belief, but added defensively, 'there is no major nation in Europe that has not'.

79 LHCMA: Bryant Papers, E/19, Gardiner to Bryant, 7 July 1941 and 17 August 1941.

80 Bryant, *ILN*, 14 August 1948, p. 170. Bryant had argued that Britain should heed an insistence from the USSR that she abrogate her right under the 1921 Convention to sit on the Commission. 'We have quite enough real grievances against Russia – many on which we must stand firm or else our civilisation and faith will perish in default – without insisting on such unrealist legalism'.

81   LHCMA: Bryant Papers, E/19, Gardiner to Bryant, 18 August 1948.

82   LHCMA: Bryant Papers, E/19, Gardiner to Bryant, 17 August 1941.

83   LHCMA: Bryant Papers, E/19, Gardiner to Bryant, 4 May 1967.

84   Stapleton, *Sir Arthur Bryant and National History*, p. 261.

85   Bryant, *ILN*, 13 November 1948, p. 534. For the reviews, see Stapleton, *Sir Arthur Bryant and National History*, pp. 149–50.

86   *ILN*, 7 September 1940, p. 294; 12 October 1940, p. 454.

87   *ILN*, 29 June 1940, p. 864; see also 25 May 1940, p. 686.

88   *ILN*, 2 September 1961, p. 356; and 'Fanaticism of German Youth', 4 May 1968, p. 16.

89   He resisted the opening of the archives on his mission to Germany in 1939 under the thirty year rule on the grounds that, taken out of the context of support for the trip by Chamberlain and Baldwin, it would be open to misinterpretation: Stapleton, *Sir Arthur Bryant and National History*, p. 136.

Part IV
Final Perspectives

11
Anti-Fascism and the Post-War British Establishment

Richard Griffiths

Introduction

One might be excused for thinking that, in the immediate post-war period in Britain, the term 'anti-fascist' had ceased to have any real meaning, in that practically the whole of British society was now opposed to fascism.[1] In the pre-war period, admiration for the fascist dictatorships had not been confined to extremist movements. Even a cursory reading of the press of that period produces myriad examples of publicly-expressed enthusiasm for fascist principles and policies, on the part of the middle and upper classes. In the Thirties, anti-fascism was essentially the province of sections of the Left and of maverick representatives of the Right. Yet now, after the war, anti-fascism had become a well-nigh universal characteristic of British society. This is hardly surprising, given the war that had intervened. Nazism had become a dirty word for all strata of polite society, and 'fascism' was tarred with the same brush; and anti-semitism, after the revelations of the excesses of the Holocaust, had in the main been driven underground.

Fascist activities continued, of course, at a lower level, with the revival of Mosleyism in the East End and in other urban centres (helped by the impetus to anti-semitism given by the Jewish terrorist attacks in Palestine, and also by discontent at the hardships of post-war Britain). Later, such people redirected their activities to the new racial minorities in Britain. But these were at best fringe activities, and there was, publicly at least, none of the kind of tacit middle-class support for fascist and totalitarian philosophies that had existed in respectable circles before the war.

To what extent, however, was this silence similar to the situation in post-war France, where the Right appeared to have ceased to exist, with the three main political parties (the Socialists, the Communists and the *Mouvement Républicain Populaire* (CMRP)) all using the rhetoric of the Left; but with representatives of the pre-war Right infiltrating the MRP, while awaiting the moment to re-emerge? Was there still, in Britain, a pro-fascist core at the heart of the Establishment,[2] which was merely keeping quiet in the new situation? It is hard to assess this, particularly in the absence of public pronouncements, but the situation does appear to have been more complicated than it seemed at first sight, and by about 1950 the re-emergence of organised anti-fascist protests seems to show that it appeared to the people in such groups that there was cause for alarm.

To examine this phenomenon properly, we will need to distinguish between those people whom, pre-war, we would have described as 'upper-class extremists', and those who, in the same period, could have been described as 'fellow-travellers of the Right'.

Upper-class extremists

This group consisted essentially of those who not only, like so many other members of the Establishment, expressed admiration for the policies of Nazi Germany and Fascist Italy, but also became activists, often in extremist movements such as the Right Club, the Nordic League, the English Array or The Link. Within such groups there were, however, people of varying degrees of commitment, and it is worth looking at the moments, and the events, which caused members gradually to fall away from such activities.

As early as 1939–40, many people whose pro-Nazism or pro-Fascism was (paradoxically) a product of their innate patriotism naturally put their country first when the choice came between it and the regimes they admired overseas. Many of the Right Club, for example, immediately volunteered for service, as did some of the most vociferous pro-Nazi apologists, from prominent aristocrats to rank-and-file members of the British Union of Fascists. That such a change of attitude was not merely for public consumption is shown by the private correspondence of a man such as Rolf Gardiner, whose admiration for Nazism was now tempered by mistrust of Hitlerian expansionism, and by a belief, despite his desire for peace, that it was impossible to negotiate with Hitler.[3] Even more significantly, that arch-publicist for the fascist powers Francis Yeats-Brown now exulted in Britain's patriotic effort, declaring that the English were 'no longer arrogant bleating pacifists, but English again', and praising 'the RAF, magnificent young fellows.'[4]

During the 'phoney war' period, however, many others had, as we know, continued pro-fascist activities.[5] The next series of defections from the pro-fascist stance appears to have been caused not so much by patriotism as by self-protection. The series of arrests of leading fascists in May–June 1940 caused many of those who had been active in pro-Nazi activities to put their heads hastily below the parapet. Typical of these was Lord Lymington, who in May, in the wake of a press attack on the Information and Policy movement, decided to expel from his English Array his old and tried collaborator Norman Hay (who had been involved in Information and Policy):

> In view of the reports appearing recently in the press ... it is necessary that I excommunicate you from the Array forthwith. ... In a time of peril to the country I have no other choice.[6]

Hay's protest at this shows just how difficult he found it to credit that Lymington could change his spots so rapidly:

> You know the Jew racket as well as I do and I think it very poor support I have had from you just at the moment that mass-hysteria began. I did not expect people on our side to lose their heads as well. I was very shocked that after ten years of political collaboration you should have taken the line you did.[7]

And Hay was essentially right in his assessment of Lymington. Though Lymington was careful about any public utterance of his previous views, by late 1943 he, together with a number of his old pro-fascist cronies (Lord Sempill, General Fuller, Admiral Domvile, Ben Greene, Bertie Mills, and so on) was regularly meeting in a body disarmingly called the 'Constitutional Research Association' (CRA), which had grown out of Ben Greene's English National Association (ENA), which in turn had replaced Edward Godfrey's British National Party (BNP). Both of these earlier bodies had been backed by the Duke of Bedford, whose adherence to pro-Nazism had remained public and insistent right through the War.

The BNP (1942–3) had been 'strongly nationalist and anti-Semitic', and held the view that 'the system of International Finance' was 'the main cause of this war'. Its organiser was Edward Godfrey, an ex-sailor who had served under Admiral Sir Barry Domvile and who was an ex-member of the British Union of Fascists (BUF).[8] It was mainly a working-class movement made up of ex-BUF members, but it attracted a number of upper middle-class adherents such as Lymington's pre-war sidekick Ben Greene (who was particularly enthusiastic),[9] Major-General Fuller, Norman Hay, the leading journalist Collin Brooks,[10] – and of course the Duke of Bedford.

The ENA (1943–5) was the BNP's direct successor, with Ben Greene at its head.[11] It held very much the same views as the BNP, but was a far more upper middle-class organisation. Already, such figures as Lord Lymington and Lord Sempill were associating themselves with Greene in his ventures.[12] Perhaps because of this changed class element, and certainly because of the current state of wartime opinion, the ENA felt that its views on race should only be expressed in a disguised form. Early in the ENA's existence Greene and his supporters had a difference of opinion with Godfrey, with 'the latter wishing to adopt a policy of open anti-Semitism, the former, supported by his associates, insisting on working secretly and underground'.[13] Greene won, and Godfrey withdrew from the ENA. Greene's policy, though 'in his words in private he [was] violently anti-Semitic', was for ENA utterances to 'play down this fundamental part of their policy so as to avoid a Fascist imputation'.[14] The ENA, funded generously by the Duke of Bedford, pretended to have no connections with fascism or anti-semitism, though the reality proved to be different. The CRA, of which we shall see more later, was to be similarly discreet both in the last years of the war and in the first years of the peace.

In 1945 there was a further powerful wave of anti-fascism, which affected even such extreme figures as the Duke of Bedford. This came at the end of the war, when the full extent of Nazi atrocities became public. In face of the evidence of the Holocaust, even the most inveterate anti-semites had to change their tack. To take Bedford as the most prominent example: as late as May 1945 he was still publicly proclaiming that the 'glorious victory' had been won solely for 'Soviet tyranny and Big Finance', and that 'Hitler's virtues [had] caused his destruction to be ordained by the financiers of the City and Wall Street', while Roosevelt, who had just died, had been 'an inveterate and unscrupulous warmonger, and a tool of Big Finance' (Big Finance being the term Bedford and people like him used for the Jewish influence).[15] Yet within a couple of months his attitude to fascism and anti-semitism had changed, because of his concern about public opinion. At a 'very private meeting' with a number of leading fascists in July 1945, he declared 'that his attitude had been misunderstood, and did not indicate any sympathy with Fascism; he strongly objected to anti-Semitism'.[16]

MI5 noted that there was nevertheless 'no change in the Duke's general outlook, but circumstances have brought a change in his activities'.[17] The same was true of a great many members of the former extreme Right in these immediate post-war years. Publicly, they tended to denounce the very things that they had previously supported. There seems at times to have been a kind of collective amnesia, as they rewrote history in their memoirs. The journalist George Ward Price, for example, who had in 1937 described Hitler as having 'a human, pleasant personality' and 'a strong vein of sadness and tenderness in his disposition', after the war described him as 'a man of neurotic character and limited perceptions'. Similarly, in 1937 he had praised Hitler's intellectual abilities to the skies; post-war, he described his surprise at the deference accorded Hitler by 'so many Germans who were his superiors in education, intellect and experience'.[18] Many other accounts, by people who had previously been seduced by Hitler's charm, now produced the stereotypical picture of 'those strange mad eyes, lit up by a fanatical glare'.[19] Somebody like Diana Mosley, who continued to flaunt her admiration and affection for the Führer, was an extreme rarity. Even Captain Ramsay MP found it expedient to present a somewhat lower profile; in March 1945 he at the last minute decided not to attend a big 18B party that had been organised. Admiral Domvile confided to his diary: 'Jock has cried off the party tonight. Frightened by his brother MPs – I think a mistake, though he professes it is *pro bono publico*, as a fuss would have been made in the House.'[20]

Such changes of mind tell us much about the prevailing mood of society as a whole, with whose assumptions such people felt they had to fit in publicly; but they tell us little about the actual views and activities of the people concerned. In fact, a number of these pre-war pro-fascists did continue to pursue their activities in secret. The Constitutional Research Association, for example, continued its meetings throughout the last years of the war and the first years of the peace, the attendance including not only old stagers such as General Fuller, Admiral Domvile, Lord Sempill, the Earl of Portsmouth (the former Lord Lymington), Arthur Rogers, Ben Greene, Norman Hay, Philip Farrer, John Scanlon, etc., but also some new and surprising recruits in the form of Lord Hankey (the former Cabinet Secretary), Lord Bennett, Sir Alliott Verdon Roe, Commander Russell Grenfell, Harold Vesey Strong, and others. At a meeting in November 1944, those attending deplored the fact that the collapse of Germany meant that 'the old financial gang, which is behind the whole of this show, will be back in power.' At the same meeting, they applauded the assassination of Lord

Moyne in Palestine as a 'bloody good thing' which would equate the terms 'Jew' and 'terrorist' in the public mind.[21] By early 1945 they were extolling the virtues of Magna Carta. This would on the surface of it seem to have been merely an innocuous example of the ostensible aims of the group, in other words constitutional research; but their admiration for Magna Carta was in fact based on their view that it was 'a way of pursuing a policy of anti-semitism', and that it 'contained a clause protecting the English from the Jews who, in those days, were regarded as aliens and infidels'.[22] A new recruit to the group was praised in the following terms: 'He knows Jock [Ramsay] and Ben Greene, and is a hundred per cent on our side, and knows the Jewish question.'[23] The continual references to 'international finance' at CRA meetings are a typical use of the traditional code to denote Jewish power.

The Duke of Bedford, despite his 1945 qualms about association with fascism and anti-semitism, was soon reviving, with John Beckett, the pre-war British People's Party. In the April 1945 number of its journal *The People's Post* there was an article typical of the ruses of anti-semitism in the post-war atmosphere. Called 'Justice for the Jew: The British People's Party Policy', it was ostensibly pro-Jewish, claiming that 'No Christian can accept a policy of discrimination owing to race and creed ... Our test must be that of the actions of the individual and it must not be applied *en masse* to any section of the population.' Soon, however, the true colours began to appear. First, the alien nature of the Jews was stressed: 'It is undoubtedly true, and it should not be offensive to say so, that the presence of this large number of people of Eastern origin with an outlook very different from our own creates a grave problem.' Thereafter, the link between the Jews and Usury (which 'must go!') was pointed out. The final sentences of the article trod an unconvincing path between tolerance and racial abuse:

> We cannot indulge in racial abuse which can only end, if successful, in stimulating lawless treatment of the Jewish people, nor can we shut our eyes to much of the evidence of unhelpful Jewish activities we see around us. If there are good Jews, we wish them peace and happiness; those who abuse our hospitality have no right to expect to continue doing so, and it is difficult to understand why Jews who claim that they are good citizens insist on spoiling their own cause by shouting 'Jew-baiter' whenever the less desirable sections of their community are exposed.[24]

This was far less immediate than Beckett's pre-war fulminations against the Jews. The need to pay lip-service to tolerance, and to appear to be defending the Jews, was something new. Beneath it, however, the old animosities still lurked.

Bedford's own attitude to this was equally complex. In his auto-biography *The Years of Transition*, which came out in 1949, he spent several pages on the 'alleged anti-semitism' of his Party, which had led to many attempts by 'Jewish extremists', many of whom had 'Communist sympathies', to break up the BPP's meetings. While denying that the Party was anti-semitic, he did admit that 'it is quite true that a small minority of our members are very conscious of the harm done by the anti-social practices of certain Jews'. He then proceeded to echo many of the points made by Beckett.[25]

The fact that Beckett and Bedford needed to dress up their views in this way, and even to pretend that their views had changed; the secrecy of the Constitutional Research Association and its dressing up of the fascist and anti-semitic dimension of its views on Monetary Reform as 'constitutional research'; all this shows that the public mood to which they were reacting no longer had any truck with such views. And, indeed, the fate of the British People's Party shows just how little future there was for such movements at this time. Despite the consider-able financial support given to it by Bedford, it had little success. On 9 October 1953 the Duke of Bedford died of gunshot wounds on his Endsleigh estate in Devon. Though the coroner's verdict was accidental death, there seems little doubt that he had committed suicide.[26]

Though the upper middle-class element in the extremist Right was later to re-emerge in such movements as the League of Empire Loyalists, it was never to do so to a significant extent. In the immediate post-war period, as Richard Thurlow has pointed out, the 'extremely negative perception of all kinds of fascist activity after 1945' meant that such people were 'very wary and security-conscious.'[27] The antics of such people as Portsmouth, Sempill, Fuller and Hankey show us, however, that a clandestine continuation of pre-war fascism and anti-semitism, clothed in monetarist rhetoric, could still exist in Establishment circles.

Fellow travellers of the Right

To assess the new position of the pre-war 'fellow travellers' (those respect-able middle-class people who admired the fascist regimes without belong-ing to any 'fascist' group or undertaking any political activity) we need to bear in mind the great variety of opinions that were involved. There were those who had fervently admired the achievements of the Third Reich, and the internal policies of the Nazi Party. Some of them condoned or even admired Nazism's anti-semitic policies; but a far greater number were uncomfortable about them, even though they did not let this stand in the way of what they thought to be more important issues. There were also a large group (including Sir Charles Petrie and most of the *English Review* group) who differentiated between Mediterranean Fascism and Nazism, praising the one and denigrating the other. And when it came to the Spanish Civil War, there were strong pro-Franco attitudes on the part of a great many people, and particularly Catholics who, influenced by the Nationalists' propaganda, saw the War as a 'crusade' against the atheistic and anti-Christian forces of Communism. Many of these people would not have seen their support for Franco as in any way related to attitudes towards 'fascism' in general, even though contemporary opinion (and indeed Franco himself)[28] saw Francoism as part of the European fascist surge.

In the post-war situation, the new, more universal 'anti-fascism' that reigned in society made little in the way of distinction between the various fascisms. While it was Hitler's Germany and its excesses that had caused this universal view, Mussolini's Fascist Party was seen as having been a willing partner in what had happened (even if the new Italy that had changed sides was now viewed with less suspicion). Franco's Spain, which though neutral had been heavily sympathetic to the Nazi cause, similarly suffered great opprobrium, in particular because Franco was a living dictator who was still in power – the last remnant, as it were, (with Salazar, who had a lower profile) of the pre-war fascist Establishment.

Yet what became of the former British sympathisers with Mussolini and with Franco? The answer is, that they kept, for the time being, a low profile. The sins of the Nazis had meant that the War, which had started as a reaction to German aggression, had turned into a crusade against the forces of evil, embodied not only in the Nazi Party but also in 'international fascism'. It was difficult, in this atmosphere, to make the kind of distinctions that these people had been making in the Thirties.

Not that they ceased making such distinctions in private. I personally remember a drinks party given by a former Conservative MP who had in the Thirties had Fascist sympathies, at which I met a number of the old *English Review* group, including Sir Charles Petrie. In the course of conversation, I was informed that though they viewed Nazism with distaste, they still considered Mussolini to have been one of the greatest politicians of modern times. In the same way, Franco's Spain still had its adherents, particularly in Catholic circles. Monsignor Alfred Gilbey once informed me that the Strafford Club, a very agreeable dining club which

I had joined in the early 1960s at his invitation, and which appeared to be in no way political, had originally been founded in the late Thirties for those 'who held the right views about the Spanish Civil War.'

Revised attitudes to Spain, and the re-emergence of an anti-fascist front

It was the question of Franco which appears to have revived the anti-fascist efforts of the Left, which by the beginning of the Fifties became aware of a resurgence of British right-wing sympathy for Franco's Spain. Spain was beginning to lose its pariah status, partly as a result of the emergence of the post-war Communist threat. Gradually it was becoming accepted in the post-war family of nations. Much of this was, of course, American-led. American bases were established there from 1953 onwards, Spain became a member of UNESCO in 1952, and so on.

In this country, the first signs of this thaw were to be seen from 1950 onwards, with the controversies over the restoration of diplomatic relations with Spain, the relaxation of the Spanish arms ban, and the possibility (short-lived) that Spain might be admitted to NATO. The last two years of the post-war Labour Government, 1950–51, were marked by increasing pressure from the Americans, and from the Foreign Office, for the Government to adopt various conciliatory policies towards Spain. The Government was, however, painfully aware of the potential reactions of its own supporters, many of whom, as a resolution by the West Lewisham Labour Party in December 1950 showed, were convinced that the Government was, at best, dragging its feet in relation to defending their views:

> The General Council places on record its protest at the failure of the British delegation to the United Nations Assembly, to take a more courageous stand against the proposal to restore full diplomatic representation to the Fascist government of Spain as well as admitting Franco's administration to certain advantages of United Nations membership. We consider that the Spanish Government of 1950 is the same as that which destroyed democracy in 1936 and aligned itself with Hitlerism during the second world war and should still be treated as outside the comity of free peoples. We urge His Majesty's Government not to send an Ambassador to Spain.[29]

By January 1951, however, the Government had appointed an Ambassador to Spain, Sir John Balfour. It is interesting to note the line-up of those who wrote to the Government to oppose this move. They included the International Brigade Organisation (deploring sending an ambassador to 'the bloody tyrant of Spain'), a large number of local branches of the Labour Party, a large number of Trades Unions, various Trades Councils, and the ILP. What is significant is the almost total absence of other kinds of protester. The anti-fascist front had by now, it appears, reverted to the kind of left-wing membership it had had in the Thirties, and had lost its more universal appeal.

The Communist Party of Great Britain (CPGB), which had played such a large part in pre-war opposition to fascism, was now taking an important role in the opposition to the street-level activities of the Mosleyites and others in the East End and other urban centres. Behind the scenes, too, they were lending their support to the protests against the easing of sanctions against the Franco regime (in particular, through the International Brigade Association). But, on the rest of the Left, there was by this stage a certain amount of embarrassment at Communist involvement. In the emergent 'Cold War' situation the Labour Party, whose Government was busy banning Communist Party members from certain kinds of public office, on the whole felt a need to distance itself from Communist activity. This perhaps explains the lack of open reference to the CPGB amid the vast correspondence engendered by the Left, and directed to the Foreign Office, about the Spanish moves.

This concern comes out clearly in a covering note written by Robert Mellish, MP, to Herbert Morrison the Foreign Secretary, which accompanied a protest by the Bermondsey Trades Council. It shows the mistrust felt in Parliamentary Party circles for such left-wing diatribes, and the new fear of Communist infiltration in the Labour movement. The protest ran: 'This Trades Council deplores the action of the Government in exchanging Ambassadors with Fascist Spain, and regards such action as an insult to the working class of this country.' Mellish's covering note ran 'My dear Herbert ... May I first of all emphasise that my Trades Council is *not* Communist.'[30]

The new Conservative Government, which came to power in October 1951, pursued even more amicable policies in relation to Spain, lifting the arms ban in July 1952. The *New York Herald Tribune* remarked that this denoted that they were adopting 'a more conciliatory and friendly policy toward the Franco regime'.[31] Again, the Government received a large number of protests at this; but again, those protests came in their entirety from trades unions and from branches of the Labour Party.[32] Anti-fascism appeared to have become the purlieu of a restricted portion of society once more.

The absence of other protests was matched by a growth in pro-Spanish and pro-Franco statements. Many of those who had supported Franco's cause before the War were now re-emerging. Signs that right-wing public opinion had begun to soften towards Spain had begun to emerge by late 1950, when a new society was formed in London, called 'Friends of Spain', whose aim was 'to work for the re-establishment of full diplomatic relations with Spain'. Its president was Sir Alexander Roger, Vice-President of the Federation of British Industries, whose own companies had strong links with Portugal and the Iberian peninsula. Prominent members included Lord Selborne, who had been Minister for Economic Warfare from 1942 to 1945; Sir Patrick Hannon, the right-wing Conservative MP who had been prominent in pro-fascist circles before the War; Sir Robert Hodgson, who had been British Agent in Nationalist Spain from 1937 to 1939, and later the British Chargé d'Affaires to the Nationalist Government in Burgos; and an array of Admirals, Generals and Air Marshals.[33] A similar society was also founded in Scotland, which had of course been, in the pre-war period, one of the most fertile recruiting-grounds for the Friends of National-ist Spain. Both societies appear to have relied strongly, in their membership, on those who had been pre-war supporters of Franco. By 1952 the London society was known as the Anglo-Spanish League of Friendship.[34]

The Governments, Labour and Conservative, received, in relation to the measures for which we have already noted the protests from the Left, a good number of missives calling for more favourable treatment for Spain. So did the press. One typical argument was:

When are we going to end the farce of keeping up diplomatic relations with an enemy country (Communist China)? And when are we going to resume diplomatic relations with a friendly country (Spain)?[35]

Another, voiced in the letter-columns of *The Times*, was:

From a political point of view, is it not time that misplaced sentiment for the International Brigade gave way to a foreign policy bearing some relation to the facts? Spain had been governed for over eleven years by the present regime. Is that proud nation to be discourteously boycotted? ... British ideals of democracy are not necessarily the ulti-mate goal of all mankind. ... The people of Spain to-day prefer peace and order to the chaos of 'democratic' rule that preceded the rebellion of June, 1936, a reversion to which so many mistaken idealists in this country would appear to advocate.'[36]

While most of these effusions clearly came from the Right, there were others which stemmed from the Left.[37] For example, one Scottish Labour Party activist wrote to Ernest Davies, the Labour Under-Secretary for Foreign Affairs, warning him that rejection of Spain could lead to a loss of Labour votes:

> Why the unjust and unsympathetic attitude to Spain? I have written to Miss Herbison ... I know how much some of her supporters resent this attitude to Spain. ... If seats are lost to the Labour cause at the next election, it will be due in no small amount to your Government's attitude to Spain.[38]

The fact remains, however, that most of the pro-Franco activity came from expected circles. The Roman Catholic Church, for example. A letter to *The Times*, in June 1950, from Dom Columba Cary-Elwes of Ampleforth Abbey, produces some typical arguments:

> International social justice demands a reversal of our present policy. ... Peoples, like individuals, have a right to have justice and friendliness shown them. It is, therefore, surely time that a voice should be raised in defence of this Christian and humanitarian attitude. [Given our recognition of Communist China, of Tito, of the new Czechoslovakia] it can scarcely now be maintained that we should cold-shoulder Spain for being authoritarian. ... It should not be forgotten that General Franco emerged as ruler after a frightful civil war, and that, therefore, any return to some sort of representative government is bound to be slow. ... Spaniards, as our fellow men, fellow Europeans, and fellow Christians, sharing a common heritage, undoubtedly have a right to normal friendly relations in the diplomatic and economic fields.[39]

And then, of course, there were the 'usual suspects' who had carried over from the Thirties, including Professor E. Allison Peers of Liverpool University (writing to *The Times* a plea for understanding of Spain),[40] and Lord Saltoun (calling in the House of Lords for a renewal of 'our ancient friendship with the Spanish people').[41]

The fact that so much of this support for Spain was publicly proclaimed in the letter columns of the newspapers shows just how far things had moved from the post-war anti-fascist consensus. Of course, this was also the time at which strenuous efforts began to be made to prove that Franco was not really a 'fascist', but was in fact an old-fashioned conservative. As I have shown elsewhere, such a distinction would not have been understood either by Franco's contemporaries, or by Franco himself.[42] But it served to muddy the waters a little, and excuse the inexcusable[43] – and in the process succeeded in creating one of the enduring myths of modern 'Fascist' scholarship.

Conclusion

For a very short period, after the War, there appeared to be an anti-fascist consensus in Britain over almost the whole range of political activities. This was mostly due to the effects of the War, which had been waged against the fascist powers (from now on to be fascist equalled being unpatriotic, where in the Thirties fascism had been compatible with patriotism), and also to the post-war realisation of the enormities of the Holocaust. And much of that consensus was to last, as enthusiasm for Nazism remained confined to small extremist groups, and anti-semitic statements, even of the 'socially anti-semitic' type which had been so widespread even in non-political circles before the War, became taboo. There had been, however, many people who had been favourable in the pre-war situation to one or other of the non-Nazi 'fascist' regimes, such as Italian Fascism or Franco's Spanish regime, and these people tended to continue their views in private. Gradually, as the post-war situation changed, such people were able once more to voice their sympathy for the Spanish and Portuguese regimes, which were now the surviving examples of 'strong government', and which could be excused from their 'fascist' associations. What is particularly interesting, however, is that anti-fascist protests against such attitudes were now confined to the traditional anti-fascist groupings to which the pre-war scene had been accustomed: the Labour Party, the Communist Party and movements to the Left of it, and the trades unions. The post-war consensus had been lost, and the vast majority of the British public did not appear to care either way.

Nevertheless, a more fundamental consensus remained, in that the general public tended to deplore the excesses of 'fascist' racism, and the violence of neo-fascist movements. The new, more coherent extreme Right that emerged in Britain from the Sixties onwards (the National Front, the British National Party, etc.) has thus had little connection with the British Establishment, and has continued, in its various forms, to be a fringe activity. Against it there has been an equally coherent, but equally 'fringe', deployment of anti-fascist forces, around for example the newspaper *Lobster*. What is missing from the contemporary scene is that vast range of sympathy for fascism that was to be found in the British society of the Thirties.

It is that lack of sympathy, on the part of the general public, for fascist ideas and policies that has produced, in Britain and elsewhere, two parallel phenomena. On the one hand, there are the fringe movements, unconcerned about general acceptance, which are founded on nostalgia for a fascist past. While it is natural that this should be central to some of the movements that have emerged in Germany, Austria and Italy, it is nevertheless surprising to find such a widespread nostalgia for Hitler and the Nazis outside these countries, on international websites of Nazi memorabilia and in the detailed paraphernalia surrounding so many movements of the new Right. This obsession with Hitler and his movement make the modern 'neo-fascists' very different from their predecessors in the Thirties, whose central concerns were usually national and/or ideological, and who looked forwards rather than backwards. Often, the symbolic connections seem almost trivial. In Britain, for example, Jordan and Tyndall's National Socialist Movement (later the British Movement) was founded on the anniversary of Hitler's birthday in 1962, and the 'Combat 18' movement, founded in the early Nineties, takes its title from the initials of Adolf Hitler's name, the first and eighth letters in the alphabet. Such extremist movements, across Europe, all share a racism that is fed by Holocaust denial. There is usually, in these movements, a tacit acceptance that their destiny is to remain a minority interest.

Movements that wish to progress to a more prominent role in national politics can take on, however, a more ambiguous role. One finds a certain amount of 'hedging' coming into play. This is particularly true of Italy, France, Germany and Austria, where at various times what we would term 'neo-fascist' movements have achieved political prominence. The best example is Italy, where the neo-fascist MSI from 1969 onwards set about changing its image, aiming to 'make [the] party look modern, law-abiding and respectable in order to widen its appeal and end its isolation'. Yet they needed to tread a tightrope, to persuade their original supporters that the aim was the same, even if the image had changed. Luciano Cheles has brilliantly shown how the visual material used in the MSI's posters and literature skilfully incorporated images (allusions to Mussolini and the Fascist past) which could be understood by the faithful, but which would be unnoticed by others.[44] The party that grew out of the

MSI, the *Alleanza Nazionale*, went even further in the direction of an appeal to the centre, its watchwords being 'freedom, democracy and solidarity',[45] and its reward has been a place in various governing coalitions.

In Britain, the 'modernisation' of the British National Party (BNP) shows a similar concern to reassure the general public – a concern which shows how much the post-war anti-fascist consensus continues, so that any movement looking, like the BNP, for electoral success needs to take account of it and adjust its policies and/or propaganda accordingly. However, unlike the *Alleanza Nazionale* the BNP shows no sign of a substantial breakthrough, despite these efforts. The reasons for this appear to be twofold: firstly, the leadership has found it difficult to restrain its followers (and indeed to restrain itself) from recorded statements in which the 'old Adam' of racism figures, and which alienate the general public (except in certain geographical areas where racial tension reigns); and secondly, because the anti-fascist consensus is still stronger in Britain than in Italy. The leaking to the internet of the BNP's membership records in November 2008 has shown that, though the party by its more restrained policies has widened its appeal to a certain extent, its new members seem still to be taken above all from the working and lower middle classes.

All in all, whether 'neo-fascism' manifests itself in unsuccessful fringe movements, as in Britain, or in more successful political movements which have adapted to the democratic consensus, as in Italy, the prospect for any kind of revival in Europe of a successful and integral fascism, as was seen in the inter-war period, seemed, when I was last writing about this subject in 2000, a very distant one.[46] European public opinion, and in particular British middle-class public opinion, appeared to have moved on. There was no need for complacency, however. Reading what I had written, a Marxist friend of mine, Ian Birchall, wrote to me to warn that there was danger of a new situation emerging as a result of changes to the underlying nature of our civilisation, such as climate change. He wrote:

> At the moment they [the extreme Right] have mainly a nuisance value, though they give comfort and encouragement to individuals (probably not under their direct control) who want to make physical attacks upon blacks or asylum-seekers. But in the event of serious economic crisis and rising unemployment they could grow very quickly. And if global warming produces massive population

movements, the appeal of fascist/nationalist rhetoric will be very strong.[47]

And the early signs are that Ian Birchall may be right. One has only to look at the first signs, such as the violent reactions of Italian right-wing politicians, and of the general Italian public, towards the gypsy immigrants from across the Adriatic, to realise that such tensions can release emotions freed from the inhibitions of the post-war consensus. Though we in Britain can console ourselves with the knowledge that, here, such reactions still do not form part of any national political activity, there is nevertheless enough disquiet in those areas of our country particularly affected by Eastern European immigration for the BNP to score, already, some minor but significant successes. What will happen in Europe as a whole, however, if in a more distant future climate change means that millions of people from Africa and the Mediterranean try to seek a tolerable climate in central and northern Europe? By then the 'appeal of fascist/nationalist rhetoric' could once more become very strong. Perpetual vigilance is needed.

Notes

1 As is customary in literature on this subject, I will be using a capital letter to designate the specifically Italian movement 'Fascism', and lower-case for the general idea of 'fascism', and for the many movements throughout Europe and elsewhere that have been described as 'fascist'.

2 By 'the Establishment' I mean those areas of the upper and upper-middle classes which, by reason of their position in society, wielded an influence far out of proportion with their numbers.

3 [L]iddell [H]art [C]entre for [M]ilitary [A]rchives: Bryant Papers, E/19, Gardiner to Arthur Bryant, 8 October 1939. See also [T]the [N]ational [A]rchives: KV 2/2245, letter from Gardiner to the Prime Minister, 24 September 1939.

4 LHCMA: Bryant Papers, Francis Yeats-Brown, letters to Arthur Bryant, 8 August 1939 and 20 December 1940. Quoted by kind permission of the Trustees of the Liddell Hart Centre for Military Archives, King's College London.

5 See Richard Griffiths, *Patriotism Perverted: Captain Ramsay, the Right Club and British Anti-Semitism 1939–40* (London: Constable, 1998).

6 Letter from Lymington to Hay, 30 May 1940 (Portsmouth Papers, Hampshire Record Office, 15M84/F189). For permission to quote from this letter, and from Hay's letter (Note 7) I am grateful to the Hampshire Record Office.

7 Letter from Hay to Lymington, 5 October 1941 (Portsmouth Papers, Hampshire Record Office, 15M84/F189).

8 TNA: HO 144/21845, Special Branch Report, 23 February 1943.

9 TNA: KV 2/491, MI5 Report, 8 October 1942. He acted in an advisory capacity to Godfrey, and proudly carried around a visiting card in the name of the BNP.

10 TNA: HO 144/21845, Special Branch Report, 25 October 1942. See also Special Branch Report of 23 February 1943.

11 TNA: KV 2/492, MI5 Report of 17 June 1943.

12 TNA: KV 2/492, MI5 minute of 6 February 1943.

13 TNA: KV 2/492, MI5 Report of 4 February 1945.

14 TNA: KV 2/492, Report of 17 June 1943.

15 Obituary of Hitler in *Talking Picture News*, 25 May 1945; article in *The Word*, May 1945, p. 10.

16 TNA: KV 2/795MI5, Note, 4 July 1945.

17 *Ibid.*

18 George Ward Price, *I Know these Dictators* (London: G. G. Harrop & Co, 1937), pp. 16–23; *idem, Extra-Special Correspondent* (London: G. G. Harrop & Co, 1957), p. 213.

19 Meriel Buchanan, *Ambassador's Daughter* (London: Cassell & Co, 1958), p. 225.

20 Admiral Sir Barry Domvile, Diaries (National Maritime Museum, DOM 57), Entry for 24 March 1945. Published by kind permission of the National Maritime Museum, Greenwich.

21 TNA: KV 2/874, MI5 Report of meeting on 8/11/44.

22 TNA: KV 2/492, MI5 report, 5 March 1945.

23 Description of the artist Barney Seale, in Admiral Sir Barry Domvile's diaries (National Maritime Museum, DOM 57), entry for 14 June 1945. Published by kind permission of the National Maritime Museum, Greenwich.

24 *The People's Post*, 20 April 1945.

25 Hastings, Duke of Bedford, *The Years of Transition* (Dakers, 1949), pp. 227–9.

26 Richard Griffiths, 'Russell, Hastings William Sackville, 12th Duke of Bedford', in *Oxford Dictionary of National Biography*.

27 Richard Thurlow, *Fascism in Britain: A History, 1918–1985* (Oxford: Blackwell, 1987), p. 236.

28 See Richard Griffiths, 'Fascists or Conservatives? Portugal, Spain and the French Connection', *Portuguese Studies* 14 (1998), 138–51.

29 TNA: FO 371/96173.

30 TNA: FO 371/96174.

31 *New York Herald Tribune*, 5 July 1952.

32 TNA: FO 371/102043.

33 *The Times*, 14 August 1950.

34 *The Times*, 26 November 1962.

35 TNA: FO 371/96173, Letter from D. J. Curran to Secretary of State, 28 December 1950.

36 Letter from J. Clive Forster, *The Times*, 27 February 1952.

37 This is not necessarily surprising. Srebrnik notes that, in the inter-war period, the strong support for Franco's 'crusade', on the part of the Irish Catholic Labour activists who dominated the East End Labour Party, was what led many London Jews 'thoroughly disillusioned by the official Labour Party representation', to turn to the Communist Party. See Henry Felix Srebrnik, *London Jews and British Communism, 1935–1941* (Ilford: Valentine Mitchell, 1995), pp. 32–4.

38 TNA: FO 371/96174, letter from Mary Lavery to E. Davies, MP, 26 February 1951.

264 Anti-Fascism and the Post-War Establishment

264 *Anti-Fascism and the Post-War Establishment*

39 Letter from Dom Columba Cary-Elwes, *The Times*, 15 June 1950.
40 E. Allison Peers, Letter to *The Times*, 26 November 1951.
41 *The Times*, 27 July 1950.
42 Richard Griffiths, *An Intelligent Person's Guide to Fascism* (London: Duckworth, 2000), pp. 98–105.
43 In a different context, I observed an attempt to classify Salazar in the same way (as a 'conservative' and not a 'fascist'), at a conference held in Paris on 'Salazar et l'Estado Novo' shortly after the fall of the Salazar regime. But here the aim was more understandable. The participants contained both former opponents of the regime, and former supporters and members of it, and the reclassification was an attempt to build bridges, and to agree on the comparative harmlessness of things under the Salazar regime.
44 Luciano Cheles, '"Nostalgia dell'Avenire". The new propaganda of the MSI between tradition and innovation', in Luciano Cheles, Ronnie Ferguson and Michalina Vaughan (eds), *Neo-Fascism in Europe* (London and New York: Longman, 1991), p. 43.
45 Roberto Chiarini, 'The Italian Far Right: The Search for Legitimacy', in Luciano Cheles, Ronnie Ferguson and Michalina Vaughan (eds), *The Far Right in Western and Eastern Europe* (Harlow: Longman, 1995), p. 20.
46 Griffiths, *An Intelligent Person's Guide to Fascism.*
47 Ian Birchall, letter to Richard Griffiths, 2000.

Index

270 *Index*